Modernism and Ireland

Stan Smith holds the established chair of English at the University of Dundee. He is the author of several books on twentieth–century literature, including *Inviolable Voice: History and Twentieth-Century Poetry* (1982), *W.H. Auden* (1985), *Edward Thomas* (1986), *Yeats: A Critical Introduction* (1990) and *The Origins of Modernism: Pound, Eliot, Yeats and The Rhetorics of Renewal* (1994). He is also general editor of Long–man Critical Readers and Longman Studies in Twentieth–Century Literature.

Anne Fogarty is a lecturer in the Department of English, University College, Dublin. She has written several essays on Renaissance literature and on twentieth-century Irish women writers. She is currently working on a study of colonial writings about Ireland 1534–1634.

Trevor Joyce co-founded New Writers' Press in 1967, and his first book of poetry, *Sole Glum Trek* (1967), was NWP's first publication. His other collections include *Watches* (1969), *Pentahedron* (1972), *The Poems of Sweeny Peregrine* (1976) and *stone floods* (1995). Until the early 1970s he was co-editor of NWP's journal *The Lace Curtain*. He is currently a business analyst for Apple Computers in Cork.

W.J. Mc Cormack lectures in English at Goldsmith's College, London. His recent publications are *Sheridan Le Fanu and Victorian Ireland* (2nd ed. 1991), *The Dublin Paper War of 1786-1788* (1993), *Dissolute Characters: Irish Literary History Through Balzac, Le Fanu, Yeats and Bowen* (1993) and *From Burke to Beckett: Ascendancy, Tradition and Betrayal in Literary History* (1994). He has also edited Austin Clarke's poems for Penguin (1992). He is general editor (with Marilyn Butler) of a twelve-volume edition of the works of Maria Edgeworth, to be published in 1997.

J.C.C. Mays is Professor of English at University College, Dublin. He has written on a number of modern Irish writers, among other topics, and is an editor for the Collected Coleridge and the Cornell Yeats. He is also general editor of Devlin's poetry for Dedalus Press, and editor of *The Collected Poems of Denis Devlin* (1989).

Thomas Dillon Redshaw is Associate Professor of English at the University of St Thomas, St Paul, Minnesota. Since 1989 he has been the editor of *Éire-Ireland*. He is the author of essays on Clarke, Kinsella, Montague, O'Brien and Reavey, and recently edited *Hill Field: Poems and Memoirs for John Montague* (1989).

Susan Schreibman is currently Faculty of Arts Fellow in Modern English at University College Dublin. She is editor of MacGreevy's *Collected Poems* (1991).

Notes on Contributors

Tim Armstrong lectures in the Department of English Literature at the University of Sheffield. He has edited a selection of Thomas Hardy's poems for Longman Annotated Texts (1993), and co-edited *Beyond the Thunderdome: Writing and Addiction from the Romantics* (1994), and *The Cultural History of the Body* (forthcoming, 1996). He is currently completing a study on modernism and the body.

Terence Brown is Professor of Anglo-Irish Literature at Trinity College, Dublin. He has written many articles on Anglo-Irish literature and is the author of *Louis MacNeice: Sceptical Vision* (1975), *Northern Voices: Poets from Ulster* (1975), *Ireland: A Social and Cultural History* (1981 and 1985) and *Ireland's Literature: Selected Essays* (1988). He is currently working on a critical biography of Yeats.

Patricia Coughlan lectures in the Department of English at University College, Cork. She has edited a collection of essays, *Spenser and Ireland* (1989), and published articles on seventeenth-century English writings about Ireland and many aspects of Anglo-Irish literature, including Mangan, Maturin, Le Fanu, representations of femininity in modern Irish writers, and narrative in Beckett.

Alex Davis lectures in the Department of English at University College, Cork. He has published articles on twentieth-century Anglo-Irish and British poetry, and is currently working on a study of Anglo-Irish poetry 1922–1966.

Editors' note:

Thomas MacGreevy altered the spelling of his name, originally 'McGreevy', to 'MacGreevy' following his return to Ireland in 1941; this collection adopts the latter spelling. All words in languages other than English are italicized in the text, except where they are part of quotations from non-English works.

Abbreviations

Aldington	Thomas MacGreevy, *Richard Aldington: An Englishman*, Dolphin Books, No. 10, Chatto & Windus, London, 1931.
CPB	Samuel Beckett, *Collected Poems 1930–1978*, John Calder, London, 1984.
CPD	*Collected Poems of Denis Devlin*, ed. J.C.C. Mays, Dedalus, Dublin, 1989.
CPM	*Collected Poems of Thomas MacGreevy*, ed. Susan Schreibman, Anna Livia Press, Dublin, 1991.
Devlin	Denis Devlin, *Collected Poems*, ed. Brian Coffey, Dolmen Press, Dublin, 1964.
Disjecta	Samuel Beckett, *Disjecta: Miscellaneous Writings and a Dramatic Fragment*, ed. Ruby Cohn, John Calder, London, 1983.
Dream	*Dream of Fair to middling Women*, eds. Eoin O'Brien and Edith Fournier, Black Cat Press, Dublin, 1992.
Eliot	Thomas MacGreevy, *T.S. Eliot: A Study*, Dolphin Books, No. 4, Chatto & Windus, London, 1931.
I	Denis Devlin, *Intercessions*, Europa Press, Paris, 1937.
Murphy	Samuel Beckett, *Murphy*, Routledge, London, 1938.
N&M	Austin Clarke, *Night and Morning*, Orwell Press, Dublin, 1938.
Pilgrimage	Austin Clarke, *Pilgrimage*, Allen & Unwin, London, 1929.
PV	Brian Coffey, *Poems and Versions 1929–1990*, Dedalus, Dublin, 1991.
QP	George Reavey, *Quixotic Perquisitions*, Europa Press, Paris, 1939.
TP	Brian Coffey, *Third Person*, Europa Press, Paris, 1938.
Yeats	Thomas MacGreevy, *Jack B. Yeats*, Victor Waddington Publications, Dublin, 1945.

Contents

v

First published in 1995 by
Cork University Press
University College
Cork
Ireland

© The editors and contributors 1995

British Library Cataloguing in Publication Data
A CIP catalogue record for this book is available from
the British Library.

ISBN Hardcover 0 902561 86 3
Paperback 1 85918 061 2

Typeset by Tower Books of Ballincollig, Co. Cork
Printed by ColourBooks of Baldoyle, Co. Dublin

Modernism and Ireland
The Poetry of the 1930s

edited by

Patricia Coughlan and Alex Davis

CORK UNIVERSITY PRESS

Acknowledgements

Alex Davis would like to thank the following for their kind assistance, encouragement and critical insight into his work for this volume: the staff at the Manuscripts Room of TCD Library; the library staff at Le Moyne College, Syracuse; the students in his M.A. seminar on Irish poetic modernism; Graham Allen, Michael and Susan Davis, Trevor Joyce, Donal and Margaret Murphy, Emily Murphy, Charles Norris, and Susan Schreibman.

Patricia Coughlan thanks Edward Beckett and The Board of Trinity College Dublin for permission to quote from Samuel Beckett's letters to MacGreevy; Mary Bryden and Mike Bott of the Beckett Archive at Reading University Library, and the staff of the Manuscripts Room and Trinity College Dublin for their courteous and efficient assistance during the research for this volume. She also recalls with gratitude the insights into Beckett's writings offered by students in her M.A. and B.A. seminars over several years. She wishes to express her appreciation of the many kindnesses and various forms of inspiration and help which she received from the following people during the long-term conception and the execution of this project: Tim Armstrong, Ellen Beardsley, Mary Breen, Garin Dowd, Liz Dunne, Anne Fogarty, Kathy Glavanis, Máire Herbert, Catherine La Farge, Piaras Mac Éinrí, Phillippa McInerney, Ulf Messner, Paddy O'Donovan, Catherine Sanborn and Rita Sisk.

Both editors wish to thank M. Noël Bourcier of the Association pour la diffusion du Patrimoine photographique, Paris, for his kind assistance in procuring the cover photograph, and Piaras Mac Éinrí for having so ably effected the necessary communication with

M. Bourcier. Finally, they wish to thank the contributors, the staff of UCC library in general, and in particular of Inter-Library Loans and the staff at Cork University Press.

Introduction

Patricia Coughlan, Alex Davis

I

There has been insufficient exploration of the fate of modernism in Irish literature after the first modernist generation. This collection seeks to explore that fate specifically in poetry, by focusing attention on that group of poets – Thomas MacGreevy, Brian Coffey, Samuel Beckett, Denis Devlin, and the publisher-poet George Reavey – who, coming to maturity during the decade of the 1930s, turned their eyes to European and, to some extent, Anglo–American modernisms for their formal and thematic inspiration. Interacquainted, in some cases intimately, and mutually supportive, these poets shared an admiration for the anti-realist and internationalist writing of Joyce, and found a common intellectual and aesthetic focus in the cosmopolitan cultural life of Paris, with its café society, its highly developed bohemianism, and its surrealist and other experiments in art and life. All except Reavey were more or less self-exiled by their common dissatisfaction with the narrow, anti-intellectual culture of the new Irish state and with what they felt to be its coercively nationalist, ruralist and bigoted ideology, and by their rejection both of Yeats as poetic ancestor-figure and of the latter-day Irish Yeatsian poets. Reavey too, part-Belfastman and part-Russian, in gravitating to France was putting a distance between himself and the culture in which he had been schooled since early adolescence, mainly in England; both MacGreevy and Beckett lived less than contentedly for periods in London and shared Reavey's alienation from mainstream British literary and cultural life, in Beckett's case to an extreme extent.

This volume sets out to reassert the importance in Irish literary history of these writers, and to further study of them within their social, literary and cultural contexts. Critical interest in their projects has been gradually increasing, and the accompanying work of editing and annotating their writings has been gathering pace over the last decade. Bringing together essays by a range of these critics and editors, the collection aims to advance the debate about the role of modernism – in the various forms it takes in these poets – in Irish twentieth-century writing. It also furthers discussion of two complex issues which have long needed more sustained discussion. One is what our current evaluation of their work should be; the other is the related and somewhat vexed question of their reception both by later genera-tions of poets and by the Anglo-Irish critical establishment over the last twenty years. All these poets published their first collections in the 1930s but their work, of course, continued into later decades: in Coffey's case, as we shall see, there is a lengthy silence between his two sustained periods of poetic endeavour, and a similar aporia, at least in terms of published work, marks MacGreevy's output. Thus these poets have had a presence continuing, however marginalized at times, into later generations and have functioned as models for suc-cessive groups of later literary dissidents from the dominant forms of Irish poetry.[1] Current debates in Irish cultural discourse over revisionism, feminism, nationalism, and the application of post-colonialist perspectives to criticism, are all, of course, relevant to these issues, as we shall see below. Of primary importance, however, is that the writings of the thirties' poets be recovered and contextualized as fully as possible for contemporary readers and that we learn to attend with increasing care and tact to their aims and achievements in their own temporal context. The volume has, accordingly, avoid-ed imposing a single theoretical or ideological position on the contributors, who represent a range of critical viewpoints.

II

Though it would be misleading to consider them a 'group' in the sense of sharing a strongly unified or codified poetic, MacGreevy,

Coffey, Beckett, Devlin and Reavey clearly held related views about modern poetry. Before considering the preoccupations that link these poets' work, and the critical reception their poetry has received, it is important to recognize the extent of their interrelationships. The following biographical details show that not only were they friends, but also that their careers as writers interpenetrated to a considerable degree, frequently at formative moments in each writer's literary development.

Thomas MacGreevy (1893–1967) was born in Tarbert, County Kerry. He entered the civil service in 1910, and spent the earlier part of the First World War working for the Intelligence Department of the Admiralty. From 1917 to 1919 he served in the British army, and was twice wounded at the Somme. He studied at Trinity College, Dublin immediately after the war, then, in 1924, moved to London, where, as well as some lecturing at the National Gallery, he contributed criticism to leading journals and began writing poetry in earnest. In 1927 MacGreevy moved to Paris, staying there until 1933 when he returned to London. His friendship with Joyce and then with Beckett in those years extended into shared literary values. Both MacGreevy's and Beckett's names appear beneath the 1932 manifesto 'Poetry is Vertical', printed in Eugene and Maria Jolas's avant-garde magazine *transition*. In the pages of the same journal MacGreevy's essay on Joyce's *Work in Progress* first appeared in 1928, later reprinted in *Our Exagmination Round His Factification for Incamination of Work in Progress* (1929), a volume to which Beckett also contributed. In 1931 he published two books of criticism, *T. S. Eliot: A Study* and *Richard Aldington: An Englishman;* and in 1934 his *Poems* appeared. The year 1941 saw him back in Dublin, where in 1950, he became director of the National Gallery, working there until his retirement in 1963. An art historian as well as a poet and literary critic, MacGreevy also wrote studies of Jack B. Yeats and Poussin, and catalogues of paintings in the National Gallery, Dublin. His *Collected Poems*, edited by Thomas Dillon Redshaw, was published in Dublin by New Writers' Press in 1971. An expanded collection of his poems, edited by Susan Schreibman, was published in 1991 by Anna Livia Press in Dublin and, in Washington D.C., by the Catholic University of America.

Brian Coffey (1905–1995) was also drawn in the 1930s to Paris, where he met MacGreevy and was memorably introduced to Joyce across the hospital bed in which Beckett was recovering from being stabbed in the chest by a pimp. Born at Dún Laoghaire, County Dublin, Coffey studied mathematics, physics and chemistry at University College Dublin. Living mainly in Paris from 1930 to 1939, he pursued studies in scholastic philosophy under the famous Neo-Thomist philosopher, Jacques Maritain, commenced doctoral research in philosophy at the Institut Catholique, and published *Three Poems* (1933) and *Third Person* (1938), as well as reviewing for the English magazine *The Criterion*. During the Second World War Coffey taught intermittently in London, and after the successful submission of his doctoral thesis in 1947 he took up the position of assistant professor in the Department of Philosophy at St Louis University, Missouri. For the next five years Coffey taught at St Louis, publishing a number of reviews and articles in *The Modern Schoolman*. Increasingly disenchanted with the college's administration, and faced with the financial difficulties of trying to support his wife and nine children on a small salary, he resigned from the college in 1952, moved to England and resumed school-teaching. In 1961 he recommenced publishing poetry: *Missouri Sequence* appeared in the *University Review* (Dublin) in 1962; three years later Dolmen Press published his translation of Mallarmé's *Un coup de dés*. During the 1960s Coffey edited both Devlin's *Collected Poems* for the *University Review* (1963) and *The Heavenly Foreigner* for Dolmen Press (1967); and, from 1966 on, produced, under his own imprint, Advent, a number of works. In 1971 New Writers' Press issued a *Selected Poems*; in 1975 *The Irish University Review* devoted a special issue, edited by J.C.C. Mays, to his work, including his major sequence *Advent*. His 1979 long poem, *Death of Hektor*, was succeeded, in 1985, by a collection of shorter poems, *Chanterelles*. In 1991 Dedalus Press in Dublin published an extensive selection of Coffey's work, *Poems and Versions 1929–1990*.

The existence of Deirdre Bair's biography of Samuel Beckett (1906-1989) makes it unnecessary to trace the broad outlines of Beckett's life in this context. However, the details of his life in the 1930s, and especially the fact of his connections with MacGreevy, Coffey, Devlin and Reavey, have not yet been the objects of sufficient attention. Beckett's links with Coffey and Devlin, and indeed, in the first instance, with Joyce, came through MacGreevy, whom he met, in 1928, when he succeeded MacGreevy as English *lecteur* at the Ecole Normale Superieure in Paris. Their close friendship, which lasted throughout MacGreevy's life, produced a correspondence of great intimacy during the 1930s. Beckett's letters to MacGreevy, who was twelve years older than him, trace the development of Beckett's reading in German philosophy, French poetry, and English fiction, and discuss many paintings, recording his tour of art museums in Germany in 1936 and 1937. From 1928 to September 1931 Beckett lived in Paris, then returned to teach French at Trinity College, Dublin, an unsuccessful move which at the end of 1931 he reversed in a state of personal crisis. During the following years he yawed uneasily between Dublin, Paris and London, where in early 1934 he entered a two-year psychoanalysis with W.R. Bion. During all this time, he was publishing criticism and poems, the latter appearing in all three cities: in Ireland in *The Dublin Magazine*, in *The New Review* in London, and, in Paris, in forms edited or published by Reavey, in *transition*, and with the patronage of Nancy Cunard. Beckett's *Collected Poems 1930–1978* (1984) contains a good deal, but by no means all, of the poetry Beckett wrote.

Beckett's first agent was George Reavey (1907–1976) who attempted, somewhat ineptly in Beckett's opinion, to find a publisher willing to accept *Murphy*. Reavey is the least known of the poets discussed in this collection; hence Thomas Dillon Redshaw's essay, below, devotes several pages to filling in the biographical details of Reavey's life. Here, it is important to realize the extent to which this Russian-born son of a Belfast flax engineer was involved in the lives and careers of MacGreevy, Coffey, Beckett and Devlin following his move from London to Paris in 1929 and his subsequent return to London in 1934. A fluent Russian speaker (his own childhood was spent in Russia), Reavey translated a good deal of the Russian section of Samuel Putnam's grandiose *The European Caravan* (1931), a projected two volume anthology of 'the New Spirit in European Literature', the first, and only, published volume of which also contained work by MacGreevy and Beckett. As a publisher, Reavey produced, under his Europa Press imprint, Beckett's *Echo's Bones* (1935), a selection of Paul Eluard's poetry, *Thorns of Thunder* (1936) – which included translations by Beckett, Devlin and himself – Devlin's *Intercessions* (1937), and Coffey's aforementioned *Third Person*. As well as his role in the early publishing history of his Irish contemporaries – a frequently turbulent one by all accounts – Reavey also published his own collections of poetry during the 1930s: *Faust's*

Metamorphoses (1932), *Nostradam* (1935) and *Quixotic Perquisitions* (1939). His later poetry includes *Colours of Memory* (1955).

Like his friend and contemporary Brian Coffey, Denis Devlin (1908–1959) attended University College, Dublin, his family having moved back to Ireland from his birthplace in Scotland in 1920. In 1930, while Devlin was reading for an MA in French, he and Coffey jointly published *Poems*. From 1931 to 1933 Devlin lived in Paris, studying at the Sorbonne, and, like Coffey, made the acquaintance of, among other literary figures, MacGreevy. Devlin first embarked on an academic career, becoming a demonstrator in the Department of English at University College, Dublin in 1934. However, in 1935 he joined the Irish Department of External Affairs, thus inaugurating what became a highly successful career as an overseas diplomat, culminating in his appointment as minister plenipotentiary and, later, ambassador to Italy. George Reavey's Europa Press published Devlin's *Intercessions* in 1937, the volume receiving a highly favourable review by Beckett in *transition*. His translations from St-John Perse (whom Devlin met, along with other writers who had left France, while working in Washington during the war) appeared in the latter half of the 1940s. His final collection, *Lough Derg and Other Poems*, came out in America in 1946. After his premature death from leukaemia, two of Devlin's American admirers, the distinguished poets Allen Tate and Robert Penn Warren, edited a *Selected Poems* which was published by Holt, Rinehart and Winston in 1963. In the same decade Coffey's editions of Devlin's work, mentioned above, appeared. In 1989 J.C.C. Mays edited a new *Collected Poems*, for Dedalus Press, which was followed in 1992 by Roger Little's edition of Devlin's numerous translations from French and, to a lesser extent, German and Italian poetry. Two further volumes – the first containing Devlin's translations from, principally, French poetry into Irish, and vice versa, the second collecting unpublished juvenilia and later work – are promised from Dedalus.

III

As the above sketches illustrate, after a considerable period of neglect, reliable editions of these writers' work are now to hand or forthcoming (Reavey is the obvious exception, while Beckett's poetry still awaits a full collected edition). This resurgence of interest on the part of publishers, however, should be placed in the context of the fitful representation of these writers in certain influential anthologies of Irish poetry. Thomas Kinsella's 1986 *New Oxford Book of Irish Verse* contains six poems by Beckett and six by Devlin, but omits the other writers entirely.[2] In *The Faber Book of Irish Verse* (1974), edited by John Montague, they fare better: it contains two poems by MacGreevy, a scrap of Coffey's *Missouri Sequence*, three poems (and, rather oddly, a couple of brief extracts from prose texts) by Beckett, two poems by Reavey and five by Devlin. Brendan Kennelly's *Penguin Book of Irish Verse*, second edition (1981), excludes MacGreevy, Coffey and Reavey, but finds space for one poem by Beckett and two by Devlin. Of the anthologies given over solely to twentieth-century Irish poetry, Maurice Harmon's *Irish Poetry After Joyce* (1979) provides a generous selection of poetry by Devlin, while Paul Muldoon's tendentious *Faber Book of Contemporary Irish Poetry* (1986) includes Kavanagh and MacNeice but does not acknowledge the existence of their Paris and London-based contemporaries from the Free State. More judicious is Anthony Bradley's *Contemporary Irish Poetry*, revised edition (1988): opening with five poems by MacGreevy, it also reprints two short poems and two extracts from longer works by Coffey, three poems by Beckett and six poems and an extract from a long poem by Devlin. Bradley's anthology, published by the University of California Press, is, incidentally, difficult to obtain in Ireland.

The point of this exercise is not to lambaste particular anthologies for failing to acknowledge adequately certain poets. Indeed, Devlin's poetry has fared fairly well at anthologists' hands, and receives praise in both Montague's introduction and Kennelly's note to the revised Penguin edition. Likewise, when these writers are admitted, the number of poems accorded them by the relevant anthologist is frequently in fair proportion to that granted other poets. Rather, the lack of consensus the anthologists show with regard to whom to include and whom not is indicative of the lack of sustained critical reflection these writers — including Beckett as *poet* — have received, with the exception of pioneering articles by, most notably, J.C.C. Mays and Stan Smith.[3] Their work has tended to be viewed, in the main, as of minor import beside the achievements of Kavanagh and Clarke, thus showing the greater ease of the critical establishment with work which can be more readily accommodated under the

rubric of a more literalist and self-proclaimed Irishness. The modern-
ist vision, with its various formal realizations, which are quintessential
to these poets, has accordingly been explicitly cold-shouldered by
many literary historians. Robert F. Garrett's judgement, in *Modern
Irish Poetry: Tradition and Continuity from Yeats to Heaney*, is representat-
ive in this respect: 'their modernism seems strained, too wilful, and
certainly too imitative to demonstrate the sincerity that Beckett and
Coffey themselves demanded.'[4]

   The narrowness of this opinion was first challenged seriously in
the late 1960s and early 1970s by Michael Smith's New Writers' Press,
a small Dublin publishing house which throughout its sporadic
history has remained antagonistic to the spuriously homogeneous
'tradition and continuity' which has sustained the narratives of most
critics and anthologists of Irish poetry. For Smith, the work of these
poets offered a salient example of resistance to absorption within
what he calls the '*Irish literary thing*' (author's italics). He identifies
that '*thing*' as the maintenance of a nostalgic backward look evident
in Brendan Kennelly's introduction to *The Penguin Book of Irish Verse*
(1970), in which, Smith argues, Kennelly posits an improbable con-
tinuity in Irish poetry from the seventh to the twentieth centuries.[5]
Smith's abrasive attack on Kennelly's anthology was delivered in
a 1970 editorial to *The Lace Curtain*, platform of Smith's New Writers'
Press, which from Autumn 1969 to Autumn 1978 sought both to
promote interest in emerging young poets and to recover neglected
poets whose practice, in the eyes of its editors, ran counter to prevail-
ing literary currents. Trevor Joyce's essay below gives an account
of the history of New Writers' Press, with which he was closely
associated, and provides useful documentation of the poetry the press
sought to disseminate. This shows a concerted attempt to provide,
often in a spirit of combative insistence and a somewhat overstated
antagonism towards prevailing literary fashions, what Smith
rather disturbingly called 'a corrected history' of modern Irish
poetry. To this end, several of his essays chart the influence of
MacGreevy — and Joyce via MacGreevy — on Coffey, Devlin and
Beckett. This counter-tradition, Smith claimed in 1975, could be
traced down to poets such as Trevor Joyce, Geoffrey Squires and
Augustus Young, 'who have now begun to look back upon [the
1930s poets] as progenitors'.[6] Consideration of those younger
writers, and of the exact nature of the relationship between their

work and that of their 'progenitors', falls beyond the purview of this book. However, Smith's 'corrected history' of the 1930s is signifi-cant to the present discussion in positing 'a whole generation of Irish poets whose work is positively unaccommodating to lovers of Anglo-Irishism [*sic*] in literature',[7] having shed an obsession with national identity in order to explore subjectivity in modern terms. Their poetry, he maintains, dispensed with a ruralist ethos, 'a poetry of the parish pump,'[8] in order to concentrate on broader ontological and epistemological issues, and is marked by formal experimentation, derived from high modernism, rather than an adherence to traditional forms. Smith's work, done partly under the influence of Coffey as mentor, certainly contributed to the keeping alive of the work of the thirties during a period when a poetic centring on Kavanagh and his latter-day avatars (including the early Heaney) was dominant: the reprinting in *The Lace Curtain* of Beckett's crucially important essay 'Recent Irish Poetry' alone was a major service to literary history. However, Smith's criticism, while undeniably lively, is rough at the edges and flawed by its acrimony. It is also marked by the persistence (which in the circumstances is ironic) of a less than modernist con-ception of the lyric speaker as unified and dominant in poetic utterance, a misunderstanding of the late-modernist dismantling of the Romantic category of subjectivity.

As for Smith's central argument, his counter-tradition and its designated antithesis – the 'poetry of the parish pump' – is open to an objection that can be also levelled at J.C.C. Mays's distinction between a peripheral Irish experimental poetry and a poetry dominated by a derivative and conservative 'pattern-book' uniform-ity.[9] One should point out that, no doubt in the interest of his own polemical position in the 1970s, Smith, in particular, fails ad-equately to register the importance of Derek Mahon's or Thomas Kinsella's work, both poets who cannot be fairly said to be inno-cent of modernist influences. In general, it might be argued that both he and Mays ride a little roughshod over the complexities of the Irish cultural landscape, postulating a poetic uniformity and, pitted against it, an avant-garde, that are equally paper tigers. In a reply to Mays's *Irish Review* essay, Edna Longley makes precisely this point, countering that 'Neither the Irish poem nor its reception is quite the unitary phenomenon that Mays seems to think.'[10] Longley con-tends that Mays's notion of a marginalized Irish poetic set against a traditional orthodoxy 'presumes that there is only one margin and the centre holds'.[11] Her principal objection to Mays's representation of Irish poetry is that it treats a partitioned Ireland as a cultural whole, and thus ignores the ambivalent UK/Irish status of Northern Irish poets. To which tradition do these poets belong? As Longley neatly puts it, 'the axis changes, the axle tilts, if Louis MacNeice is seen as more central than Austin Clarke'.[12] No doubt a situation of intensely competing attempts at hegemony is inescapable where contemporary poetry and that of the more recent past is concerned; but it would be unfortunate if the result were merely to embroil the thirties writers in the contestations of the 1980s and 1990s: a more productive approach to their work would aim, as we have sought to do, to resist the whole logic of centres and peripheries and recognize in the 1930s, as today, a situation of complex and shifting identities and assertions of difference: a study of MacGreevy's subtle combination of nationalism, modernism and Catholicism (explored below by both Tim Armstrong's and J.C.C. Mays's essays) is instructive in this regard. This volume does not threfore align itself with the counter-hegemonic claim of Michael Smith to 'correct' history and to assert the *centrality* of the neo-modernists here discussed: indeed their whole enterprise during that decade was predicated upon a creative peripherality and a conscious and willed self-marginalization. Further, there are other poets of the period in Ireland who are inevitably squeezed out of the binary accounts (whether Revivalist/modernist or Northern/Free-State-based) and who for various reasons deserve the attention of scholars, readers and historians: Lyle Donaghy, Geoffrey Taylor, Blanaid Salkeld, to name but a few.

Along these lines, Longley's own mild deconstruction of Mays's polarity of centre and margin, traditionalism and experimentation does have the usefulness of demonstrating that what is viewed as marginal depends on the perspective one takes and from where. The essays in this volume discuss poets born into the twenty-six counties that were to become the Irish Free State and later the Republic of Ireland, with the exceptions of Devlin, who returned to Ireland in adolescence, and Reavey, reared in Nizhninovgorod, Belfast and London. All of them, as we shall see, are linked, not only through biographical contact and Irish background, but also through their poetic theory and practice.

Louis MacNeice falls outside the range of this book, because, despite his poetry's complex negotiations with his Irish background, his adult life was spent, and his entire literary career conducted, largely in England and within English cultural problematics. His quizzical attitude towards both modernist 'abstraction' and formal self-consciousness also differentiates him from his contemporaries discussed herein, with their intense interest in continental experimentalism. It does not, however, follow from his omission that Clarke occupies the 'centre' or that his poetry is to be read as in any way normative of Irish poetry in the 1930s. As W.J. Mc Cormack's essay below establishes, Clarke's position within the literary culture of that decade was, in Mc Cormack's words, 'profoundly anomalous'. In contrast to Longley's characterization of Clarke's position within Irish poetry of the 1930s as 'axial', Mc Cormack reveals a writer caught in the generation gap between what Frank Kermode calls the 'paleo-modernism' of Yeats – and by extension, the Irish Literary Revival as a whole – and the 'neo-modernism' of Beckett.[13] Mc Cormack's examination of Beckett's satirical engagement with Clarke in the character of Austin Ticklepenny in *Murphy* reveals a lampoon of 'Celticism', which the novel presents as the Revival's variation on reactionary modernism's familiar distaste for the 'modern'. Clarke becomes a complex projection, by Beckett, of an aesthetic which, once experimental in its 'primitivism', had, in Beckett's eyes, hardened into an orthodoxy.

The example of Clarke already suggests what a more general examination of Irish writing in the 1930s clearly illustrates: that there was no straightforward opposition between a cultural centre and a 'revolutionary' margin. The ruralist, Catholic nationalism of Irish Ireland's ideology, promulgated by the likes of by D.P. Moran in the early days of the Free State and later in a more nuanced version by Daniel Corkery, was constantly challenged by a number of writers themselves disparate in ideology and style: the elder Yeats, Sean O'Casey, Seán O'Faoláin, Frank O'Connor, Patrick Kavanagh and Elizabeth Bowen, to name a few of the most prominent. As John P. Harrington observes: 'To be alienated from the pragmatic ideology of Ireland in the Free State was not to be rendered solitary and marginal . . . rather, it was to be part of one contentious and generally ineffectual faction in a natural debate over cultural priorities.'[14] That Irish Ireland found antagonists of various persuasions among writers and intellectuals stemmed from its restricting cultural horizons and its own increasingly monolithic nationalist values, promoting the fallacious belief that there is a specific 'essence' in Irish writing to which Irish writers should be faithful.

Along with many other writers, the poets in this volume were resistant to official and populist Free State ideology, but their opposition took a very different course from that of the most considerable of their poetic contemporaries in the South, Clarke and Kavanagh. Clarke's deployment of mythic and legendary material and Celticizing atmosphere is an aspect of his work prior to *Night and Morning* (1938) to which many critics have drawn attention; and W.J. Mc Cormack further reminds us of the nature of Clarke's project in his essay below. In the case of Kavanagh, the 1930s saw the publication of *Ploughman and Other Poems* (1936), a collection singularly untouched by the receding tides of high modernism, and his autobiographical memoir, *The Green Fool* (1938), a light-hearted work he grew to despise. However, as Kavanagh's finest critic Antoinette Quinn has demonstrated, the late 1930s saw Kavanagh working towards the formal experimentation of *The Great Hunger* (1942), a work which has been proffered as *the* poem which most successfully imports the techniques of *The Waste Land* into Irish poetry. Quinn considers the 'multifaceted' technique of *The Great Hunger* as 'modernist',[15] while Longley, in an explicit recent attack on Smith's counter-tradition, bluntly states that 'to deny Kavanagh's innovatory shock is to imply that all natural or country images, whatever their purposes, belong to a single reactionary aesthetic'.[16] Kavanagh's formal radicalism in a poem like *The Great Hunger* is unquestionable. Yet it is an approach governed by Kavanagh's positivist adherence to the *facts* of Irish rural experience, which he felt had been falsified by writers of the Irish Literary Revival, and thus subservient to the 'authenticity of representation' which Quinn identifies with the 'parochial' vision he was to develop in subsequent years.[17] *The Great Hunger*, in other words, ultimately represents an aesthetic of 'savage realism'[18] profoundly at odds with modernism's 'textual indefiniteness or incompleteness, epistemological doubt, [and] metalingual skepticism'.[19] It is perhaps not irrelevant in this context to recall that Kavanagh read *Ulysses* as 'almost entirely a transcription from life'.[20]

IV

At this point it is necessary to isolate the distinguishing features of MacGreevy's, Coffey's, Beckett's and Devlin's poetry as it is discussed in this volume; features which connect their work to one another's and set it apart from that of Clarke and Kavanagh, for whom the 1930s were of equal importance in their search for new modes of poetic expression. One avenue of enquiry is to consider the background against which their writings stand. Terence Brown's essay in this volume draws attention to the kinship between the Irish Literary Revival and international modernism. Brown questions the commonplace identification of the Revival as itself a late Romanticism; he notes the striking parallels between the break which both modernism and the Revival made, not only with Romantic conceptions of individual creativity, but also with realism's fidelity to its historical moment. Like modernism, the Revival sought its own version of Mallarmé's *Le Livre*, a search that, wedded to cultural nationalism, took the form of 'the book of the people' to which Yeats wistfully refers in 'Coole and Ballylee, 1931'. Yet though the emergence of the Free State in 1922 coincides with a key date in modernism, and represents a modernist 'event' in its own right, Brown argues that the nationalism that had fed the Revival's literary experimentation and rejection of nineteenth-century literary forms ultimately stultified the further development of such art forms. This blocked the influence of European and Anglo-American modernism in literature, architecture, music, film; and generated resistance, in the theatre, to the Gate's modest attempts to move beyond the insularity of the Abbey's repertoire.

The channelling of the Revival's ambitions into the narrow conduit of Corkery's Irish Ireland is presented, in Tim Armstrong's essay, as due to the 'split', in an independent Ireland, between the revolutionary aspirations of the political and aesthetic avant-gardes. Armstrong explores the manner in which this division informs MacGreevy's aesthetic and poetic practice, partly trammelling his desire for a Catholic modernism that would be flexible enough to accommodate both a public and private voice. It is a division which equally characterizes the work of MacGreevy's successors, Devlin and Coffey. The characteristic 'distance' established in Devlin's poetry, through irony or other means, from a public

or political role registers the presence of the impasse reached by
MacGreevy,[21] while Coffey's complex negotiations with history
have to be read alongside his poetry's aspiration to the condition
of prayer and a space beyond temporality.

As both Armstrong's and Brown's essays illustrate, the denudation
of the modernist dimension to the Literary Revival, in post-
independence cultural nationalism, stultified the further develop-
ment of second-generation modernism in Ireland, truncating or
interrupting the careers of several of the poets discussed in this collec-
tion. This curtailed the development of a poetic which is stated at
its most formulaic in Beckett's 1934 article in *The Bookman*, 'Recent
Irish Poetry', an essay referred to by many of the contributors to
this collection. At the opening of that essay Beckett, in a by now
well-known distinction, divided Irish poets into 'antiquarians' and
'others' (*Disjecta*, p. 70). The 'antiquarians', unsurprisingly, include
Yeats, F.R. Higgins, Monk Gibbon, James Stephens and Clarke; the
'others', Coffey, Devlin and by implication Beckett himself, with
MacGreevy, for reasons explored in Armstrong's and J.C.C. Mays's
essays below, lying somewhere between the two groups. Beckett's
division, as Mays has observed, is 'an exacerbated analysis, which
. . . bears the same relation to reality as an infra-red photograph
which obliterates contours' (*CPD*, p. 26) and, specifically, does little
justice to the complexities of Clarke's use of 'Celto-romanesque'
material in his 1929 collection, *Pilgrimage*. Nevertheless, Beckett's
reductive approach has the value of noting two important elements
present in the work of the 'others'. Firstly, it identifies the influence
of French modernist poetry, as well as the work of Eliot and Pound,
on Devlin's and Coffey's early work. Secondly, and more significant-
ly, it pinpoints the centrality to the work of the 'others', and to
MacGreevy's, of the problematic relationship between the subject
and the object-world, knowledge of both entities stripped, in these
poets' writings, of empirical certainty. Beckett's pronouncements
in the essay build upon the 1932 'Poetry is Vertical' manifesto, refer-
red to above, in which the co-authors resist 'a world ruled by the
hypnosis of positivism' and champion, in a quasi-idealist fashion,
'the hegemony of the inner life over the outer life'.[22] The 'rupture
of the lines of communication' Beckett speaks of in 'Recent Irish
Poetry', stemming from the rejection of positivist or realist conceptions
of knowledge, leads, in the work of the 'others' and MacGreevy, to

the realization that traditional, shared literary forms are no longer adequate: hence the characteristic fragmentation of their texts, their use of montage, and the elliptical, oblique manner in which their poems explore their chosen themes.

Despite the similarities between these poets' neo-modernist techniques and modernist assumptions about subjectivity and language's representational capacity, there are considerable divergences in other areas of their poetics, particularly in their respective views on the relationship between poet and nation or, in more general terms, poetry and the cultural sphere as a whole. David Lloyd has rightly stressed the extent to which Beckett's essay constitutes a 'rejection of the already ossifying obsession of Irish writers with . . . the recurrent reproduction of Celtic material as a thematic of identity'.[23] For Lloyd, Beckett's modernism continues a critique of nationalism's emphasis on racial identity that reaches back to James Clarence Mangan, writing at the dawn of Irish romantic nationalism.[24] This suggestive interpretation, resting on the controversial thesis that Ireland constitutes a post-colonial social formation, grants Irish second-generation modernism, in Beckett's work at least, the status of *Ideologiekritik*: a post-colonial discourse that one might also see as gesturing towards the 'hybridity' that Homi Bhabha celebrates as the most powerful way in which a cultural artefact can question the monologic discourses of imperialism and nationalism alike.[25] Patricia Coughlan's contribution to this volume explores the validity of this claim in relation to Beckett; in the work of the Catholic modernist MacGreevy, however, there is considerable tension between the international, avant-garde aesthetic to which he adhered and his broadly nationalist fidelity to ideas of Ireland, as the newly-emergent nation-state increasingly drove a wedge between cultural nationalism and the modernist experimentation of the Irish Literary Revival.

The partial failure of MacGreevy's aesthetic programme is examined in J.C.C. Mays's careful contextualization of the reception of his work, in an argument that expands upon and refines his more polemical discussions cited above. Mays sees MacGreevy as having been misjudged both by the lukewarm response his poetry received in Ireland on first publication and by his championing in the 1970s as a 'John-the-Baptist figure' for later poets disaffected with the modern Irish poetic canon. Mays's re-reading of MacGreevy centres instead on the convergence in his writing of a modernist poetic with a distinctly non–internationalist set of beliefs, namely, his cultural nationalism. This combination of what many would see as incompatible elements is, according to Mays, the signature of MacGreevy's work.

During his close reading of a representative sample of MacGreevy's poems, Mays draws our attention to the importance of studying the revisions this minimalist poet made to his texts. Susan Schreibman's meticulous consideration of his unpublished poems substantiates Mays's point. The unpublished poetry, she observes, foregrounds an aspect of MacGreevy's poetic voice easily overlooked when reading the 1934 *Poems*: an 'immediate emotional' quality to his work at variance with modernist notions of artistic 'impersonality'. Of particular interest in these poems is MacGreevy's suppressed engagement with, and frustration at, Irish politics in the 1930s, the poems casting light on the difficulty MacGreevy found in arriving at a poetic space free from political wrangling, but one nevertheless sensitive to the independent Irish nation with which he identified himself.

Brian Coffey's correspondence with MacGreevy during the 1930s shows a young poet for whom poetry is equally problematic, though for different reasons. Alex Davis's essay argues that Coffey's poetic reservations are informed not only by his mistrust of the example of Yeats and of Irish cultural nationalism as a whole, but also, and perhaps more profoundly, by his Neo-Thomism. Between 1934 and 1961 Coffey published no poetry (though he did resume writing in the 1950s). This prolonged silence is, arguably, coloured by the influence of the Catholic philosopher Jacques Maritain, who from the 1920s on meditated on the difficulties, for the Christian, of modernist aesthetics' worship of 'pure form', the correlative of which is modernism's crippling inability to do more than reflect, in a negative sense, on the separation of art from ethics and politics in modernity. Davis shows how Coffey's later poetry provides a self-reflexive commentary on issues raised by Maritain, articulating the difficulties of developing a Catholic modernism in ways that bear fruitful comparison with MacGreevy's poetic dilemmas: both poets sought a way for poetry to engage in the public sphere, but without complicity.

This latter explicit 'public' dimension, or aspiration, in the work of both Coffey and MacGreevy distinguishes it from that of Beckett.

As Patricia Coughlan demonstrates, throughout Beckett's writings in the 1930s, in his poetry, articles, reviews and letters, the evidence of his attitude towards Ireland and towards contemporary Irish cultural priorities is clear and consistent. Firmly opposed to poets following in the Yeatsian Revivalist tradition, as he understood it, he himself turned away consciously and deliberately from the path that would have led him to participation in *national* cultural work. Unlike MacGreevy, he was unmoved by the notion of nationhood, and attended instead to a set of international aesthetic imperatives which were formulated, for Beckett, above all in certain modern French poets and in the work of Joyce. By the end of the 1930s Beckett felt very clearly his own definitive divergence from MacGreevy on questions of national identity. Without a rupture in their friendship, Beckett nevertheless establishes his distance from MacGreevy's desire to put his own talents to the service of his nation-alist conviction while retaining modernist aesthetic aims. This project was eventually realised in MacGreevy's return to Ireland. It was a path on which Beckett, already engaged (as his French poems late in the decade show) on his own anatomy of subjectivity in modern-ity and its internal aporias, did not intend to follow him. Ruefully charting their difference of perspective about Jack Yeats – they would praise him for different reasons, Beckett's modernist, MacGreevy's nation-minded – he describes his 'chronic inability to understand as member of any proposition a phrase like "the Irish people"'.[26]

Written by a diplomat for an independent Irish state, Devlin's poetry, which neither ceases nor suffers a rupture in the 1930s, might perhaps be expected to comprehend Beckett's 'proposition' and find it a ground of departure. On the contrary, however, Devlin's work is scored throughout by a sense of existential perplexity Terence Brown has described as 'metaphysical anxiety'.[27] This prompts, in the poems, an obsessive meditation on the self and its relationship with an extra-subjective reality and an elusive, silent Godhead whom Devlin terms 'the heavenly foreigner'. As Stan Smith argues in his essay below, the poetry evinces a marked sense of dislocation and displacement in its search for a poetic 'ground', as Devlin's poetic speakers seek an epistemological certainty that their temporal placing denies them in advance. In contrast to the Neo-Thomist under-pinnings of Coffey's writing, this aspect of Devlin's work is deeply coloured, Smith argues, by the poet's Jansenist leanings, yet one also finds, in this dimension of Devlin's poetry, signs of that sense of 'rupture', albeit differently inflected, that Beckett explores in 'Recent Irish Poetry'.

Anne Fogarty's essay explores Devlin's problematic representation of female figures, which function as 'intercessors' in his poetry's attempts to mend this rupture. Furthermore, her general examination of gender and modernism reveals a limitation on the extent of the Irish modernists' difference from either Revivalists or socially-conscious English poets of the period. A masculinist bias informs both modernist conceptions of literary creation and the Catholic perspectives which are such strong sustaining influences on Coffey, Devlin and MacGreevy. In the case of Beckett, reared in a devout Evangelical Protestantism, as Patricia Coughlan shows, the representation of women and femininity is also pervaded by distancing otherness and governed by intense anxieties and fears. Fogarty further points out that while the male poets encountered considerable resistance in their attempts to articulate a modernist poetic shorn of the traits of Revivalism, female poets in the period such as Blanaid Salkeld, Sheila Wingfield, Rhoda Coghill and Mary Devenport O'Neill suffered the additional problem of the exclusions commonly affecting women's writing, producing a set of evident dislocations in their work.

V

It remains to consider the relation between the poetry discussed in this volume, and that of Yeats, undeniably an Irish modernist. His omission from this collection rests not only on the grounds that he belongs to an earlier generation of writers, but also on our belief that his work contains aesthetic premises that differ considerably from those of the poets we and our fellow contributors have chosen to discuss.

Yeats's modernism has its roots in his early combination of Celticism and a theory of symbolism he derived, at least in part, from Arthur Symons. The resulting poetic, as Frank Lentricchia persuasively argues, connects his *fin de siècle* work to that of Mallarmé (or Symons's Mallarmé), and parallels the phenomenology of Husserl. Husserl's philosophical distrust of scientism, the 'natural standpoint', is at one with the implicit idealism of the symbolist project in poetry.[28] Both constitute a response to that crisis in representation which is a crucial spur to the projects of philosophical and aesthetic modernism. Husserl's process of phenomenological reduction aims to liberate the philosophical subject from exterior determinants in a manner comparable to the transcendence Mallarmé sought in a poetic discourse sufficient unto itself. Yeats's early poetry and prose evinces a similar distrust of scientism, and his consequent search for a non-positivist method or language is comparable to that of Mallarmé and Husserl. For all the transformations in Yeats's work between the 1890s and the 1930s, this search remains fundamental to his thought. It forges a continuity between the aestheticism of 'The Autumn of the Body' (1898) and the arcane metaphysics of *A Vision* (1926, second edition 1937) and links collections as diverse in tone and theme as *The Wind Among the Reeds* (1899) and *The Winding Stair and Other Poems* (1933). To this extent there are indeed parallels to be drawn between the ways in which Yeats's work and that of the Irish neo-modernists each confront the 'breakdown of the object', to which Beckett refers in 'Recent Irish Poetry'.

Nevertheless, despite these important and overlooked resemblances, Yeats's mature aesthetic modernism is different from that of the younger poets in certain key respects. Notably, none of these writers viewed their poetry within a Yeatsian paradigm of literary modernism — indeed, Mervyn Wall reports that, while his friends Coffey and Devlin 'read and examined Eliot and Pound', he 'never heard them quote a line of Yeats'.[29] (This does not, of course, preclude the fact that Coffey and Beckett, in particular, wrote in acute consciousness of Yeats's work and out of an agonistic reaction to his example, one most vehemently expressed in Coffey's reiterated condemnations of Yeats as, in his words, 'a power-hungry seducer'.)[30] Yeats's fidelity to traditional metrical and stanzaic forms, his belief that 'ancient salt is best packing', is clearly at odds with the neo-modernists' various experiments with *vers libre*, devices of fragmentation and, in some cases, surrealist techniques.[31] For the neo-modernists, Yeats's 'ancient salt' had lost its tang.

Similarly, their conception of literary history and of their own place therein diverged decisively from the 'tradition' to which Yeats adhered and on which, in 'Coole and Ballylee, 1931', he bestowed his famous valediction: 'We were the last romantics. . . .' As late as 1936 Yeats was still making the essentialist claim that modern Irish poetry belonged to 'a different story' from that of Britain, and must stay connected to its origins in 'folk thought', and avoid what he called 'impersonal philosophical poetry' (by which he probably meant T.S. Eliot's later work).[32] Certainly the Irish 1930s' modernists belong to a 'different story' from Auden and the other *engagé* poets in Britain, but their determined urban internationalism removes them from the prescribed closeness to 'the common people'. However, these poets firmly resist Yeats's prescription for the severance of subjectivity ('the personal') from philosophical reflexivity. This is amply shown by Beckett's castigation of the Revivalists' 'flight from self-awareness' and his eminently philosophical insistence on 'the act, and not the object of perception'; by Coffey's complex exploration within modernism of scholastic aesthetics; by the epistemological scepticism Devlin directs at his own frenetic search for *symboliste* transcendence; and by MacGreevy's many 'metaphysical bereavements' (*CPM,* p. 42). Their work, in short, is based on aesthetic presuppositions divergent from those of Yeats, is influenced by both philosophical and literary writings of which Yeats knew little, and reflects the alienated modernity of great cities (notably Paris and London) after the First World War.

VI

The essays in this collection make a step towards a richer consideration, in the context of their time, of poets who did not take their bearings from Yeats. These poets, for reasons which we have already given, have received far too little attention in the critical writings on modern Irish poetry. The intention of this volume is to further the enquiry into the fate of modernism in Irish literature, clarify the relationships between some of its practitioners, and stimulate greater appreciation of a body of poetry that, in both its formal exactness and thematic complexity, merits and rewards the closest scrutiny.

Notes

1   See the polemical article by J.C.C. Mays, 'Flourishing and Foul: Ideology, Six Poets and the Irish Building Industry', *The Irish Review,* 8, 1990, pp. 6-11, for a spirited and informative example of the deployment of the thirties modernists in the critical battle about value in contemporary Irish poetry.
2   Interestingly, the *Oxford Book of Irish Verse,* edited by Donagh MacDonagh

and Lennox Robinson (1958), which Kinsella's anthology superseded, contained MacGreevy's 'Aodh Ruadh'.

3 See Stan Smith, 'On Other Grounds: The Poetry of Brian Coffey', *The Lace Curtain*, 5, 1974, pp. 16-32; reprinted in Douglas Dunn, ed., *Two Decades of Irish Writing: A Critical Survey*, Carcanet, Manchester, 1975, pp. 59-80; Smith, 'Frightened Antinomies: Love and Death in the Poetry of Denis Devlin', *Advent VI*, Denis Devlin special issue, Advent Books, Southhampton, 1976, pp. 24-30; Smith, 'Precarious Guest: The Poetry of Denis Devlin', *Irish University Review*, 8, 1, 1978, pp. 51-67; reprinted, with revisions, in the present volume; Smith, 'From a Great Distance: Thomas MacGreevy's Frames of Reference', *The Lace Curtain*, 6, 1978, pp. 47-55; Smith, 'Against the Grain: Women and War in Brian Coffey's "Death of Hektor"' *Etudes Irlandaises*, 8, 1983, pp. 165-73; and J.C.C. Mays, 'A Poem by Denis Devlin, with some Questions and Conclusions', *Advent VI*, Denis Devlin special issue, Advent Books, Southampton, 1976, pp. 9-13; Mays, 'Biographical Note and Introductory Essay', *Irish University Review*, Brian Coffey special issue, 5, 1, 1975, pp. 9-29; Mays, 'Passivity and Openness in Two Long Poems by Brian Coffey', *Irish University Review*, 13, 1, 1983, pp. 67-82.

4 Robert F. Garrett, *Modern Irish Poetry: Tradition and Continuity from Yeats to Heaney*, University of California Press, Berkeley, 1986, p. 100.

5 Michael Smith, editorial, *The Lace Curtain*, 3, 1970, p. 6. Smith's target, it should be said, is the *first* edition of the Penguin anthology (1970). For the enlarged and revised edition of 1981, however, Kennelly chose simply to reprint the introduction to the first, adding a brief note that, among other concerns, makes reference to his admiration for Devlin's poetry.

6 Michael Smith, 'The Contemporary Situation in Irish Poetry', *Two Decades of Irish Writing*, ed. Douglas Dunn, Carcanet, Manchester, 1975, p. 160. See also his essay 'Irish Poetry Since Yeats: Notes Towards a Corrected History', *Denver Quarterly*, 5, 1971, pp. 1-26. Joyce (1967), Squires (1969), and Young (1969) had all already published collections when *The Lace Curtain* and Smith's series of articles praising the thirties poets began appearing; the explicit adoption of MacGreevy and the others as spiritual fathers therefore would seem to have postdated the early work of these poets.

7 Michael Smith, editorial, *The Lace Curtain*, 4, 1971, p. 3. The issue is given over entirely to 'the thirties generation of Irish poets'. For precise details of its contents see Trevor Joyce's essay below.

8 Smith, 'The Contemporary Situation in Irish Poetry', p. 156.

9 Mays, Flourishing and Foul', p. 11.

10 Edna Longley, 'The Irish Poem', *The Irish Review*, 9, 1990, p. 55.

11 Longley, 'The Irish Poem', p. 56.

12 Longley, 'The Irish Poem', p. 56.

13 John Wilson Foster has drawn attention to the often under-emphasized modernist dimensions of the Literary Revival in his essay 'Irish Modernism'. Despite the inclusiveness of his title, however, Foster does not consider the poets discussed in this volume. See his *Colonial Consequences: Essays*

in Irish Literature and Culture, Lilliput Press, Dublin, 1991, pp. 44-59. Frank Kermode's distinction between 'paleo-modernism' and 'neo-modernism' is drawn in his essay 'The Modern', reprinted in *Modern Essays*, Fontana, London, 1971, pp. 39-70.

14 John P. Harrington, *The Irish Beckett*, Syracuse University Press, Syracuse, 1991, p. 86.

15 Antoinette Quinn, *Patrick Kavanagh: Born-Again Romantic*, Gill and Macmillan, Dublin, 1991, p. 143.

16 Edna Longley, *The Living Stream: Literature and Revisionism in Ireland*, Bloodaxe, Newcastle, 1994, p. 204.

17 Quinn, p. 199.

18 The phrase is Terence Brown's; see 'After the Revival: Seán O'Faoláin and Patrick Kavanagh', *Ireland's Literature: Selected Essays*, Lilliput Press, Gigginstown, 1988, p. 105.

19 Brian McHale, *Postmodernist Fiction*, Metheun, London, 1987, p. 8. McHale is here drawing upon Douwe Fokkema's *Literary History, Modernism and Postmodernism*, John Benjamins, Amsterdam, 1984.

20 Patrick Kavanagh, 'Diary', *Envoy*, April 1950. Quoted in Quinn, p. 203.

21 On 'distance' in Devlin's poetry see also Brian Coffey, 'Denis Devlin: Poet of Distance', *Place, Personality and the Irish Writer*, ed. Andrew Carpenter, *Irish Literary Studies 1*, Colin Smythe, Gerrards Cross, 1977, pp. 137-57.

22 Hans Arp *et al.*, 'Poetry is Vertical', *Transition*, 21, 1932, pp. 148-9; reprinted in Thomas MacGreevy, *Collected Poems,* ed. Thomas Dillon Redshaw, New Writers' Press, Dublin, 1971, p. 73.

23 David Lloyd, *Anomalous States: Irish Writing and the Post-Colonial Moment,* Lilliput Press, Dublin, 1993, p. 56.

24 See David Lloyd, *Nationalism and Minor Literature: James Clarence Mangan and the Emergence of Irish Cultural Nationalism,* Univeristy of California Press, Berkeley, 1987, pp. xi-xii.

25 On the topic of 'hybridity' in post-colonial discourse see the essays collected in Homi Bhabha, *The Location of Culture*, Routledge, London, 1994.

26 Samuel Beckett, letter, 31 January 1938, Beckett Correspondence, Trinity College Dublin Library.

27 Terence Brown, headnote to 'The Counter-Revival 1930-65: Poetry', *The Field Day Anthology of Irish Writing*, gen. ed., Seamus Deane, Field Day, Derry, 1991, vol. 3, p. 132.

28 Frank Lentricchia, *After the New Criticism,* Methuen, London, 1983, p. 68. See also W.J. Mc Cormack, *From Burke to Beckett: Ascendancy, Tradition and Betrayal in Literary History,* Cork University Press, Cork, 1994, pp. 307-23.

29 'Michael Smith asks Mervyn Wall Some Questions About the Thirties', *The Lace Curtain,* 4, 1971, p. 82.

30 Quoted in Smith, 'Irish Poetry Since Yeats', p. 7. Beckett's 'agon' with Yeats is apparent in the extent to which 'Recent Irish Poetry' alludes to and quotes from Yeats's *The Winding Stair* (1929) and *Words for Music Perhaps and Other Poems* (1932).

31 W.B. Yeats, 'A General Introduction for My Work' (1937), *Essays and Intro-ductions,* Macmillan, London, 1961, p. 522. The passage follows soon after a quotation from 'Burnt Norton'.
32 W.B. Yeats 'Modern Poetry' (1936), *Essays and Introductions,* p. 506.

1

Ireland, Modernism and the 1930s

Terence Brown

The *annus mirabilis* of literary modernism was 1922, when *Ulysses* and *The Waste Land* were first published in two metropolitan centres, Paris and London. In Ireland 1922 saw the founding of the Free State, a coincidence of chronology that ought to have stimulated more reflection than it has. For the moment when a national revolution achieved even a partial success represented an experiment in social and cultural expression just as the publication of those two works represented experiment in the artistic sphere. Each event, the founding of a post-imperial state, the publication of a novel which set in question the adequacy of realist fiction to the present moment and the issuing of the poem which sought to exploit a 'mythical method' the better to comprehend the 'immense panorama of futility and anarchy' of 'contemporary history', were symptomatic occasions, signs of the times, manifestions of, and reactions to, the general crisis of post-war Europe.

Ulysses and *The Waste Land* are of course customarily entered in the roll-call of modernist masterpieces even by those who suspect that modernism is so capacious a term, so 'completely lacking in positive content', that it is 'the emptiest of all cultural categories'.[1] The Irish revolution and the foundation of the Free State have not, by contrast, been considered in the context of the international modernism of the period, however accommodatingly conceived. And this despite the fact that the Irish society which in 1922 embarked on its own national experiment was the same society which gave to the world the Oscar Wilde whose *fin de siécle* art and criticism was a precusor of modernist aesthetics, two major modernist writers in Yeats and Joyce and would in Beckett produce a writer whose preoccupations would be largely defined by modernist achievement.

The reasons are not far to seek. Modernism, in as much as it can as a term provide descriptive insights on widely variegated phenomena, is radically internationalist in scope and vision, cosmopolitan in its *dramatis personae*. Its characterizing conditions are literary and artistic exile, *deraciné*, cosmpolitan and metropolitan rather than national foci, a highly self-conscious eclecticism and near-universality of cultural forms. A nationalist revolution values none of these things and the state it inaugurates may be reckoned to contribute to a movement like modernism only through provoking that exile which so evidently marks the sociology of the twentieth-century European avant-garde.

Artistic and cultural expression in the Irish Free State in the 1920s and especially in the 1930s would certainly give the cultural historian apparently sufficient ground for concluding that modernism and post-colonial nationalism (another capacious and acccommodating term) are antithetical in their particular manifestations. The predominant literary form of the period was the short story which for the first time in Ireland employed a sustained realism to assses the condition of the country in its new-found and less than inspiring freedom. Its principal practitioners were antagonistic to literary experimentalism. Both Frank O'Connor and Seán O'Faoláin entered objections, for example, to Joyce's *Work in Progress*. In painting, a fascination with landscape which in the early work of an original painter like Paul Henry had involved avant-garde interest in post-impressionism, by the 1930s had hardened into convention and stereotype which was readily exploited by less able painters. Indeed Henry remembered of the 1920s in Dublin that there was a deep-rooted 'ignorance and prejudice . . . against any form of art which savoured, even remotely, of modernism'.[2] By 1937 John Dowling in *Ireland To-day* could hail Seán Keating, who was aggressively opposed to modernism in painting, as the chief glory of the Irish school. Sculpture was entirely academic and architecture almost unaffected by the experimentalism of the Bauhaus (though a few houses in Dublin's suburbs built in the 1930s suggest that modernist ideas were not completely unknown). Furthermore in 1920s and '30s

Ireland symphonic music was scarcely established and no real audience existed for it. Aloys Fleischmann, the country's leading musicologist, in 1936 declared '*this* is the land without music, a land that is literally music starved. . . . The intelligentsia does not give music a thought' (author's italics).[3] In 1937 Eamonn Ó Gallchobhair concurred. He declared 'musically speaking Dublin is a city of barbarians.'[4] So while composers like Fleischmann himself were aware of develoments in twentieth-century European art music and sought to make them known in Ireland, there were few opportunities, beyond those afforded by occasional broadcasts and gramophone records, for interested individuals to hear such large-scale works as Stravinsky's *The Rite of Spring* which had announced itself as the harbinger of modernist iconoclasm in music as early as 1913. Nor was there much chance that Irish audiences could get to see the great modernist experiments in cinema, where such radical techniques as *montage* had defined for modernism as a whole its quintessential structural method (though the Irish-made *Guests of the Nation* does show the influence of Eisenstein).[5] Liam Ó Laoghaire, that notable and in the thirties almost unique Irish cineaste, wrote in 1932 that 'the quality of creative film work shown in Ireland, particularly in recent years, has been as drops in an ocean of comercialised vulgarity'.[6] In 1937 he reported that only the 'cheapest and most inferior products of modern film production' were screened in Dublin.[7]

A very telling indicator of the Irish cultural condition in the 1930s is the achievement and reception of the Gate Theatre company in the Dublin of the period. Founded by Micheál Mac Liammóir and Hilton Edwards in 1928, to explore the international repertoire that the Abbey felt unable on account of its brief to stage, the Gate endured constant disapproval. Writing in 1932 in *Motley*, the theatre's journal which ran for a couple of brief years during what Micheál Mac Liammóir called 'these early drab days of the present drab decade',[8] a contributor commented of the Gate's repertoire:

> Since this theatre was founded we have presented comparatively few realistic plays, and have already avoided realism in production. We consider that realism has been badly overdone, and if the drama has a future that that future will not be found to lie in a realistic direction.[9]

Perhaps this unfashionable espousal of non-realistic modes when the Abbey was effectively patenting Peasant Quality in its realist

plays as the indigenous dramaturgy, accounted for the state of affairs
the journal had reported on earlier in the same year:

> From the very first moment of its inception in this city, the Gate
> Theatre has suffered more carping criticism from friend and foe
> than any other Little Theatre in these Islands. Perhaps it is the
> modern progressive element in us.[10]

Not that even the Gate was in any very real sense dedicated to
modernist experimentalism. In its journal the idea of an avant-garde
is certainly bruited and the word 'modern' is employed quite fre-
quently in positive contexts. There is no evidence, however, that the
critics and writers ready to assocciate with the Gate venture were
the dedicated vanguard of a movement which took seriously the
radical engagement with disorientating aesthetics that modernism,
through movements like vorticism, cubism, futurism, surrealism,
had sponsored. Certainly, as Richard Pine has argued, the influences
which had complicated Mac Liammóir's *fin de siècle* aestheticism as
a stage designer had included an 'affinity with Gordon Craig'[11] and
a fascination with the colour effects of Leon Bakst whose work with
the Russian Ballet he so admired where he saw the dancing of
Nijinsky, heard the music of Stravinsky and Ravel under the inspired
management of Diaghilev. Yet reading through the files of *Motley*
and considering the repertoire of the early seasons when the Theatre
was striving to distinguish itself from its competitor in Abbey Street,
one is struck by the odd mixture of classics, experiments, inter-
national successes and potboilers that graced the boards and the lack
of a ruling engagement with ideas. What this suggests is a theatre
whose ethos was style for style's sake rather than a theatre that shared
the modernist movement's intense desire to be present at the birth
of the 'Savage God'. Nor indeed does one gain a sense that the theatre
was directed by individuals truly aware of modernism's crusading
aspirations. For all its brilliance, its bravura cosmopolitanism, one
detects in the Gate Theatre of the 1930s the subversive energies of
both the decadence and of the modern becoming somehow un-
threatening in the provincial Irish air.

   In fact what now strikes the reader of such literary periodicals
as there were in the period is an absence of that urge to make it new
which so informed the manifestoes, treatises and prophesies which
had publicized modernist ambition since early in the century. A

curious atmosphere, for example, pervades the pages of *The Dublin Magazine* (the only well-established literary periodical in the period) in the 1930s. Work by experimental poets such as Lyle Donaghy appears in its pages; Samuel Beckett's early remarkable poem 'Alba' was published there in October 1931. But the overall impression is not of an editorial engagement with the way modern letters since the era of the French symbolists had sought to represent strikingly original modes of human consciousness in new poetic forms, but of literary and artistic connoisseurship. The shock of the new is absorbed in the general atmosphere of cultivation and informed, self-consciously urbane taste.

A tendency to absorb and discharge the energies of the most original modernist texts and techniques may in the Irish context be the most persuasive evidence that Ireland and modernism were antithetical congeries of feeling and sensibility in the 1930s. An in-triguing case in point is a work of Thomas MacGreevy. A poet who in the 1930s composed a small body of rhythmically exquisite verse indebted to the experimentalism of Pound and Eliot (which stimulated an admiring celebratory essay from the young Samuel Beckett and the respect of Wallace Stevens), MacGreevy's volume of 1931, *T.S. Eliot: A Study*, is a very odd performance indeed. MacGreevy's essay is an early attempt (eight years in advance of Cleanth Brooks's classic, more subtle Christian account in *Modern Poetry and the Tradition*) to read *The Waste Land* in positively Chris-tian terms. 'The subject' MacGreevy announces 'that overtook him was nothing less than death and resurrection. What he made of it is *The Waste Land*, a poem which, in its own more nervous way, has influenced us all almost as much as Mr Joyce's *Ulysses*' (*Eliot*, p. 34). It is not, however, the poem's nervousness that MacGreevy emphasizes in his literal-minded account but the worthy Christian conclusions the poem can be read as attaining. *En route* to this happy terminus MacGreevy opines of the famous prophetic passage in 'The Burial of the Dead': 'For my own purposes I take the broken im-ages to be the weakened churches of to-day, the dead tree to be dead faith, and the cricket to represent the inadequacy of mere natural companionship (or perhaps sermonless, message-less natural science)' (*Eliot*, p. 42). But what is even more surprising is the critic's deter-mination to read Eliot as formally nothing very new – certainly nothing to get excited about. It is as if the orthodox believer in him, who as poet learned from Eliot how modern free verse can be written, must make his precursor a questing man of the spirit and deny to him any really disturbing originality of form, inappropriate to one who is to be recruited by the critic to the secure, unshakeable traditions of Catholic faith and art. Apropos of Eliot's 'associative way of writing' MacGreevy is at pains to insist 'the method is not really very new', continuing

> In France it is at least as old as Arthur Rimbaud. Mr Pound got it in France, and it is possible that it is amongst the things for which Mr Eliot acknowledges his indebtedness to Mr Pound in the introduction he wrote to his selected poems. Mr Joyce uses it also. It forms an inherent element in the 'interior monologue' for which he acknowledges his indebtedness to the French novelist, M. Edouard Dujardin. But it is not, in reality, very important. . . . For what it sets out to be, it seems to me, therefore, that *The Waste Land* is practically beyond mere literary criticism, and to criticise the religious and moral attitude expressed in it would be to criticise the strictest Christianity (*Eliot*, p. 56).

So there is, according to MacGreevy, nothing new under the literary sun and Eliot's poem simply employs an existing method to produce 'this Old, almost Jacobean, if not Elizabethan, English (and above all, London) shorthand masterpiece' (*Eliot*, p. 57), in which the devout reader may find nothing at variance with the 'strictest Christianity'. To read MacGreevy's *T.S. Eliot* is to be reminded of how perspicacious was Wallace Stevens when he wrote to MacGreevy, 'You were . . . a young man eager to be at the heart of his time' but that he had also been affected by 'the nostalgie du divin' (which is obviously endemic in Dublin).[12] In that endemic Dublin state of feeling the dangerous implications for the Christian world-view of the major modernist texts can be rendered anodyne in an oddly Olympian conception of tradition which may in fact be the symptom of a certain self-protective provincialism of mind before the arresting challenge of true and threatening originality.

It was possibly the unruffled conservatism of Irish intellectual and cultural life in the 1930s, rather than more obvious indignities such as the Censorship of Publications Act of 1929 (which had begun to work its absurd will in the country in the banning of books by Irish and international authors alike) and regular episcopal fulminations against the cinema and the dangers of jazz, which gave their

special tone to the two indisputably modernist manifestoes issued
by Irish artists in that decade. I am thinking of Mainie Jellett's
'Modern Art And The Dual Ideal of Form Through The Ages',
published in *Motley* in 1931 and Samuel Beckett's 'Recent Irish Poetry'
published in *The Bookman* in 1934. Jellett, the disciple of and fellow-
worker with Albert Gleizes, who had begun to show her cubist
works in Dublin in the 1920s and who would achieve only limited
recognition in the 1930s, writes in 1931 with the painstaking cau-
tion of one who expects to be misunderstood:

> A picture or work of art evolved with the mobile non-materialistic
> ideal of form is, first and foremost, a complete formal organism
> in itself; and secondly, if the forms are derived from nature,
> descriptive. If the work of art is a painting, it is considered two
> dimensionally as a flat surface to be filled and made alive by forms
> born of its own shape and obeying the natural laws of the surface
> and the shape of the surface they are filling. If the work of art is
> sculpture, then the third dimension is recognised, it being the
> material property of the sculptor's material. His ideal would be, first
> and foremost to make his block of stone or marble live as an har-
> monious mass of form and secondly to introduce description.[13]

She continues, somewhat wearied in tone, as if having to explain
what should be well-known by 1931, even in Dublin:

> In Western art since the Renaissance, the tendency has been more
> and more towards realism and materialism, but with the opening
> of the twentieth century came the first sign of reaction. The reac-
> tion started with Cézanne in France, and the Italian Futurist group,
> and has continued with the Cubist movement and Expressionist
> movement. . . . When a work of art which is striving towards a
> different ideal of formal expression than that which is commonly
> accepted at the moment, is being judged, it should be approached
> with the same ideal of form as that with which it is conceived.[14]

By contrast the young Samuel Beckett, knowing that the gulf bet-
ween subject and object, so necessary to all forms of realism, has
broken down in modern epistemologies, inveighs against those mired
in artistic anachronism with the intemperance of the prophet who
knows he will be without honour in his own country. Addressing
a 'rupture in the lines of communication' he advises, in what J.C.C.
Mays has precisely identified as 'an exacerbated analysis' (*CPD*, p. 26):

The artist who is aware of this may state the space that intervenes between him and the world of objects; he may state it as no-man's-land, Hellespont or vacuum, according as he happens to feel resentful, nostalgic, or merely depressed. A picture by Mr Jack Yeats, Mr Eliot's 'Waste Land' are notable statements of this kind. Or he may celebrate the cold comforts of apperception. He may even record his findings, if he is a man of great personal courage. Those who are not aware of the rupture, or in whom the velleity of becoming so was suppressed as a nuisance at its inception, will continue to purvey those articles, which in Ireland at least, had ceased to be valid even before the literary advisers to J.M. Synge found themselves prematurely obliged to look elsewhere for a creative hack. These are the antiquarians, delivering with the altitudinous complacency of the Victorian Gael the Ossianic goods. (*Disjecta*, p. 70)

Modernism requires definition; we must identify its salient features the more convincingly to assess the justice of our view that 1930s Ireland was largely bereft of its artifacts and the prevailing culture apparently unmoved by its concerns. Eugene Lunn lists four primary characteristics of modernist art forms: 1. Aesthetic Self-Consciousness or Self-Reflexiveness; 2. Simultaneity, Juxaposition, or 'Montage'; 3. Paradox, Ambiguity, and Uncertainty; 4. Dehumanization.[15] Michael Bell also suggests that modernism as well as manifesting 'aesthetic self-consiousness' involves issues pertaining to 'the transcendence of realism,' (a variant of Lunn's second and third set of terms); 'the presentation of identity' (related to Lunn's fourth definition) and 'the treatment of time'.[16] Simply to list these, reflecting as one does how they bear on works as diverse as *Ulysses, The Tower*, the *Cantos, A la recherche du temps perdu, To the Lighthouse* without even considering developments in music, painting and film, is initially to be confirmed in the judgement arrived at above that Ireland in the 1930s was not significantly attentive to modernism. Yet in the 1930s Yeats was still at Work, Joyce was to complete *Work in Progress* and Samuel Beckett was at the start of his career, as if to rebuke any too summary assumption that the matter is simple and can without further thought be put down to the invincible provincialism of Irish cultural reality. For to list these several characteristics of works which find themselves enumerated under the general rubric of modernism is to realize how the Literary Revival in Ireland in its symbiosis with Irish nationalism (which was in part responsible for the foundation of the Irish Free State in which modernism apparently foundered) shared many of the attributes more generally associated with the presumably internationalist artistic movement.

It is commonplace to account for both the Irish Literary Revival and Irish nationalism, when they are set in other than a local context, as late versions of European Romanticism. The obssession with the past, the veneration of the primitive and the rural, the cults of the hero and of blood sacrifice, give both a genuinely Romantic inflection.[17] What is less frequently addressed is the degree to which nationalism and the Literary Revival, itself so imbricated with that nationalism, allow parallels to be drawn with modernism. This is not, I hasten to add, to state that the Revival in its Irish nationalist context is a version of modernism, but rather to observe that the relationship between that movement and the modernist movement is complex, since both share the figure of W.B. Yeats, and in an even more complex way, that of James Joyce.

In nationalism the nineteenth century's sense of time is challenged. No longer a secular, sequential process in which progress unfolds, time becomes an element in which the sacred national saga of ancient glory and recurrent defeat can be played out in iterative and, it is hoped, climactic fashion. The past intrudes on the present to offer typologies and prophetic instances. Vast stretches of mere chronological time can be elided as Cuchulain stalks in the Post Office. Past and present instances are significantly juxtaposed like images in some symbolist text. Historical time and mythological timelessness are woven together in a seamless garment of national imagining. Time is not only the individual's possession but the shared reality of the collective. Literary production conducted in the context of nationalist feeling accordingly revives and translates texts from the dim past not for antiquarian reasons but to allow them to exist again in the timeless spirituality of the nation's continuous being. 'The best that has come out of Ireland in my time' portentously avers Yeats when he introduces Lady Gregory's *Cuchulain of Muirtheimne* 1902, investing her book with timeless, classic status and impersonlity at the very moment of its publication. Stan Smith has recently written that translation is 'not just one of several activities for modernist writers. It is, rather, a key to all their activities';[18] and in a suggestive analysis of a representative modernist text, Pound's 'translations' from the Chinese in *Cathay*, he notes how 'in the many mediations between Li Po and Pound, a wholly imaginary "intellectual and emotional complex", has been created, transcending cultures and histories, which is entirely contemporary: the *illusion* of unmediated rapport with the dead' (author's italics). In the literature of the Irish Literary Revival, we are reminded as we read Smith on modernism that texts translated from the Gaelic past and present, in Hyde's *Love Songs of Connacht* for example, in O'Grady's prose-poetry versions of the sagas, live as if again, in a permanent national present tense. 'Real time', comments Smith, reflecting on the Poundian and the modernist sense of time (strikingly similar it will now be clear to that stimulated by nationalism)

> is an eternal present where all that is truly living coexists. Literature provides privileged access to it, for literature offers us the subjective interior of dead lives as if *we* were living them for the first time. It is a kind of spiritual possession, and indeed the vocabulary of mediumship recurs in the theorising of the Modernists.[19]

As of course it is present in the very notion of a Literary Revival and in the spiritualist interests of many of its apologists.

Smith highlights how past subjectivities become contempories in Poundian theory and practice. But in his suggestion that the works of the past come to us in the 'translations' in *Cathay* as if 'unmediated' he alerts us also to the way modernism sponsored an ideal of objectivity and impersonality in art. The instant of permanent present tense in which the 'translation' lives is neither an achievement through which the translator expresses himself or herself, nor a carrying over of a past moment of self-expression into the present, but an illusion. It is a fabrication. The writer's role in this is not that of a self-expressive creator, but that of a maker, one who impersonally fabricates (*The Waste Land*, famously, is a work of two hands). Modernist works accordingly both offer a moment 'when the reader is brought fully alive . . . by instantaneous co-presence of the actual writer . . . with that of his imagined persona'[20] and clear indications that the work is a made thing. We are arrested by its magic, even as we know it to be an illusion. *Cathay* is signalled on the title page to be a co-operative scholarly and literary venture. We are convinced by the trick even as we know the magician does it all with mirrors.

The Literary Revival offers parallel occasions. Indeed a literature so dependent on versions, redactions, editions, translations could scarcely have avoided making literature itself seem a matter of construction rather than creation, of objective, impersonal work, rather than an opportunity for personal expression. The ubiquitous ambition of writers in the period to provide the nation with a sacred, magical book of the people (which would exist in its own ideal time), involved revisions and reworkings, fabrications in, for example Yeats's volumes *The Wind Among the Reeds* or *The Secret Rose*. But such ambition was simultaneously an idealisation of the movement's elevation of literature's national provenance over its personal significance. Such works as made things, which sought to function as powerful illusions, inevitably drew attention to the fact that a literary artifact is not simply to be reckoned an apparent reflection of a contemporary or historical social world in the manner of a realist text. Rather they advertised how writing obeys its own internal laws of narrative structure, employing as it does juxtaposition, temporal and contextual elisions, reiterated motifs and conventional descriptions of locale and *personae*. As such it broke the canons of classical realism as well as undermining the Romantic notion that a text is an expressive phenomenon rooted in the unitary, organic self of an originary creator. That the Revival depended for its sources as a revived national literature on the ancient Celtic sagas, on folktale and on the self-conscious interlacing narratives of the story-teller's oral art, as well as on the revelatory capacities of myth, assuredly meant that the defining characteristics of its key texts would have little in common with the prevailing literary norms of Victorian literature where the realist novel, the discursive essay and the subjective lyric met the expectations of a bourgeois audience.

Through what initially seems an historic accident therefore, the Revival's distinguishing literary forms in its nationalist context were those which in several respects anticipated and paralleled what commentators have isolated as the nexus of features which allow the term modernism such critical valency as it possesses. Nationalist consciousness cut across conventional awareness of time and Revival texts in effect were entered in a temporal zone akin to that which works like *Cathy* and *The Waste Land* would so compellingly occupy. They revealed themselves as literary constructions (even sometimes admitting their fragmentary nature) which must obey their own laws of narration, presentation and a self-reflexive trajectory. Their sources in various modes of discourse and textuality were made plain to the reader. As works which aspired to the condition of myth, they represented meaning as ambiguous and uncertain, only available in the irrational structures of primitive imagining and in the depths of communal consciousness. They denied to the literary artifact the authority of an originary creative mind, situating it in the dimension of the collective, thereby setting in question the significance of individual identity and the coherence of the self. Realism was rarely admitted as a governing possiblity.

Sociolgists of modernism tend to adopt the internationalism of the phenomenon they investigate. Notable among them is Perry Anderson, who has set the agenda for some important recent theorizing. For Anderson, modernism emerges in the context of a crisis in European capitalist society. What he calls 'a *conjectural* explanation' (author's italics) has modernism as 'a cultural force-field "triangulated" by three decisive coordinates'.[21] These are, in summary, formalized academicism in the arts complicit with the *ancien régime*, modern technologies of communication and the expectation of revolution. In a pan-European context modernism emerges as a non-national, internationalist art movement exhibiting the characteristics we have noted above. What is not explained in such accounts is why such circumstances result in such aesthetic effects. Though by associating modernism with the city, in which new technologies in communications and visual representation of experience were taking place in cinema and advertising, such explanations suggest that high art was readily adapting to the novel means of communication rapidly becoming available in the capitals of the continent as a whole.

What such a thesis ignores is what W.J. Mc Cormack has called elsewhere in this volume the 'issue of national, regional or local provenance' in modernism. Alex Callinicos in a sympathetic critique of Anderson does indicate how such matters of 'local provenance' can be of import when we consider why modernism as an international event of the period 1890 to 1930 is not uniformly thick on the ground in the various parts of Europe. For Callinicos, England made a very limited contribution to the movement because 'Britain by the late nineteenth century did not offer the sharp contrast between old and new provided by the comparatively sudden onset of industrial capitalism in genuinely *ancien régime* orders such as Prussia, Russia, and Austria-Hungary'.[22]

A task exists then to establish the socio-cultural construction of modernism which takes account of the varying levels of European modernization and identifies how elements deriving from different local contexts coalesce into the more general movement. From such a perspective it may be possible to isolate two things as particularly salient: the adoption of techniques based on the new means of communication, film, wireless, advertising – with montage as a unifying preoccupation – and the employment of techniques deriving in part from cultural developments of a less general kind, of which the Irish Literary Revival is one telling example. Indeed for all Joyce's and Beckett's documented antagonism to the cultural limitations of the Revival their sense, as often impatient readers of its products, of what might constitute a literary text was obviously more akin to that of the Revival itself than to, for example, that sponsored in the tradition of the nineteenth-century realist novel. Nor did they merely exploit procedures becoming available as the pace of technological change quickened, though both were highly attentive to these. Joyce indeed in 'Cyclops' may satirize the textual forms of the Revival, but he registers in doing so the highly textual nature of the phenomenon he is himself satirizing in a work which announces its own undeniable, labyrinthine, even scholastic sense of ubiquitous textuality on every page. Beckett uses in the first trilogy the self-reflexive, interlacing procedures of Irish anecdote and tale to deconstruct the very basis of narrative itself. And both writers shared with Yeats an awareness that time, as history in Ireland would have had them know, is a matter of repetitions, an endless present tense, comic, tragic, a matter of pathos by turns. Riverrun. What stalked through the Post Office? Another happy day.

What I have been arguing is that the Irish Literary Revival in its nationalist context was contiguous with modernism rather than merely concurrent. Context and text formed a culture in which the kinds of technical devices and the sense of reality modernism would internationalize were contemporaneously aspects of the Revival project and probably influenced, consciously and unconsciously, the Irish contribution to the general movement. As John Wilson Foster has reminded us in his pioneering essay 'Irish Modernism', it was to that quintessential Revival writer James Stephens (possibly the closest in practice of all Revivalists to the fabular, folkloric indigenous tradition) that Joyce turned to invite him 'to complete *Finnegans Wake* ... in the event of his own death'.[23] By such a proposal Joyce, however eccentric it seemed to his biographer,[24] gave notice that the experimental qualities of his own art were not so very far removed from what the local tradition had generated in the work of Stephens. He could hope in the man who shared with him a Christian name and day-of-birth for comprehension of his most radical experiment in fiction and a sufficiently sympathetic sensibilty in a writer who might on superficial examination appear to lack appropriate modernist credentials. It was on reading Stephens's *Deirdre*, it should be noted, that Joyce conceived this idea.

In sum, the Revival and modernism can be seen as exhibiting parallels of outlook and method. At moments in the work of the Irish modernists the literary historian is conscious of overlappings, points of contact as well as parallels and similarities. And the Revival context can be seen as one likely to produce writers who, formally at the very least, can be reckoned as contributors to the international phenomenon of modernism.

Most post-Treaty Irish writers reacted against the Romantic idealism of the Literary Revival which seemed too intimate with the political wave which had broken on the rocks of civil war and republican failure. Seán O'Faoláin (a highly representative figure, as ex-IRA man, language-enthusiast and caustic post-revolutionary social critic), in his biography *Vive Moi!* recalls how in the 1930s he attended four Irish Academy of Letters dinners. He calls them to mind the better to 're-evoke the sense I gradually got of a tide receding about me'.[25] Yeats, the presiding genius of those occasions, as he was the doyen of the Revival itself, struck O'Faoláin as one whose nature required him as man and poet 'to live a foot off the ground, a foot or two or more, away from common life'.[26] O'Faoláin was determined to be true to that common life and to employ realism as the instrument of his integrity. In rejecting the idealism of Yeats and his confederates, O'Faoláin and others who shared his post-revolutionary disillusionment also by the same token rejected the forms in which that idealism had apparently most readily expressed itself − saga, heroic narrative, translated antique text, folklore and myth. Character returned with a vengeance to Irish fiction. Self-obsessed young men would come of age again and again in a depressed Irish environment that demonstrably allowed for none of the mythic and structural fictional complexity of Joyce's classic Irish

Künstlerroman, A Portrait of the Artist as a Young Man. It was as if the challenge to realism effected by both the Revival writers and the modernist movement had not taken place. A debilitating air of anachronism hangs over the whole of what gets called in the literary histories 'the Irish short story'. It reads as if Joyce had not already in *Dubliners* and in that short story writ large, *Ulysses*, taken the form to its limits. And in poetry Austin Clarke, who wished to establish himself as a post-Revival writer, after his youthful infatuation with its achievement, opposing the unstable heteroglossia and fertile invention of the preceding period, turned to the tradition of Irish-language religious poetry – 'another imaginative world which remains entirely neglected'.[27] He found there 'a world of art in which emotion is pure, choice and disciplined'.[28] Anything but Romantic, and certainly not modernist. Indeed Clarke, identifying the learned tradition he wished to emulate, spoke of a desire to express 'our own casuistic mentality as deeply as we can.'[29]

So disillusioned, post-revolutionary literary Ireland seems to have thrown out the the modernist baby with the Romantic bathwater of the Literary Revival, leaving the 1930s to produce only a few writers, like genetic sports, who wrote in varying degrees of awareness of the Revival's formal originality or of modernism's revolution of the word. At the very least, until Flann O'Brien in 1939 published *At Swim-Two-Birds*, there did not occur that curious co-incidence of literary taxonomies in which a work rooted in aspects of Revival poetics (I am thinking of the parodic Revival epic descriptions and the version of *Buile Suibhne* which it contains) is also an entry in the modernist canon.

Irish nationalism and literary modernism in the 1930s do however share some parallel concerns, even if their aesthetics appear markedly antithetical. Both responded to a perceived international crisis and sought in history explanations for, and solutions to, the challenge of the present momement. Accordingly, it may be that the paucity of an explicit, developed interest in modernism in Ireland in its post-independence phase also has to do with the fact that nationalism itself as a structure of feeling allowed for the expression of what elsewhere became identified with the reactionary cultural politics of the general movement. Irish writers and ideologues could dispense with the formal originality of the Revival's poetics, with its links to, and parallels with, modernist experiment, but could nevertheless indulge themeselves, in the midst of general crisis, in conservative ideological accounts of past and present which were elsewhere the basis of modernist sociological and historical expatiation. A crucial figure in this respect is Daniel Corkery, the principal ideologue of independent Ireland in the 1930s.

It would be instructive to attempt a comparative analysis of the social and historical thought of Corkery and Yeats in the 1930s, that decade in which Yeats became increasingly obsessed by European history and the role Ireland must play in it. It would, I believe, be evident in such a study that what in Yeats is a characteristically modernist set of reactionary political and social theses (culminating in the second version of *A Vision* in 1937, and *On the Boiler* in 1938) in Corkery is paralleled by Irish nationalist convictions and preoccupations. The fact, however, that Yeats frequently expresses his essentially modernist world-view through meditations and polemics on Irish reality, and shares a basic Irish nationalist outlook with Corkery would make such a comparison seem less interesting than a comparison with that other modernist ideologue at work in the 1930s and '40s, T.S. Eliot, on whom Irish nationalism had no impact whatsoever (to ignore an Irish nurse in a St. Louis childhood).

Corkery published his *Hidden Ireland* in 1924, a study of Gaelic poetry in eighteenth-century Munster. It is prefaced by a general reflection on the nature of a national literature which must, if it is to express the national life, eschew the false cosmopolitan values of the European Renaissance. For Corkery, the Renaissance represented a fall from the pre-lapsarian world of national culture which could be restored in modern writing where 'everything is creeping back to the national hearth'.[30] It might be thought that it would be difficult to find a more anti-modernist set of observations (and indeed Corkery seems to oppose T.S. Eliot's elevation of Dante over Shakespeare in the course of his argument) than the critic offers in this introduction to his subject. Yet Corkery and Eliot share an assumption that the European rot set in with the Renaissance. Then, for the American modernist, a 'dissociation of sensibility' occurred which thereafter sundered fact and value, mind, emotion and body. For the Irish nationalist the Renaissance introduced a 'common strain into the art-consciousness of all European countries' that

> was certainly brilliant, shapely, worldly-wise, strong, if not indeed gigantic, overbounding in energy, in life! Yet all the time there

was a latent weakness in it, a strain, a sham strength, an uneasy
energy, a death in life.[31]

In Corkery's bizarre reading of things, Shakespeare as an Englishman
was free of the malign influence of the Renaissance: 'what did
Shakespeare's native wood-notes wild know of tbe Unities. Happy
England! — so naively ignorant of the Renaissance at the close of
the sixteenth century'.[32] It is a theme he returns to in his second
book *Synge and Anglo-Irish Literature*, published in 1931. There he
deems England a 'normal country' where writers are 'at one with
what they write of'.[33] Ireland in this text is not such a happy place
for its writers are almost all alien to the real experience of the people.
In Corkery's thinking, Renaissance moulds were external things.
Thus in *The Hidden Ireland* Romanticism is read as 'a protest against
the externality of Renaissance moulds'.[34] In Ireland, *Synge and
Anglo-Irish Literature* insists, the 'literary Irishman' knows of Anglo-
Irish literature that 'whatever moulds exist in this literature are
not the inevitable result of long years of patient labour by Irish writers
to express the life of their own people in a natural way'.[35] As a
consequence, the Irish endure a condition remarkably akin to that
identified by Eliot as a 'dissociation of sensibility'. Corkery writes
of the education of a typical Irish child: 'No sooner does he begin
to use his intellect than what he learns begins to undermine his
emotional nature. . . . His surroundings begin to seem unvital'.[36]

What is most revealing is that Corkery, like Eliot, cnvisages culture
both as a whole way of life and as a collective experience. For the
Irish critic/prose writer, culture can, if literature expresses it, heal
the nation's broken psyche. For the American poet/critic, culture,
expressing as it does the whole life of the people, can unify the
fragmented self of the modern individual. Corkery in 1931 writes:

> I recall being in Thurles at a hurling match for the championship
> of Ireland. There were 30,000 onlookers. They were as typical of
> this nation as any of the great crowds that assemble on Saturday
> afternoons in England to witness Association football matches are
> typical of the English nation. It was while I looked around on that
> great crowd I first became acutely conscious that as a nation we
> were without self-expression in literary form.[37]

And he goes on to imagine the defining constituents of the typical
Irish culture which Irish writing has not yet expressed — 'the fair,

the hurling match, the land grabbing, the *priesting,* the mission, the Mass'.[38] Eliot in 1948, in his *Notes towards a Definition of Culture,* writes of culture as comprising

> all the characteristic activities and interests of a people: Derby day, Henley regatta, Cowes, the twelfth of August, a cup final, the dog races, the pin table, the dart board, Wensleydale cheese, boiled cabbage cut into sections, beetroot in vinegar, nineteenth century Gothic churches, and the music of Elgar.[39]

The nationalist and the modernist can it seems share, as well as convictions about a historic fall from some previously existing state of European grace, a nostalgic, evasive vision of an integrated way of life (neither admits industrialism or the city to his thumbnail sketch of the national culture). They thereby indicate, in this precise conjunction of preoccupations, how parallels could exist between the two movements which can seem entirely antithetical. For in Ireland impulses which elsewhere could find expression in reactionary modernist stances and polemics were channelled into nationalist feeling and the exposition of its sustaining ideology.

Notes

1 Perry Anderson, 'Modernity and Revolution', in *Marxism and the Interpretation of Culture,* eds. C. Nelson and L. Grossberg, Macmillan, London, 1988, p. 332.
2 Paul Henry, cited by S.B. Kennedy, *Irish Art and Modernism*, The Institute of Irish Studies, Queen's University of Belfast, Belfast, 1991, p. 20.
3 Aloys Fleischmann, 'Ars Nova: Irish Music in Shaping', *Ireland Today*, 1, 2, July 1936, p. 42.
4 Eamon Ó Gallchobhair, *Ireland Today*, 2, 9, September 1937, p. 62.
5 See Kevin Rockett, '1930s Fictions', *Cinema and Ireland*, eds. K. Rockett, L. Gibbons and J. Hill, Syracuse University Press, Syracuse, New York, 1988, p. 61.
6 Liam Ó Laoghaire, *Motley*, 1, 5, October 1932, p. 3.
7 Liam Ó Laoghaire, 'Irish Cinema and the Cinemas', *Ireland Today*, 1, January 1937, p. 74.
8 Micheal Mac Liammóir, *Motley*, 1, 7, December 1932, p. 11.
9 'Realism', *Motley*, 1, 7, December 1932, p. 3.
10 'An Open Letter to the Leader', *Motley*, 1, April 1932, p. 12.
11 Richard Pine, in *Enter Certain Players*, ed. Peter Luke, Dolmen Press, Dublin, 1978, p. 74. See also Richard Pine, 'The Gate Theatre 1828-1978', *All For Hecuba*, ed. Richard Pine, Hugh Lane Gallery, Dublin, 1978.

12   Cited in Stan Smith, 'From A Great Distance: Thomas MacGreevy's Frames of Reference', *The Lace Curtain*, 6, Autumn 1978, p. 54.
13   Mainie Jellett, 'Modern Art And the Dual Ideal of Form Through the Ages', *Motley* 1931, p. 8.
14   Jellett, p. 9.
15   Cited in Alex Callinicos, *Against Postmodernism: A Marxist Critique*, Polity Press, Cambridge, 1989, pp. 12-13.
16   Michael Bell, 'Introduction: modern movements in literature', *The Contexts of English Literature 1900-1930*, ed. M. Bell, Methuen, London, 1980, p. 3.
17   See Giovanni Costigan, 'Romantic Nationalism: Ireland and Europe', *Irish University Review*, 3, 2, Autumn 1973, pp. 141-52.
18   Stan Smith, *The Origins of Modernism: Eliot, Pound, Yeats and the Rhetorics of Renewal*, Harvester Wheatsheaf, London, 1994, p. 6.
19   Smith, *The Origins of Modernism*, p. 5.
20   Smith, *The Origins of Modernism*, p. 7.
21   Anderson, p. 324.
22   Callinicos, p. 44.
23   John Wilson Foster, 'Irish Modernism', *Colonial Consequences: Essays in Irish Literature and Culture*, Lilliput Press, Dublin, 1991.
24   See Richard Ellmann, *James Joyce,* Oxford University Press, London, 1959, p. 604, where he describes Joyce's proposal as the 'one of the strangest in literary history'.
25   Seán O'Faoláin, *Vive Moi!*, Rupert Hart-Davis, London, 1963, p. 270.
26   Ó'Faoláin, p. 277.
27   Austin Clarke, 'Irish Poetry Today', *The Dublin Magazine*, 10, 1, January-March 1935, p. 31.
28   Clarke, p. 31.
29   Clarke, p. 32.
30   Daniel Corkery, *The Hidden Ireland*, Gill and Macmillan, Dublin, 1970, p. 15.
31   Corkery, *Hidden Ireland*, pp. 12-13.
32   Corkery, *Hidden Ireland*, p. 13.
33   Daniel Corkery, *Synge and Anglo-Irish Literature*, Cork University Press, Cork, 1966, p. 13.
34   Corkery, *Hidden Ireland*, pp. 13-14.
35   Corkery, *Synge*, p. 12.
36   Corkery, *Synge*, p. 14.
37   Corkery, *Synge*, p. 124.
38   Corkery, *Synge*, p. 13.
39   T.S. Eliot, *Notes Towards the Definition of Culture,* Faber and Faber, London, 1948, p. 31.

2

Muting the Klaxon:
Poetry, History and Irish Modernism

Tim Armstrong

In the winter of 1923–24 a periodical called *The Klaxon* appeared in Dublin. It was the only issue of what was hopefully announced as a 'seasonal' quarterly. The table of contents makes interesting reading:[1]

Confessional	L.K.E.
Beauty Energised	F.R.H.
The Midnight Court (from the Irish)	Percy Ussher
North	H. Stuart
Cheese	John W. Blaine
The Will of God	Sechilienne
The Ulysses of Mr James Joyce	Lawrence K. Emery
Cleopatra	F.R. Higgins
An Inghean Dubh	G. Coulter
Picasso, Mainie Jellett and Dublin Criticism	Thomas McGreevy

Seeking, as its editorial note suggests, to link itself to international modernism, *The Klaxon* has a Brancusi-like cover device and a 'Negro sculpture in wood' as frontispiece. The 'Confessional' by Lawrence Emery which opens this Irish *Blast* has a fine ranting tone: 'We railed against the psychopedantic parlours of our elders and their old maidenly consorts, hoping the while with an excess of Picabia and banter, a whiff of Dadaist Europe to kick Ireland into artistic wakefulness.' The aggressive modernism of the doomed journal, and the harshness of the context it expects to insert itself into, is evident in its defense of Joyce and Picasso against philistine taste. The inclusion of Ussher's translation of *The Midnight Court* also carries a political weight – its bawdy tone invoking a different Irish tradition from that of the Celtic Twilight (it was to be republished in 1926 with a polemical introduction by Yeats).

Thomas MacGreevy's piece, the longest in the journal, is a defence of Dublin artist Mainie Jellett, 'the first resident artist to exhibit a Cubist picture in Dublin'. Citing Gauguin's dictum that 'Symbolism is only another name for sentimentality', he points out that the Irish tradition (the Book of Kells) supports the use of abstraction and pattern. The resistance to such art among the Dublin art-fraternity he blames on 'the English tradition'. A fierce attack on English art and literature follows:

> That Gainsborough could make such concessions is a sign of the curious inability of the Englishman ever to be more than half an artist. Spencer, Marlowe, Dryden, Landor, and Keats are perhaps the only exceptions; and Webster, who may have been an Irishman. Practically all the others are moralizing snobs as much as they are artists, Chaucer and Shakespeare and Shelley and Reynolds as well as G.F. Watts and Mr John Galsworthy and the detestable Dr Johnson.

'There is', he adds, 'no artistic conscience in the country whose greatest genius could write both *King Lear* and *King Henry V*.' What is wanted is 'Irish artists and French artists', equated with the progressive Municipal Gallery, rather than the 'dead Dutch boors and English gentlemen' in the National Gallery of Ireland. That the future director of the National Gallery could launch a youthful diatribe against the institution which he would later head is an unsurprising incident in the battle of the generations, here linked to an animus against 'English' values designed to clear a space for Irish work. MacGreevy continued to dislike Reynolds and to argue for an Irish tradition. But he also offers a hostage to fortune in the form of his implicit programme for an Irish modernism: formalist and rigorous, it is to be unencumbered by the agenda of the state (*Henry V*), by bourgeois morality, by the necessity to embody a symbolic reality. At the beginning of his career, MacGreevy raises vital questions about the coordination of modernism, nationalism, religion, class, and tradition.

In this essay, I will use MacGreevy's writings, and the later work of Denis Devlin and Brian Coffey, to investigate the way in which an Irish (and particularly Catholic) modernism seemed possible in the 1930s, and the way in which its promise was at best partially fulfilled. The essay will focus on the split between public and private voices, between the desire to 'sound the Klaxon' for a reformed culture and a sense of personal estrangement from the existing culture.

MacGreevy and Irish Modernism

Thomas MacGreevy's position within modernism is fascinating for the literary historian: a poet living in Paris and then London who knew Joyce, Eliot, Beckett; author in 1928 of the text of a ballet by Constant Lambert; regular contributor to *transition;* translator of Valéry and others; later a cultured art historian; correspondent of Wallace Stevens. His status as an up-and-coming writer at the beginning of the 1930s is reflected by his appearances in the prestigious Dolphin Books – his 1931 monograph *T.S. Eliot: A Study* (no. 4 in the series) placed him in the company of Aldous Huxley, Richard Aldington, R.H. Mottram, T.F. Powys, Sylvia Townsend Warner and Samuel Beckett. It was followed by a study of Aldington, published the same year as Dolphin Books no. 10.

In the book on Eliot, MacGreevy sees a reflection of 'the fresh wind of Irish poetry that was blowing when Mr Eliot appeared above the horizon' in those lines in *The Waste Land* from the sailor's song in *Tristan and Isolde:*

> Frisch weht der Wind
> Der Heimat zu,
> Mein Irisch Kind,
> Wo weilest du?   (*Eliot,* p. 43)

McGreevy had already incorporated Wagnerian borrowings into 'Crón Tráth na nDéithe', invoking a mutual interchange between Eliot and himself. That, operatically, is how it still seemed at the beginning of the thirties, with Captains Joyce and Eliot at the helm, MacGreevy and Beckett on board, the wind at their backs. But for all that, MacGreevy's subsequent career as a poet was disappointingly truncated. By the time he published the superb *Poems* in 1934 he had stopped writing poetry; the moving gratitude at the renewal of voice in a few poems written decades later bears witness to the length of intervening silence. Instead he became a pioneering art historian and curator, writing on Jack B. Yeats, Poussin, and Irish collections. A number of questions thus hang over MacGreevy and his context. How symptomatic is his career? Why did Ireland fail to nurture an experimental modernist movement?

One obvious answer (which I want to avoid accepting prematurely) lies in the conservative nature of Irish culture in the 1920s and 1930s — typified by a prurient Catholic nationalism manifested in the Carnegie Library scandal, the protests over *The Plough and the Stars* (1926), and by the Censorship Act of 1929. This harsh context has been the staple of discussions of the problems facing writers in the period from 1922 to 1950, and of experimental writers in par-ticular.[2] One pitfall of such arguments lies in their tendency to perpetuate the idea of Irish exceptionalism — as if writers elsewhere were not faced with such pressures in the 1930s (conservative aesthetics were advocated from the left in the USA and the right in Germany). As J.C.C. Mays points out, the Irish experience can be compared with the failure of the early modernist impulse in America, Britain, and Ireland. He argues that Irish writers, in a post-colonial situation, faced a choice between international ex-perimentalism and a conservative, representative aesthetic associated with 'true' Irishness — but with little of the political inflections at-tached to those positions elsewhere (*CPD*, p. 24-5). One could com-pare post-revolutionary Mexico, in which the yoking of an artistic and political avant-garde — at least up to the suppression of the Com-munist Party in 1928 — produced an extraordinary body of work, particularly in the circle around Diego Rivera and Frida Kahlo, whose influence on international modernism has barely been assessed.[3]

In that case, the split between the political and the aesthetic avant-garde which Andreas Huyssen sees as definitional to later modernism happened rather earlier in Ireland than elsewhere, as a result of the rapid post-independence vitiation of those revolutionary pressures which might sustain an oppositional aesthetic.[4] Indeed the potential for such a split can be seen at the height of the strug-gle for independence: Arthur Clery commented, in a 1918 volume celebrating the *Poets of the Insurrection*, that 'To speak of a Catholic Revolution is practically an oxymoron. Yet Pearse's movement in-evitably claims that epithet' — a declaration followed by a critique of the secularizing modernism associated with Nietzsche, Ibsen, etc.[5] A 'Catholic revolution' will involve, that is, a return to older forms of cultural authority. The pre-existing role of the Revival (and the associated Gaelic League) as the vehicle for a national culture is important here: for all its nostalgic contradictions it formed a ready-made basis for an Irish literature outside the urban mainstream of Anglo-American and European culture, which in its narrow form fed into Corkery's 'Irish Ireland'. The comparison with Mexico is again illuminating: there, a hybrid art incorporating European, American and pre-Colombian elements flourished – as in Rivera's murals in Detroit or Kahlo's extraordinary 'Self-Portrait on the Borderline Between Mexico and the United States' (1932); in Ireland the use of 'native' materials was more constrained, and defined in terms of a 'return' to purity rather than a reformist sense of the need to incorporate and move on.

More locally, Susan Schreibman suggests that MacGreevy's problems in the Dublin world to which he returned in 1941 included the difficulty of access to publication, reflected in the hesitancy with which, even from abroad, he submitted work to Irish magazines. The obscurity of his poetry can even be linked to that self-protective stance, she argues (*CPM*, pp. xxix–xxiv). That seems paradoxical: less obscurity would have brought more ready publication, and MacGreevy's poetic difficulty was clearly programmatic and self-willed. A range of texts provides evidence that MacGreevy *did* have a confidently-promulgated programme for an Irish, Catholic, modernism, connected to a wider European modernism, and registered by an allegiance to Eliot and Joyce. For that reason, we need to study MacGreevy's programme and consider its relation to the period. But we might also wonder how it was that by the mid-1940s he had descended to the position of a pillar of establishment rectitude, to writing articles on church fittings (including realist sculpture) for the *Capuchin Annual* – in which he cites Degas's comment on Velasquez in relation to them, advocating silence before the sublime: 'There are no words. No, there are no words.'[6] For all that he was just making a living, the journalist over-praising national art is uncomfortably close to the compromised English artists whom he had criticized in 1923.

MacGreevy's Criticism: A Catholic Modernism?

In his monographs of 1931, MacGreevy feels his way towards an
analysis of what a writer's relation to society should be in a new
republic. America provides one point of reference, as a grossly
materialist culture: 'Where they do not worship money they wor-
ship power' (*Eliot*, p. 4). The American writer, he argues, is trapped
in an attitude of 'reaction' to this dynamic but morally-blind culture,
rather than being an organic intellectual. The result is the young
Eliot's cynicism:

> The masses can take themselves humorously but will not stand
> personality except in the matter of energy, the [intellectual] classes
> cannot take themselves humorously and will only stand person-
> ality when its energy has been subdued to mere nervous in-
> tensity (*Eliot*, p. 5).

The masses are energy and comedy; intellectuals, particularly the New
England élite, are 'nerves' (recalling George M. Beard's famous
diagnosis of 'American nervousness'). MacGreevy's vision of the
American writer caught between a philistine mass culture and a man-
darin high culture is a local and nuanced version of Eliot's own
'dissociation of sensibility', a fracture between art and the common life:

> There are literally dozens of writers of extraordinary verbal talent
> in America today who cannot find their own subjects because of
> the attitude that is imposed on them by a state of civilization that
> is on the one hand blatantly objective and on the other primly
> emasculate (*Eliot*, p. 40).

The characteristic American reaction to this 'spiritual bankruptcy'
is satire, which MacGreevy sees as essentially reactive and defensive.

For all that this is located in America, and in poets like the
early Eliot and Wallace Stevens, the same antinomies dominate
MacGreevy's *Richard Aldington: An Englishman*. MacGreevy portrays
his friend as representative of his own 'lost' war-time generation,
whose writers are doubly skewered: in chronological terms 'bet-
ween the stupidity of the elders and the mocking indifference of
their [often slightly younger] contemporaries' (*Aldington* p. 71), and
in terms of stance between the familiar poles which (in terms bor-
rowed from Aldington's *The Colonel's Daughter*) he calls 'Stimmism',

money-making philistinism, and 'Eastcourtism', the disengagement of the aesthete typified by Lytton Strachey. The war generation can accept neither a cynical pragmatism nor the abstraction of Eliot and others: 'reality' has, he argues, a particular weight for the writer who remembers the war.

The predicament of the modern artist is thus a focus of both books, and clearly relates to the Irish situation (in which the memories of a bitter war also intruded). In lamenting the isolation of the artist MacGreevy enters familiar modernist territory. But he attempts to avoid doing so on the terms laid down by Eliot, Pound, and Yeats, whose response to claims of the cultural inadequacy of the 'masses' is to cling to aristocratic culture and the authority of the classics (often combined with a eugenic desire to purge the socially inferior). Instead, MacGreevy criticizes both extremes: that of mass culture, and that of a cultural élitism associated with the Ascendancy. His aim might be said to be to plot a route between Stimmism and East-courtism – a middle way between disengagement and popularism, abstraction and 'reality', high and mass culture; to provide a sensibility which is not 'dissociated'. Accordingly in *Richard Aldington* he defends a specifically bourgeois art against modernist writers who reject it. The bourgeoisie has, he suggests, carried the responsibility for tending the 'Great Tradition' for only a century, and needed more time to live up to it, to produce an art of 'revolutionary humanity' (*Aldington*, pp. 11-12).

We need to notice the shift in attitude here: if in the *Klaxon* piece of 1923 the Dublin middle classes are criticized, in modernist fashion, for their philistinism, by 1931 MacGreevy now advocates an art which avoids élitist terms. If earlier he had said 'Symbolism is only another name for sentimentality', he now desires something like a common culture with a shared symbolic repertoire. In this he follows Eliot, who by 1930 had moved from the fragmented hostilities and framed 'hysteria' of *The Waste Land* to the tentative collective pieties of *Ash Wednesday*, from the position of outsider to the more inclusive role of editor of the *Criterion*.

Given the alienation inherent in the modernist stance, the best possible basis of this inclusive art for MacGreevy is Catholicism. Satire is more readily avoided within the collectivity of the Catholic tradition, which (implicitly) furnishes a set of shared symbolic resources and practices:

> Catholics, who have the habit of accusing themselves of their own
> sins in confession, are less inclined to be satirical about the other
> fellow than non–Catholics are. That is why the literature of
> indignation flourishes more in Protestant than in Catholic societies.
> It is why Mr James Joyce is, philosophically, a more just writer
> than say Mr Wyndham Lewis . . . It is why Mr Eliot's verse has
> purified itself of merely social elements as he has moved towards
> Catholicism . . . (*Eliot*, p. 16).

The mature Eliot becomes the candidate for the title of the coming
Catholic poet, plotting his way through despair and cynicism to
affirmation, finding his subject in 'nothing less than death and resur-
rection' (*Eliot*, p. 34). *The Waste Land* is ultimately 'practically beyond
mere literary criticism' because of its spiritual content, which is like
that of 'the strictest Christianity' (*Eliot*, p. 56). That does not imply
that it is simply doctrinal – MacGreevy worries about 'The Hollow
Men' because of its over–literal use of prayer (*Eliot*, p. 59), and has
doubts about Eliot's later devotional turn in general.[7] Rather he
values *The Waste Land* for its sense of sorting through a crowded
cultural terrain to where it can seek a truth outside itself. That point
is of utmost importance here (and will remain so as we look at Devlin
and Coffey). The aesthetic which MacGreevy champions suggests
that the meaning of a work of art can lie outside that work, in the
spiritual or religious. Art, which belongs to the fallen world, *quid-
ditas*, must reach beyond itself; it is not (as it was in the 1923 essay)
self–sufficient, it can find its meanings and framework in the larger
context of Christianity.

  MacGreevy's earlier essay on 'The Catholic Element in *Work in
Progress*' in *Our Exagmination Round his Factification for Incamination
of Work in Progress* (1929) presents another version of the Catholic
tradition. Joyce encompasses the darker aspects of existence which
canonly be subsumed within the open spiritual vocabulary of
Catholicism. The search for that vision skews MacGreevy's interpre-
tation of *Ulysses*, however: necessarily, he reads Stephen Dedalus as
the hero, journeying through 'the inferno of modern subjectivity':

> In this inferno from which Stephen is ever trying spiritually to
> escape, for he, unlike the Jewish Bloom, knows the distinction bet-
> ween the law of nature and the law of grace and is in revolt against
> the former however unable he be to realize the latter [,] even the
> most obscene characters are viewed with a Dantesque detachment
> that must inevitably shock the inquisitorially minded.[8]

Most modern readers of this passage are probably shocked not at Joyce's obscenity, but by its blunt, even 'Dantesque', view of hierarchy: the Catholic above the Jew with the latter among the damned (nature, the body), and Molly Bloom presumably further down the scale. The phrase used for Eliot — 'purged of all merely social elements' — explains the choice of Stephen: Bloom is a social creature; Stephen is the embodiment of an allegorical and spiritual quest. MacGreevy's interpretation of *Work in Progress* is also skewed by his programme. Where Jolas and other contributors to *Our Examination* see its constantly shifting, polyglossic languages as part of a revolution in poetic languge, MacGreevy sees the fact that 'the characters speak a language made up of scraps of half the languages known to mankind' as related to the 'purgatorial, transitional' nature of the text. It is of this world: 'Purgatory is not fixed and static like the four last things, death, judgement, heaven and hell.' MacGreevy expects Joyce, that is, to move beyond the satire and play of *Work in Progress* to the eternal verities: 'The questions of the law of grace triumphant and of a modern Paradiso will probably be more appropriately raised in some years' time.' This, it seems to me, is an opportunity lost. In the post-colonial situation in Ireland, one obvious pressure was to locate a linguistic purity in the national language: Irish. But a more inclusive gesture, not simply imposing a fixed language, is suggested by Joyce's strategy of incorporation (as by the hybrid styles of the Mexican artists).[9] MacGreevy ultimately rejects polylogue, not for the 'lost poetry' of the Celt, but for the truths of the Church and the idea of epic art.

That programme fits uncomfortably with the parallel demands of the state for a monologic culture. Writing in the year of the Censorship Act, the founding of what he calls an 'Inquisition', the distance between his ideal European Catholic vision and Irish actuality is all too obvious. The opposition between society and the writer which MacGreevy had located elsewhere — in America — threatens to come home. As Terence Brown has argued, much of the best Irish writing in the 1920s and 1930s is characterized by a satirical distance from official discourses: O'Casey's drama, O'Flaherty's *The Informer*, Denis Johnston's *The Old Lady Says 'No!'*, and the work of Seán O'Faoláin in particular.[10] The lack of a middle ground on which intellectuals and the 'masses' could meet is particularly apparent on the issue of censorship — as O'Faoláin complained, censorship is inherently divisive, splitting the intelligentsia who may know and judge from the 'masses' who are protected. (The fact that *Ulysses* was never banned in Ireland is revealing: the split was already in operation by virtue of its being a 'difficult' text.) Liam O'Flaherty was even more scathing about the paternalism of censorship:

> The tyranny of the Irish church and its associate parasites, the upstart Irish bourgeoisie, the last posthumous child from the wrinkled womb of European capitalism, maintains itself by the culture of dung, superstition and ignoble poverty among the masses.[11]

Obviously, MacGreevy was aware of these pressures, self-consciously creating in his criticism a utopian version of Catholic modernism. He argues, for example, that Aldington's anti-Catholic comments can be discounted – including the 'extraordinary historical defence of Protestantism' on the basis of its tolerance in *Death of a Hero* (*Aldington*, p. 54). His exhaustive refutation of the imputation of intolerance to the Catholic tradition (Spain aside) suggests an uneasiness, however, as do other comments about bourgeois puritanism. His Catholic, bourgeois, aesthetic is built on a ground which seems as riven by divisions between actual and real as deep as any he had seen in America.

MacGreevy's Poetry: Waiting for the 'Object'

How does MacGreevy's own poetry fit into the conceptual framework outlined above, in which the writer plots a path through 'the inferno of modern subjectivity' and emerges into truth, 'purged of all merely social elements'? Does MacGreevy the poet find the middle ground he desired as critic? Beckett's answer to the latter is yes: in his 1934 essay on 'Recent Irish Poetry' he sees MacGreevy as responding to the modernist 'rupture of the lines of communication' which cast the experiencing self and poetic objects equally into doubt. If poets can be divided into 'antiquarians' and the 'poor fish' gasping on the shores of modernity, MacGreevy occupies

> a position intermediate between the above [antiquarians] and the poor fish, in the sense that he neither excludes self-perception from his work nor postulates the object as inaccessible. But he

knows how to wait for the thing to happen, how not to beg the fact of this 'bitch of a world' — inarticulate earth and inscrutable heaven (*Disjecta*, p. 74).[12]

The process which produces awareness here is waiting and prayer. In his review of the *Poems* (1934), 'Humanistic Quietism', Samuel Beckett praised MacGreevey for his ability to reach towards prayer and affirmation, even in the 'darkest' poems (*Disjecta*, p. 69).[13]

Poems as a whole moves in that direction: from longer poems on World War I, the Easter uprising, and the period of the Irish Civil War, to the satire of 'Anglo-Irish' and 'The Other Dublin', and finally to the series of short, painterly, epiphanic poems which ends the volume. We might see this as a shift, according to MacGreevy's own project, away from satire to affirmation. Yet the basis of that affirmation is often personal and obscure, for all that these poems incorporate formal prayer. Many late poems end in declarations of small redeeming individual activities, centred on the lyric 'I': 'I hear . . .' ('Recessional'), 'I begin my rounds' ('Saint Senan's Well'), 'I recede, too,/Alone' ('Giorgionismo'), 'I rake the fire' ('Nocturne'). 'Nocturne of the Self-Evident Presence' is a good example, its obvious precursor Shelley's 'Mont Blanc', with its evocation of Alpine nothingness. Shelley's idealistic disappointment is replaced by minimalism; anything said in the face of nature's 'inarticulate' silence goes on the dump of poetic apparatus:

> I see no immaculate feet on these pavements,
> No winged forms,
> Foreshortened,
> As by Rubens or Domenichino,
> Plashing the silvery air,
> Hear no cars,
> Elijah's or Apollo's
> Dashing about
> Up there.
> I see alps, ice, stars and white starlight
> In a dry, high silence.   (*CPM*, pp. 42-43)

The silent epiphany which ends the poem is echoed elsewhere, in the 'vast, high, light-beaten plain' of 'Seventh Gift of the Holy Ghost', for example. MacGreevy shares this mode in a wintery minimalism with Wallace Stevens, with the St-John Perse of 'Snows', with the

Coffey of 'How Far from Daybreak' – muted tones, first of all those of the Ypres Salient and the Somme, then Whistleresque nocturnes in shades of white, ash, silver, grey, lead, and black. 'Gray' is a constant in his poetry, as in 'Homage to Jack Yeats': 'Grayer than the tide below, the tower;/The day is gray above' (*CPM*, p. 28).

Often this acts as the painterly wash on which a sparse colour signalling the moment of epiphany is applied. What Beckett called a 'spasm of awareness' is conveyed in splashes of gold, green. Even in the death of an airman: 'A delicate flame,/A stroke of orange in the morning's dress'(*CPM*, p. 3) – the pun on 'mourning' indicating the access of grief in the poem's Beckettian tentativeness before its object. 'Gloria de Carlos V' is a meditation on the way in which art can produce a moment of transfiguration. MacGreevy's world, formed in Flanders (the grotesqueries of Grünewald and gas masks), is mapped onto the difference between the agonistic and the paradisaical in Christianity, as he explains how Titian's masterpiece in the Prado affected him:

> My rose of Tralee turned gray in its life,
> A tombstone gray,
> Unimpearled.
> But for a moment, now, I suppose,
> For a moment I may suppose,
> Gleaming blue,
> Silver blue,
> Gold,
> Rose,
> And the light of the world.   (*CPM*, p. 36)

The move from 'But for a moment, now, I suppose' to the more declarative 'For a moment I may suppose' encapsulates Beckett's sense of poise: waiting and arrival.

The ability to wait spans the huge silence in MacGreevy's poetic career between 1930 and 1960. His major late poem 'Breton Oracles' (1961) returns in pilgrimage to 'the Brittany of the tender legends', the territory of Renan, of Celtic purity, in order to wrestle a final image from the world. If the 'Gigantic red rocks' which he finds there, with their 'drowsing menace', remind one of *The Waste Land*, the pilgrimage amongst stone crosses is closer to the spirit of 'Little Gidding'. The poem finds its redemptive moment in a characteristic streak of colour:

You were there;
And, in the half-light,
The dark green, touched with gold,
Of dream leaves;
The light green, touched with gold,
Of clusters of grapes;
And, crouching at the foot of a renaissance wall,
A little cupid, in whitening stone,
Weeping over a lost poetry.   (*CPM*, p. 70)

For all the almost irresistible plangency of this image, we need to note its elegiac nature; it is an epitaph. The little stone angel is not an actual angel, but an image for a 'lost tradition' of Celtic monasticism. MacGreevy echoes Devlin's tendency to anchor his Catholicism on its places; on the stones of the cathedrals which are the loci of *The Heavenly Foreigner*. The quest is for the object which will act as the container of meaning, but that meaning is located in the past.

Thus, MacGreevy became a guardian of the past: as a social being a curator and churchman, but a silent poet. His major poems were written with a full consciousness of the pressures of history: 'De Civitate Hominum', 'The Six Who Were Hanged', 'Homage to Hieronymus Bosch', 'Crón Tráth na nDéithe', 'Aodh Ruadh Ó Domhnaill' — all respond to the sense of fragmentation produced by the Civil War and its aftermath, often with a bitter satirical pungency. Yet beyond them we have poems reaching towards silence, to a meaning which they could not contain. If MacGreevy's Catholic aesthetic had suggested an affirmation of religious truth, he could not, in general, follow Eliot into the world of 'Ash Wednesday' and the *Four Quartets*. It is difficult to say why: perhaps simply that his rose *was* gray, conditioned by historical realities to which he could not cease to bear witness, and which precluded any movement beyond the individual epiphany.

The struggle for a voice which negotiates between public and private, which MacGreevy returns to again and again, is endemic to modernist texts. One solution adopted by a number of writers is to split public and private voices, as in John Dos Passos's *U.S.A.*, in which the subjective 'Camera Eye', representing an authorial interiority, alternates with passages of conventional narrative and the 'Newsreels' that chronicle public events. Another solution is the

dialogism of texts like *Ulysses* and Lowry's *Under the Volcano*; yet
another the modernist collage-text from which the subject is
(theoretically) expunged, as in much of *The Cantos*, and in which
the power to integrate the material is passed over to the reader or
located in an absent centre ('history').[14] MacGreevy did write
poems in the 1920s which could in a manner of speaking be called
dialogic: 'Crón Tráth na nDéithe' in particular incorporates citation,
discord, fragments of musical notation, extending the aesthetics of
The Waste Land in formulating its sense of malaise.[15] But as a
general tendency MacGreevy shows no sign of abandoning lyric;
it is the poet's voice – the 'I' – which bears the burden of witness-
ing to his times, taking the burden of petition and at its best finding
a confluence of personal and collective feeling, as at the end of 'The
Six Who Were Hanged', with its insistent time and place:

> And still, I too say,
> *Pray for us.*
> *Mountjoy, March, 1921*

The consonance here is of a particular revolutionary moment. Beyond
such points of crisis the lyric voice falters and becomes isolated as
politics and the avant-garde peel apart. The only option, apart from
silence, is to join those forces which say 'I too' within a true Catholic
collectivity – and that is the road to the *Capuchin Annual.*

Art Criticism: Jack B. Yeats and the Historical Style

It is in MacGreevy's study of Jack Yeats, published in 1945 but much
of it written in London in 1938, that he finds an image of the Irish
artist. He declares that the 'secularist tendency' of English criticism
offends him, as it had Professor Clery in 1918 – 'secularism' signal-
ling aesthetic individualism (*Yeats.* p. 3).[16] The Protestant Yeats
hardly seems a promising model for the non-secular Irish artist; yet
it is, one could speculate, his Protestantism that attracts MacGreevy,
since it generates an immanence which seeks symbolic objects located
in the world of 'reality'. For MacGreevy he bridges the multiple
divisions in modern Irish society – between the subjective and
objective, individual and social, between imagination and reality, and

between different political groupings: 'In the life of Ireland fact and poetry have parted company. Jack Yeats's work became a passionate recall to poetry — to the splendour of essential truth' (*Yeats*, p. 27). Yeats paints 'the Ireland that matters' (*Yeats*, p. 5), an common humanity unstratified by class (*Yeats*, p. 15).

Elsewhere, MacGreevy uses his art history to formulate a genealogy for the Irish painter who will avoid both abstraction and satire. *Pictures in the National Gallery* (1945) attacks Dutch art, with its 'snobbism' in using comic peasants, as well as the aristocratic British tradition and the stylization of Lucas Cranach. His imaginary genealogy of Irish painting takes in Mantegna and Poussin. The former's 'Judith With the Head of Holofernes', painted amidst Italian political turmoil, becomes 'a woman condemned to be an assassin for the honour and salvation of her countrymen', as if she were a republican heroine. Poussin, like Mantegna, combines religiousness with intellectual passion on an epic scale. The Irishman James Barry (1741–1806) forms a third rung in this ladder, though limited by his market: 'Barry dreamed of being a great European "historical" artist like Mantegna or Poussin. He despised professional portrait painting as an inferior branch of art. But English society only wanted pictures of itself . . .'[17]

It is worth pausing over MacGreevy's stress on the term 'historical'. Associated with eighteenth-century France and the Académie, with the line from Le Brun to David, the historical style elevates the representation of public action (particularly conflict). The historical mode is a didactic art dedicated to the ideological needs of the state, often linking itself, as Norman Bryson shows in his *Word and Image*, to the body of a figure who incarnates it. Its mode in Bryson's fascinating account is what he calls *discursive*; that is, it sees painting as the achievement of an embodied or narrated meaning, seemingly independent of the process in which meaning is produced, in contrast to the *figural* work which stresses the painter's brushwork, or the surface of the painting, and which privileges the image rather than the symbol.[18] Like the Catholic work, the discursive painting gestures outside itself.

The 'historical' is what MacGreevy sees in Jack Yeats; the first great national painter in the line of Poussin and Barry. As in the case of Benjamin West in early national America, the historical style, in MacGreevy's programme, is to create a landscape-with-figures, suffused with heroic resonances.[19] He insists that Yeats has found a *new* balance between the figures and the landscape, not seen in previous painters, creating a mythology which is both personal and collective — particularly in his later, more sketchy and dramatic technique. In recent works 'the balance between observation and imagination has, in fact, altered' (*Yeats,* p. 28), moving away from that mere realism which one might associate with the detailed and self-suffient surface of the still life (the book on Aldington had praised *nature vivante* over the *nature morte*). The 1945 'Postscript' to *Jack B. Yeats* singles out the recent large-scale mythological paintings, implicitly in terms of their aspiration to the historical style. 'Tinker's Encampment — the Blood of Abel', for example, provides an adequate symbol of the war in Europe which combines Irish reality with an epic, biblical scope which would be appropriate to Poussin or Barry. These are not works of 'withdrawal', he argues, pursuing art for art's sake. Rather they are engaged by virtue of their recourse to a mythology consciously embodied in 'reality', an 'objective correlative'.

MacGreevy and Wallace Stevens

In his stress on the meditative lyric, MacGreevy can be compared to a poet with whom he had connections in later life: the American Wallace Stevens. Stevens and MacGreevy knew each other's work in the 1930s, and began to correspond in April 1948 after their mutual friend Barbara Church mentioned to the Irish poet that Stevens enjoyed his work; MacGreevy sent a copy of *Poems*, and they continued to exchange letters regularly, only meeting each other in July 1954 at the Churchs' apartment in New York. The correspondence was productive for Stevens, directly inspiring his poem 'Tom MacGreevy in America', influencing 'The Westwardness of Everything' and 'The Novel', and providing material for essays. As Peter Brazeau tells the story, the gregarious MacGreevy also saw the reclusive, private side of Stevens, who stuck to home in Hartford: when the Director of the National Gallery of Ireland visited the Hartford Athenaeum the local poet-lawyer was not at the reception, rigidly isolating the world of the imagination from that of work.[20]

Yet as recent critics have suggested, much of the force of Stevens's greatest poetry comes from the points where that isolated stance was most under threat: for example in the fierce debates in the 1930s, continuing into the war, about artistic 'involvement' versus abstraction, which prompted Stevens's most productive attempts to write a poetry adequate to the demands of history. That concern persisted into the post-war period, for example in the questions about the viability of (America's) 'bearing the weight of Europe' in 'Imago'. These issues are taken up in the correspondence, with a debate on American involvement in post-war Europe in which MacGreevy took an independent line with respect to those bearing gifts, Marshall and Stalin alike. Ireland was, he said, already 'lousy with money'.[21] This sense of self-sufficiency after the 'Emergency' contrasts sharply with Stevens's war, the pressures of which compelled him to produce a poetic equivalent of Yeats's 'History' paintings, mythical and real, while MacGreevy (whatever he felt about the position) could not mediate between the poet and journalist-curator.

In 'Nocture of the Self-Evident Presence', as we saw, MacGreevy rejected the poetic apparatus of Elijah's chariot in favour of silence. Stevens also declared that the solar chariot was junk, and in 1938 wrote 'The Man on the Dump.' This poet of the junk-heap is noisier:

> One sits and beats an old tin can, lard pail.
> One beats and beats for that which one believes.
> That's what one wants to get near. Could it after all
> Be merely oneself, as superior as the ear
> To a crow's voice? Did the nightingale torture the ear,
> Pack the heart and scratch the mind? And does the ear
> Solace itself in peevish birds? Is it peace,
> Is it a philosopher's honeymoon, one finds
> On the dump? Is it to sit among mattresses of the dead,
> Bottles, pots, shoes and grass and murmur *aptest eve:*
> Is it to hear the blatter of grackles and say
> *Invisible priest*; is it to eject, to pull
> The day to pieces and cry *stanza my stone?*
> Where was it one first heard the truth? The the.[22]

As James Longenbach comments, neither sceptical empiricism (the Johnsonian 'stanza my stone') nor the romantic optimism of the 'invisible priest' are appropriate here, since both 'forsake the work of manufacturing a world that has the value we grant it'.[23] Where

MacGreevy reduces the world to silence and frost in order to clear a way for prayer, Stevens does so (as in 'The Snow Man') in order to build it up anew from the materials he finds around him.

For Stevens, this method is supported by his reading of Nietzsche and Vaihinger, and by the American pragmatist tradition. His particularity ('the the'), like that of William Carlos Williams, eschews universal truths. Or at least, it delays them — the story of deathbed conversion to Catholicism which emerged in the early 1980s suggests at best a last-minute entry. 'St Armourer's Church from the *Outside*' is his title. We can say that as a critic MacGreevy made a choice between models. Stevens represented a nativist modernism (Protestant, personal, and local; immanent and flexible in approach); whereas Eliot represented an international Anglo-Catholic modernism (transcendent, authoritarian, and impersonal — in aim, at least). Critical of Stevens in 1931, MacGreevy argues for Eliot's importance. But his difficulty with the orthodoxy of Eliot's later work suggests that Stevens's mode, which represents the road not taken, offered a potentially fruitful set of possibilities, closer to those realized in Jack Yeats. In order to explore the implications of that choice, we can look at two Irish modernist poets who followed MacGreevy: Denis Devlin and Brian Coffey.

After MacGreevy: Denis Devlin and Brian Coffey

The careers of Denis Devlin and Brian Coffey begin with the jointly-authored *Poems* of 1930, praised by Beckett in his 1934 article on 'Recent Irish Poetry'. Both show the influence of Eliot. Coffey's work is less mature than his friend's and far from his later style, yet fascinating for the way in which Eliot's disturbed voices infect them:

> Let us consider once more, you and I,
> The sorrows beaded on the chainéd years
> Lonely as tears
> Unheeded wilfully . . .
> Let there be frankness underneath the sky
> Truth in our eyes as each questions why.
>
> Who walks beside me plucking at my hand
> Arousing thoughts I will not understand . . .
>
> O robed lady, clothed in light and rose. . . .[24]

Other early poems are equally fitted with the furniture of Eliot: demotic complaints, geraniums, granite rocks. Significantly, *Poems* as a whole does not have an identifiable politics; unlike MacGreevy's major poems, it is less driven by the historical pressure of the decades which precede it, and more concerned with the problematics of voice.

If Coffey begins in the shadow of Eliot, Devlin's dense, ironic poems already signal a mature distance – partly, as his editor J.C.C. Mays suggests, under the influence of Hart Crane, but perhaps also suggesting a stance of self-protective alienation: 'O Paltry Melancholy', for example, is concerned with the rejection of positions rather than their adoption. A certain guardedness was to remain with Devlin. Like MacGreevy, he could mount an attack on the English – as in the comments against Milton, Marvell, and 'the toady, Horace' in 'Encounter' (*CPD*, p. 136) – but as Mays points out he less readily falls into an identifiable literary or political position. Indeed, one could see Devlin's earlier work as dominated by a satiric distance. 'Bacchanal', originally entitled 'News of Revolution', works through its grotesque, anaphoric rhetoric to a point of satiric disillusion which parodies the poetry of Audenesque excitement. His 'Forerunners', running 'naked as sharks through water', are a breed reminiscent of Wyndham Lewis's 'Tyros', savage revolutionaries made for a new world, but Devlin holds out no hope of 'intelligence from a brave new State' (*CPD*, p. 65). The piled sentences make this a difficult poem to follow, as does the tangling of post and pre-revolutionary perspectives; but that difficulty is, perhaps, the point. Devlin's poetic mode is inherently catacrectic, jumbling discordant registers and abandoning any sense of clear progression, often to the point that sense is threatened. The 'difficulty' is created at the semantic level: his sentences usually seem grammatical, he does not simply arrange words in juxtaposition; it is as if one language were struggling to emerge from beneath another.

Devlin, then, does not seem a ready candidate for the position of MacGreevy's Catholic poet. He did, of course, go on to write 'Lough Derg', 'The Passion of Christ', and other devotional poems, *The Heavenly Foreigner* the greatest of them, but even they are marked by distance (for example, the satire of pietism in 'Lough Derg'). It is as if he could not accommodate himself to a public role, a declarative poetry. The idea of the public statue is a useful way into that question (remembering MacGreevy's final image of the stone angel). Mays suggests a comparison between Devlin's 'The Statue and the Perturbed Burghers' and Wallace Stevens's *Owl's Clover*, a sequence written in response to 1930s' demands for a politicized art. In fact Stevens meditated on the possibility of a public, monumental art throughout his career, in essays like 'The Noble Rider and the Sound of Words' as well as in poetry. And while that attempt was ultimately to fail, given the difficulty for the modern poet of achieving a collective voice, Stevens's repeated attempts at commemorative art contrast with Devlin's sharply accented sense of discomfort in the face of burgherly values. His 'fluttering boy in tight marble' exists amidst the sarcastically described:

> People of worth and wealth
> Glancing with care at their modes of life
> Walls cradles windows amber orchards.   (*CPD*, p. 54)

Stevens, on the other hand, never ceases to attempt a dialogue between the values of art and the bourgeoisie.

If the comparison seems unfair, then 'Argument With Justice' – one of Devlin's most political poems of the 1930s – provides another example, opening in the manner of Keats and Hopkins with a series of rhetorical questions to the abstract figure of blind Justice, a goddess who has 'abandoned' her reign. The questions take in most of the poem, and only find a resolution in the final teasing imprecation:

> Come down, let there be
> Justice though the heaven's fall, be virtue of our
> Temporary measure.   (*CPD*, p. 89)

The final line, deliberately stranded with its leaden official term for the state's edicts, seems to accentuate the distance between one language and another. Like Walter Benjamin's Angel of History, Devlin's blind Justice is blasted by the wind of events – but in this case the Angel does not feel the wind and see its results with Benjamin's pity and terror.[25] Instead, she is isolated, distant from the chaos, more like Keats's *Mnemosyne*: 'Blown, see, against thy portals, centuries of mortals mouth blasphemy righteous.' We get no further than the portals, while the statue on her 'column transcendental' remains distant. There is no possibility of the epic-historical here.

Devlin remains sceptical about public symbolism, often constructing his poems around a private set of preoccupations and memories which only reluctantly achieves a realization in the world – as in the moving final lyric of 'The Colours of Love'. The only basis on which he could accept public discourse was that identified by MacGreevy, within a Catholicism whose meanings are already externalized – in the extended versions of the Stations of the Cross in 'The Passion of Christ', in the cathedrals of *The Heavenly Foreigner* (whose meaning is so fixed that starting an argument about Bath vs. Chartres can stand for Protestantism in general). *The Heavenly Foreigner* achieves a brilliant fusion of personal experience, religious aspiration, and formal effectiveness. Yet many readers of 'The Passion of Christ', I suspect, find it a dry performance (particularly compared to Coffey's version in *Advent* 8). The rigidity of form is suggested by the dedication to Allen Tate, who was in that period busily writing himself into an American version of Eliot's Anglo-Catholic impasse. Devlin's work more often takes the opposite path of distance, difficulty, and resolute individuality; his status as a 'historical' poet is at best problematic.

Coffey and History

Brian Coffey's poetry maps the public-private, political-personal, satiric-affirmative in a different and more complex way. We can begin with *Missouri Sequence,* the poem which, it seems to me, best balances public and private preoccupations to provide something like the stance which MacGreevy praised in Jack B. Yeats, and which Devlin achieves in *The Heavenly Foreigner.*

Coffey was a slow starter as a poet, with (like MacGreevy) a long period in which he completed little – between *Third Person* (1938) and *Nine a Musing* (1961).[26] It was only with *Missouri Sequence* (1962) that he attempted a sustained piece, more open to personal and collective history. The sequence spans a period of crisis in 1952, in which Coffey was forced to leave his teaching post in America, and to re-forge his poetic vocation. At the centre of the poem is the meditating voice of the poet at his desk at night, considering the balance between the ideal world of poetry and experience, but it also evokes larger forces around that space: the natural world and the cycle of

the seasons, the Irish diaspora, family life, and a web of friends created
in the dedications of individual sections (to MacGreevy, Leonard
Eslick, Devlin, and Coffey's wife Bridget).

Missouri Sequence is most compelling when Coffey evokes what
he calls the 'distraction' of concrete experience:

> Tonight the poetry is in the children's game:
> I am distracted by comparisons,
> Ireland across the grey ocean,
> here, across the wide river.
>
> ★ ★ ★
>
> We live far from where
> my mother grows very old.
> Five miles away, at Byrnesville,
> the cemetery is filled with Irish graves,
> the priest an old man born near Cork,
> his bloss like the day he left the land.   (*PV*, p. 69)

To be 'distracted' is to notice suddenly, to enter that present which
'Missouri Sequence' recognizes as in time rather than timeless, for
all its appeal to an abstract wisdom. At the moment of loss, poetry
appears:

> Watch the slender swallow flash its wings,
> dive, sheer sky in two,
> never before, never again
> and such is poetry.   (*PV*, p. 86)

Coffey is constantly 'distracted' in the sequence – again in section
1 by the sunfish that play on the surface of a pool, by winter in sec-
tion 2, from the contemplation of his muse in section 3, by love and
anger in section 4, and more globally, by his forced abandonment
of the place his children have grown up in. In each case he brings
a startling attention to his being in the world, measuring himself
against the parables he includes, and pouring himself into his poems
as he lives beyond their scope. Among other things, this is a poetry
of small detail – frogs among iris leaves, the weather last month,
a catalogue of the trees that grow in Missouri. These things work
against the discursive, producing a texture against which myth stands

out as 'poor alien symbols'. In the opening section of *Missouri Sequence* he had set out an opposition which his poem dilutes:

> No servant, the muse
> abides in truth,
> permits the use of protest
> as a second best
> to make clean fields
> exults only in the actual
> expression of a love,
> love all problem,
> wisdom lacking.   (*PV*, p. 73)

Protest comes to seem intrinsic to the 'actual'. Protest and love, by poem's end, have been subsumed to wisdom and poetry. Thus Coffey refuses any distinction between the 'merely social' and 'truth'; he recognizes the pressures of time, place, history and season, while balancing pattern against impulse, a desire to symbolize against the needs of existence.

Coffey's 'hard' poems are also political and historical, though in a pessimistic sense which sees all experience as flawed. Indeed, *Advent* and *Death of Hektor* remind me most strongly of Shelley's despairing political apocalypses, *Prometheus Unbound* and *Hellas*, in which the ages roll on despite the poet's cry:

> But we blank through ages to Earth's crying out 'how long'
> may note not at all Earth's fairest day-show of beauty
> fudging even the dreams which keep us asleep   (*PV*, p. 136)

It is section 3 of *Advent* in which Coffey turns to the question of history and addresses Klio, its muse. This figure, like Devlin's in 'Argument with Justice', has become seemingly distant and statue-like:

> what have they done to Klio what have they done to our Muse
> of History Muse Klio of Memory daughter and set
> out of place and time on a plinth to reign of silence queen
>
> As if in opened bunker one faced numberless suppliant bones
> and awed by that silent thunder wanted words

> What would we call on you for Klio if your style
> were finger on lip to crawl through cunning corridors
> fumbling behind the arras for what was not there   *(PV,* p. 122)

This silent muse seems to accede to the terrors of history, to imperialism and nationalism. The muse of 'cunning corridors' (which seems to allude to Eliot's in 'Gerontion') is impotent. Yet history offers no redemption, and the desire for order in history is itself a snare, with no meaning outside its accidents:

> The veil of randomness attracts lawseeking yen
> constants to find to make necessity of
> while history works still against the rounded tale   *(PV,* p. 126)

The final lines of part 3 take in Ireland's history, 'compromise partition . . . civil war', but conclude that the tangled story is 'earth's unfinished business', not to be plotted before its completion, even within a Christian framework ('no necessary thought will usher in final night').

Similarly in *Death of Hektor* (which has a number of links with *Advent* 3) Coffey denies the possibility of any panoptic view:

> We can not hold time fast in our sights
> as if judging events in a moment unique
> like hill-top watcher taking Battle in at a glance   *(PV,* p. 152)

The perspective denied here is that of a particular type of heroic painting, typified by Velasquez's 'The Surrender of Breda', as well as the god's-eye views of the *Iliad.* The point made at the opening of *Death of Hektor* is that history is sealed off from us, that we have only the poet's myth – the story of violence which Coffey proceeds to deconstruct by insinuating it into the modern world. Section 10, for example, refers to 'Doom now in the air like a cloudy mushroom' above Troy (followed by a reference to 'white blood cells'). Section 11 castigates the vanities of public life in language evoking Nazi Germany:

> Doom's rank perfect days   the false assumptions of security
> doom as rot of joists beams partner's treachery slave ways
> coinage falsified   Niagara's   of fairy cash corpses candles
> chalices gold teeth spendthrift scrip to jack up naked power
>
> *(PV,* p. 161)

Thus, Coffey's mature poetry pictures a radical incompletion in the field of history, a 'point to point' (*PV,* p. 153) awareness of its fragmentary and negotiated nature. *Death of Hektor* begins with a personal memory and ends with not with epic scope but with Andromache amidst her linen, pots and pans:

> the years it took to put a home together living against the grain
> of great deeds   her woman's life   in her heart
> much held fast   word hidden for all   (*PV,* p. 165)

One might be suspicious of another image of woman as the outside of history; yet this is a position in which Coffey places himself in *Missouri Sequence,* claiming no privileged point of view and 'living against the grain' around him — creating in the difficult textures of his poetry a different grain. Like Shelley, Coffey protests against and finally accedes to necessity — from the 'Say — could it indeed be otherwise' of 'Exile' (1933) to the 'Must it be this way / How would one better have had it done' and final 'So be it' of the last section of *Advent,* forty-two years later (*PV,* pp. 14, 148, 150).

Even outside the strong structures supplied by the biblical and classical myths, Coffey's poetry aspires to something more like Beckett's condition of prayer. Yet often it seems to flee from any located place, in contrast to the careful placing of *Missouri Sequence* — and it is here we see the cleaving of two modes in Coffey. We find ourselves where, as Stan Smith puts it, 'exile is not so much a social condition as an ontogical given'.[27] Smith's comment is directed at *Missouri Sequence,* to which it seems to me misapplied: the answer to Coffey's question in the sequence, 'Does it matter where one dies, / supposing one knows how?' is 'yes' — where the Irish immigrants died, Byrnesville, is just the point. But the flight within to a no-place of retreat is apparent elsewhere, as in 'How Far from Daybreak':

> There was a sort of place
> call it a bowl
> encompassed a maze
> of growing walls
> Let's say there was no way out
> all ways led within
> There walls grew strong

> around a central waste
> grew petrified
> 'til small distant soul
> curled in wordless haven
> and withdrawal   (*PV*, p. 103)

'Withdrawal' is what MacGreevy had defended Jack Yeats against; localized here in a wasteland from which Coffey's poem plots its tenuous path to freedom, love, and the 'green light' of dawn. An allegorical space constructed in patterns of layered words, it is one of those modernist zones whose origin lies in Mallarmé's *Un Coup de dés* (which Coffey has translated): 'forcefields of hurt and bruising' (*PV*, p. 103), 'parks of emptiness or supposition' (*PV*, p. 104).[28] The dark, grey-and-white place, covered in sand or snow, recurs in many poems — 'For What for Whom Unwanted', 'The Prayers', as well as in *Advent* itself. In many cases it recalls MacGreevy's characteristic spaces, with their splashes of colour — 'one touch of poppy-red' (*PV*, p. 173) — though Coffey's meditative mode is more pessimistic, and his epiphanies more framed.[29]

There are also harsher moments. The split in Coffey's later career, it seems to me, is between the abstract poems described above and a broad satire. *Advent* appeared in the wake of the self-published children's alphabet *ABECEDARIAN*.[30] Only the poem for 'V' offers a sardonic comment on the wider field of literature:

> I'm a Viper.
> Sunning
> on a stone I lie.
> 'Horseman, pass by!'   (*PV*, p. 215)

This is not, of course, to criticize Coffey for writing children's literature. But it is necessary to recognize a divide between these modes. Equally, for a public political voice we could look at *The Big Laugh* (1976), Coffey's reading of the seventies and particularly the 'Winter of Discontent' in England, where he now lived. It is a family story of apocalypse in which two hand-drawn Jarryesque characters, the ultra-fat Glutz and the rakish Coil, conspire to end the universe — Glutz having taken over first Iceland then the world to regain Coil's love, before blowing it up with 100-megaton cobalt bombs. Though the story is prefaced by rhythmical grumbling about the decline of commercialised society – 'strawberry jam/shouldn't taste/like fish' – and the slogan 'HANDS OFF/THE/UNIVERSE'. Coffey's political discontent seems most readily located in his interpolated one-page 'Playlet by Anne Ankay', which has a cast including an 'Enclave of Stewards' and an 'Envy of Lads', and contains the following speech:

> Topman to Nation: Cool it LADS. We've just found under the
>   HOUSE a multiplying gear we didn't know we'd got that
>   fits the BANKNOTEMACHINE. Will you accept quad-
>   rupled wages and quartered work?[31]

Whether this inset play is ironized is difficult to say (the title suggests not). Coffey's preoccupations in Southampton in the late 1970s seem disturbingly similar to Philip Larkin's in Hull: national decline and the unions, disgust at junk. The opinions of a conservative teacher distressed at the way the world is going, even in the idiom of Jarry and Beckett, are unsettling reading, the 'merely social' with a vengeance.

The Big Laugh has its rewards (including those of narrative and humour), but it reflects a conservatism, coupled to a suspicion of all state apparatus, apparent elsewhere in Coffey's late works – in poems like 'Leader', 'Eleison II', and 'Call the Darkness Home'. The bitter title piece of *Topos and Other Poems* (1981) describes 'Tiber Topman' who hires 'Angus MacSorass of that Ilk' to kill the poets unhappy enough to have become ad-men:

> MacSorass to bellow the slogan
> 'Self to itself is the Same
> Novelty Fiction Supreme.'[32]

Are these satires 'mistakes'? Certainly, they seem evidence of the relative failure of a public voice for the later Coffey, outside the context of the intense sacramentalism and experimentalism of *Advent* and 'The Prayers'. The confluence of writing, personal, and public history in *Missouri Sequence* is abandoned in favour of more divided modes in which political life is either a horror, or distanced in time or concept. Coffey becomes *both* of the poets MacGreevy identified: the alienated satirist preoccupied with the social, and the poet of religious 'truth'.

Conclusion

What we have observed is a defining uncertainty in the Irish modern-ist tradition. If the *Klaxon* blasted existing values, MacGreevy quickly moved to a position in which he wished the poet or artist to be central to national cultural aspirations, representing a broader base. That in turn involved the creation of a symbolic repertoire, like that which he saw in Jack B. Yeats, which was at least potentially shared. Yet for MacGreevy and for the writers who follow, that communality was most readily located in Catholicism. The result was poems which often locate their meanings beyond the 'merely social', and often beyond the poem itself – in MacGreevy's silences, in Devlin's places, in the religious fulfillment implied by Coffey's *Advent*. The linguistic difficulty of Devlin and Coffey serves not to break a language (the original intention of the avant-garde) but to conserve it in a space beyond the always compromised world of social action. The figural (in Bryson's terms) becomes discursive; it can be read as an index of the difficulties and rewards of truth, and as symptomatic of a fallen world.

There is always, however, a counter-pressure from the social and historical which informs the best poems of all three writers, and turns them into profound meditations on the nature of human experience. What Coffey calls being 'distracted' sees the poet measure ideals against bitter reality – a reality which MacGreevy could not expunge from his poems. If Devlin often strives to distance reality in his poems (to make it a little harder to see, as Wallace Stevens put it), then that indicates the danger inherent in the Catholic idealism which begins with MacGreevy: a fall into satire or silence as the social world comes to seem polluted.

The long period between 1938 and 1961 in which only Devlin, of the three poets here, was producing significant work is indicative of the problems of that social world, of a delay between MacGreevy's programme for an Irish poetry and the possibility of its fulfillment – a story which lies to a large extent outside the scope of this essay, in the work of Kinsella and others as well as Coffey. It is as if the political call could not be matched by a sustaining structure (factors like the encouragement offered by Michael Smith at the New Writers' Press and others in the 1970s would need to enter the story here). One might compare post-colonial America, in which the call for an 'independent' literature to match political independence came after the revolution, and was arguably only matched by a literary response decades later — a literary response whose sense of dislocation from the state is (in Melville in particular) already responsible for a modernist irony.[33]

It is at this point that MacGreevy's move from poetry and literary criticism to art becomes important. In a post-colonial struggle the oppositional forces are partly those of tradition, inherent in the language and its influences as in a shared history. MacGreevy's complicated alignment with respect to Eliot and Aldington, and modernism itself, derives from that fact; it is hard to escape a language. In moving to art history and forging a genealogy for the Irish historical painter incarnated in Jack B. Yeats, he was able to work on a different ground — and to escape modernism's pre-occupation with the figural, with surfaces, and find the discursive, national, art which he sought. The cost may have been a narrowly defined language — implicitly monologic rather than dialogic — and his own poetic silence: there is little room in such a view of art for either the intense but dwindling lyric voice of the nocturnes, or for grotesque, stylized, satirical and surreal effects like the dancing rats in 'Homage to Hieronymus Bosch'.

Devlin, and particularly Coffey, both aspire to something like an equivalent in poetry to this historical style. But the careers of both poets are marked by the ambivalence which MacGreevy sought to escape — ambivalence about the bourgeois public sphere, ambivalence about the state, and about history itself. Both share the Catholic lexicon which MacGreevy celebrated, but in both cases the satirical impulse erupts elsewhere; the 'merely social' returns as a supplement, in the Derridean sense, to the 'truths' of the devotional mode. Arguably all three poets produce their best poetry when most challenged by the force of experience and history, at those points where they are not merely relying on an established mythology out-side the poem to create a sense of ambient meaning. In that sense an (Irish) Catholic modernism remains, as Professor Clery described it in 1918, most productive when most an oxymoron.

Notes

1 *The Klaxon*, 1, Dublin, 1923-4, title page. MacGreevy's piece is pp. 24-6.
2 See Terence Brown's *Ireland: A Social and Cultural History, 1922-79*, Fontana, London, 1981, chs. 1-5; Richard Fallis, *The Irish Renaissance*, Syracuse University Press, Syracuse, N.Y., 1977, ch. 12; Dillon Johnston, *Irish Poetry After Joyce*, Dolmen Press, Dublin, 1985, ch. 1; Augustine Martin, 'Literature and Society, 1938-1955', *Ireland in the War Years and After 1939-1951*, ed. Kevin B. Nowlan and T. Desmond Williams, Gill & Macmillan, Dublin, 1969.
3 Peter Wollen compares Mexico and Ireland briefly in *Raiding the Icebox: Reflections on Twentieth Century Culture*, Verso, London, 1993, pp. 200-1. The parallel group in Mexico to the poets considered here were *los Contemporáneos*, founded *c.* 1920; the diplomat-poet José Gorostiza's four-part *Muerte sin fin* (1939) bears comparison with Devlin's work.
4 Andreas Huyssen, *After the Great Divide: Modernism, Mass Culture, Postmodernism*, Indiana University Press, Bloomington, 1986, introduction.
5 Professor Arthur E. Cleary, 'Pearse, MacDonagh, and Plunkett: An Appreciation', *Poets of the Insurrection*, Maunsel, Dublin, 1918, p. 59. The articles were reprinted from *Studies*.
6 Thomas MacGreevy, 'St Brendan's Church, Loughrea, 1897-1947', *The Capuchin Annual*, Dublin, 1946/47, pp. 353-73. This was one of a series on cathedrals.
7 A related problem is the limitations of an established conceptual framework like that offered by the Church, as MacGreevy's discussion of the French royalist and fascist Charles Maurras suggests. Maurras was one of Eliot's acknowledged influences in the preface to *For Lancelot Andrewes*, which declared that his attitude was classicist in literature, royalist in politics, and Anglo-Catholic in religion. But Maurras's polemics have cheated Eliot:

> When the Lord God gives an American the gift of poetry he ought
> to stick to it and and not bother himself and us with his discovery
> that the mere 'isms' of Europe are better than those of his own
> country.   (*Eliot*, p, 68)

8 Thomas MacGreevy, 'The Catholic Element in *Work in Progress*', *Our Exagmination Round his Factification for Incamination of Work in Progress* (1929), Faber, London, 1972, pp. 117-27.
9 Dialogism in relation to the post-colonial is discussed by Graham Pechey, 'On the Borders of Bakhtin: dialogisation, decolonisation', in *Bakhtin and Cultural Theory*, ed. Ken Hirschkop and David Shepherd, Manchester University Press, Manchester, 1989, pp. 39-67.
10 Brown, *Ireland*, p. 124; see also his 'After the Revival: The Problem of Adequacy and Genre', *The Genres of the Irish Literary Revival*, ed. Ronald Schleifer, Wolfhound Press, Dublin, 1980, pp. 153-78.
11 Seán O'Faoláin, 'The Mart of Ideas', *The Bell*, 4, June 1942, pp. 153-7; Liam O'Flaherty, 'The Irish Censorship', *The American Spectator*, 1, Nov. 1932,

p. 2. Reprinted in Julia Carlson, ed., *Banned In Ireland: Censorship and the Irish Writer*, Routledge, London, 1990, pp. 147-50, 139-41.

12 His essay, 'Recent Irish Poetry', first appeared in *The Bookman*, August 1934, under the pseudonym 'Andrew Belis'.

13 This essay, 'Humanistic Quietism', first appeared in *The Dublin Magazine* July-Sept. 1934.

14 See Carol T. Christ, *Victorian and Modern Poetics,* University of Chicago Press, Chicago, 1984.

15 Defining dialogism in poetry is a problem on which Bakhtin offers little help; for a consideration of the multi-vocal and poly-vocal traditions in modernism, see Marjorie Perloff, *The Dance of the Intellect*, Cambridge University Press, Cambridge, 1989.

16 MacGreevy makes Burke's 'Essay on the Sublime and the Beautiful' the source of that secularizing tradition – reversing the valuation of Yeats's Anglo-Irish hero.

17 Thomas MacGreevy, *Pictures in the Irish National Gallery*, Batsford, London, 1945, pp. 9, 13, 57. The essays first appeared in *The Capuchin Annual* in 1943.

18 See Norman Bryson, *Word and Image: French Painting of the Ancien Régime*, Cambridge University Press, Cambridge, 1981, chs. 1-2. This is not, it should be noted, an opposition between realist and abstract modes: as Bryson points out, realism and abstraction may create images which are equally self-sufficient, which refuse outside reference.

19 See Joann Peck Krieg, 'The Transmogrification of Fairie Land into Prairie Land', *Journal of American Studies*, 19, 1985, pp. 199-223.

20 Peter Brazeau, 'The Irish Connection: Wallace Stevens and Thomas MacGreevy', *Southern Review*, 17, 1981, pp. 533-41.

21 Alan Filreis, *Wallace Stevens and the Actual World*, Princeton University Press, Princeton, 1991, pp. 211, 334; the letters are at the Huntington Library.

22 Wallace Stevens, *Collected Poems,* Faber, London, 1955, pp. 102-03.

23 James Longenbach, *Wallace Stevens: The Plain Sense of Things*, Oxford University Press, New York, 1991, p. 207.

24 Brian Coffey and Denis Devlin, *Poems*, Printed for the Authors by Alex Thom & Co., Dublin, 1930, p. 21.

25 Walter Benjamin, 'Theses on the Philosophy of History', *Illuminations*, trans. Harry Zohn, New York, 1969.

26 The lack of dates for many of the poems in *Selected Poems* (New Writers' Press, Dublin, 1971) and of details of the composition of the longer poems leads one to suspect this; it is confirmed in his letters to MacGreevy (see Davis, pp. 150-51 below). Coffey himself writes in *Missouri Sequence* that 'I have grown slowly into poetry.'

27 Stan Smith, 'On Other Grounds: The Poetry of Brian Coffey', *Two Decades of Irish Writing: A Critical Survey*, ed. Douglas Dunn, Carcanet, Manchester, 1975, p. 59.

28 Brian McHale attempts to define the Zone as a post modern space in his

Postmodern Fiction, Methuen, New York, 1987.

29   J.C.C. Mays comments on the Edenic nature of such moments in 'Passivity and Openness in Two Long Poems by Brian Coffey', *Irish University Review*, special issue: The Long Poem, 13, 1, 1983, p. 71. Mays's comments on detachment and 'the gap which is filled by prayer' (p.76) in *Advent* are also pertinent here.

30   Brian Coffey, *ABECEDARIAN*, Advent Books, Southampton, 1974. Cited from the text in *Poems and Versions*. The 'split' I am describing is to some extent suppressed by the choice in *Poems and Versions*.

31   Brian Coffey, *The Big Laugh*, Sugar Loaf, Dublin, 1976, p. 8.

32   Brian Coffey, *Topos and Other Poems*, Mammon Press, Bath, 1981, np. (Not reprinted in *Poems and Versions*.)

33   See Larzer Ziff, *Literary Democracy: The Declaration of Cultural Independence in America*, Viking Press, New York, 1981.

3

Austin Clarke:
The Poet as Scapegoat of Modernism

W.J. Mc Cormack

I have endured
The enmity of my own mind that feared
No argument; but O when truth itself
Can hold a despairing tongue, what recompense
To find my name in any mortal mouth? (*N&M*, p. 21)

I

Although the Irish contribution to Anglophone modernism was disproportionately large, efforts to define (or even comprehensively describe) the modernist movement have rarely engaged with the issue of national, regional or local provenance. Similarly, schemes by which modernism in general has been periodized into early and late phases have paid little attention to the manner in which paleo-modernism depends heavily upon the pioneering work of Yeats in the 1890s *and* ignored the extent to which a 'neo-modernism' in the 1930s requires the existence of Beckett. In part, these omissions result from the lack of interest in particular provenances displayed even by radical commentators such as Perry Anderson. However, Irish commentators (not necessarily excluding Anderson) have also tended to ignore the larger issues thrown up by the complex phenomenon of literary modernism, perhaps feeling that the famous works speak for themselves.

Literature written within Ireland in the 1930s does not evidence a vast body of modernist poetry, fiction or drama. On the contrary, the notable figures of Joyce and Beckett were living abroad, and even Yeats passed substantial stretches of time in England, France, Italy, and Spain. Their high profile was no less visible at a distance. The situation of the resident writer in Dublin or Cork or Belfast was affected by other pressures which may have mitigated against the implantation of modernist notions. By this is meant no endorsement of the serial *non sequiturs* proffered by Maurice Harmon in his study of Austin Clarke as poet, dramatist and novelist. Harmon argued that:

> One reason why Irish fiction, with the exception of Samuel Beckett and Flann O'Brien, is not experimental and did not follow up on the innovations of James Joyce, is that novelists are preoccupied with trying to understand Irish life as it emerged about then out of the confusions of the revolutionary period. Because of the changed circumstances, including the social shrinkage that had taken place with the virtual disappearance of an upper-class, the novel in its traditional, socially representative form did not flourish.[1]

We are invited to deduce that experimental novels failed to appear because traditional fiction did not thrive, both of these lamentable omissions occuring because writers were attempting to understand post-revolutionary confusion. Instead, it is more likely that the establishment of the Irish Free State constituted a modernist *success* in that the society thus formalized as a self-governing nation had broken away from the industrialized, urbanized and (allegedly) dehumanized world of the United Kingdom, in apparent compliance with Yeats's early primitivist version of modernism. On these grounds, modernism as a literary project might have been thought redundant in Ireland after 1921. Against this argument there remains the case of Northern Ireland, where urbanization and industrialization were closer to the centre of society's self-image, where no break with the rest of the United Kingdom was effected, and where no discernible modernist campaign persisted.

The situation, north and south, altered in 1920/21. Even if the detection of literary generations is fraught with imprecision, it is fair to say that in Samuel Beckett (*b.* 1906), John Hewitt (*b.* 1907), Denis Johnston (*b.* 1901), Louis MacNeice (*b.* 1907), Seán O'Faoláin (*b.* 1900), a new phase of literary endeavour was seen to follow on from that which had powerfully collected round Yeats (*b.* 1865), Synge (*b.* 1871), and Joyce (*b.* 1882). Among these younger writers, only Beckett and Johnston could be plausibly linked with the modernist movement. Not only a preference for experimentation in literary form, but a willingness to confront the agreed order of things generally, differentiates them from writers (as different from each other as Hewitt and O'Faoláin) who still nurtured hopes of reconciliation with their societies and/or an improvement in those societies as such. The first publications of this generation emerged in the shadow of the War of Independence.

In all of this, the figure of Austin Clarke is profoundly anomalous. Born in 1896, he was only fourteen years younger than Joyce, and yet was ten years older than Beckett. Though his novels were banned in Southern Ireland, and he was for many years at loggerheads with the Catholic Church, his brand of Celtic Revivalism lay very close to the imagery used by the new state to endorse its political independence and its acknowledgement of a distinguished cultural pedigree traceable to pre-Reformation Europe. Leaving aside issues of personal difficulty, medical and marital (which complicated his career in the early 1920s), we may find external reasons for Clarke's anomalous relationship to both the older and younger generation of writers. Commencing to publish poetry with *The Vengeance of Fionn* in 1917, he was seen to be part of a late Victorian/Edwardian/Georgian continuity rather than a contributor to the newer, more hard-bitten school soon to be associated with the short story writers. It is true that he personally favoured the anti-Treaty side in the Civil War of 1922 – as did (more actively) O'Faoláin, Francis Stuart and other prentice writers. *The Cattledrive in Connaught*, published several years after the Civil War was deemed (even by the losers) to have ended, still maintained the Yeatsian epic mode. But Clarke's political leanings involved no left-wing ideological commitments of the kind sometimes discerned in the republicanism of Liam Mellowes or even Éamon de Valera. He was simply in favour of breaking the link which bound Ireland to England, and of breaking it as neatly as possible.

Initially, Clarke's difficulty lay less with the new men than with the old. His epic hero, Fionn, came straight from central casting, without the permission of the overseer, W.B. Yeats. Thus, he was not only potentially isolated from the concerns which O'Faoláin and

Frank O'Connor were to pursue in a body of fiction where Roman-
ticism and disillusion sustained a dialogue, he was already in com-
petition with senior figures associated with the Abbey Theatre. Many
years were to pass before his poetry found itself in finding original
imaginative and intellectual themes. To make matters worse, Yeats
himself was in the process of shifting ground, of whetting a sharper,
more aggressive line. Clarke was in a sense the imitator of a Yeats
who had ceased to exist.

Consequently, it is customary to date his real commencement from
Pilgrimage and Other Poems, published in 1929. But the appearance
of a premature *Collected Poems* in 1936 had the effect of disguising
the recent change in his work by prefacing these new poems with
the lengthy verse-epics of which *The Vengeance of Fionn* was only
one. Published in the middle of a crucial, and highly self-conscious
decade, the *Collected Poems* 'dated' Clarke in the idiomatic sense of
assigning him to the past. In addition, he had moved from Ireland
to England, and redirected his attention from poetry to drama. As
a result, his contribution to poetry in Ireland in the 1930s seems
on the surface to be slight. (*Night and Morning*, his only collection
of the decade, did not appear until 1938.) The drama, it should be
emphasized, took the form of verse-plays, and shortly would in-
clude experiments with radio-broadcasting. But, living in St Albans
and hacking on London's Grub Street, Austin Clarke did not register
strikingly as a contemporary poet of great consequence in Ireland.
It was thus very easy, and also very convenient, for Yeats to exclude
him from *The Oxford Book of Modern Verse*, published in 1936, while
cronies like Oliver Gogarty and Dorothy Wellesley were puffed.

The subject-matter of Clarke's 1930s' plays is not directly rele-
vant to the present argument, though in retrospect the coherence
of what he was doing is palpable. His exile, if so emotive a term
can be used of life in Hertfordshire, had been prompted mainly by
personal difficulties, the breakdown of his first marriage, his dismissal
from a lectureship in University College, Dublin, the need to pro-
vide for a young family. Behind these practical problems lay his com-
plex relationship with Irish Catholicism, a relationship which for
much of his life was not conducive to the earning of a livelihood
at home. Yet it is wrong to see in the elderly satirist a legacy of thir-
ties' radicalism. Clarke's dissent from Irish orthodoxies involved no
blinding encounter with Marx or Freud, nor does he seem to have

bothered very much about Abyssinia and the Spanish civil war.

His circle of literary friends and acquaintances in England did not include Auden and MacDiarmid. His close associates were poets who do not excite much interest now – Gordon Bottomley (1874–1948), Caradoc Evans (1879–1945), and Herbert Palmer (1880–1961). These are not the names which make Alvarez bristle like Housman's whiskers. Nevertheless, Palmer's poetry had absorbed certain Celticist themes and tonalities from a reading of Synge and James Stephens; its author is a rare example of an English writer concerning himself with Irish disengagement from the United Kingdom as a major factor in post-war cultural upheavals and readjustments. Evans, as his name suggests, was Welsh and had his own difficulties with the religious orthodoxies of his homeland, while Bottomley shared with Clarke an interest in verse drama. Palmer lived in St Albans and provided an element of agreeable company for the exile who was, it might be noted, considerably younger than his three English associates.[2] If, collectively, they seem an insignificant band, unlikely to provide an illuminating context for Irish literary criticism, one may approach the problem of assessing Clarke in relation to the poetry of the 1930s through a problem purely textual – or nearly so.

II

As against the seclusion implicit in the image of Austin Clarke among marginalized British poets, Samuel Beckett's novel *Murphy* (1938) advances a caricature of the poet as Austin Ticklepenny, 'a distinguished indigent drunken Irish bard' (*Murphy*, p. 88),[3] sexually ambiguous, pathetic but aggressive nonetheless. Given the hero's fatal taking up of a post in a mental hospital, the context of this verbal assault by Beckett's narrative is highly suggestive. As if the distinctive Christian name of the character were not enough to alert the reader to the possibility of near-libel – and a clerk/Clarke might be thought of as someone who tickles pennies – then Beckett had thrown caution to the winds by quoting Clarke verbatim. But not quite *all* caution.

In the chapter but one following after the introduction of Ticklepenny, Beckett recounts an encounter between a character called Wylie – sometimes Needle Wylie – and a Miss Counihan who loves Murphy:

> Wylie did not often kiss, but when he did it was a serious matter. He was not one of those lugrubrious persons who insist on removing the clapper from the bell of passion. A kiss from Wylie was like a breve tied, in a long slow amorous phrase, over bars' time its equivalent in demi-semiquavers (*Murphy*, p. 117).

The middle sentence of this passage draws directly on the technical annotations which Austin Clarke had provided for *Pilgrimage and Other Poems* in 1929:

> Assonance, more elaborate in Gaelic than in Spanish poetry, takes the clapper from the bell of rhyme. In simple patterns, the tonic word at the end of the line is supported by a vowel-rhyme in the middle of the next line. The poems in the present series are more formal than those in *The Cattle-drive in Connaught*, though still approximate (*Pilgrimage*, p. 43).

Even the most sceptical opponents of intertextuality can hardly deny the reality of relationship (however verbally restricted) between the collection of poems and the novel.[4] The question is vexed, however, by the displacement wherein the novel separates Austin Clarke's words from the fictional character (Austin Ticklepenny) who is unambiguously introduced as an Irish poet. Having provided a brief *résumé* of his medical history, the narrative continues:

> This view of the matter will not seem strange to anyone familiar with the class of pentameter that Ticklepenny felt it his duty to Erin to compose, as free as a canary in the fifth foot (a cruel sacrifice, for Ticklepenny hiccuped [*sic*] in end rimes) and at the caesura as hard and fast as his own divine flatus and otherwise bulging with as many minor beauties from the gaelic prosodoturfy as could be sucked out of a mug of Beamish's porter (*Murphy*, p. 89).

For good or – obviously – ill, Clarke is associated in the novelist's mind not with the lyrics of *Pilgrimage* but rather with the epic poems beginning with *The Vengeance of Fionn* (1917), *The Fires of Baal* (1921), *The Sword of the West* (1921), and *The Cattledrive in Connaught* (1925). For the sake of comic effect, the techniques of epic and lyric are thoroughly confused in the account of Ticklepenny's style, but the *mélange* conveys a strong impression of fusty antiquarianism on the one part, and of deep-rooted personal antagonism on the other.

One diplomatic way of accounting for the relentless satirizing of Austin Ticklepenny in *Murphy* would refer to Clarke and Beckett as modernists of conflicting generations. Accordingly, the former approves all the anti-modern prejudices of modernism, its rejection of democratic mass-civilization, its detestation of industry and mechanical inventions, its cults of mediaevalism and primitivism, and the convenient accommodation of these preferences in what was taken to be the programme of the Irish Free State. Beckett, in contrast, is cosmopolitan, disaffiliated and prosaic, a polyglot individualist of the avant-garde. In this reading, *Murphy* involves a series of textual betrayals — of Synge and Yeats notably, and (now it seems) of Austin Clarke also — just as *More Pricks than Kicks* had 'betrayed' Joyce by rewriting the final paragraph of 'The Dead' in 'A Wet Night'. It was by such textual betrayals that Beckett's fiction liberated itself from the incumbrances of the Literary Revival.[5] In less obscure terms, this betrayal (or textual violation) is memorably encoded in the novel when Neary assaults the statue of Cuchulain in the General Post Office, Dublin (*Murphy*, p. 42). Second-generation modernism declared independence from the first generation and, unfortunately for Clarke, it required a victim who mediated between the two generations in order to thoroughly ridicule the Celtic themes and techniques which it associated with its precursor. The attack on Cuchulain might be read as a purely internalized version of the attack on Clarke.

But the animus directed against Ticklepenny only occasionally refers to poetic technique, and then simply to drive home an identification with Clarke. A ferocious energy of characterization is devoted to establishing certain practices or phobias in Ticklepenny which can be summarized under the three headings — alcohol, insanity and sex. Thus the reader initially encounters him by means of a visiting-card thrust against Murphy's nose 'which was at once withdrawn so that he might read':

Austin Ticklepenny
Pot Poet
From the County of Dublin

Confronted with the transcription centre-page, the reader is obliged also to read, a crude strategy which momentarily aligns the reader with Murphy's perspective. No sooner has this ostentatious introduction been effected, however, than the narrative is instantly anxious to cancel any sense of importance in the character, despite the prominent way in which his identity, profession, habits and origin have been presented:

> The merest pawn in the game between Murphy and his stars, he makes his little move, engages an issue and is swept from the board. Further use may conceivably be found for Austin Ticklepenny in a child's halma or a book-reviewer's snakes and ladders, but his chess days are over (*Murphy*, pp. 84-5).

Whatever critics of Beckett's fiction may wish to say about the role of the character Ticklepenny in the structure of the novel, the over-determination of the passage anticipates the frustration of its aims. For Ticklepenny is not swept from the board. On the contrary, Murphy (killed by an explosion in the pot-poet's former room, then cremated, and finally used as a football in a public house) is

> swept away with the sand, the beer, the butts, the glass, the matches, the spits, the vomit (*Murphy*, p. 275).[6]

That Murphy should end up where the narrative insists Ticklepenny has emerged from (the dregs of former drinking), and that he should do so as a direct consequence of his taking over Ticklepenny's job, gives the lie to the narrative's insistence that 'this creature does not merit any particular description' (*Murphy*, pp. 84-5).

A further detail, hinting at a *roman-à-clef* factor, may be noted before we consider the broader significance of alcohol, insanity and sex in the misrepresentation of Clarke in *Murphy*. When the pot-poet first thrusts his card under Murphy's nose, the two of them jointly recall the place of their first encounter – the Gate Theatre, Dublin, at a performance of *Romeo and Juliet* : ' "*Romiet*', said Ticklepenny, "*and Juleo . . .*" ' (*Murphy*, p. 86).[7] Both admit to having been drunk on the occasion, and it must seem that this circumstance explains the terse narrative remark that 'Murphy dimly remembered an opportune apothecary' (*Murphy*, p. 86). However, instead of providing a cure for drunkenness, the apothecary may well have been part of the company – may have been James Starkey (the poet, Seumus O'Sullivan), a pharmacist by profession and editor of *The Dublin Magazine*, for whom both Beckett and Clarke had written.[8] If a blurred reference to this real person is acknowledged by the reader of *Murphy*, then a significant step is taken towards reducing the seemingly absolute antagonism between Murphy and Ticklepenny.

Both Beckett and Clarke had written for *The Dublin Magazine*, and were associated with *Motley*, an occasional publication of the Gate Theatre in Dublin.⁹ When Murphy concedes that it was in the theatre he and Ticklepenny had met, a further minum of evidence is added to the suggestion that Austin Clarke is lampooned in Austin Ticklepenny. Yet the most powerful evidence – the note to Clarke's *Pilgrimage* volume directly cited – is deflected away from Ticklepenny as poet, on to Wylie as kisser. In terms of libel law, such a manoeuvre might frustrate an action, in that the recognizable features of Austin Clarke (his distinctive Christian name and his learned annotation) are related to different named characters in the fiction. Or it might not. But in terms of Freudian analysis, these textual strategies of the narrative can be regarded as projections.

The relevance of psychoanalysis becomes immediately obvious when one discovers a further deflection and projection in Ticklepenny's assessment of Murphy. Having made his way back to an attic room in the Magdalen Mental Mercyseat which he had very recently vacated in Murphy's favour, Ticklepenny is prompted by something in Murphy's appearance to make a telling comparison:

> 'Do you know what it is?' said Ticklepenny, 'no offence meant, you had a great look of Clarke there a minute ago.'
> Clarke had been for three weeks in a catatonic stupor.
> 'All but the cackle', said Ticklepenny.
> Clarke would repeat for hours the phrase, 'Mr. Endon is *very* superior' (*Murphy*, p. 193).

Thus a perfect circle, whether evading libel or projecting identity, is completed: the narrative ascribes Clarke's Christian name to Ticklepenny, and Ticklepenny ascribes Clarke's surname to a catatonic patient in the mental hospital in which he finds work for Murphy by giving it up himself. Not surprisingly, this is the only occasion on which the reader encounters the name Clarke, for it is a formal device only.

Alcohol is prominently and disruptively present in the representation of Ticklepenny. The visiting-card, already noted, effects the introduction in a most self-conscious fashion, while also insisting on Ticklepenny's self-description as a 'pot-poet'. It is possible to argue that Ticklepenny is so abject a figure as to confess to alcoholism in this way, but the term 'pot-poet' fails to harmonize with pathetic confession; on the contrary its external and satiric tonalities belong to the novel's brutally impersonal narrative. Already a structural ambiguity shadows that narrative's attitude towards Clarke/ Ticklepenny – even transcribed documentary evidences are permeated with an antagonism as yet impersonal, with a disembodied animus. Ticklepenny's mental condition, implicitly compared to his fussy poetic manner, is attributed 'less to the pints than to the pentameters' (*Murphy*, p. 88).

Employed in a menial capacity 'in return for a mild course of dipsopathic discipline', Ticklepenny apostrophizes himself as one 'who for more years than he cares to remember turned out his steady pentameter per pint, day in, day out', and who, 'is now degraded to the position of male nurse in a hospital for the better-class mentally deranged'. It is, he continues, 'the same Ticklepenny, but God bless my soul *quantum mutatus*' (*Murphy*, pp. 87-7). His main difficulty at the Mercyseat lies in his fear of insanity – in what the narrative starkly calls his 'pompous dread of being driven mad by the spectacle constantly before him of those that were so already' (*Murphy*, p. 91). This potential resemblance between nurse and patient is transferred promptly when Murphy offers to substitute for Ticklepenny, an offer made with the appropriate mimicry of the qualities needed for the post. The antagonism between the two characters is already refined towards a limited interchangeability.

But it is in the sexual domain that Murphy is most determined to resist any negotiation with Ticklepenny. The two are sitting at a café table when the job-swap is proposed. 'These words sent the whole of Ticklepenny into transports, but no part of him so horribly as his knees, which began to fawn under the table' (*Murphy*, p. 92). Earlier, Murphy had ordered the pot-poet to cease his 'clumsy genustuprations' under the table at which 'Murphy's memory began to vibrate.'[10] And it was this unwelcome prompt which revived recollection of the Gate Theatre encounter and 'the opportune apothecary'. Murphy's fear of, or great distaste for, Ticklepenny's excitation of the knees is explicitly associated with possibilities of homosexual liaison –

> with some high official, the head male nurse for example. Short of being such a person's minion, Murphy was inclined to think

there was nothing Ticklepenny could do that he could not do a great deal better . . . (*Murphy*, pp. 92-3).[11]

But it is only when Murphy is dead that such liaisons are openly conceded in the narrative. 'Ticklepenny and Bim, wreathed together' in the mortuary. . . . 'Bim and Ticklepenny lifted the sheet' from the corpse. . . . 'Bim and Ticklepenny raised their heads together, their eyes met in a look both tender and ardent, they were alive and well and had each other', whereas Murphy was dead. . . . 'Bim and Ticklepenny had gone, already they were far away, behind a tree, in the sun' (*Murphy*, pp. 259, 261, 264-5, 270). The emergence of these micro-incidents of homosexual pleasure after Murphy's accidental death in Ticklepenny's room resembles a further narrative strategy, just as Clarke's name is dispersed between separate characters and his learned footnote negatived and reassigned to Wylie's heterosexual zeal. In this domain also is it possible to see projection at work, this time in a circle which is less than perfect. For, on the occasion where Ticklepenny had remarked on Murphy's resemblance to the obligingly catatonic Clarke, Murphy had sustained a longer dialogue than quoted above:

'You want to watch yourself.'
'In what way?' said Murphy.
'You want to mind your health,' said Ticklepenny.
'In what way do I remind you of Clarke?' said Murphy.
'You want to take a pull on yourself,' said Ticklepenny. 'Good night' (*Murphy*, p. 194).

Does 'want', in these exchanges, denote desire or need? The question raises issues of verbal register which are rife with ambiguity, as key terms hover between colloquial and technical, or banal and subversive, registrations. The passage begins by smuggling in the notion of sustained visual inspection (of the kind mental patients are subjected to) while seeming simply to advise caution. Murphy's responses persistently take the conversation into new areas, demanding specificity. Finally, the desire or need 'to take a pull on yourself' is suspended between the commonplace vocabulary of Ticklepenny (i.e., get a grip on yourself, or, pull yourself together) and that of sexual indulgence in 'self-abuse'. The very area of transgression, which has been projected on to Ticklepenny, under Murphy's questioning recommends itself to Murphy.

It is clear from this last analysis that the involuntary role of Austin Clarke in *Murphy* is activated at what one might term the level of 'the sexual unconscious'. The animosity displayed by the narrative towards his various textual surrogates never relaxes: no character, apart from the obliging Bim, adopts anything like a positive attitude towards him. Indeed no character encounters him while Murphy is alive, apart from Murphy. Far from being 'the merest pawn in the game between Murphy and his stars', Ticklepenny is central to the most significant incident of Murphy's life — his death. Even the dismissive metaphor, which the narrative insists on, proves to be central. Once established as Ticklepenny's locum in the Magdalen Mental Mercyseat, Murphy is able to indulge his passion for chess by playing against the patient, Mr Endon, whom Ticklepenny had thought '*very* superior'. If we look ahead to Beckett's later fiction and drama, we can recognize in Murphy and Ticklepenny an instance of what will be more explicitly treated as 'the pair', a recurring feature of characterization in which schizoidal dualities are sustained under double names or twin identities. This feature of the pair arises more obviously in *Murphy* in the case of the Clinch twins, Bim and Bom, who work in the Mercyseat: the sexual pairing of Bim with Ticklepenny should be read, however, as the rearrangement of two former pairs — the brothers constituting one, Murphy and Ticklepenny the other.

III

It is no secret — though the facts as yet are poorly documented — that both Beckett and Clarke underwent treatment for mental disorders in their youth, Clarke in St. Patrick's Hospital, Dublin, and Beckett at the Tavistock Clinic in London.[12] In the former case, treatment was involuntary, a factor which — together with the passage of decades in which little or no scholarly interest was evinced in the patient — has limited the extent of presently available information. However the poet's son, Dardis Clarke, has not only authorized the publication of some primary material resulting from his father's treatment, but has also provided a useful gloss on the matter.[13]

It can be established without too much difficulty that Clarke suffered a mental collapse in 1919 and that he spent almost a year in

St Patrick's Hospital, the institution founded under the terms of Jonathan Swift's will. In his autobiographies, *Twice Round the Black Church* (1962) and *Penny in the Clouds* (1968), he provided some details of the psychological difficulties, intimately involving his relationship with – and subsequent, brief, marriage to – Geraldine (or Lia) Cummins, which resulted in his collapse. But the notable literary consequence of this experience was the long poem, or sequence of poems, called *Mnemosyne Lay in Dust* published in 1966. In the context of Clarke's relationship to the 1930s, however, it should be noted that at least part of the long poem had been written close on thirty years earlier – section 8 appeared as a self-contained poem ('Summer Lightning') in *Night and Morning* (1938).

The existence of this poetic material, or poetic project, of Clarke's at the time that Beckett was writing *Murphy* raises a further distinctly unpleasant possibility. For, in addition to Austin Ticklepenny's being a direct ridiculing of Austin Clarke, it may be that details of aberrant conduct employed in the novel were obtained by Beckett from Clarke either in conversations which might have been deemed confidential or even in a manuscript carelessly made available. As against this near-allegation, it should be immediately recognized that the novelist had his own access to institutions treating mental disorder, not only at the Tavistock (where he was analysed by Wilfrid Bion[14]) but also at the Bethlehem Royal Hospital, at Beckenham in Kent. Apart from anything else, the alliteration of Bethlehem and Beckenham, together with the biblical provenance of the first name, is clearly echoed in the fictional Madgalen Mental Mercyseat. Yet there is a lingering unease in the seemingly disarming comment made by Beckett to John Fletcher in the 1960s that, 'lest an action for libel should lie' the Kent hospital served 'only as a point of departure' for the Mercyseat.[15]

The unease is compounded if we return to Beckett's acknowledged critical references to Clarke and to certain details in *Murphy*. In his review of 'Recent Irish Poetry', he had devoted three sentences to Clarke in the course of which severe comment on poetic technique among 'the antiquarians' merged into personal innuendo:

> Mr Austin Clarke, having declared himself, in his 'Cattle-drive in Connaught' (1925), a follower of 'that most famous juggler, Mannanaun', continues in 'The Pilgrimage' (1929) to display the 'trick of tongue or two' and to remove, by means of ingenious

metrical operations, 'the clapper from the bell of rhyme.' The ful-
ly licensed stock-in-trade from Aisling to Red Branch Bundling,
is his to command. Here the need for formal justifications, more
acute in Mr Clarke than in Mr [F. R.] Higgins, serves to screen
the deeper need that must not be avowed (*Disjecta*, pp. 72-3).

If the last phrase makes sense only as a laboured re-writing of 'the
love that dares not speak its name', then the detail about 'the Red
Branch Bundling' as part of Clarke's mythological stock-in-trade
will be echoed in *Murphy* at the point where Neary explains his
assault on Cuchulain:

'The limit of Cork endurance had been reached . . . That Red
Branch bum was the camel's back' (*Murphy*, p. 46).[16]

The role of Cuchulain as the pre-eminent hero of the Red Branch
knights is well known from many sources available to Clarke and
his predecessors in the Literary Revival.[17] Beckett's choice of the
obtrusive word 'bundling' , instead of the Victorian 'knights' regular-
ly employed in translations of the Gaelic material, reflects his
awareness of the German noun *Bund*, meaning league or confedera-
tion, a term with distinctly political overtones in the 1930s. However,
the novel's substitution of 'bum' not only concentrates attention on
a single figure but also on the precise anatomical area which Neary
assaulted – 'seized the dying hero by the thighs and began to dash
his head against his buttocks, such as they are.' It is for this reason
that Wylie, rescuing Neary from the police, goes to such lengths
to suggest that the statue is female – 'not a feather out of her' (*Murphy*,
pp. 42-3).

Oddly enough, Clarke had voiced his own resentment of
celebratory sculpture. In 1928, he won a national award for poetry
at the Tailteann Games. Obliged to return to England and employ-
ment, he took delivery of the trophy at Westland Row railway station
in Dublin, making the bitter remark that 'My grateful country of-
fers me a statuette, but I have to emigrate to earn my bread.'[18]
Beckett's review in 1934 had ridiculed Clarke's *Pilgrimage* annota-
tion and and proceeded to hint at a love that dared not speak its
name: his novel four years later not only distributes these details
(as we have seen) between Wylie as kisser and Bim as Ticklepen-
ny's partner, but it also insinuates a sexual reference to the Red Branch

aspect of what had been established as Clarke's poetic material. Illuminated by the 1934 book review, *Murphy* no longer manifests a purely textual and wholly internalized interest in Clarke.

IV

Nor can the discussion of Clarke's poetry, relevant to this atrocious malrepresentation, be constricted to a rigid definition of the 1930s. The volume, *Pilgrimage and Other Poems*, published in 1929, clearly constitutes the point of departure for that aspect of Beckett's ridicule which has a textual provocation. The final poem of the collection, immediately preceding the much-quoted note on technique, is 'Aisling', a detail also echoed in Beckett's 1934 review. The second poem in the collection, 'Celibacy', starkly contradicts the general view of the collection presented by Clarke when he incorporated the 1929 volume into *Later Poems* (1961): there he speaks of the poems as 'written in exile, when the future of our new State seemed so hopeful that Irish writers could delay for a while in the past.'[19] The third stanza of 'Celibacy' balances visionary brightness, an awareness of sexual temptation, and (potentially at least) terror:

> Eyelid stood back in sleep,
> I saw what seemed an Angel:
> Dews dripped from those bright feet.
> But, O, I knew the stranger
> By her deceit and, tired
> All night by tempting flesh,
> I wrestled her in hair-shirt.[20]   (*Pilgrimage*, p. 12)

If Beckett's *Murphy* seeks to escape into the privacy of his own mind, Clarke's obsessional interest in the separation of consciousness from body (in sleep) is more often fixed on experiences of terror, violent constraint, and a sense of sin. There is, however, no allusion whatever in *Murphy* to a religious dimension, either by reference to Ticklepenny's 'pompous fear' or by reference to any difference of denomination between the two protagonists. The conversation between Murphy and Ticklepenny, which culminates in the introduction of Clarke's surname, had opened with the latter surprising his deputy in the Mercyseat attic at night. Murphy being engaged in one of

his characteristic retreats from the phenomenal world, Ticklepenny
— not unreasonably perhaps — assumed he was sleeping. But with
a difference — Murphy appeared to be 'fast asleep in the dark with
[his] eyes wide open' (*Murphy*, p. 192). To be sure, this is not a verbal
echo of 'Celibacy' in anything like the sense that Wylie's kissing is
based on a reversal of Clarke's rhyming technique. What is signifi-
cant is the sustained concern with sleep in Clarke's poetry, the poetry
written before and after *Murphy*.[21] Five of the ten poems in the
1929 series (Clarke's own term) employ the word in one form or
another: these are 'Pilgrimage', 'Celibacy', 'The Confession of Queen
Gormlai', 'The Scholar', 'The Young Woman of Beare'. Though the
length of individual poems varies considerably in *Night and Morn-
ing* (1938) — and they do not form a series in the same sense — one
still finds five of twelve items alluding to sleep, two to the state of
waking, and others less directly implicating sleep: one of the five
is 'Summer Lightning', harbinger of *Mnemosyne Lay in Dust*.

It is of course relatively easy to interpret this thematic continuity
in terms of a puritanical fear of sexuality, especially of female sexu-
ality as feared by Irishmen. Clarke himself had attempted an
interpretation of Parnell's influence on Irish culture in just such terms,
and the comments on 'Margaret', and on his own painful matura-
tion, contribute to this familiar topic of Irish male incompetence and
anxiety, all heavily overlaid with the fulminations and anathemas
of the Catholic Church. But the occurrence of 'Summer Lightning'
both in the collection of 1938 and in the late sequence of 1966
provides the opportunity to consider a less localized mode of inter-
pretation or to move to such by means of a re-examination of the
one collection Clarke published in the 1930s.[22]

'Repentance' opens with lines which indicate that Beckett's ac-
cusation of parochial antiquarianism might still be apt in 1938:

> When I was younger than the soul
> That wakes me now at night, I saw
> The mortal mind in such a glory —
> All knowledge was in Connaught.   (*N&M*, p. 13)

Yet the Hibernian landscaping of the first stanza should be read only
as a kind of courtesy to the poems of ten years earlier. More signifi-
cant is the business of seeing ('I saw/ The mortal mind') as an indicator

of informed innocence, a state in which knowledge and purity are at one. 'Martha Blake' employs the same basic trope, though in quite a different direction, to suggest how faith can retain this condition, though not (it is clear) in the case of the soul articulated in 'Repentance'. It is well known that Martha Blake was based on Clarke's sister, Eileen, and on her spiritual life. In the poem simply bearing that name, the earlier of two examining the paradoxes of her faith, the pious woman is found praying:

> She does not see through any saint
> That stands in the sun
> With veins of lead, with painful crown;
> She waits that dreaded coming,
> When all the congregation bows
> And none may look up.   (*N&M*, p. 10)

The faithful individual sees the saint without seeing through him, and is thus to some extent marked off from the generalized congregation more closely associated with the moment when 'none may look'. But in 'Summer Lightning', the business of looking and seeing is wholly altered:

> Napoleon took his glittering vault
> To be a looking-glass.
> Lord Mitchell, pale and suffering,
> Fell to the floor in halves.
> The cells were filling. Christopher
> O'Brien, strapped in pain,
> For all the rage of syphilis,
> Had millions in his brain.   (*N&M*, p. 22)

The prostration of Lord Mitchell has only the outer shape of that observed among the devout in 'Martha Blake', but then 'Martha Blake' had employed a limitation, or short-focusing, of sight to indicate the harmony of knowledge and purity, whereas 'Repentance' had found such harmony only in a long-lost vista. From *Mnemosyne*, we now know that 'Summer Lightning' alludes to the poet's incarceration in a mental hospital; thus informed, we can re-read other details in the 1938 collection, for example the final lines of 'Repentance':

> Could I unbutton mad thought, quick-save
> My skin, if I were caught at last
> Without my soul and dragged to torment,
> Ear-drumming in that dreadful place
> Where the sun hides in the waters?   (*N&M*, p. 14)

The antiquarian landscape of the first stanza is now challenged, as much by the suspended conditional clause ('could I . . .') which bluntly terminates in a question, as by anything else. If, in 1938, few were able to recognize the imagery of clinical derangement and strait-jacketed confinement (which one cannot unbutton), the astute critic should still find in the precipitous nine-line stanza employed throughout the poem an objective correlative of truncated discourse, suppressed knowledge. One can now move backwards and forwards between 'Summer Lightning' and 'Repentance', recognizing a common concern with the horror of not-being-seen. Recounting the impact of a storm on hospital inmates, 'Summer Lightning' opens:

> The heavens opened. With a scream
> The blackman at his night-prayers
> Had disappeared in blasphemy . . .   (*N&M*, p. 22).

The blackness of this figure already prefigures his invisibility, just as his derangement is aggravated by 'somebody in white' who had removed the one image – 'his photograph' – in which black and white are harmonized intelligibly. The photograph is ambiguously 'his' in the cryptic text, neither specified as an image of him nor an image he possesses: between these possibilities he is vulnerable to disappearance. Though 'Summer Lightning' speaks of blasphemy and sin, the deliberate confusion of plausible names (Christopher O'Brien) and deluded self-identifications (Napoleon, Lord Mitchell) has the effect of secularizing the implied context of the storm. In 'Repentance' such terms as 'Connaught' and 'blessed Patric' – not to mention 'the last Gospel' and 'that book in Heaven' – emphasize a religious preoccupation that masks the clinical allusions in the final five lines. But, in connection with the horror of non-existence or not-being-seen, the second stanza maintains the 'Celtic Church' landscape of purgatorial exercises while specifying that Patrick drove out 'a crowd / Of fiends that roared like cattlemen':

>   Until they stamped themselves out
>   between the fiery pens . . .   (*N&M*, p. 13)

The fiends of heroic Christianity are the deranged of Swift's hospital, but the two terms of this analogy are most tensely compacted in the 'fiery pens' of 'Repentance'. The sudden latter-day word 'cattle-men' may bring with it notions of a frenzied pursuit of money while retaining some dim memorial echo of *The Cattledrive of Connaught*. To stamp oneself out is a form of obliteration with suggestions of uncontrolled physical repression – trampling, extinguishing, etc. – while the phrase harbours a slight implication of an imprinted sign, a stamped image, albeit in the mucky environs appropriate to cattle-pens. But the 'pens' in which these cattle/men stamp themselves out refuse to signify only the corrals in which beasts are herded. Like the photograph in 'Summer Lightning' the word occupies no one place or moment in the poem. If 'pens' is also metonymic of writing and so of poetry, then the possibility is raised of some extinction in expression. These fiends, likened to cattlemen in 'Repentance' but more familiar as beasts – Gaderene swine (Matthew 8: 28-34) or scapegoats (Leviticus 16: 8) – carry the projected anxieties of the community and are banished from it. In the New Testament story, it is worth noticing that Christ too is promptly besought 'that he would depart out of their coasts'. These communities of the biblical narratives might well be likened to the institutions – paramedical, ecclesiastical, legal, etc. – which Clarke's poems at once reproduce and subvert.

V

In addressing Clarke's poetry of the 1930s in this manner, one is negotiating with two intimidating bodies of commentary, neither of which adverts to Clarke or his work. One of these is the mass of exegetical and speculative writing devoted to Samuel Beckett, whose reputation as international modernist, anti-hero of existential-ism, and stealthy philanthropist leaves no room for the 'local complainer' Clarke characterized himself as. The other, held in check more effectively here, is the equally bulky literature devoted to the work of Michel Foucault, especially his history of madness and his various accounts of the carceral structures of modern civilization. Perhaps the fact that Foucault was twenty years Beckett's junior, and that fashion changes rapidly on the Left Bank, accounts for the curious neglect of Beckett's many accounts of formal and informal institutional terror in the Foucaultian commentaries. Certainly, the critic of Austin Clarke's poetry only feels like a voice crying in the wilderness while the ghetto-blasters of rival prophets dominate the airwaves. That, however, is a situation for which Clarke himself appears to have made preparations at an early date.

Given the unrelenting hostility manifested towards him in *Murphy*, it would be understandable if sympathizers were to look for a defence, for evidence demonstrating innocence of the charges laid against him, for an effective, perhaps even an eloquent, repudiation and self-justification. To the best of my knowledge Clarke nowhere alludes to the character assassination which Ticklepenny amounts to. Nor does he take the opportunity, when the author of *Waiting for Godot* had become the butt of Grub Street jokes, of settling an old score with judicious recollections of the younger Beckett's antics in Dublin. Of course it may be that Clarke calculated that, in accusatory exchanges, any response is an admission of guilt or an embarking on damage limitation – the last resort of the blameless. Beckett himself had learned a good deal of the ironies of innocence when he appeared as a witness in the action for libel taken against Oliver St John Gogarty in November 1937; perhaps Clarke learned something from it also, for he had returned to settle in Dublin in February of that year. Neverthless, some biographical detail is not without its uses at this juncture.

Between his departure for England in 1922 and his failure in 1926 to obtain a London divorce from Cummins, Clarke took up with two English women whom he refers to somewhat coyly as Angela and Avril. These relationships were temporary affairs. In 1930, he met Nora Walker at Bulmer Hobson's house in Dublin; the following year their first son was born, and in 1932 they settled in St Albans. In 1934, Clarke successfully took a libel action against the publishers of Arnold Bennett's diaries, objecting to the wrongful attribution of a remark he denied making. He was throughout this period active both in writing verse-plays and in turning out book reviews for the *Spectator* and other English magazines. In all of this one reads the chronicle of a respectability well equipped to rebut the libels of *Murphy*. Only in the past, in the years when memory lay in the dust, was Clarke's record beyond inspection. Those years, as an examination of *Night and Morning* now suggests, also drove his poetry.

It is tempting to read 'No Recompense' as the poet's answer to the mixed maledictions of publicity. The lines appearing at the head of this essay might indeed be interpreted as an answer to any abuser of his name. But the poem had originally appeared in the *Collected Poems* of 1936: Vivian Mercier even opines that it had been written, in one form or another, as early as 1925.[23] In either case, it cannot have arisen from a reading, even an anticipation, of Beckett's novel of 1938.

Removed from a possible context of personal retaliation, the poem nonetheless presents an image of separation from informed purity, of initiation into contradictory sensations of deprivation and excess which 'Bring madness in our sleep'. As an exploration of the scapegoat's role, the poem deserves quotation in its entirety:

No Recompense

Quality, number and the sweet divisions
Of reason may forget their schoolmen now,
And door-chill, body's heat, anger of vein,
Bring madness in our sleep. I have endured
The enmity of my own mind that feared
No argument; but O when truth itself
Can hold a despairing tongue, what recompense
To find my name in any mortal mouth?

Craig Tapping reflects the general tendency among critics of Clarke's poetry when he summarizes 'No Recompense' as challenging the idea of fame and 'stating with its title and mournful conclusion that the world is nothing when a man's soul is at stake.'[24] In fact, it is one of a small minority of the poems in *Night and Morning* which do not explicitly invoke the soul, and the practice of reading a specifically religious programme into 'No Recompense' limits it drastically. There is surely an echo of Milton's 'Lycidas' here — 'Fame is no plant that grows on mortal soil' — or of Shelley — 'Such is the tyrant's recompense: 'tis just; / He who is evil can receive no good.' The question for readers of Clarke's poem focuses on the issue of infamy: if the poet can acknowledge truth to himself and yet hold silent, what recompense is to be gained if his name is spoken by others for such utterance must confirm a truth of which he despairs or state an untruth. If indeed, an echo of Milton is present, then something akin to the poet's loss of his *alter ego* in death — even of the poet's own *ego* in Clarke's de-memoried past — is central, together with a resolution to renew the self by resolving the conditions of despair. Stoic endurance is only one version, Miltonic pride another, of this mental strife.

By such a reading of a poem which likely dates back into the 1920s, one can discover in Clarke a mind already equipped for the infamous assaults of *Murphy*. The enmity of his own mind later transforms itself in forgetfulness of Yeats's enmity ('The Abbey Theatre Fire' in *Flight to Africa*, 1963), through a line which in time provides the opening for Thomas Kinsella's tribute to Clarke on his seventy-fifth birthday.[25] In the succession of enmity by magnaminity one finds a minor registration of the late flowering of Clarke's poetry, its satiric generosity, its playful religious inquiries, its mischievous sexual narratives, not to mention the development of those prosodic technicalities which so infuriated Samuel Beckett thirty years earlier. But, by the same token, the enmity which oscillates between these writers — Yeats and Beckett, Beckett and Clarke, Clarke and Yeats — also serves to emphasize the agonistic character of literary discourse, especially of that known broadly as modernism. Irish truculence is merely one local variant within a continental pattern. Exchanges do not proceed solely in the laboratory conditions dreamed up under the name, intertextuality: Eliot's review of *Ulysses* in November 1923, for example, was rife with political implications for the 1930s, just as Yeats's hieratic pronouncements on Charles Maurras in *The Irish Times* signalled the anti-democratic response of the senator to the polity he had helped to create. The ferocity of Beckett's portrayal of Ticklepenny is of a piece with his translations of André Breton and Jacques Boulanger in *The Negro Anthology*.[26] More closely aligned with conflicting political forces than even Romanticism had been, modernism was an internally violent discourse in which archaic and futuristic materials and manifestos vied for supremacy. Montage, the distinctive method of modernist textuality, was quite straight-forwardly *an imposition*, with all that mild term suggests.

We are left then with one — probably unanswerable — question:

why Clarke as the butt of Beckett's ill humour? Perhaps the biographers can offer some enlightenment by bringing out patterns of similarity in the two men — early loss of a father, a religious mother, and the dislocations and impositions implied in such patterns. Perhaps the more numerous but also anonymous victims of Beckett's energetic ridicule in 'A Wet Night' hold the key. Even in *Watt* (written during the war years in France) there are surviving cider-vinegar vignettes of Walter Starkie and other Dublin notables. But in April 1973, Beckett told Vivian Mercier that the post-war work began in ignorance — 'I realized that I knew nothing. I sat down in my mother's little house in Ireland and began to write *Molloy*.'[27] The violence of modernism had been bested by the developments Eliot and Yeats had done much to encourage. Clarke in his turn had, by the early 1950s, found it possible to direct his attention to the society in which poetry remained suspect.

Given the complex links between *Mnemosyne Lay in Dust* (1966) and various texts written in the 1930s or earlier — *The Bright Temptation* (1932), *Night and Morning* (1938) and the prose memoir described by Dardis Clarke — it is proper to end with some broad consideration of Clarke's last 'epic'. Certainly, sleeping and waking can be traced in *Mnemosyne*, where the monodrama of the patient confined in St Patrick's Hospital — he is named Maurice Devane — is related in a style at once highly disturbing and humdrum. But, if there is a feature that recurs with significant regularity and frequency, it is that of looking or of being looked at, as indeed 'Summer Lightning' has already revealed. While a great deal has been written about the 'gaze' in connection with Beckett's novels and plays, Clarke's work has rarely if ever attracted discussion of this kind. Yet Foucault's account of the constitution of modern madness, from the late eighteenth century onwards, likewise his history of incarceration, pays particular attention to the power exerted through observation. Clarke's *Mnemosyne* offers stimulating opportunities for an analysis along the lines indicated by Foucault, all the more so if one remembers that St Patrick's Hospital deserves attention as a very early example of eighteenth-century reform in the treatment of 'fools and mad'. Even if St Patrick's turns out not to be quite the kind of institution with which Foucault was concerned — he might have considered St Brendan's Hospital closer to his interests — the general topic of Ireland's treatment of mental illness and its literary registration has been oddly neglected.

More particularly urgent for readers of Clarke's poetry is some attention to Clarke's choice of title. Mnemosyne is not only the Greek word for memory but, as goddess, she was also mother of the muses. Thus, the 1966 sequence does more than treat of mental breakdown with consequential loss and recovery of memory: it also posits a genealogy of the arts, more particularly, of writing in verse. Compared to the poems in *Pilgrimage* and *Night and Morning*, it could be more effectively regarded as a modernist text, albeit a late one. Much of the material treated is quasi-factual – the names of medical staff and fellow-patients appear to be authentic – while little in the way of an ostensible narrative line can be traced. Maurice Devane's recovery occurs as it were alongside the course of the poem rather than in it, as if to indicate that chronic mental disorder is incompatible with language in its aesthetic and social forms. The reader becomes aware of altering and, ultimately, ameliorated relations between the inmate and his surroundings. No cause for this improvement is remotely suggested. If the sequence concedes a palpable design for the reader to seize on, it is a topographical one – with references to Dublin streets prefacing and post-scripting Devane's enforced residence in the hospital. In all of this, there is ample evidence of stylistic affinities with the acknowledged modernist *magna opera* – Joyce's *Ulysses*, being the most notable, Alexander Doblin's *Berlin Alexanderplatz* being a more remote, instance.

The final line of the last section of *Mnemosyne*, reading 'The house in which his mother was born', should surely be interpreted as an allusion to Mnemosyne, mother of poetry, and not simplistically to the patient or the author as tormented son. Thus, in 1966, Clarke releases into the public domain a poetic sequence which concludes with the creative possibility of that author who will write 'Celibacy', 'Aisling', and 'Summer Lightning'. As the last-named of these exists within two literary historical timetables – that of 1938 and that of 1966 – so the remaking of the poet cannot be dated exclusively to the latter period.

Notes

1 Maurice Harmon, *Austin Clarke 1896-1974: A Critical Introduction*, Wolfhound, Dublin, 1989, p. 92.

2 Palmer discussed Clarke's poetry at some length in his *Post-Victorian Poetry*, Dent, London, 1938, pp. 114-18.

3 In 'A Wet Night', Beckett had certainly played with satirizing the Dublin lower intelligentsia — among them 'the homespun Poet wiping his mouth and a little saprophile of an anonymous politico-ploughboy setting him off' — see *More Pricks than Kicks*, Calder & Boyars, London, 1967, p. 57. Though this, like the portrait of Ticklepenny in *Murphy*, combines poetry, alcohol, and a touch of homosexuality — 'the gimlet eyes of the saprophile probed his loins' — it omitted names.

4 Proof that Beckett was aware of *Pilgrimage* and its annotations can readily be found in his review-article, 'Recent Irish Poetry', *Bookman*, August 1934 (see *Disjecta*, pp. 72-3).

5 See W.J. Mc Cormack, *From Burke to Beckett: Ascendancy, Tradition and Betrayal in Literary History*, Cork University Press, Cork, 1994, pp. 378-9, for a detailed discussion of Synge and Yeats in *Murphy*.

6 Rubin Rabinovitz has noted many elaborate verbal pairings and doublings in the novel, though he has not — any more than I have — checked if the verb to sweep occurs only on the two occasions cited above, viz. the sweeping of Ticklepenny from the board and the sweeping of Murphy off the pub floor. See R. Rabinovitz, 'Murphy and the Uses of Repetition', *On Beckett: Essays and Criticism*, S.E. Gontarski ed., Grove Press, New York, 1986, pp. 67-90.

7 *Romeo and Juliet* ran at the Gate Theatre, Dublin, from 25 October to 5 November 1932, and was revived in 1936. See Peter Luke, ed., *Enter Certain Players: Edwards-MacLiammóir and the Gate 1928-1978*, Dolmen Press, Dublin, 1978.

8 Starkey (1879-1958) also ran the Dublin-based Orwell Press which issued *Night and Morning* in 1938 and thus assisted Clarke's repatriation. Other potential identifications have been noted, but not explicitly endorsed by Eoin O'Brien — Neary as H.S. Macran, Endon as Thomas MacGreevy, even Willoughby Kelly as James Joyce; see *The Beckett Country*, Black Cat Press, Dublin, 1986, p. 377 n. 83. The last of these possibilities raises serious questions, for it would implicate the identification of Celia who is in effect Kelly's adopted daughter; if any aspect of Joyce is reflected in Kelly, does Celia's determination to possess Murphy reflect Lucia Joyce's infatuation with Beckett? Given Lucia Joyce's difficult mental condition, ultimately schizophrenic, the implications are not flattering for the novelist. Of the possibilities listed by Eoin O'Brien, Neary/Macran seems most likely: Henry Stewart Macran (1867-1937) was professor of moral philosophy in Trinity College, Dublin until 1934, the author/translator of two books: *Hegel's Doctrine of Formal Logic* (Oxford, 1912), and *Hegel's Logic of World*

and Idea (Oxford, 1929); he was a notable drinker.

9   Clarke contributed a signed article 'Love in Irish Poetry and Drama' to *Motley*, 1, 5, October 1932, pp. 3-4, which dwelt on 'fear of women' as a major force in Gaelic culture recently intensified by the fall of Charles Stewart Parnell and so reactivated as painful literary influence. Christopher FitzSimon has suggested that Beckett wrote 'A Proposal for the Strengthening of the Censorship', an ironic essay appearing in *Motley*, 2, 5, September 1933, pp. 3-5, on the grounds that it resembles Beckett's 'Censorship in the Saorstat' which was commissioned by the *Bookman* in 1935 but never published until 1983. Personally I am not convinced. The entire Gate circle was hostile to censorship, and as an example of how vehemently such views were expressed see T.B. Rudmose Brown's letter in *Motley*, 2, 2, February 1933: 'The most denunciatory adversary of Joyce in Trinity College has not read a sentence of his work. Nor have I. But I don't profess to hold any opinion on the subject . . . My opposition to literary censorship is part and parcel of my opposition to all coercion, whether political, social, religious, economic, or other' (p. 16). But for evidence of Beckett's involvement with some Gate Theatre personalities, see Mary Manning's reminiscences (pp. 35-9) in Luke, pp. 35-9. Manning edited *Motley*.

10   'Genustupration' – agitation of the knees.

11   That this fear should be linked to Murphy's recollection of an encounter at the Gate Theatre is not accidental: for many years, Hilton Edwards and Micheál MacLiammóir were synonymous in Dublin gossip with homosexuality.

12   For the basic facts see Deirdre Bair, *Samuel Beckett: A Biography*. London: Cape, 1978, p. 177, etc. Maurice Harmon contributed 'Notes Towards a Biography' to the 1974 special issue of the *Irish University Review* dedicated to Clarke's memory: Mary Thompson's full-length *Life* is eagerly awaited.

13   Dardis Clarke describes a thirty-seven page manuscript, probably written in 1920. Entitled *The House of Terror*, it is a prose account of the poet's incarceration and treatment. 'The manuscript has the status of an authorial draft, at times resembling a memorandum addressed to the author himself.' Two passages from this document have been published, one about 650 words, the other shorter, in W.J. Mc Cormack, *In the Prison of the His Days: A Miscellany for Nelson Mandela on his 70th Birthday*, Lilliput Press, Gigginstown, 1988, pp. 72-5, by kind permission of Dardis Clarke (who also contributed a brief commentary, pp. 74-5).

14   For an account of the analyst's early years, see Wilfrid Bion, *The Long Weekend 1897-1919: Part of a Life*, Free Association Books, London, 1986, which does not cover the period of Beckett's association with Bion. Nicola Bion confirms that her father said little about Beckett's analysis and that his professional notes, which are almost certainly in the Tavistock, are under the embargo in the way usual for such records.

15   See G.C. Barnard, *Samuel Beckett: A New Approach*, Dent, London, 1970,

pp. 7-8; Eoin O'Brien, *The Beckett Country,* pp. 115, 371n. A.G. Thompson, an old school friend of Beckett's, worked in the Bethlehem and arranged for him to have some access to the institution. See also John Fletcher, *The Novels of Samuel Beckett,* Chatto, London, 1964, p. 45.

16 For good measure, a slightly later retelling of Neary's frenzy manages to stress the fundamental focus of his attention; he refers to 'that deathless rump' and Wylie repeats the noun twice while suggesting that the statue lacked this anatomical item, 'What chance would a rump have in the G.P.O.?' (*Murphy,* p. 57).

17 For example, T.W. Rolleston, *Myths and Legends of the Celtic Race,* Harrap, London, 1911. Yeats, though he had used Cuchulain in several plays, did not favour the Red Branch; the term only appears once, in the first version of *The Countess Kathleen* (1892).

18 Cited by Harmon, without provenance, in 'Notes towards a Biography'. Beckett, in comic imitation of Joyce's directive concerning the depth of the area in front of No. 7 Eccles Street, had written from London to ask Con Leventhal to 'measure the height from the ground of Cuchulain's arse'. Quoted from Leventhal, 'The Thirties', *Beckett at Sixty,* Calder & Boyars, London, 1967, p. 11. A hostile crowd gathered during the inspection.

19 Austin Clarke, *Later Poems,* Dolmen Press, Dublin, 1961, p. 89.

20 Clarke, *Later Poems,* p. 5.

21 Both *Murphy* and *Night and Morning* were published in 1938, but we know that Beckett's novel had been completed quite some time prior to its appearance. The business of finding a publisher had been left to George Reavey, a vigorous advocate of the kind of poetry Beckett had emphatically preferred over the antiquarianism of Clarke, Stephens, Higgins, etc. No last-minute qualms about the ridiculing of Clarke were likely from that source, even with the novelist himself abroad and unavailable for comment.

22 Harmon has also noted details in the first of Clarke's three prose romances, *The Bright Temptation* (1932), which recur in *Mnemosyne*; see *Austin Clarke: A Critical Introduction,* p. 263n.

23 Vivian Mercier, in 'Mortal Anguish, Moral Pride: Austin Clarke's Religious Lyrics', *Irish University Review,* 4, 1, 1974, pp. 91-9, points out that, though the texts of 1936 and 1938 differ, the lines quoted above remain unaltered in the later version. Only the third and fourth lines differ, reading in 1936: 'And door-chill, body's heat, a common ill,/Grow monstrous in our sleep: I have . . . '

24 Craig Tapping, *Austin Clarke: A Study of his Writings,* Academy Press, Dublin, 1981, p. 65. Of the twelve poems in the collection, all except 'The Straying Student', 'Penal Law', 'Summer Lightning' and 'No Recompense' attend specifically to the soul's fate.

25 Clarke, 'The Abbey Theatre Fire', *Flight to Africa,* Dolmen Press, Dublin, 1963, pp. 16-17; Thomas Kinsella, 'Magnaminity' in *Nightwalker and Other Poems,* Dolmen Press, Dublin, 1968, pp. 46-7.

26   *Selected Prose of T.S. Eliot,* Frank Kermode ed., Faber, London, 1975, pp. 175-8; W.B. Yeats, 'From Democracy to Authority', *The Irish Times,* 16 February 1924; on Beckett's contributions to *The Negro Anthology* (1934), see W.J. Mc Cormack, *From Burke to Beckett: Ascendancy, Tradition and Betrayal in Literary History,* Cork University Press, Cork, 1994, pp. 386-91.

27   Vivian Mercier, *Beckett/Beckett,* Oxford University Press, New York, 1977, p. 161.

4

How is MacGreevy
a Modernist?

J.C.C. Mays

It is easy to forget, and some readers may not know, that the reputa-
tions of Joyce and Beckett did not always stand as high in Ireland
as they do today. They are now the stuff of theatre festivals and tee-
shirts, commemorative postage stamps and bibliographic investment.
Their writing is as well known to the average secondary-school goer
now as the short stories of Frank O'Connor used to be some thirty
years ago. However, in the early 1960s, *Ulysses* and *Finnegans Wake*
were so little evident in bookshops that visitors habitually assumed
they were censored and wrote home about the indifference towards
or ignorance of Joyce's achievement they found.[1] Interest in Joyce's
later writing had widened somewhat by the time I came to Dublin
in 1967, but the lack of interest in Beckett in turn surprised me. There
were local champions of both writers – John Garvin and Niall
Montgomery, Alan Simpson and Alec Reid – but they did not seem
to get much of a response beyond the hospitable columns of Quid-
nunc in *The Irish Times*.

The sense of an Irish tradition in which the late Joyce and Beckett
played such an insignificant part was reflected in the syllabus and
reading-lists of the new MA in Anglo-Irish at University College,
Dublin. In this course, as it was originally conceived, the period 1890
to 1920 was pivotal. What came before prepared for it and what came
after was a consequence. Poetry and drama were central: they shared
a common attitude towards mythology and mysticism; they both ex-
plored Celtic subject matter and native techniques. The period

1920–50 was understood in terms of reaction: the thesis of the Revival, focused on the myth and folklore of the Irish countryside, produced an antithetical interest in the modern urban world; verse gave way to prose, the Romantic W.B. Yeats in term 1 was displaced by the realist Joyce in term 2, J.M. Synge by Seán O'Casey. The assumptions are summed up by Maurice Harmon:

> The literature cf the period, in reaction to the romantic, subjective and idealistic literature of the Revival, was produced by a distinctive generation, whose growth to manhood had usually paralleled and been keenly affected by the changing fortunes of the country as it passed from colonial status to independence.[2]

In this view of things, *Ulysses* is grouped with Corkery's *Threshold of Quiet* under realism and *Finnegans Wake* with Eimar O'Duffy's *King Goshawk and the Birds* under fantasy, and, while there is room for Walter Macken and George Shiels, neither Beckett's fiction nor his plays get a mention.

Maurice Harmon's *Guide* proved an invaluable handbook for students. Its value was that it did not seek to be novel – the historical schema overlaps with Frank O'Connor's *Short History of Irish Literature* and Ben Kiely's *Modern Irish Fiction*, for example – but it succeeded in stating a by then traditional view succinctly and with detachment. The fact that it has been superseded by an enlarged and revised edition does not lessen its value as an historical document. It remains a summary of how writing in Ireland appeared to have evolved during the present century, formulated at the moment when Irish writing emerged as a special course of study, and it accurately registers the distinctive emphases and exclusions this involves.

I recall this view of Irish writing in the late 1960s because it provides the context in which Thomas MacGreevy wrote and of the moment at which he was 'rediscovered'. It has been overtaken by other views and paradigms of history, and the underlying assumptions have emerged more clearly as we have become detached from them. Some of them are peculiar and worth noting.

For a start, while Yeats and his legacy are central, the view of him is a narrow one and we might now think it begs important questions. Specifically, though the figure of Yeats used customarily to be taken as a given and stable background to the period 1920–50, we might protest that this is a drastic narrowing. Irish Yeats was early Yeats, since no one was influenced by his ideal of Byzantium or of the eighteenth century. When his fame grew in the 1920s and was confirmed by the Nobel Prize, the status of his earlier poetry was enhanced but perceptions of it were not modified by the different way he had come to write. Yeats in Ireland meant Irish subject-matter, rural and lyrical and mythical, and a special modification of late nineteenth-century style. His prestige worked not to take Irish poetry with him into the symbolic mode but to preserve it in a limbo of Georgianism. Irish Yeats proved not to be the author of 'Leda and the Swan' or of *Last Poems* but was involved in a crucial dispute with Edward Dowden.

The special features of Joyce's Irish reputation are connected with this view of Yeats. Joyce was spoken of as and assumed to be representative of a stable isolable literary quality and to be the author, above all, of *Dubliners* and *A Portrait*. His place in Irish writing was as a realistic and satirical writer, and his later manner appeared irrelevant to the Irish line which continued in the realist short stories and *Bildungsroman* of O'Connor, O' Flaherty and O'Faoláin and in the verse satire of Clarke, Kavanagh and Kinsella. Illustrations and variations of this view are contained in the collection, *A Bash In The Tunnel: James Joyce by the Irish*.[3] The title is from an essay by Brian O'Nolan which strikes the characteristic note. The contributors are on the whole more impressed with Joyce's realism and humour than his art.

The older sense of a tradition involved not only a partial view of Yeats and Joyce but a special view of writing at large. Seán O'Faoláin spelled it out when he attacked *Work in Progress*, arguing that words should be simple counters for subject-matter. Art which draws attention to itself is corrupt and corrupting: 'Joyce's medium strikes at the inevitable basis of language, universal intelligibility . . . it comes from nowhere, goes nowhere, is not part of life at all.' Frank O'Connor articulated a similar belief: 'I . . . see a mind turning in on itself and not caring any longer for the business of communication. I feel . . . a sort of disintegration of the material, as though the mind behind had softened from abstraction through pedantry into mere whimsy.'[4]

Attitudes towards *Finnegans Wake* have changed and these comments position themselves in an historical time-frame. As Joyce's book comes to seem more readable and more successful, the protest that he fails the test of social realism seems to miss the point.

Similarly Yeats: the criteria of subject-matter which made his earlier poems seem more centrally Irish now seems odd. Englishmen were not obliged to maintain that *Hamlet* and *Antony and Cleopatra* are less part of English culture than *Henry IV* and *Richard III*, nor Frenchmen that *Polyeucte* and *Phèdre* are not monuments of the French tradition,[5] but Irish readers were asked to accept that the only novels of Elizabeth Bowen, say, that belong to the Irish tradition are the ones with Irish subject-matter. This sometimes caused embarrassment – for instance, when it was maintained that *Juno and the Paycock* is more central to Irish writing than *The Silver Tassie* or *Saint Joan* – but the embarrassment was endured for the sake of the presumption.

MacGreevy's sense of an alternative to the view of Irish writing I have described was, as I have said, largely ignored. He wrote largely in isolation from the dominant Irish culture of his time: 'I labour in a barren place,/Alone, self-conscious', he wrote in 'Nocturne' (*CPM*, p. 1). This needs to be recalled because the lack of support he received bears on the fragility of his achievement. Equally important, the fact that his rediscovery from the later 1960s onwards has taken place against the background of a changing attitude towards Irish writing inevitably affects the way he is seen now. He has moved back into the picture more for the picture's sake than as a result of any serious re-reading of what he wrote. His new status is as much a limbo as his former one.

His poems began to appear in anthologies of Irish verse even before they were collected in *Poems* 1934, and regularly thereafter, and one can find respectful mention of the regard in which they were held. Though Daniel Corkery described him as one who went away, Arland Ussher recalled him as one of 'our better poets' in *The Dublin Magazine* in 1947 and Beatrice Glenavy remembered 'Dechtire' being recited at dinner.[6] After he died in 1967, *The Capuchin Annual* was able to put together a small memorial by friends and acquaintances which testified to the worth of his writing.[7] At the same time, the position he had come to occupy reverberated with the knowledge that he had a reputation outside Ireland among writers like T.S. Eliot and Marianne Moore. A. Rivoallan included him in a survey of Irish writing in the late 1930s, Babette Deutsch remembered him when she reviewed Devlin's *Lough Derg* volume for the *New York Herald Tribune*, and Wallace Stevens addressed 'Our

Stars Come from Ireland' to him, thus inaugurating an important correspondence.[8] My impression is that he came to be accorded a kind of respect in Ireland, even though he was only read seriously by a few fellow-writers like Pearse Hutchinson and John Jordan.

The situation changed when New Writers' Press published *Collected Poems* edited by Thomas Dillon Redshaw, with Beckett's 1934 review as preface. They also republished Beckett's polemical essay on Irish poetry from the 1934 *Bookman* as part of a special issue of *The Lace Curtain* devoted to the 'lost generation' of 1930s writers.[9] These two publications, appearing in the same year (1971), positioned MacGreevy at a hinge-point in Irish modernism, and his poetry and what it represented supplied an historical background for other poets published by New Writers' Press. MacGreevy had written in response to O'Faoláin's attack on *Work in Progress* at the time itself. He had been intimate with Beckett from early days, Beckett who in 1969 had been awarded the Nobel Prize. He had written on Mainie Jellett and Jack B. Yeats, who were beginning to emerge as Irish modernist painters. He appeared as the man in the middle around whom a largely ignored tradition of international modernism in Ireland had happened and had been waiting to be rediscovered.

So it seemed at the time, and so it was celebrated in position-essays by Michael Smith, Augustus Young and others.[10] Time has nonetheless moved on; the idealistic, cultural enthusiasm for Europe has mutated into something more pragmatic and New Writers' Press has folded its tents. Scholarly articles on MacGreevy and his contemporaries began to appear in the cooling temperature of the 1980s,[11] and he has entered the lecture-programme of Irish summer schools. Susan Schreibman has edited a helpful annotated and enlarged edition of the poems and is at work on a comprehensive biography. Even so, despite this interest, it is not evident that his poems are read with much care or very widely. MacGreevy has emerged from obscurity to be placed in a respectful niche, but, though his name is better known than it was, I am not sure that his true provocation is understood. He was not simply a John-the-Baptist figure to the now all-conquering Beckett. His writing is something which Beckett described as transitional and it amounts to something more interesting than the mindless modernism it is sometimes taken to represent.

MacGreevy has a special place in the Irish tradition because he was a modernist, but he was a special kind of modernist because he was Irish. The disparate backgrounds which fed into his writing most obviously distinguish it from other international modernists with whom he might be compared. He acknowledged Henry James, Schubert, Valéry, Giorgione and Corneille. One could also argue that negative influences like Goethe, Wagner and George Moore were equally important. The point is that all of them, positive and negative, were idiosyncratic. He was not part of a school and his thinking about art did not go in a straight line. Someone familiar with the main traditions in Anglo-American writing might assume his poetry had been influenced by imagists like Richard Aldington and H.D. He was in fact more influenced by the *Ballet Russe* and the Latin Mass.[12]

His critical work on writing and painting is likely to disappoint the modern reader because it is untechnical. He was also conspicuously uninterested in artistic movements – those grooves in which thoughts gather momentum and become emphatic. The progress of his arguments typically moves backwards and forwards in time across a wide field of reference in a way which looks like namedropping because it is concerned more with values than analysis or the theoretical construction of a tradition. One enthusiasm merges with another, so that a poem like 'Sour Swan' incorporates allusions to Baudelaire, Mallarmé, Proust and Yeats as well as to the Bible and Dante, even while it is addressed to a younger contemporary and summarizes the argument of a monograph on T.S. Eliot.[13] Significant gaps appear: what do we make of his apparent indifference towards American writing or painting of this century?

MacGreevy stood for a position about art rather than for or against a single movement within art – for or against W. B. Yeats, for example – and this gives him an uneasy relation to those who employ such oppositions to know where they are. He appears not to have been interested in manifestos,[14] and even Beckett was more directly affected by the currents of thought of his time – surrealism, existentialism, whatever. His sense of the present was confidently non-polemic. He would have been naturally modern in any age, yet he did not feel the need to defend the past against the present.

This so-called modernist makes an odd internationalist also. His poems celebrate the republican side in the Irish Civil War; they are fed very directly by popular Catholicism, from turns of phrase to a cast of feeling; his sense of cultural nationalism runs so deep as to make that of writers like J.M. Synge (so he argued) seem like a libel. He contributed prolifically to the debate which opened and then closed during the course of the 1920s in the pages of *The Irish Statesman, The Gael, The Klaxon, The Irish Program, The Irish Independent, The Dublin Magazine* and other journals of greater or lesser fame and longevity. When he left Dublin and began increasingly to write for English and later French journals, his tone changed but his point of view did not. Distance — and living in London again, in particular — only heightened his sense of nationhood, and there is evidence that several members of the Paris international brigade found his attitude hard to take.[15]

The Irish and modernist dimensions of MacGreevy's sensibility combine in a way which is more unusual than is commonly recognized and which is fundamentally different from the better-known version deriving from Brian O'Nolan. O'Nolan, like MacGreevy, was interested in the experimental aspect of Joyce's writing at the time when this was less popular than the earlier more realist mode. His writing appears to make its bid to an international audience, and to have nothing to do with the kind of fiction presided over by O'Flaherty, O'Faoláin, and O'Connor. His gift appears as a gift for fantasy, for sheer untrammelled inventiveness and wordplay, for mimicry of style and juggling of planes of illusion. *At Swim-Two-Birds, The Third Policeman* and *The Dalkey Archive* seem to be at one with an international mode current from Buenos Aires to Brighton and not with anything that came out of Listowel. They are hardly of the stuff that would have qualified their author for full membership of Yeats's Academy.

However, though O'Nolan has been compared to Nabokov and Karl Kraus and though writers like B.S. Johnson and Tom Stoppard have expressed their indebtedness to him, he was firmly rooted in the Palace Bar in Dublin. He was at one with O'Faoláin and O'Connor in holding that art like Joyce's perverted the proper bond between literature and experience, words and life. His books, it is true, develop similar methods, but only to parody them on behalf of values he held more real. His motivation is emetic, he saw the Joycean legacy as at best pure game, and his pursuit of technique for its own sake would not have been so miraculous had he felt committed to its justifying ground.[16]

O'Nolan was a home-staying exile who wrote to undercut the pretensions of international modernism on the grounds that they embody an excess of high-flying pride. His contradictory inspiration sometimes degenerated into jeering, and one might wonder if it did not in the end, in *The Hard Life* and much of the *Cruiskeen Lawn* column, become self-destructive. When one compares O'Nolan's attitude towards Joyce with MacGreevy's, in the essay 'The Catholic Element in *Work in Progress*' and the poem 'For an Irish Book', one is made aware of MacGreevy's genuinely larger understanding of what Joyce was attempting to do. There is a dialogue between Joyce's assumptions and MacGreevy's, but there is no attempt to spoil or put down what Joyce had achieved.

MacGreevy and O'Nolan's different understanding of the relation between art and life is the same as that which divided Joyce and O'Faoláin/O'Connor in the debate about *Work in Progress*. It had been argued over a few years previously by John Crowe Ransom and Allen Tate in the pages of *The Fugitive*, and many years before that by Francis Jeffrey and William Wordsworth.[17] The grounds of the dispute can indeed be traced back to Aristotle and Longinus. MacGreevy, like Joyce and others in the Longinian tradition, understood that poetry remakes — does not need always to represent — the material world; art need not have a paraphraseable content, the standards of criticism need not be mimetic. He learned this not just from French and Spanish modernists but from his experience of all kinds of art before that, and he understood it at a level where understanding ousted mistrust. His greatest historical importance is as a witness to this permanent truth at a particular time and place.

While it would appear to be a rule that social-realist standards in art become oppressively normative in emerging nation-states (Cuba and Russia can be compared with Ireland between 1920 and 1950), MacGreevy maintained a larger understanding without compromising his commitment to Ireland. This in turn is why, at the same time that his brand of modernism needs to be distinguished from that of Brian O'Nolan and his imitators, his brand of cultural nationalism differs from other varieties current then and now.

MacGreevy's involvement in republican politics is recorded in memoirs such as Ernie O'Malley's *On Another Man's Wound*[18] and poems like 'The Six Who Were Hanged'. When one follows his continuing polemic on behalf of the Irishness of Irish art during the

1920s, one could be forgiven for recalling the tirades of D.P. Moran against the English and against Protestants in the columns of *The Leader*. The monographs on T.S. Eliot and Jack B. Yeats were too consistently Catholic and nationalist, by turns, to please those who wanted art for art's sake. Yet MacGreevy's dearest friends from the First World War were Englishmen and he resigned his post in the Carnegie Library Trust when the Protestant Lennox Robinson was unfairly dismissed for perpetrating obscene literature. This ex-British officer was a republican, this devout Catholic attended Trinity College and was the trusted friend of the agnostic Jack Yeats. This modernist was consciously a nationalist.

I do not believe I am describing a paradox. MacGreevy had an idea of the Irish mind which is at a significant remove from the kind of cultural nationalism regularly condemned by Conor Cruise O'Brien.[19] He believed what is incontrovertible, that Irish experience is unique, but he was tolerant enough to realize that other nations could claim the same prerogative on their own behalf and his sense of the Irish mind was not something to be imposed on the Irish people. His idea of national identity took other national identities into account and welcomed their fructifying influence. He differs from many other modernist writers in that he thought in nationalist terms; he differs from many Irish nationalists in the selflessness and range of his extra-national sympathies. Similarly with his other beliefs. His long correspondence with Beckett is remarkable for the level of sympathy and moral support he sustained for attitudes at odds with his own. Beckett was the more intransigent of the two, and the cruel caricature of Catholic belief in Father Ambrose (*Malone Dies*) and the nihilistic assault on all belief in *Endgame* must have wounded MacGreevy deeply. His statements of difference were nonetheless as supportive and tactful as they are in 'Sour Swan'.

The poem 'Aodh Ruadh Ó Domhnaill' (*CPM*, pp. 34–5) is an excellent example of the point at issue, combining as it does nationalist and modernist themes. It is Irish and European in a way that compromises neither. Indeed, it illustrates so many characteristic features of MacGreevy's poetry at its best that it runs the risk of becoming his 'Lake Isle of Innisfree' – as W.B. Yeats recognized.[20]

The genre is established by Unamuno's 'En un cemeterio de lugar castellano' and by Valéry's 'Le cimetière marin'. The one famously celebrates a visit to a ruined and abandoned graveyard near Arévelo in Castile, the other the cemetery at Sète on the Mediterranean. The subject is at the same time Irish in a particular way. One might have expected MacGreevy the European to have celebrated Manus O'Donnell, Red Hugh's grandfather, who was a famous translator and international scholar; or Red Hugh's companion, the visionary and charismatic Hugh O'Neill, who died in Rome. MacGreevy settled on the less attractive subject of Red Hugh simply, it seems, because Hugh stood for one cause: to expel the English. This single-mindedness imbued him with a symbolic interest for intellectual republicans following 1916.[21] Following the War of Independence and its aftermath, his relevance was subtly qualified and the Spanish context of MacGreevy's poem associates Red Hugh with the millenarian idea of a redeemer coming from Spain to liberate the Irish nation. At this point, also, one can note that de Valera was often held, in the popular imagination of his supporters in the 1920s, to combine the tradition of a redeemer from Spain with a redeemer from America. MacGreevy may or may not have intended these last meanings to enter his poem, but they could be present.

This said, his lines move very differently from Unamuno's and Valéry's and in a way which transforms their political content. They are constructed in the form of a complicated dialogue, in which the speaker is increasingly isolated as he discovers his real subject, and which comes to transcend its specific backgrounds.

The poem begins with a series of recorded observations, priest and poet trying to help one another, each restricted within his own linguistic horizon. The observations are separate, the poet is detached from the priest, they are linked only by an academic question about pronunciation. However, the staccato dialogue builds to a point where it exfoliates into a longer, more connected sentence describing the speaker's own thoughts. The reactive principle of the forward movement here is idiosyncratic. One should notice how a subsequent parenthesis '(it seemed odd)' impels the movement of the longer sentence onward into a different, less self-conscious, less precise and less clearly separated area. This is the movement the poem at large will mimic, until it reaches a point where physical failure is overwhelmed by psychic resolution.

The poem continues with the speaker now alone ('All day I passed') on his search. Rhymes create echoes in which he is further lost; his surroundings merge in the darkness, 'gloom' with 'tomb'; we accompany him inward into the world of the dead and the pace slows. The irregularity of the rhyme-words mimics his stopping and starting as we move, 'Rubbing/At mouldy inscriptions'. He asks again, but his failure only completes the sense (and the rhyme) of several lines before, hanging limply off the end of the long sentence. 'Yet' the next paragraph begins – and here the counter-movement picks up again more strongly, this time impelled by a more forceful parenthesis – and the speaker at last moves closer to the object of his quest. The lines continue first as if compressed, to emphasize the pride of a royal funeral, but we are outdoors again, among the quick and the living. So the poem opens into its conclusion, proudly spelling it out in measured, rhyming lines:

> And all Valladolid knew
> And out to Simancas all knew
> Where they buried Red Hugh.

The politics get left behind in the process I have described, the speaker creating in imagination the object he has failed to find. In effect, he creates the sense of glory he laments and establishes the sense of connection he has described as physically not there. The close of the poem is indeed heroic; the resonant names succeed one another in a way which cements their value. When Red Hugh's name is finally discovered, it is in English, which may cause surprise until one reflects that this carries more weight than the aspirated form. The Englishness is a rich irony. The poem is propped with antiquarian notes to do with Hugh's burial place[22] and MacGreevy always insisted on the Irish form of the title, but he drove his poem towards a conclusion which offsets what these things communicate. His poem is as far from being a cry of 'Brits Out' as it is from being an Irish version of a Spanish and French genre of the 1920s, though it rests on both these foundations.

It rests on others, too. A consciousness of the paintings of Jack Yeats – whose republicanism and hopes for an Irish Ireland were close to MacGreevy's – sustains the loss this poem celebrates.[23] 'Aodh Ruadh' mingles elegy and celebration in the same way as Yeats's 'The Funeral of Harry Boland' (1922) or 'The Island Funeral' (1923). One might also compare 'Aodh Ruadh' with W.B. Yeats's 'Easter 1916', which seeks to establish a similar balance between loss and gain. Yeats's poem directly assaults the vanity and foolishness of the figures it describes so as to render more self-consciously the perception of them after the event as martyrs. The difference between the two poems is between what MacGreevy called 'heroic tragedy' in Jack Yeats and W.B. called 'terrible beauty' in his own poem, and it exactly measures MacGreevy's position in the debates of his time. His view is less aesthetic than that contained by 'Easter 1916': there is less rage, less gaiety, a different sense of loss, and I should say more compassion.

The structure and movement of 'Aodh Ruadh' is characteristic of MacGreevy's poems as a whole. They typically begin with negative origins and proceed towards celebration. Some stay close to the ground and are predominantly satirical, like 'Anglo-Irish' and 'The Other Dublin'. Others like 'Recessional' and 'Nocturne of the Self-Evident Presence' are well off the ground before they begin; 'Out of the gloom', celebrating 'a dry, high silence'.

> Ready therefore, all ready, already
> For the without of glory.
>
> ('Saint Senan's Well', *CPM*, p. 44)

The mood can be sunny, as in 'Homage to Marcel Proust', or epigrammatic, as in 'Arrangement in Gray and Black'.

When Beckett wrote about MacGreevy, he emphasized this ascensionist movement and its celebratory aspect. It is certainly habitual, as MacGreevy displayed when he continually urged Joyce to write a *Paradiso* and, differently, as he acknowledged when he planned to call a collection of essays *Reactions*.[24] Beckett, however, seems to me to place too much emphasis on the pure moment of perception to which MacGreevy's verse climbs:

> But a moment, now, I suppose,
> For a moment I may suppose,
> Gleaming blue,
> Silver blue,
> Gold,
> Rose,
> And the light of the world.
>
> ('Gloria de Carlos V', *CPM*, p. 36)

In the language of Wordsworth's 'Tintern Abbey', this is the moment 'we are laid asleep/In body and become a living soul.' In Beckett's formulation, 'It is from this nucleus of endopsychic clarity, uttering itself in the prayer that is a spasm of awareness, and from no more casual source, that Mr McGreevy evolves his poems' (*Disjecta*, p. 69).

But Beckett's interests led him to understand MacGreevy as a more self-absorbed writer than he is. He went on to claim that 'for the intelligent Amiel there is only one landscape' and to describe MacGreevy as 'the Titchener of the modern lyric' — the first having evolved the image of the ideal core of the onion before Proust, the second a system of pure introspective psychology.[25] Beckett's comparisons suggest MacGreevy's effort was in one direction and was relatively colourless; that it drove towards a vacant, nameless consciousness, like the idea Valéry demonstrated in *Monsieur Teste* and completed in the final shadow of 'Le Solitaire' in *Mon Faust*. Amiel called it 'reimplication' and defined it as 'consciousness of consciousness' long before Valéry made the phrase famous.[26] The reality of MacGreevy's poetry differs from such an ideal, which approaches Belacqua's limbo and Murphy's microcosm. It is engaging because of the varied manner of his ascent to the *gile na gile* and also because of the relation of the position reached to the world which he never altogether leaves behind. W.B. Yeats is reported as saying, 'It is very hard to like men of action', but the poem in which the quotation makes up a line, 'Homage to Louis XI', is homage to several men of action who sought to link heaven and earth, the ideal being not to forsake one for the other but to conjoin them.

'De Civitate Hominum' (*CPM*, pp. 2-3) offers a ready example of the kind of compromise which can be reached. It combines the literary genres of poems based on painting — like Cendrars's 'Natures mortes', Apollinaire's 'Les Fenêtres' and Reverdy's 'L'Ombre du mur' — and the even larger body of poems arising from the First World War. Its manner might owe something to the kind of free verse centred on clearly-imaged, even painterly, subjects evolved by Juan Ramón Jiménez after 1916, and even to such special effects as Machado's *pie quebrado* or short line. The movement of the poem is a process of adjustment of the kind I traced in 'Aodh Ruadh Ó Domhnaill'. A situation is there, is described as given; an event takes place, which is horrible; but the real action in the mind of the speaker is an interior drama and reaches an unresolved stasis. At the close, though the speaker is unable to focus properly on what has happened, a sense of it remains and has been qualified.

There is a link between the last four lines of the poem (beginning 'My sergeant says'), and the provisional conclusion to the first section which winds up with an awkward pun and an affected abbreviation.

> *Morte . . .!*
> 'Tis still life that lives,
> Not quick life —

The last four lines are not more of a conclusion in the sense of having reached an answer, but they are closer to it. The response is deeper and at the same time its inadequacy is framed by a clearer recognition of what cannot be known.

> My sergant says, very low, 'Holy God!
> 'Tis a fearful death.'
>
> Holy God makes no reply
> Yet.

'De Civitate Hominum' is about the horror created by man and his inability to respond to it adequately — a failure which reflects his nature and is the condition of his relation to God. It is a failed still-life: as Waldemar George explained the distinction between *nature morte* and *nature vivante* to MacGreevy (*Aldington,* pp. 31-5), the one is humility and prayer and the other anger and involvement. As a poem of reaction in MacGreevy's sense, registering the attempt to translate life into art, 'De Civitate' is finally awkward and inadequate. The experience it describes draws a conventional response from the sergeant and a too-pat counter-response from the speaker, the witty line-break giving away his callowness, and this is the point. It is as much about limitation as achievement, about the state of humanity and the inability of art to transcend nature.

Other poems complicate Beckett's suggestion in other ways. 'Homage to Jack Yeats' (*CPM,* p. 28) is an exact reversal of the ascensionalist movement. Paragraph 1 moves quickly from a desolate land to a vision of more 'daring-delicate' days; paragraph 2 looks back and enlarges on the 'stupidity' which lurked in 'the gold years / Of Limerick life', the wastefulness in richness and recklessness in bravery,

> The brave stupidity of soldiers,
> The proud stupidity of soldiers' wives.[27]

'Crón Tráth na nDéithe' has a horizontal narrative, following the cab-journey from Broadstone Station to Merrion Square, and contains only a moment in which the gloom brightens:

> The brightness of brightness
> Towering in the sky
> Over Dublin.   (*CPM*, p. 19)

It is otherwise unrelieved satire.

MacGreevy's own sense of his poems was that they were sad, 'elegiac'.[28] So many of them are. 'Winter' describes his heart being with the dead. 'Love always fails' is the burden of 'Arrangement in Gray and Black'. 'Ten Thousand Leaping Swords' is not just about promise; as earlier titles make clear, it is also about the state of wilderness from which promise is glimpsed. Even a poem as jolly as 'Homage to Li Po' is actually about the impossibility of escaping the human condition. A sense of inadequacy and loss always stands behind his writing. The feeling is partly personal, partly the experience of the European war and its aftermath in Ireland:

> I began my rounds with the sorrowful mysteries
> Instead of the joyful   ('Saint Senan's Well')

The result is that these poems which Beckett suggested were about transcendence and art are about the conditions of life and art at the same time — that is, equally, about failure.

Another aspect to which Beckett particularly responded — over-responded, I would argue — was a tendency of MacGreevy's poetic rhythm. MacGreevy reported Beckett saying that his verse 'lapse[d] too easily into iambics'.[29] By this, I think Beckett meant something connected with his overall view that MacGreevy's verse tends in the direction of prayer; that, in its ascent to a breathless hush, it creates for itself a self-comforting surround; that upbeat becomes habitual. In fact, the length and patterning of lines is more varied than the short lines Beckett likes to quote, and, as I have argued, the movement of lines is habitually interrupted and complicated and for that reason more interesting. The white spaces to which the poems ascend are not a regressive blank; MacGreevy's *nature morte* is coloured by living awareness.

Take as an example 'Homage to Hieronymus Bosch' (*CPM*, pp. 11-13). It is far more than the lyrical utterance of a single voice, which is how Beckett would encourage us to read it. It contains and adjusts several voices, which advance and retreat and alter their position. Thus, the details of the opening observation of a woman and a boy develop until it is inevitable that the third-party, the observer himself, should be brought into the equation: 'And I, in terror, stopped, staring.' At this point, 'a group of shadowy figures' emerges behind the two he has observed, the field of perception deepens and he diverts momentarily into a sideways observation:

> It was a wild wet morning
> But the little world was spinning on.

When the observer returns to the scene before him, the woman is addressing the group in a way that causes his further estrangement and simultaneously the group begins to stir, a shadowy action begins to take place. What had seemed immoveable begins to show signs of life, is opposed by the sudden intervention of a ridiculous but nightmare 'nursery governor' figure, and films back into effigy again. From outside, above, 'Unearthly music sounded,/ Passing westwards', which is the signal for the poem to move into its last long continuous section – a loathsome vision of emerging rats which overwhelm the watching woman and the shadowy figures while the boy disappears with the governor.

Susan Schreibman has elucidated very nicely the contemporary references in the poem,[30] which turns on the stifling of republican hopes. I would emphasize here the mobility of the speaker's point of view which enables the transitions in the poem to take place. The speaker is outside and then is drawn in; from being a chance observer, he comes to make the most significant observation in the poem. The poem reads the imagined situation like an unfolding drama, cutting from scene to scene, emotional control registered by focal length. If it had not wound up to the glimpse of counter-values 'Passing westwards' at the point it does, the long final paragraph would fall flat. Vision is momentarily discovered, enough to convert nightmare into satire.

All MacGreevy's poems are masterpieces of pacing. The voice pauses, deflects and returns from different angles, recoils and picks up earlier threads to rejoin them in different ways. Paragraphing and patterns of indentation are important guides to the way poems should be read and MacGreevy took considerable care about them. Anthony Cronin has praised his ear in the highest terms: 'MacGreevy wrote, after Eliot himself, the most perfectly modulated free verse in the period in England, Ireland, or America.'[31] Such praise is not excessive, though Spanish and French poets might be more appropriate than the models suggested by Cronin and though the gift was more instinctive than learned. It is not just a matter of lyric rhythm, the sound of individual lines. It is also , as I have suggested with respect to 'Hieronymus Bosch', inherently dramatic. It comes from a conversational sense in which the speaker is aware of the effect he is making and paces his discourse accordingly. When I asked Samuel Beckett, in late years, for a comment on the sources of MacGreevy's style, he replied telegraphically: 'Talk/rhythms (his)'.[32]

This is the lesson to be learned from a study of the manuscripts and the revisions of printed texts. MacGreevy's poetry is spare. There is little ornament; he does not make adjectives or adverbs work hard or engage with elaborate rhyme-schemes and stanzaic forms; he does not strain after linguistic surprise or richness. He worked on poems as a whole, rewriting them as a whole or in whole sections at a time; his substitutions and alterations play fast and loose with sense to achieve a better sound in the service of total effect. Examples of the way he worked are provided by 'Nocturne of the Self-Evident Presence', measured by the difference between the version which was published in *The Irish Statesman* and the version which was collected in 1934; or the different versions of *Breton Oracles*, as published first in *Poetry* (Chicago) and as revised in *The Capuchin Annual*. In the first instance, the changes are nearly all to do with lineation and punctuation and phrasing for the sake of sound. In the latter, the improvement of 'grave soldiers' to 'tired' forces the change in the next line from 'timid young girls' to 'carefree' — the visual picture being sacrificed entirely to sound.

Some shorter poems are rhymed or tightly-patterned — 'Nocturne' being an instance of the first, 'Dechtire' of the second — and they are deft and balanced. The longer ones pursue the course I have described. Sometimes colour supplements or replaces rhyme as a principle of organization. The double movement of 'De Civitate Hominum' has blue and white giving way to black on white and grey, and then white and silver and blue interrupted by orange. The political and religious meanings of colour are exploited in 'The Six Who Were Hanged' and 'Gloria de Carlos V', and witty meanings in 'Did Tosti Raise His Bowler Hat?' and 'Promenade à Trois'.

One comes to recognize rhythmical habits in the way one comes to recognize a voice. I have remarked how the poems tend to begin on a level and then to ascend, to begin with a grey world and discover a golden one – 'I recede too/ Alone', as 'Giorgionismo' puts it (*CPM*, p. 48) – though I have suggested that this recessional movement can be overstressed. I have noted how parenthesis is used in 'Aodh Ruadh Ó Domnhaill' to step outside the body of a poem both to change its direction and to wind up feeling. The sergeant's comment in 'De Civitate Hominum' serves the same purpose and one might compare the uses of this penultimate parenthesis in 'Recessional', 'Exile' and 'Sour Swan'. In longer poems like 'Homage to Marcel Proust', it is usually indented – registering a moment of catch in the breath, a relief from the main action, in which expectation lifts.[33] One could also look at the unpublished plays, and compare the structuring of scenes with the dramatic structure of the poems.

MacGreevy's satirical voice is declarative and has a grammar which is different from his main tendency: 'The Other Dublin' provides good examples. He mimics what he wants to satirize, enveloping it with a voice not his own, and it has an appropriately hollow ring. 'I have heard them,/ *Muriel, do you aspire?*' he quotes in 'Sour Swan' (*CPM*, p. 54). This ventriloquism is a way of using reference to say something on his own behalf which does not always work. One might worry who asked such a question about Muriel (presumably a Protestant, like Vanessa in 'The Other Dublin') and question whether it presumes too much. MacGreevy totally absorbs the literary background of his poems – their French and Spanish models – but the manner of particular allusion can be arbitrary. He drops names and expects them to do more work than they are able to do on their own. 'Golders Green', to take another instance, sets up an opposition between districts in London and Ireland which a reader is forced to explain by sharing assumptions he might otherwise not subscribe to. The epigraph depends likewise on an unwarranted presumption that the reader shares a specially high regard for Schubert's setting of a Heine poem, whereas there is no more reason that s/he should do so than that s/he should share MacGreevy's particular disregard for Bach's *Magnificat*, in 'Anglo-Irish'.[34]

There is more to be said along these lines. The way MacGreevy's titles can at first seem oblique and subsequently, with understanding, can irradiate the meaning of a poem is like his way of using reference. They typically exist in dialogic relation with the verse they precede, not laying down a literal meaning on which subsequent lines build but instead bringing meaning into focus as the lines that follow are understood. The widely-differing titles recorded by Susan Schreibman in this way resemble the processes of verbal revision, or substitution, described above. Titles relate to poems in the way Klee's or Jack Yeats's do to their paintings, but not as in Constable or William Orpen. MacGreevy touched on the habit of mind involved when he said a postcard-reproduction of a Giorgione painting could recreate for him the experience of the original.[35] The habit is reactive rather than active. Several poems are nocturnes, recreating the world in darkened stillness. Several more are titled 'homage', celebrating not the thing itself but responses to the thing.

The mind that tuned the rhythms of these poems was tremblingly aware of occasion, and it is not surprising that, when the 1934 *Poems* did not make a splash, MacGreevy did not persist. He completed perhaps twice as many as appear in Schreibman's collection. Some were copied into letters which are now scattered round the world. Others, for the most part less finished,[36] explore the private pain which poems like 'Exile' and 'St Senan's Well' report obliquely. But, despite the existence of such other material, the 1934 collection was a sensible sifting and contains in itself the entire explanation why MacGreevy did not persist. He must have realized he did not have much more to say unless he became a poet of a different kind; that he had reached a point where he must either make a commitment he was not prepared to make or repeat himself. This reading is confirmed by the poems he published when he began writing again, from 1951 onwards.

Of the four poems — 'Homage to Vercingetorix', 'Moments Musicaux', 'Breton Oracles' and 'On the Death of Joseph Stalin' — the first and last are in MacGreevy's satirical mode, alternately extended and compressed, and the other two merit closer attention. 'Moments Musicaux' (*CPM*, pp. 65-7) has a very patterned structure:[37] in section 1, the first line of the first four stanzas is the same, before they pick up the strength to modify it in the extended fifth; parts 2 and 3 repeat the same first line, but modify it further with increasing emphasis. Advance is through repetition and reversal: 'the heart,/They that were all heart', 'They, tender as potent,/ They, potent as tender'. 'Breton Oracles' is more fluid but again moves forward by way of oppositions: Nîmes against Britanny, deepening heat and darkening menace against cool light and sparkling water. Typically, it ends with the same kind of contradiction with which 'Aodh Ruadh Ó Dohmnaill' ends: a Renaissance cupid in a Catholic graveyard, Roman merged with Celtic, 'Weeping over a lost poetry' (*CPM*, p. 70).

Both poems celebrate the return of 'She of the Second Gift', by whom MacGreevy appears to intend his muse. They proceed in different ways: 'Moments Musicaux' is more formulaic, 'Breton Oracles' more operatic. They differ from earlier poems in their more self-conscious, sectioned structures. Earlier poems of similar length worked-through a single antithesis: these poems repeat a process of dilation, like gathering waves. They state explicitly what they are about – the celebration of the poetic principle – like Denis Devlin in 'Est Prodest' or Brian Coffey in *Third Person*. 'Then, one was there/ And it was you', from 'Breton Oracles', is a phrase which could come, again, from both *The Heavenly Foreigner* and *Advent*.

These late poems are of interest, it seems to me, not as an occasion to exclaim over the interval which punctuated MacGreevy's poetic career. 'Moments Musicaux' and 'Breton Oracles' bear a poignant relation to the earlier poems but they will not gain converts because what they profess to believe is too vague. For a reader of MacGreevy's previous poems, this is indeed their interest: they manifest a continuing belief in the guiding spirit of poetry in ways which state and restate it instead of incorporating and developing it. The same tendency is apparent in his later art criticism, in which a general truth is obscured by the flurry of names which should embody it. MacGreevy's later writing in verse and prose is open to the charge that his sense of art left him little more to say than that it was generally important; he avoided the technical analysis – professed to scorn what some might call the professionalism –

which would have developed the statement. While abstraction is a viable mode for poetry, generality is not, and it seems to me that Devlin and Coffey pursued MacGreevy's theme more rigorously and more convincingly than he was inclined to do himself; in different ways, their poems take further what in MacGreevy is only a beginning. This is why Beckett is right to suggest that in terms of literary history MacGreevy is, in the end, a transitional figure.

The general truth MacGreevy insisted on needed to be heard in the 1920s and 30s. He began his reminiscences by recalling how he left his friend Beckett at the typewriter while he 'had to go out and make sure the world was where I had left it the evening before'.[38] This was not dereliction of duty or the betraying of a gift. His poems feed on an awareness of surroundings which is simultaneously delicate and wide ranging. The need for reassurance which prompted him to turn away from poetry also prompted a career in the public service on behalf of painting. The range of dedications to the poems is witness to his need and genius for friendship. He had, as Richard Aldington put it, 'all the gifts of a writer, except the urge to write,'[39] and his poetry, like his art criticism, is none the worse for being that of an amateur of genius. By amateur I mean in the shaping of his career, not the shaping of what he wrote. If he was not a total poet, he was, in the poems he wrote, a singularly perfect one.

There have been other distinguished curator-writers: in French, Jean Paulhan, André Malraux, Michel Leiris; in English, Frank O'Hara, David Antin, John Hewitt. O'Hara and Antin offer interesting comparisons as poets who also based their writing on talk, and Hewitt as a poet who returned to work elsewhere on the same island. All six I have mentioned were more prolific but I think MacGreevy wrote enough to make his point. To measure his vision against Hewitt's is to make one aware of the breadth of his sympathy and understanding. He wrote against the background of the idea of a nation, not a province, and in relation to other national cultures. In this respect, Malraux offers a more fruitful comparison, grandiose though it might at first seem.

As I tried to explain with reference to Brian O'Nolan, MacGreevy's poems embody different values from modernism as it appears in Irish writing today. Despite New Writers' Press, the regnant version is composed of either verbal high jinks or Nabokovian dandyism, lashings of fun or bevelled reflections on the art of fiction.

MacGreevy's modernism is as remote from this as from the low mimetic realism it defines itself against — indeed, more so, despite initial assumptions. In the present context, where festivals and tee-shirts have helped assimilate Joyce and Beckett to the regnant version with a welcoming laugh, MacGreevy is specially valuable because the terms on which he asks to be read are less easily distorted. The vein he opened has been pursued by very few, and they have not yet found an audience, but their isolation has been productive.[40]

Whatever conclusion can be reached needs to be stated with care. There are many poems in English by minor lyricists which possess the classic ring of 'Aodh Ruadh Ó Dohmnaill' and 'Homage to Marcel Proust' yet I believe MacGreevy is more important than, say, Henry King ('Exequy upon His Wife') or Stevie Smith ('Not Waving But Drowning'). I would not claim on nationalist grounds that he is more than a writer of anthology pieces: why should I, since I am neither Irish nor a nationalist. Nor am I saying in a patronizing way that he wrote well for an Irishman but that his poems have no claims on a larger stage: the acknowledged greatest poet of the time was Irish. Nor anything like that he was a big fish in a small pond. But I am saying that his view of Irish nationhood and art, which is expressed in a small body of poems, casts a long shadow. I hope I have suggested not just why but how, because it is time he ceased being rediscovered and began to be more closely read.

Notes

1   See Robert S. Ryf, 'Letter from Dublin', *The Nation*, 191, 7, 10 September 1960, pp. 138-9; and J.C.C. Mays, 'Beckett and the Irish', *Hibernia, 33*, 21, 7 November 1969, p. 14.
2   Maurice Harmon, *Modern Irish Literature 1800-1967: A Reader's Guide*, Dolmen Press, Dublin, 1967, p. 41.
3   *A Bash in the Tunnel: James Joyce by the Irish,* ed. John Ryan, Clifton Books, Brighton, 1970.
4   Seán O'Faoláin in comments first published in 1929 and 1928, quoted in *James Joyce: The Critical Heritage*, ed. Robert H. Deming, Routledge and Kegan Paul, London, 1970, vol. II, pp. 392 and 397. Frank O'Connor, 'James Joyce: A Post-Mortem', *The Bell*, 5, 5, February 1943, p. 374.
5   A point made famously by Jorge Luis Borges, 'The Argentine Writer and Tradition', *Labyrinths. Selected Stories and Other Writings*, eds. Donald A. Yates and James E. Irby, New Directions, New York, enlarged edition, 1964, pp.177-85 (180-1 specifically).

6   Daniel Corkery, *Synge and Anglo-Irish Literature,* Cork University Press, Cork, 1966, p. 4; also Arland Ussher, 'The Contemporary Thought of Ireland', *The Dublin Magazine,* 22, 3, July– September 1947, pp. 24–30 (26 specifically); Beatrice Lady Glenavy, *'Today we will only Gossip',* Constable, London, 1964, p. 152.

7   'In Tribute to Thomas Mac Greevy, Poet and Connoisseur of the Arts', *The Capuchin Annual,* 35, 1968, pp. 277-97.

8   A. Rivaollan, *Littérature irlandaise contemporaine,* Hachette, Paris, 1939, pp. 123-5; Babette Deutsch, 'A Learned Craftsman of Verse', *New York Times Herald Tribune,* 28 July 1946, p. 3; Peter Brazeau, 'The Irish Connection: Wallace Stevens and Thomas McGreevy', *The Southern Review,* 17, 1981, pp. 533-41.

9   Beckett's comments are now most easily to hand in *Disjecta,* pp. 68-9 and 74.

10   Michael Smith, 'Irish Poetry Since Yeats: Notes Towards a Corrected History', *Denver Quarterly,* 5, 4, Winter 1971, pp. 1-26; Augustus Young, 'Letters from an Irish Poet', *The Niagara Magazine,* 3, Summer 1975, pp. 7-19; Hank Schau, John Jordan, Eamonn Wall, James Liddy, Billy Brooks, Liam O'Connor, *The American Friends of Thomas MacGreevy,* privately published, New Orleans, 1975.

11   For instance, Hugh J. Dawson, 'Thomas MacGreevy and Joyce', *James Joyce Quarterly,* 25, 3, Spring 1988, pp. 305-21.

12   MacGreevy's disapproval of the Imagistes (as well as of Eliot's later poetry) was confirmed by his publisher at Heinemann and friend (to whom 'De Civitate Hominum' is dedicated), A.S. Frere (letter to me dated 17 June 1974).

13   I should explain. The references which situate the poem in its genre combine that elegy of all exiles, Baudelaire's 'Le Cygne', with Mallarmé's poem about the swan-artist, 'Le vierge, le vivace et le bel aujourd'hui'. The exile theme is particularized by echoes of swans in Yeats and of Irish Wild Geese. Also, as Baudelaire's poem is dedicated to Victor Hugo, so one must understand MacGreevy to be addressing his fellow artist, Beckett, who wrote a monograph about Proust's Swann (an earlier title was 'Sweet Swann of Bayswater' – TCD MS 789 (1) f. 118) At this point, the texture of reference begins to bear on MacGreevy's argument. His claim that 'the first virtue' does not necessarily contradict 'the greatest' – viz. to faith and charity (1 Corinthians 13:13), belief and pity – connects with another of his poems, 'Fragments'. This turns on the line in *Inferno* XX 28, 'qui vive la pietà quando è ben morta', on which Beckett's 'Dante and the Lobster' also turns. MacGreevy's position here is that Beckett should 'moderate' his sense of contradiction and 'Go to God'.

     In short, the concluding poem in MacGreevy's 1934 collection is a counter-statement of his position against his most articulate critic. His monograph on T.S. Eliot had celebrated the supercession of Puritanism by humility, and he no doubt hoped Beckett would follow the same course. Beckett's early poems pursue a complicated dialogue with MacGreevy's which terminates with the portrait of MacGreevy as Mr Endon in *Murphy*. Joyce alludes to the dialogue in his vaudeville conjunction of Slippery Sam and Tomtinker Tim ('the seers are the seers of Samael but the heers are the heers of Timoth') in *Finnegans Wake*, Faber, London, 1939, pp. 341-2.

14   I have not forgotten he was a signatory to Eugene Jolas's manifesto on verticalism in *transition*, 21, March 1932, pp. 148-9, but so also was Beckett. As a matter of fact, the manifesto suits Beckett's view of MacGreevy's verse very well.

15   See the responses to his Eliot book by Edward Titus, 'Editorially: Criticism à l'Irlandaise', *This Quarter*, 3, 4, April-May-June 1931, pp. 569-84; and Richard Thomas, 'Island Without Serpents', *New Review*, 1, 3, August-September-October 1931, pp. 119-21. The London reviews (e.g. *The Times Literary Supplement*, 19 March 1931, p. 226; *Spectator*, 14 March 1931, p. 427) were by comparison kind.

16   These points of difference are further elaborated in my 'Brian O'Nolan and Joyce on Art and on Life', *James Joyce Quarterly*, 11, 3, Spring 1974, 238-56.

17   Details of the Ransom / Tate debate are supplied by John M. Bradbury, *The Fugitives: A Critical Account*, University of North Carolina Press, Chapel Hill, 1958, pp. 53 ff.; also Louise Cowan, *The Fugitive Group: A Literary History*, Louisiana State University Press, Baton Rouge, 1959, pp. 63-94; of the earlier debate by Russell Noyes, *Wordsworth and Jeffrey in Controversy*, Indiana University Publications Series no. 5, Bloomington, 1941.

18   Ernie O'Malley, *On Another Man's Wound*, Rich and Cowan London/The Sign of the Three Candles, Dublin, 1936, pp. 215-16.

19   For example, 'The Nationalist Trend', *TLS*, 4309, 1 November 1985, pp. 1230-31.

20   See the letter to M.E. Barber quoted by Schreibman, *CPM*, pp. 134-5. The version of the poem given by Seán O'Faoláin 'Irish Poetry Since the War', *The London Mercury*, 31, April 1935, pp. 545-52 (550-1 specifically), can be added to Schreibman's list of reprintings.

21   Compare the poem by Moireen Fox, 'Aodh Ruadh in Prison', *New Ireland*, 6, 10, 13 July 1918, p. 155. Pádraig de Brún and Stephen MacKenna (to whom MacGreevy subsequently dedicated his 'Aodh Ruadh') were writing for the magazine at the time. I owe the information on Irish millenarianism to a conversation with Dr Daithí Ó hÓgáin and Professor Augustine Martin, both of University College, Dublin, in January 1986. Compare my suggestion about de Valera with Schreibman's interpretation of a line in 'Crón Tráth na nDéithe' (*CPM*, p. 111).

22   The poem was not accompanied by a note when it first appeared in *The Irish Statesman*, 6, 8, 1 May 1926, pp. 204-5. The note combines information contributed in subsequent issues – by Lennox Robinson, 8 May, p. 234; C.P. Curran, 15 May, p. 270; and Ignatius McHugh, 5 June, p. 352. MacGreevy went on elaborating on the note in his own copy of the Heinemann 1934 *Poems* (now in private hands).

23 See the letter quoted by Schreibman, *CPM*, p. 107. The phrase 'heroic tragedy' comes from MacGreevy's 'Three Historical Paintings by Jack B. Yeats', *The Capuchin Annual*, 13, 1942, pp. 238-51 (240 specifically).
24 MacGreevy read *Ulysses* and *Work in Progress/Finnegans Wake* as Inferno and Purgatorio in his *Exagmination* essay, and the idea that Joyce should write a Paradiso grew from there. Though Richard Ellmann entertained a hope that the idea received some encouragement from Joyce, I found no proof of this among MacGreevy's copious published and unpublished references. The *Reactions* project is discussed in a correspondence with David Nolan of Anvil Books, Tralee, dating from February-March 1966, and compare TCD MSS 7994, 7995. The title derives from a comment by W.B. Yeats: 'MacGreevy, you are a reactionary.'
25 For Amiel, see *Journal* for 18 September 1862; and also the discussion by Georges Poulet, *The Metamorphoses of the Circle*, trans. Carley Dawson and Elliott Coleman, with the author, Johns Hopkins Press, Baltimore, 1966, pp. 203-48. For Titchener, see Edwin G. Boring, *A History of Experimental Psychology*, Appleton-Century-Crofts, New York, second edition 1957, p. 417 specifically. The book is dedicated to Titchener, and contains a large section on his 'new' psychology.
26 Compare Amiel, *Journal* for 7 April 1869; discussed by Poulet, p. 224.
27 W.B. Yeats had written of his Ballylee tower, 'I have set/A powerful emblem up' and 'I declare this tower is my symbol' ('Blood and the Moon', *The Poems: A New Edition*, ed. Richard J. Finneran, London, Macmillan, 1984, p. 237). It figures so extensively in poems he wrote in the 1920s that it was surely in MacGreevy's mind when he addressed his thoughts on Norman pride to W.B.'s brother.
28 Introductory remarks on a gramophone record made by the St Stephen's Green Studio in 1956 for the Harvard University Poetry Library (in private hands). Oddly, there was no trace of the record having reached the Harvard collection when I searched for it in 1978.
29 Letter to Babette Deutsch, from 49 Morehampton Road, 13 February 1960 (Olin Library, Washington University, St Louis).
30 I can only think of adding to her notes that Joyce was busy adding St Laurence O'Toole into *Work in Progress* at the time of his friendship with MacGreevy. O'Toole appears in a way which suggests Joyce influenced the choice of MacGreevy's earlier title, 'Treason of Saint Laurence O'Toole'.
31 Anthony Cronin, 'Thomas MacGreevy: Modernism not Triumphant', *Heritage Now. Irish Literature in the English Language*, Brandon Books, Dingle, 1982, p. 157. Cronin is off the mark with Pound, I think. The only thing MacGreevy liked was *How to Read*, mainly to argue with it: see his review in *New Review*, 2, 5, April 1932, pp. 45-8. The dust-jacket of the Heinemann poems (written by Aldington) was more astute in naming 'the younger Spanish poets' as MacGreevy's models, as I have tried to show.

Cronin's essay is a much-expanded version of his review 'Something for the Locals', *Hibernia*, 36, 20, 5 November 1971, p. 14.

32 Beckett's reply is postmarked Paris, 27 October 1975.

33 MacGreevy's usage may be compared with the examples collected by John Lennard's splendid *But I Digress: The Exploitation of Parentheses in English Printed Verse,* Clarendon Press, Oxford, 1991. Compare also Robert Grant Williams, 'Reading the Parenthesis', *Sub/Stance,* 22, 1, 1993, 53-66. The plays (*One Fair Daughter,* with Meredith Clarke; *Old Time New Time,* with Geraldine Cummins; etc – now TCD MSS 8016-33) for the most part postdate his return to Dublin. He had, before, produced, acted in and translated plays for the Dublin Drama League.

34 Some of these assumptions reflect the shared prejudices of a particular time and circle. Compare Padraig Colum's preface to *Journal and Letters of Stephen MacKenna,* ed. E.R. Dodds, Constable, London, 1936, pp. xv-xvi on the Catholic nationalist view of Goethe; also Thomas Kettle, *The Day's Burden: Studies Literary and Political and Miscellaneous Essays,* Maunsel and Co, Dublin, 1918, p. xii.

35 Thomas MacGreevy, *Amateur Humanist: A Gossiping Autobiography and Highbrow Chronicle,* p. 254 (in private hands). The 497-page typescript, dated January 1965-February 1967, covers only four of the projected nine parts.

36 The largest number is included in TCD MSS 7989 (2) and 10381 (186-203). There are others elsewhere (e.g. TCD MS 8080) and in other collections.

37 The title derives from Schubert and his imitators, which is relevant to its form – a point which Schreibman for once misses.

38 MacGreevy, *Amateur Humanist,* p. 2. The whole opening paragraph is of interest and given in *CPM.*

39 Richard Aldington, *Life for Life's Sake: A Book of Reminiscences,* Viking Press, New York, 1941, p. 352. The concluding sentence in my paragraph alludes to two reviews of the New Writers' Press edition: Michael Hartnett, 'Not a Total Poet', *The Irish Times,* 36021, 20 November 1971, p. 10; and Brian Coffey, 'Thomas MacGreevy: A Singularly Perfect Poet', *Hibernia,* 37, 3, 4 February 1972, p. 10. The Coffey piece was reprinted from *The Capuchin Annual* (see above note 7) perhaps to bolster Cronin's first response which was less enthusiastic than his revised one (see above note 31).

40 Besides Devlin and Coffey, of course, I refer to the writers I describe in my 'Flourishing and Foul: Six Poets and the Irish Building Industry', *The Irish Review,* 8, Spring 1990, pp. 6-11 – to which I would now add the name of Catherine Walsh.

5

The Unpublished Poems of Thomas MacGreevy: An Exploration

Susan Schreibman

> Imagination is primarily the faculty of
> relating the ephemeral to the unchanging
>
> Thomas MacGreevy

Thomas MacGreevy wrote poetry steadily over a relatively short period of time, from 1924–1934. At the tail end of this period *Poems*, MacGreevy's only collection of poetry published during his lifetime, was brought out by Heinemann. About ten years before this period, during the autumn of 1915, coming up to the second winter of the First World War, he wrote his first poem. It was about the 'beauty of the world and the tragedy of war', and although he had 'some appreciation' of the one, he (as yet) had no 'first-hand knowledge of the other'. Years later, when coming across the poem in his family home in Tarbert, County Kerry after his mother died in 1936, he discounted it as intellectually 'negligible'. His first inclination was to throw it away – but as his mother treasured it, he left it.[1] If that poem exists somewhere in MacGreevy's substantial collection of papers, it has not been identified.

Except for several references in MacGreevy's memoirs to poems written during the war, the earliest poem that can be dated with accuracy is six lines written during the Hilary Term 1919 while MacGreevy was enrolled as a student at Trinity College, Dublin. It was written in his logic notebook and, not surprisingly, began by positing the premise that God is a 'differential equation'. It was never published. It is one of about forty poems by and large catalogued under TCD MSS 7989/2 and 10381/183–203 which contain most of the typescript and manuscript drafts of MacGreevy's unpublished poems.[2] There are also many manuscript drafts of unpublished poems on the backs of letters, on envelopes and in notebooks scattered throughout MacGreevy's papers.

When Anthony Cronin wrote of MacGreevy in his 1982 essay 'Modernism not Triumphant' that 'assuming he began to write poetry in his early twenties what is remarkable is that he made no false starts'[3] he was right – as far as he could have known. Even if Anthony Cronin had gone to Trinity College, Dublin to examine MacGreevy's papers (the bulk of which had been recently deposited by MacGreevy's executors)[4] he would probably only have had access – due to the massive job of cataloguing the collection – to a portion of the unpublished poems. Over ten years after Mr Cronin's book was published, and after many years leafing through notebooks, collections of letters and drafts of poems, I can confidently say that MacGreevy made 'false starts'. And he made a lot of them. What is extraordinary about MacGreevy is that unlike many a poet who rushes to get every scrap into print, he chose not to publish them.

When editing MacGreevy's collected poems for publication in the late 1980s, I also chose not to publish them, concentrating instead on his published work. This was decided because it was impossible to ascertain from MacGreevy's papers (and because nobody had thought to ask him in his lifetime) which of his unpublished poems he would have liked to see in print. In addition, before including his unpublished work in book form, there loomed the very real aesthetic quandary of how or whether to 'finish' many of MacGreevy's poems for him. The vast majority of his unpublished poems were left in varying stages of completion; and perhaps the only way to represent MacGreevy's unpublished poetry fairly would be in a facsimile edition. Yet, now that there is more interest in MacGreevy's poetry than there was five years ago, an exploration of some of his unpublished work, along with the publication of some of these poems in a diplomatic edition, is not only appropriate, but timely.[5]

At some level, the selection of poems included in this essay is somewhat arbitrary and should not be taken as representative of

MacGreevy's unpublished *oeuvre*. In some cases, what seemed to be his most finished work (i.e. typescript with little or no emendations), and/or poems which seemed similar in spirit to the published work were chosen. In other cases poems which might not be considered amongst MacGreevy's best but, nevertheless, demonstrate a particular point were selected. Yet, even this small sampling of unpublished poems re-contextualizes MacGreevy's published work, making it clear that it is impossible to appreciate fully what MacGreevy chose to include in *Poems* without some understanding of what he chose to exclude. And perhaps by understanding what he chose to exclude, it is possible to inch that much closer in understanding the enigma of why he published so little in his middle years, and then virtually stopped writing poetry in his later years.

What strikes the reader of MacGreevy's unpublished poetry is that there are many poems which, while maintaining his poetic voice, differ substantially from the published work. One of the major differences is that the unpublished poems are what one might term unmediated: they do not rely on a narrator relating events from a self-conscious socio-historical perspective. Yet, it is this very perspective which provides *Poems* with its remarkably cohesive narrative voice: MacGreevy, the Everyman, whose purpose is to witness (not necessarily to comment)[6] and to record. Thus, the effect is of a narrator who moves freely through time and space to relate events from a perspective not unlike that in Titian's *La Gloria*. This disembodied narrative positioning concurrently creates the illusion of an ' "aesthetic" distance'[7] as Stan Smith implied in his 1978 article in *The Lace Curtain*, 'From A Great Distance', which borrows a line from Wallace Stevens's tribute to MacGreevy, 'Our Stars Come from Ireland'. The quotation comes from Stevens's last stanza:

> The stars are washing up from Ireland
> And through and over the puddles of Swatara
> And Schuylkill. The sound of him
> Comes from a great distance and is heard.[8]

The focus of Smith's article, implicit in the last line of Stevens's poem, is not only that MacGreevy's poems travelled a great distance to reach Stevens (they were sent 'by registered ordinary post'[9] from Dublin to Connecticut) but that the aesthetic distance MacGreevy maintained as a poet was not lost on Stevens. The notion that

MacGreevy maintained such a distance in his poetry, however, rein-
forces the reader's diversion away from the immediate emotional
response to so many of the incidents recorded in Poems:

> Tired of sorrow,
> My sorrow, their sorrow, all sorrow,
> I go from the hanged,
> From the women,
> I go from the hanging;
>
> ('The Six Who Were Hanged', *CPM*, p. 9)

> In the absurdity of ugliness
> Some found quick doom
> And some of us
> Saw.
>
> ('Crón Tráth na nDéithe', *CPM*, p. 16)

> And I find I am thinking:
> Supposing I am drowned now,
> This tired, tiresome body,
> Before flesh creases further,
> Might, recovered, go fair,
> To be laid in Saint Lachtin's
>
> ('Recessional', *CPM*, p. 41)

In these moments of heightened emotion, the self-realization is often
lost within a poem which draws the reader's attention instead to
the perceived as it is embodied in the historical, the literary, the
political, or simply the obscure. The result is that the distance bet-
ween narrator and narrative seems to widen, foregrounding the
modernist doctrine of impersonality and overshadowing the intimate
self-disclosure at the nucleus of the poem. 'Recessional' is a good
example of this. Here MacGreevy locates his meditation on suicide
in the breathtakingly beautiful Swiss Alps where it is easy to be
distracted from the event's emotional import by the first six lines:

> In the bright broad Swiss glare I stand listening
> To the outrageous roars
> Of the Engelbergeraa
> As it swirls down the gorge
> And I think I am thinking
> Of Roderick Hudson.

A reader unskilled at reading Thomas MacGreevy's poetry would immediately look for meaning through the perceived. Armed, however, with the knowledge that Engelbergeraa is a waterfall located about 30 km from Lucerne, and that Roderick Hudson is the protagonist in a novel of the same name by Henry James, the reader has been diverted by MacGreevy from what has triggered the impulse to write: 'Poetry is not a turning loose of emotion, but an escape from emotion; it is not the expression of personality, but an escape from personality'. MacGreevy, true to the dicta set out by T.S. Eliot in his 1919 essay 'Tradition and the Individual Talent', attempted to 'escape from personality'[10] through poetic mediation. Yet, in many of Mac-Greevy's unpublished, expurgated poems, the mediation that he so artfully maintains in the published work breaks down and seems perilously close to the confessional, albeit in a modernist sort of way. His unpublished 'Nel Mezzo' is a good example of this.

The poem was written in March or April 1930, during his father's last illness, or perhaps soon after his father's death on 19 April. His father's death touched a raw nerve with MacGreevy who, at the age of thirty-seven, had not published a book, had no home of his own, nor had anything in the traditional sense resembling a career. That his father died before MacGreevy was able to demonstrate at least some outward signs of success, at least by Tarbert standards, in either his personal or professional life, must have weighed heavily on the younger man's mind. Thus, it is not surprising that he scribbled on the back of a letter sent to him by Stephen MacKenna, the Irish journalist and translator of Plotinus, (who was himself not in the best of health and would die four years later) notes for a poem beginning with the line, 'Of course you look sorry'. Raw and intensely personal, the poem, eventually entitled 'Nel Mezzo', was Mac-Greevy's statement about having 'journeyed half our life's way',[11] about coming home, and about faith:

Nel Mezzo

Mein Auge und Herz

~~I know~~   But I'm sure you feel sorry
~~You look sorry all right~~ It's all right.

Only
~~But~~ that was the last spark of kindling
Amongst the cold ashes

And the dreary cinders.
It has gone out.
You had no breath for it.

But perhaps you were right,
Knowing,
As I know,
That neither that chimney
Nor any in the house
Drew well
This half-a-man's lifetime.

Why should you be sorry?
Why should I be angry?
Blessed breath that may never inform me,
Blessed eyes whose beatitude I may not see with,
You were probably right.

(God, Father, Creator,
Let this house of ~~my~~ life
                   is
That, if fair, ~~has been~~ no house of joy,
Crumble quickly).

Now,
When those cold ashes
        — This last poor ash too —
And the dreary cinders
Are covered at last
With dirt
And wet soot,
When the cold grate has rusted,
Is bent,
Broken in pieces,
By infalling masonry
And stones,
When damp mould is on all,
The departing inhabitant,
Not turning,
May say,

End,
End to death,
To half a life's death,
A death that came after

> *An uncomprehended youth*
> *And so, unperversely,*
> *Thanks be . . .*
> *For release.* [12]

Here there is little aesthetic distance: nothing to distract our attention away from the very intimate details of the poem – no hangings, no airmen being shot down, no Alps, no literature, no burials: just one man meditating about having 'journeyed half our life's way' and the concomitant struggles of that journey. And although there are several versions of 'Nel Mezzo' amongst MacGreevy's papers, the changes from the first draft to the nearly finished poem above, are, in fact, slight. Two final holograph changes in stanza 5 do, however, alter meaning, and continue to alter meaning as we can never be certain which version MacGreevy might have chosen had he published the poem. The revising out of 'my' life in line 2 seems to be typical of MacGreevy's revision towards impersonality; yet, the change to the much stronger 'is' in line 3 instead of the earlier 'has been' focuses the reader's attention in the opposite direction. The only part of the poem that did see its way into print was the line 'Blessed eyes whose beatitude I may not see with' which, in 'Ten Thousand Leaping Swords' was contextualized within the framework of a love poem (*CPM*, p. 29).

It seems, however, that on two occasions the 'blessed breath' did inform MacGreevy. He attempted to record these experiences, but like 'Nel Mezzo', this text was never published. Indeed, it never made it out of manuscript form. Like several early poems by T.S. Eliot (particularly one entitled 'Silence' in which the street Eliot was walking upon in Boston suddenly shrank and divided, and all his 'everyday preoccupations, his past, all the claims of the future fell away and he was enfolded in a great silence'), [13] this untitled draft was aborted by MacGreevy before an editor (or a reader in the 1920s, equivalent to the poetry workshop) could reject it. It was written and reworked on the back of a draft of 'Nel Mezzo', and is about an experience which Eliot later in life termed 'communion with the Divine' or 'temporary crystallization of the mind'. [14] The joys which in 'Nel Mezzo' were absent are converted here into the joys of communion:

A translation of the altar at benediction time
A transport to an opening ~~in the~~
      pale starred
In a ~~[?] night~~ sky

The only joys I've had have been aesthetic
    knowledge   is
My ~~vision~~ of the City of God ~~was~~ limited
                      views
To two aesthetic–[?] seeming ~~openings in the sky~~
               though [?] first time shut
If the body fell away my eyes remained
The first ~~time It~~ was lemon yellow
The second silver white
And there was no substantial element
So why should I have shame ~~before the Catholics~~
Of being aesthetic
Before those who are but the body of the Church
Not even the body
Merely the body's excrement[15]

In her critical biography of Eliot's early life, Lyndall Gordon ventures the opinion that for Eliot, 'the memory of bliss was to remain a kind of torment, a mocking reminder through the years that followed that there was an area of experience just beyond his grasp, which contemporary images of life could not compass.'[16] These experiences for MacGreevy were of similar import. It is no coincidence that 'A translation of the altar' was penned on the back of 'Nel Mezzo'. These two poems work in counterpoint: 'Nel Mezzo', a dialogue between MacGreevy and his dying father, recounts the externality and divide between MacGreevy's and his father's lives; 'A translation of the altar' recalls the internality and divide between MacGreevy and his God. The ambiguous 'God, Father, Creator' of stanza 5 of 'Nel Mezzo' is a plea to both the heavenly and earthly fathers:

       (God, Father, Creator,
       Let this house of life
       That, if fair, is no house of joy,
       Crumble quickly).

Yet in these two poems, neither God nor Father answers, unless the closing lines of 'Nel Mezzo' constitute a reply:

And so, unperversely,
Thanks be . . .
For release.

'A translation of the altar', on the other hand, closes, not by narrowing the divide, but by creating a new one: one between MacGreevy and society. The poem abruptly shifts at line 11 from a recollection of one of those rare moments in which 'our first world'[17] is glimpsed, to an angry and somewhat pugnacious defence of the experience. Here, private significance is transmuted into a defensive dismissal of the experience itself. Without the cockiness of Joyce or the desperation of Beckett, MacGreevy began a retreat into silence. Perhaps his ultimate act of writing was his not writing. The poem was left abandoned in manuscript form, too risky, too personal, too unmediated to finish, still less publish. If MacGreevy's poetry is indeed, as Beckett described it, prayer, 'an act of recognition' (*Disjecta*, p. 68), it is the prayer of the 'anti-self' – the 'other self, of the studious "imitator", one who might disclose to him what he sought'.[18]

Thus, the anti-self is the narrating voice in many of MacGreevy's published poems; the self having retreated into a position of safety, though not a position safe enough to have stopped writing altogether. MacGreevy's poems are written from the point of view of the Observation Officer in his 'O Pip' (Observation Post) positioned at the verge of No Man's Land: ahead lies confession, behind lies silence. The emotion necessary to link reader to poem edited out by the poet as being outside the Observation Officer's range – a 'turning loose of emotion'. The opposite of a turning loose of emotions is like sleeping with one's boots on, and we are left with the impossibility of expression suggested by very Beckettian ellipses. Some of these ellipses appear in published poems, such as 'Seventh Gift of the Holy Ghost':

The end of love,
Love's ultimate good,
Is the end of love . . . and
Light

We never find the answer to what comes after 'the end of love'. It could possibly be the end of light, if the sentence is read syntactically as such. Yet, it is just as valid to read 'Light' as belonging to the sentence that follows, in which the narrator musing upon the end of love, also muses on the end of

> Light
> On a towering wall
> Yellow villages
> In a vast, high, light-beaten plain

in which the *you* and the *I* of the poem imagine

> The pity we had to learn
> And the terror –
> The ultimate terror.   (*CPM*, p. 33)

Here, the brilliance of the vision coalesces with the 'pity we had to learn', leading, not to light, but to the 'ultimate terror'. And it is here, at the juxtaposition of light and dark, at the ellipse, that MacGreevy comes closest to what he considers the true currency of poetic discourse: 'knowledge of life, personality and humility' (*Eliot*, p. 16).

Sometimes 'knowledge of life' is precluded in a world of fragmentation and discontinuity making the right choice impossible. The sense of the absurdity of the absolutes of right and wrong might have had its beginnings in MacGreevy's war experience: in the salient '[m]ost moving objects were under observation.'[19] In No Man's Land, whether one goes left or right, towards the enemy or away, one is equally in danger of being hit by a five-nine. What seems like a contradiction, is not; it is simply an ellipse, the last bit of information necessary for understanding unstated, like the tacit agreements made between soldiers at war, or the closing lines of 'Sour Swan': 'Song is dead. Yes. Song/Is dead. Long live song!' (*CPM*, p. 55). Sometimes, on the other hand, 'knowledge of life', implying some degree of rationality, is sought in a communal past, such as in MacGreevy's unpublished poem, 'Diarmuid of the Beautiful Hands'.

Contemporary versions of Diarmuid and Grania's story were popular long after the Celtic Renaissance had ended. In 1917 Austin Clarke's epic poem *The Vengeance of Fionn* was published, and in 1928 Micheál MacLiammóir staged his own play, *Grania*, in Galway. The idea of using Irish mythology as symbolic of a disaffected self, however, did not seem to be a particularly tempting poetic road for MacGreevy to travel down, particularly after 1927, the year which marked the beginning of his friendship and collaboration with James Joyce. Rather than locating his source of national identity in Irish mythology, MacGreevy gravitated towards the literary and the political. Thus it is no surprise to find that 'Diarmuid of the Beautiful Hands' is the sole experiment (at least amongst MacGreevy's remaining papers) in a manner derivative of Yeats's style. Yet, this poem could also be seen as an attempt, like Austin Clarke's poems of the mid-1920s, to reincorporate Irish mythology into a more self-conscious poetic style which acknowledged rather than ignored the sense of discontinuity between an irredeemable past and an uncertain future.[20]

In MacGreevy's version of the myth, Diarmuid is on the run from Fionn Mac Cumhaill, the leader of the Fianna, after having eloped with Grania during her betrothal feast to Fionn. At first, Diarmuid was reluctant to elope with her out of loyalty to Fionn, but when she threatened him with *geis* – a magical injunction or spell, the infringement of which could lead to death – he acquiesced to her demand. During the subsequent pursuit, Diarmuid is torn between two conflicting loves, that of Grania and that of Fionn:

> the proffered
> If I took ~~Grania's~~ body
> I should have outward peace
> But inward torment
>
> Had I Finn's love again
> I should have inner peace
> But suffer torture
> At Grania's instance
>
> here I am   lost
> Alas ~~that I may not have~~ Finn's love
>
> Alas for resentful
> ~~That I may not take~~ Grania's
>
> ~~And~~   am
> ~~That~~ I ~~must be always~~ chaste

            e
I who know love's delight
~~And alas~~   And
That I must be wandering ~~always~~
By tree and field and river
By blue-roofed white
~~By slate-blue white~~-walled towns
~~And on again~~
By ~~level~~ plains and lifted hills

I who despised Rousseau
And distrust the art of Orpen[21]

The legend, long used as a story representative of male bonding, reflects a theme prevalent in MacGreevy's unpublished creative writing: the choice between artistic fulfilment and matrimonial vows. In few, if any, of MacGreevy's unpublished writings, could the two cohabit successfully. The last three lines of the poem represent another uneasy cohabitation: the self-consciousness of these lines make a mockery of the inheritance of the Celtic Renaissance. For MacGreevy, the very act of retrieval only reinforced the futility of self-discovery within a shared past. Instead, the self-consciousness of the narrative voice transcends the idea that self-identification can be found either in reality or in a pre-Christian mythology. The last two lines of the poem reflect the auto-destructive dimension of Dadaism or surrealism – on second reading the poem, no longer bound by time and space, becomes decontextualized, and meaning (if meaning is to be sought) must be gleaned within a self-referential context. It should also be borne in mind that MacGreevy's first impulse to write (and I would venture to add many subsequent ones) was as a direct result of the First World War: that many of his poems mirrored the essential irrationality of war, and that no matter how heartfelt any attempts to recapture that idyllic past which preceded the war (and which may have only existed outside time as in a poem such as 'Homage to Marcel Proust') must, by necessity, end in failure.

   Contrary to a poem like 'Diarmuid of the Beautiful Hands' are poems like 'Elections' and 'Homage to Ruteboeuf' which are patently bound by both time and space. They take the political as their inspiration. Yet, unlike MacGreevy's published poetry, these poems bespeak little outside a narrow political context. They were the medium, largely unsuccessful, through which MacGreevy worked out frustrations with Irish politics that never made the transition into a finished product: they just seem too personal or too private; too petty perhaps, or too angry. MacGreevy and politics were uneasy bedfellows, and by the late 1920s, political poetry was the last thing he wanted to write. Yet, he was drawn to it over and over like a moth to light. In an undated manuscript letter to W.B. Yeats,[22] written from Paris, most likely late in 1927 or early 1928 (somewhere around the time another version of 'Diarmuid of the Beautiful Hands' was being composed), MacGreevy tried to come to terms with the intertextuality of Irish politics and poetry, and his place within the Irish literary canon:

> I think ~~the fact that~~ my indignant poems ~~demons which seem to me to have life~~ show demonstrate in their bareness a certain belief that I in common with other writers of ~~my~~ generation have come to the belief that indignation in general politics in general and ~~political~~ indignat~~ion~~ant politics in particular ~~is~~ are unsuitable material for poetry. . . . in spite of the marvellous improvement in ~~treatment~~ technique brought about by you in modern Irish poetry the [worldly?] preoccupations of Davis ~~had~~ are still dominat~~ed~~ing all of us who were interested in literature and that I was anxious to get away from what unfortunately had dominated me ~~as well as everyone else~~ to something that was more fundamental material for poetry. You had pointed out the way ~~in much~~ in many a line and passage ~~Mr Joyce had gone further along it~~ but we in Ireland were all still too aware of the world.~~the world was too much with us.~~ Poetry is not yet for us Irishmen. Poetry, ~~Poetry independent~~ one of the gifts of God to man as important as the desire for political liberty and entirely independent of it, a preoccupation for free and civilised people. We are ~~not~~ possibly freer under your Free State. Under English law we lost much of our civilisation but I think the time has come for us who care about [?poetry] to try and ~~drop~~ shed ~~not Ireland~~ the last vestiges of ~~all~~ political preoccupations from our writing. ~~We may even drop Ireland.~~ It is only when we have done so that we shall be truly Irish at last.[23]

Here, MacGreevy prefigures much Irish writing that would emerge after the Second World War, as well as the current post-colonial debate: over sixty years later David Lloyd, in the introduction to his *Anomalous States: Irish Writing and the Post-Colonial Moment*, reposits MacGreevy's statement:

> The problem is not the questioning of identity, a process which can . . . be imbued with quite radical consequences, but rather the way in which the theme of identity saturates the discursive field drowning out other social and cultural possibilities.[24]

It is this 'drowning out' process that MacGreevy realized was the central theme of his generation. It was only when Ireland, in the narrowest of political constructs, whether the construction of national identity be through mythology, Romanesque Catholicism or as Beckett only half tongue-in-cheek put it, 'spook', was purged from the poetic imagination, that Irish writers could turn to what MacGreevy felt was the true nature of poetic discourse: 'relating the ephemeral to the unchanging' (*Yeats*, p. 28).

In his essay 'Imagination as Value', Wallace Stevens argued for something similar:

> When we speak of the life of the imagination, we do not mean man's life as it is affected by his imagination but the life of the faculty itself. . . . The imagination that is satisfied by politics, whatever the nature of the politics, has not the same value as the imagination that seeks to satisfy, say the universal mind . . .[25]

MacGreevy's belief that 'indignant politics . . . are unsuitable material for poetry' is similar to Stevens's statement that the 'imagination that is satisfied by politics . . . has not the same value as the imagination that seeks to satisfy, say the universal mind'. In other words, poetry that does not bear witness to 'more fundamental material', what Stevens calls 'the universal mind', what Beckett calls the poet's 'unfailing salute to his significant' (*Disjecta*, p. 68), what MacGreevy calls 'relating the ephemeral to the unchanging', is not worth writing. It is certainly not worth publishing.

Yet, MacGreevy was the first to realize that the world was too much with him to retreat from it. As a survivor of the First World War, he never forgot that it was only by chance he was not in a British graveyard somewhere in Flanders. 'If you have been placed suddenly on the other side of the grave and left there for months and years, you do not forget it' (*Aldington*, p. 6). Like that moth that flies into the light until his wings get so singed he can no longer fly, MacGreevy gravitated towards 'indignant politics'. In several of his unpublished poems, such as this fragment from 'Elections', he was not able to relate post-civil war politics to anything outside his immediate feelings of frustration:

> Up the Republic!
> Up the Free State!
>   ~~Trade Unionists~~
> Up ~~the Clergy! Socialists~~ Farmers
> No hate
> For those patriots either
> Who make of the race-course, the card-room, the slum pub
> Their hub . . .[26]

MacGreevy felt betrayed by the Treaty, the Civil War, and its aftermath, and indignation is the predominating expression in the opening lines of 'Homage to Ruteboeuf':

> I ought to write a whereas
> To the perjured civil warriors
> Who set up to be God's just men
> Loving their enemies
> With the loves of cravens
> And letting down their friends
> In the very best tradition
> Of the self-righteous puritans they revere . . .[27]

MacGreevy quite rightly withheld these poems from publication. They do not, as do some of MacGreevy's most successful poems, negotiate with deftness his engagement with the private, the historical and the political to transform them into near perfect poetic expression, as in 'Aodh Ruadh Ó Domhnaill'. In this poem, MacGreevy's futile search for the dead prince's grave in Valladolid reveals the 'painful consequences of action imagined and the painful consequences of inaction felt' (*Eliot*, pp. 29–30), while 'Elections' and 'Homage to Ruteboeuf', grounded in 'impotent rage', never lift themselves out of limited social possibilities; never achieve what Beckett called 'grace of humility "founded" – to quote from Mr McGreevy's *T.S. Eliot* – "not on misanthropy but on hope"' (*Disjecta*, p. 68).

There are other poems which MacGreevy chose not to publish, or to republish in *Poems*, although it is not clear why. One such poem, 'For an Irish Book, 1929', was first published in *transition* in November 1929, and although it is as skilfully executed as the other poems comprising *Poems*, MacGreevy opted not to include it in the collection.[28] While looking through his unpublished work I discovered what seems to be a companion poem, 'La Calunnia e un Venticello'. Like 'For an Irish Book', the poem is an apologia for Joyce. It is also an attack on Wyndham Lewis. It was written in the late spring or early summer of 1928, and as Geoffrey Taylor pointed out to MacGreevy, 'The poem indeed is good. Obscurish of course unless you explain it's about Windam Luis [sic] . . .'[29] And in its final typescript form there is no allusion to Lewis, except for one small but exceedingly evidential detail: '[t]he apes'.

For several years before Lewis published *The Apes of God* (1930), apes figured predominantly in his work. To Lewis, they represented the pseudo-artists, particularly those working between the wars.[30] Lewis, who had once been a literary admirer of Joyce, around 1927 became a foe: the change of tactics resulted in many bitter attacks on Joyce, cumulating in 'An Analysis of the Mind of James Joyce' first published in *The Enemy* (vol. II) in February, and in September of that year in *Time and Western Man*.[31] And by the late 1920s, it might have indeed seemed to Joyce that Lewis had the upper hand, particularly when *Time and Western Man* received praise from 'nearly all' its reviewers.[32] When Joyce chose to counter attack, he couched it in the night language of his most difficult literary work, *Finnegans Wake* (then known only as *Work in Progress*) thus making it accessible to only a small readership. His most famous reply was published in the March issue of *transition* (in which *Work in Progress* was then being serialized) in the form of a fable about the Ondt (a composite character predominantly made up of Lewis) and the Gracehoper (Joyce). But when counter-attacks were to take the form of literary criticism, Joyce, always wary of covering his left flank, did not respond directly, but made sure his captains and lieutenants were at the front line. The final product was a group of essays (the writing of which was directed by Joyce himself) collected under the title *Our Exagmination round His Factification For Incamination of Work in Progress*. MacGreevy's contribution, 'The Catholic Element in *Work in Progress*', was written during the same period as 'La Calunnia e un Venticello', and its closing lines reposit the premise of MacGreevy's poem:

> The London master of spaces should read Mr Joyce's fable. He might learn from it that Gracehopers, for all their seeming timeness are much more in space than the Ondts who decide that they

will 'not come to party at that lopps'. . . . If he would read the story of the Ondt and the Gracehoper, not impatiently but patiently he might learn from it how to write satire not like a barbarian, ineffectively but like an artist, effectively.[33]

La Calunnia e un Venticello

The apes of the
fanaticisms
Grow facetious
And think to confuse the issue
By whispering blackhearted
othernesses
in obscure galleries.

But that is not the end.

They whispered similarly
About Molière
Who routed them
And about Racine
And about Cézanne

Two who defeated them
By allowing them immediate
victory.[34]

This poem also has much in common with the best of MacGreevy's published poetry in its juxtaposition of sound and meaning, its modulation of *vers libre*, and its ability to encompass the inevitable whorl of history. Unlike Lady Gregory's belief that MacGreevy possessed 'the Roman Catholic soporific . . . [which excluded him from speculating] on the ideas of things and [from using] poetry to express' those speculations,[35] he might have only been waiting, as Beckett remarked, 'for the thing to happen, how not to beg the fact of this "bitch of a world" – inarticulate earth and inscrutable heaven' (*Disjecta*, p. 34).

The question still remains. Why did MacGreevy not publish 'La Calunnia e un Venticello' or 'Nel Mezzo', or for that matter republish 'For an Irish Book, 1929'? Perhaps MacGreevy himself best described the reasons for his holding back so many poems from publication, and the reasons why he, by and large, gave up writing poetry after the mid-1930s. Some of MacGreevy's unpublished poems might best be described as poems that he felt unworthy as the quintessence of poetic discourse as they ran counter to a theory that he had spent his most artistically productive years developing. The most concise definition of this poetics is set out in his monograph of Jack B. Yeats (published in Dublin in 1945, but completed — except for a short postscript — in London a year before the outbreak of the Second World War) as a means of identifying some of the technical and thematic changes in Yeats's paintings after 1924. According to MacGreevy's thesis, it was only when Yeats's paintings sought to represent, not the externality of Irish life — its politics and its social problems — but what Beckett identified as its 'great solidarity . . . its insistence upon sending us back to the darkest part of the spirit that created it'[36] — that Yeats found his mature style. Writing in terms of the Irish artist, MacGreevy divided art into the 'objective' and the 'subjective'. Objective art located its source in the temporality of literary or political affairs; in the need 'to insist on . . . a definitive solution of Ireland's political and, more particularly, social problems'. This bifurcated concept of objective and subjective echoes MacGreevy's earlier letter to W.B. Yeats in which he advocated shedding 'the last vestiges of political preoccupations from our writing'.

Subjective art, on the other hand, used 'such liberty [from the post-Civil War period] as has been achieved to attain greater abundance of individual life' (*Yeats*, p. 26). Thus, after 1924 the 'artist particularises less, generalises more. At times he will make some quite humble scene look positively apocalyptic' (*Yeats*, p. 28). This is not unlike the method MacGreevy himself employed in several of his published poems including 'Homage to Hieronymus Bosch' and 'Sour Swan'. After MacGreevy's distinction between objective and subjective art in Jack B. Yeats, he continues with his most concise definition of the role of the imagination in the creative process: 'Imagination is primarily the faculty of relating the ephemeral to the unchanging' (*Yeats*, p. 28). Yet, if the task MacGreevy aspired to in his art was relating 'the ephemeral to the unchanging' why were such poems as 'Nel Mezzo', which MacGreevy might himself have categorised as 'subjective art', held back from publication? Could it be, as I have suggested, that they were simply too raw, too 'unmediated', too counter to the modernist cult of the impersonal that MacGreevy, at least superficially, subscribed to? MacGreevy was not, as Wallace Stevens speculated in his second letter to him, 'a man eager to be at the heart of his time', but, as Brian Coffey knew, someone who has known the 'love of Ireland/withering for Irishmen', and 'the pain between/its fruiting and the early dream' (*PV*, p. 70).

MacGreevy's early dream, filled with both personal aspirations and his aspirations for a newly independent Ireland, knew by his fruiting, his artistic maturity, 'the pain between'. There is no doubt that a more thorough exploration of his unpublished writings would reveal the extent of 'the pain between', and the enormity of the task he set himself as an artist aware of the public discourse of a nation struggling towards renewed self-definition:

> Though I may appear to have defaulted,
> I still hope —
> More — let me not be dishonest, I believe —
> That, in time,
> My name will serve as a rampart
> To the integrity of an Ireland
> Which appearances are always against.[37]

This last stanza from the unpublished poem, 'Appearances', demonstrates how firmly MacGreevy tied his own personal fortunes to Ireland's. Yet, as confessional, as free from the 'intolerable wrestle with words and meanings' as it sounds, is 'Appearances' just another guise for 'indignant politics'? That old monster kept rearing its head in MacGreevy's poetry. It is however here, at the juncture of 'the pain between' and 'indignant politics' that much of MacGreevy's unpublished poetry exists. Both their similarity to and their differences from MacGreevy's published poetry must, by necessity, recontextualize our reading of the published poems. Why they were never published can only be partially teased out in an essay of this length and scope. Their fortunes were, no doubt, tied to the wider issue of MacGreevy's small poetic output, and to that enigmatic cupid in 'Breton Oracles' 'crouching at the foot of a renaissance wall . . . /Weeping over a lost poetry' (*CPM*, p. 70).

Notes

1 Thomas MacGreevy's memoirs, private collection, p. 278.
2 TCD MS 7989/2 contains the majority of unpublished poems, while 10381/183-203 contains the mixture of published and unpublished poems.
3 Anthony Cronin, 'Modernism not Triumphant', *Heritage Now, Irish Literature in the English Language*, Brandon, Dingle, 1982, p. 156.
4 MacGreevy's executors deposited MacGreevy's papers at TCD over a thirteen-year period, first in 1976, then in 1978 and most recently in 1989.
5 The conventions used throughout this essay are as follows: strikeout indicates a holograph crossout; smaller typeface indicates a holograph correction in the case of typescript, or in the case of manuscript, an addition to the original text.
6 Interestingly, when MacGreevy chooses to comment, his comments are couched in such surreal imagery, such as in 'Homage to Hieronymus Bosch', that 'understanding' is all but impossible.
7 Stan Smith, 'From a Great Distance: Thomas MacGreevy's Frames of Reference', *The Lace Curtain*, 6, Autumn 1978, p. 50.
8 Wallace Stevens, *Collected Poems*, Faber, London, p. 455.
9 Letter from Thomas MacGreevy to Wallace Stevens, 27 April 1948, property of The Huntington Library.
10 *Selected Prose of T.S. Eliot*, ed. Frank Kermode, Faber, London, 1975, p. 43.
11 Dante, *The Inferno*, trans. Allen Mandelbaum, Bantam Books, New York, 1982, p. 3.
12 TCD MS 7979/2/8.
13 Lyndall Gordon, *Eliot's Early Years*, Oxford University Press, Oxford, 1977, p. 15.
14 Gordon, p. 15.
15 TCD MS 7989/2/6.
16 Gordon, p. 15.
17 T.S. Eliot, *Four Quartets, Complete Poems and Plays*, Harcourt Brace Jovanovich, New York, 1971, p. 118.
18 Thomas MacGreevy, *Nicolas Poussin*, Dolmen Press, Dublin, 1960, p. 15.
19 MacGreevy, memoirs, p. 345.
20 I am indebted to Mary Thompson for her comments on Austin Clarke and the use of mythology in post-Irish Renaissance poetry and drama.
21 TCD MS 7989/2/42.
22 It is not clear whether MacGreevy ever posted this letter. It does not seem to have been preserved in Yeats's papers now deposited at the National Library of Ireland, nor does it appear in *Letters to W.B. Yeats*.
23 TCD MS 8068.
24 David Lloyd, *Anomalous States: Irish Writing and the Post-Colonial Moment*, Lilliput Press, Dublin, 1993, p. 3.
25 Wallace Stevens, 'Imagination as Value', *The Necessary Angel: Essays on Reality and the Imagination,* Faber, London, 1984, pp. 144–5.

26 TCD MS 7989/2/37.

27 TCD MS 7989/2/48.

28 It is one of only two poems which had been published prior to 1934 that MacGreevy chose not to reprint in *Poems*. The other poem is 'Transition'.

29 TCD MS 8117/94.

30 See Paul Edwards, '*The Apes of God:* Form and Meaning', *Wyndham Lewis: A Revaluation*, ed. Jeffrey Meyers, Athlone Press, London, 1980, p. 134.

31 See Jeffrey Meyers, *The Enemy: A Biography of Wyndham Lewis*, Routledge & Kegan Paul, London, 1980, p. 135.

32 Meyers, p. 136.

33 Thomas MacGreevy, 'The Catholic Element in *Work in Progress*', *Our Exagmination round His Factification For Incamination of Work in Progress* (1929), p. 127.

34 TCD MS 7989/2/47.

35 Letter from Thomas MacGreevy to Wallace Stevens, 26 May 1948, property of The Huntington Library.

36 Samuel Beckett, 'Hommage à Jack B. Yeats', *Jack B. Yeats: A Centenary Gathering*, ed. Roger McHugh, Dolmen Press, Dublin, 1971, p. 75.

37 TCD MS 7989/2/49.

6

'Poetry is Ontology':
Brian Coffey's Poetics

Alex Davis

In 1938 George Reavey's Europa Press published Brian Coffey's short sequence of poems *Third Person*, a volume that brought to a close the first phase of his career as a poet. His preceding work included *Poems* (1930) — which collected his and Denis Devlin's juvenilia — *Three Poems* (1930) and *Yuri-Hira* (1933), a Christmas-card poem. For the following two decades, until 1961, Coffey published no poetry, his interests, it would appear, becoming increasingly governed by his philosophical and theological preoccupations. The relationship between Coffey's mature Catholicism, with its philosophical underpinnings, and his later poetry, has remained relatively unexplored, despite the fact that his three major sequences, *Missouri Sequence* (1962), *Advent* (1975) and *Death of Hektor* (1979), develop a poetic deeply imbricated with the scholastic ideas with which Coffey came into contact in Paris during the 1930s. In the years 1933–36 Coffey was studying at the Institut Catholique de Paris, principally under the Neo-Thomist philosopher, Jacques Maritain (1882–1973). Coffey's familiarity with, and interest in, Maritain's work is considerable. In 1937, upon his return to Paris, he began work on his doctoral thesis, 'De l'idée d'ordre d'après saint Thomas d'Aquin', submitted in 1947. From 1948 to 1952 Coffey, then an assistant professor in philosophy at St Louis University, Missouri, contributed a number of articles and reviews to the neo-Thomist journal *The Modern Schoolman* (including an English translation of a portion of his thesis),[1] essays that are indebted to Maritain, principally to his careful differentiation between the epistemological claims of science and faith, the 'degrees of knowledge' that, in their respective spheres, each confers.[2]

During the period of his initial contact with Maritain, and three years before *Third Person* appeared, Coffey had written to his friend Thomas MacGreevy of the difficulty he was experiencing in being both a poet and a Christian.[3] Interestingly, a tension between art and faith is central to Maritain's analysis of modernist poetry. In *Art and Scholasticism* he explicitly states that, for the modern poet, Christianity is arduous.[4] His essay, 'The Frontiers of Poetry', contends that this is due to the fact that, since Mallarmé, poetry has increasingly 'arrogat[ed] to itself the aseity of God' in its search for pure form: 'What makes the condition of modern art tragic is that it must be converted to find God again'.[5] The 'spiritual experience' of European and American modernism is 'tragic' because it is haunted by the question Baudelaire poses, but leaves unanswered, in 'Hymne à la beauté': 'Viens-tu du ciel profond ou sors-tu de l'abîme,/ô Beauté?'[6] Modernism, in Maritain's eyes, severs the link between beauty and God: beauty becomes, in the words of *Creative Intuition in Art and Poetry*, 'the all-exacting idol of art' but 'reigns *separate* in our human heaven' (author's italics).[7] The reification of poetry into pure form Maritain views as a highly ambivalent phenomenon in the arts. If formal self-consciousness is indicative of modernity's secularization of beauty and poetry's divorce from lived experience, it, nevertheless, harbours a suppressed longing for divine 'Beauté'. Beauty's terrible gaze, in Baudelaire's words, is both 'infernal' and 'divin'.

Though it would be overly reductive to equate Coffey's lengthy abstention from poetic composition with the tension between experimental artistic form and religious faith postulated by Maritain, it is noteworthy that, after resuming writing poetry in the 1950s, Coffey's work recurrently interrogates the function of the artwork and the role of the poet in a fashion which bears striking comparison with Maritain's aesthetic views. The difficulty Coffey had outlined in his 1935 letter to MacGreevy becomes, in some of the later poetry, a stimulus to a highly self-referential analysis of the poetic a Christian modernism requires. That poetry, and its relation to Maritain's opinions on modern art, I examine in detail in the latter part of this essay. Firstly, however, I shall draw together Maritain's views on the ontological status of the artist and artwork, and Coffey's scattered, and hence less programmatic, reflections on poetic composition and the formal properties of the completed poem.

The *Artifex*

Asked to describe the 'creative process' in a 1978 interview, Coffey replied that 'the Scots are nearer the mark when they call the poet a "macher", a maker rather than a creator'.[8] Coffey's comment illustrates his antipathy towards the Romantic and post-Romantic preoccupation with 'creativity' as formulated, for example, in Shelley's claim, in *Defence of Poetry*, that 'Poets are the hierophants of an unapprehended inspiration.'[9] This strain of Romantic aesthetics had been regalvanized, for Coffey's generation, through the experiments of the surrealists. Coffey is suspicious of the irrationalism he detects in the latter's poetic, arguing that the work of a poet like Paul Eluard 'was the result of deliberate choices; it could never have been the uncorrected resultant of spontaneous regurgitations (or would it be gurgitations?) from the vasty depths within the person'.[10] Coffey's mistrust of this kind of reach-me-down Romanticism derives, at least in part, from his Neo-Thomism. In *Art and Scholasticism* Maritain places 'The sphere of Art' within 'the sphere of Making'. Art, while belonging to the intellectual order, is practical rather than speculative; its maker is not a hierophant but the '*artifex*, artist or artisan', a craftsperson who 'devote[s] all the strength and intelligence of his manhood to the thing which he is making'.[11] Maritain's industrious *artifex* is of a piece with his idealized evocations of medieval Europe: yet he is a figure equally at home in the modernist cultural landscape, to the literature of which Maritain devotes many sympathetic pages. Fredric Jameson and Jerome McGann have argued that a celebration of 'individual production' is central to modernist aesthetics. The modernist artist, working on the Great Book, provides an after-image of the pre-industrial artisan, his or her labour directed at the production of handiworks resistant to the degrading effects of commodification.[12] Coffey's emphasis on the poet as maker, whose craft involves 'practice, deliberate composing of metaphor and image and figure', and his concurrence with the Greek idea of 'knowing an art or trade (techné), in the sense of an outwardly turned integration of the craftsman or artist or tradesman in the direction of a good performance',[13] are at one with the importance Maritain lays on the labour exerted by the *artifex*. Likewise, the establishment of his own press, Advent, in 1966, the aim of which was to publish finely-crafted limited editions, can be viewed as further evidence of the centrality of 'individual production' to Coffey's work.

The artisanal nature of poetic composition is also raised in Coffey's reflections on Mallarmé. Mallarmé's *Livre* is an exemplary instance of the idea of the text-as-artifact: 'a book', in Coffey's words, 'which would be architectural, premeditated – not a mere collection of chance-born inspirations and insights, were they never so marvellous'.[14] But Coffey's esteem for Mallarmé's aspiration towards the definitive act in poetic making is tempered by his awareness that The Book can exist only as a 'dream'. Coffey does not state explicitly why *Le Livre* is unrealizable, remaining content to quote the French poet's comment: 'Il faudrait être je ne sais qui pour cela.' Maritain, in contrast, is quite clear about the impossibility of achieving – and the dangers of yearning for – the absolute in pure art. In 'The Frontiers of Poetry' he states that the 'logical extremes' of pure or abstract art require the idea of an artwork 'separate and exempt from, and perfectly disinterested in regard to man and things'. In a striking image Maritain likens such craving to 'The suicide of an angel – through forgetfulness of matter'. The obliviousness of the advocates of aesthetic purity to the matter of their craft is, according to Maritain, an instructive lesson for art in general:

> [It] remind[s] it that 'poetry is ontology', that, being *of man*, it can no more fence itself off from things than he; that being *in man*, art always ends by confessing in some way the weaknesses of man; . . . that being in a way *for man* . . . it will in the end decay if it rejects either the constraints and limitations required from without by the good of man or the service of our common culture. (author's italics)[15]

The making of art, in this aesthetic, is finally inseparable from, and is responsible to, its 'conditions of existence, the sum of which is: humanity'. In a not unrelated vein Coffey has said that in encountering a new poem one is 'meeting another human person': 'Everything, now, emanates from the person, including the human intelligence, the will, the human emotions, and terminates in a literary work.'[16] In summary, both Maritain and Coffey are committed to a poetic in which an Aristotelian conception of artistic labour – art is a shaping of sensible matter through the imposition of form – entails that the existential 'conditions' of the *artifex* are indelibly stamped upon the finished artifact. Further, the material 'constraints' upon poetry have an ethical dimension: to avoid 'decay' poetry is bound by 'limitations' that, in a sense to be developed, are in 'the service of the common culture'.

Nevertheless, the Mallarméan 'dream' has another, seemingly contradictory, lesson to teach. The drive towards purity warns art that, in Maritain's words: 'A too flabby resignation to its conditions of existence is also suicide for art; the sin of materialism'. This 'sin' ensues from Maritain's belief that art is 'ordered to an object transcending man . . . whose fullness is without limit, for beauty is as infinite as being'.[17] The artist is therefore beset by a painful siege of contraries: gripped by an awareness of the immaterial essence of art, its 'beauty', he or she is all too cognizant of the fact that the *artifex* cannot transcend the sphere of Making by repudiating the matter upon which he or she works. Coffey's philosophical prose is silent on this issue. In his reviews and articles for *The Modern Schoolman* he, like Maritain, views materialism as a 'sin': he berates Marxism, logical positivism, 'the unabashed materialism of the *Encyclopedia and Unified Science* [*sic*]',[18] even the procedures and conclusions of the Kinsey Report, which studies 'human sexuality from the standpoint of the material cause alone'.[19] However, these pieces, by the very nature of their subject-matter, do not venture into the aesthetic realm. We have to turn to Coffey's poetry to find an extended commentary on the dilemma confronting the earthbound maker of beauty.[20]

Missouri Sequence

Coffey's self-reflexive ponderings on poetry in *Missouri Sequence* comprise a poetic close in substance to that of *Art and Scholasticism* and 'The Frontiers of Poetry'. The sequence places great weight on *both* the situatedness of the poet's making *and* the transcendent, transcontextual being of art in itself. The poem has its origins in the early

1950s (though it was not published until 1962), a period of Coffey's life in which the all-too-human context in which a poem is made was brought home to him through distressing financial circumstances.[21] The sequence preserves the biographical facts in a series of references to the domestic and economic circumstances of the poet, portraying the act of composition as impinged upon by 'family cares and crises' (*PV*, p. 82). Coffey's depiction elsewhere of Mallarmé, beleaguered by teaching commitments, 'administrative duties, household cares, financial demands', stealing from sleep 'for the demands of the Muse',[22] finds a parallel in another teacher-poet beset by 'bitter necessity' (*PV*, p. 71) trying to 'write verses at [his] desk' (*PV*, p. 82):

> I am seated here
> hoping the weightless flight
> of a poem born aright.   (*PV*, p. 84)

The deployment of autobiographical details throughout the sequence bears comparison with the 'confessional' quality of the poetry of Coffey's American near-contemporaries, Robert Lowell and John Berryman. However, like those poets' work, *Missouri Sequence* cannot be reduced solely to the biographical data it culls. In the sly words of Berryman's 'Message': 'This is not autobiography-in-verse, my friends.'[23] Instead, autobiography in *Missouri Sequence* serves a poetic function akin to that which the Russian formalists dubbed 'the motivation of the device'. [24] The 'cares and crises' and consequent 'writer's block' which comprise the subject-matter of much of the sequence are a 'pretext', or point of departure, for the poem's meditative form — it is a 'metapoem', a poem which reflects upon poetry and/or poetic composition. (Another, more famous, Irish example is Yeats's 'The Circus Animals' Desertion'.) The troubled ruminations of the 'I' in the poem are not 'explained away', as it were, by reference to Coffey's psychological make-up at the time of the poem's conception. For while it is true that with *Missouri Sequence* Coffey broke a considerable period of poetic silence, that silence as documented in the poem itself underlabours — provides the motivation for — the metapoetic device.[25]

The foregrounding of this device (it is present in each of the poem's four sections) has the effect of transforming the speaker's individual crisis into an exploration of the historically 'embedded' nature of poetry *per se*. Coffey's concern with the ontological status of poetry *in general* explains the apparent inconsistency of his distaste for the metapoetic device as found in the work of Wallace Stevens. Stevens's 'false step', he said in interview, is to make 'the poem itself the subject of the poetry'.[26] While this remark unquestionably does little justice to Stevens, it underscores the extent to which the genesis of *Missouri Sequence* is not the poem's dominant concern. Rather, the sequence's focus on the difficulties Coffey experienced in the composition of this particular poem become a vehicle for a broader examination of the ways in which the products of the *artifex*, the works of *any* artist or artisan, are shaped by circumstantial forces.

The antics of the speaker's children, running from room to room of his house, passing his desk 'each minute' (*PV*, p. 69), come to represent the dictum 'poetry is ontology'. The solitary maker is shown to be not only circumscribed by but also a construct, to a degree, of his environment and culture:

> If memory were an ice-field
> quiet as all outside!
> Tonight the poetry is in the children's game:
> I am distracted by comparisons,
> Ireland across the grey ocean,
> here, across the wide river.   (*PV*, p. 69)

The 'bitter necessity', that having once driven him to Missouri is now forcing him to leave, raises disturbing, distracting memories for the speaker, which include a reflection on the shaping influence of his nationality: 'there is a love of Ireland/withering for Irishmen' (*PV*, p. 70). Yet the poem is alive to the fact that such love is a culturally acquired rather than an inherent property of the individual. Coffey's children, raised in America, 'know nothing of Ireland,/they grow American' (*PV*, p. 70), their sense of national identity at odds with their father's. These familial concerns, however, are not the only distracting 'comparisons' troubling the poet. The 'children's game' that has possessed his poetry becomes a metaphor for the 'cares and crises', socio-political and/or economic, which in the past brought other Europeans to this region. 'Bitter necessity' is at the core of the collective memory of Missouri, in its history of immigration, of the 'Irish, German, Bohemian' peoples who populated it 'more than one hundred years ago' (*PV*, p. 69). The speaker's peregrinations are thrown into relief upon this historical backdrop, exhibiting the *artifex* as subject, like the early settlers, to forces which delimit his individual agency. Hence the poem's emphasis on the cultural foundations that support human activity: 'We face a testing/based on other grounds than nature's' (*PV*, p. 77).

Stan Smith sees in this stress on the contextualization of selfhood a rigorous attention to the contingencies of human existence: 'For Coffey, where one finds oneself is the result of an accumulation of circumstances, accidents and omissions, not a willed and single act of defiance or flight.'[27] As Smith further notes, this view of human existence is bound to a paradigm of the artist different from that expressed in Stephen Dedalus's desire to 'fly by' the 'nets' of 'nationality, language and religion'.[28] Such 'nets', for Coffey, are not to be eluded through self-imposed exile but constitute inescapable necessities which are 'no monopoly/of Irish soil' (*PV*, p. 71). This point is given poignant expression in the 'comparison' *Missouri Sequence* draws between the speaker's predicament and that of the older Irish poet, Thomas MacGreevy:

> Dear Tom, in Ireland,
> you have known
> the pain between
> its fruiting and the early dream
> and you will hear me out.   (*PV*, p. 70)

MacGreevy's 'fruiting', a single, thin collection of 1934 (and a handful of uncollected poems), can be taken as a salutary lesson that the 'dream' of an Irish avant-garde poetry could not withstand the realities of 1930s' Ireland. Terence Brown has drawn attention to the ideological reasons that lay behind the lack of interest in the formal experimentation and 'cosmopolitan' preoccupations of MacGreevy (and of Coffey and Denis Devlin) shown by the Irish reading public of that time.[29] Coffey's comments on this topic are simpler, and more forthright. The specific pressure he locates in the cultural context in which he began writing is the presence of Yeats: 'a power-hungry seducer who gathered a right gang of praisers around him, and who blocked off the kind of talent he didn't like.'[30] A draft of *Missouri Sequence*, sent to MacGreevy, includes a milder, if not unrelated, criticism of the poet:

> And I will say that William Butler Yeats
> was a great poet who failed
> when he advised our Irish poets.[31]

The allusion, presumably, is to the exhortation of 'Under Ben Bulben': 'Irish poets, learn your trade,/Sing whatever is well made . . .',[32] to which Coffey has objected, understandably, that it is difficult to be 'tolerant of the idea that it is an Irish poet's business to sing of peasants and country gentlemen, of monks and porter-drinkers in their respective avocations, of the uppercrust of a mere seven centuries past'.[33] Nevertheless, in the published version of *Missouri Sequence* these polemics, while present, remain subordinate to a broader discussion of the ontological situation of the poet. Coffey's long absence from Ireland, his isolation from literary circles and his position in St Louis as a professional philosopher rather than a published poet, may well lie behind Coffey's projection of his own plight as an existential given.[34] Be that as it may, *Missouri Sequence* implies that the discrepancy between the poetic 'dream' and its material fruiting is due to the general condition of poetry: '*in man*', as Maritain has it, poetry necessarily confesses 'the weaknesses of man'. The movement of the remainder of the poem is to identify the strength that resides in poetry being '*for man*', and thus in the 'service of the common good'.

The parabolic narrative of the 'poet as a hunter' (*PV*, p. 78), in section 3 of the sequence, is central to this movement. It begins immediately after another reference to the finite, temporal character of human activity:

> All the passions meet at the dinner table,
> all men's history ever was or will be
> uncoils its features while we serve the food.   (*PV*, p. 78)

The hunter-poet represents the desire to transcend 'constraints', whether domestic 'cares' or the constricting coils of one's historical conjuncture. He is, in the speaker's words, 'one who would not let me be/among the children' (*PV*, p. 78). The poem portrays him in pursuit of an elusive female, 'a slip of light' (*PV*, p. 79), over whom he ultimately believes he has gained poetic mastery:

> In song he poised her,
> lauded victory
> over his muse.   (*PV*, p. 80)

His triumph, however, is wholly illusory; he is, in fact, 'astray from the perfect scene' (*PV*, p. 80). It is not without relevance to the nature of the hunter's ruined quest-romance that this section of the poem is dedicated to the memory of Coffey's contemporary Denis Devlin. In Devlin's *The Heavenly Foreigner* (first published, in full, in 1950; edited by Coffey, for Dolmen Press, in 1967) women function as ambivalent intercessors between the poet and the transcendental titular figure. The poem is structured around recollections of these women, each of whom becomes the poet's 'emblem', 'the absolute woman of a moment' (*CPD*, p. 266).[35] Yet these moments never yield the certainty of revelation. The speaker remains tied to his temporal circumstances: 'Time', he cries, 'is volumed round me, thick with echoes, things/I cannot see throughout' (*CPD*, p. 269). Fixated by the 'Beauty! Beauty!' (*CPD*, p. 260) he glimpses in the female figures, the poetic subject becomes the hollowed-out echo-chamber of his past, leafing vainly through the library of his erotic past for insight.

The conclusion of section 3 of *Missouri Sequence* suggests that the failure charted in a poem like *The Heavenly Foreigner* is antithetical to the self-deluding 'victory' of the poet as hunter:

> The true muse fleshed
> nor was, nor shall be,
> is a torment of oneself,
> cannot be done without.   (*PV*, p. 80)

The 'torment' of a Devlin is the condition that the hunter-poet must attain: 'he must run, must implore/her veiled features in desperate race . . .' (*PV*, p. 80). Devlin's theological preoccupations, his unremitting attempt to grasp infinite Beauty in the finite forms of women, become in Coffey's text analogous to pure art's refusal to resign itself to its 'conditions of existence'. If the 'labour' of the *artifex* will never lead him or her to the 'perfect scene', still 'The never perfect work/[is] its own reward' (*PV*, p. 80).[36] This we have seen to be Maritain's thesis in 'The Frontiers of Poetry', for 'to aim too high' is essential for any art ordered towards beauty: the work should '*tend* to abstract art like a curve to its asymptote . . .'[37] *Missouri Sequence* differs from *The Heavenly Foreigner* in the hard-pressed stoicism with which it finally accepts art's dependence on matter and the consequent antinomy between art's essential being and the material constraints on the *artifex*. Section 3 ends with a return to the embeddedness of the artistic act: the speaker's children once again break in upon his thoughts, on his meditation on the 'true muse', 'scattering/[him] everywhere' (*PV*, p. 80). Caught between his knowledge of the ineluctably contextualized character of the poetic process, represented by the children's 'scrambling play' (*PV*, p. 80), and a fidelity to the longing for poetic purity, symbolized in Devlin's 'torment', the speaker simply states the impassability of this poetic Scylla and Charybdis:

> This much is certain:
> he will not forget her beauty,
> he must not attempt escape
> from here and now.   (*PV*, p. 81)

The sequence's final section attempts to turn this realization to positive ends. The section includes an account of an enigmatic dream which recasts, allegorically, the above quotation's bald final clause. In the dream the poet, a 'white knight', repeatedly challenges a dragon while a woman looks on. While this scenario echoes that of the 'desperate race' of the previous section, it differs in its connotations. In the dream the speaker asks himself whether the quest (for purity or transcendental beauty) 'confused for him an afternoon/with key to open silver moon' (*PV*, p. 83). The naivety of that final image is contrasted with the facticity of the poet's lived experience, that offers him 'love's every shape/in all earth, all sky':

> until I ceased to think of escape,
> until I sit here solely,
> damp in strident summer's
> cloud of small pests,
> making poetry.   (*PV*, p. 83)

Here poetic 'making' is not fuelled by the desire to 'escape' the matter of art. Coffey foregoes pure art's aim of somehow *representing*, in

Renato Poggioli's words, 'a state of beatitude and grace, a condition of perfection and stasis fixed forever, by the severe ethos of form'.[38] Yet the poem insists that to rest content with the 'shapes' present in the earth and sky of this world is *not* to celebrate contingency and champion the accidental. That, after all, was precisely the aim of the surrealists, to whose aesthetic we have already seen Coffey antagonistic. André Breton and others argued that the 'gurgitations', as Coffey felicitously calls them, from which surrealism claims to derive the matter of its art, should be rendered in all their formless inarticulateness – in automatic writing, for instance. The surrealist gesture, in theory at least, is thus the polar opposite of the idea at the heart of pure art. Surrealism endeavours, according to Poggioli, to 'realize . . . a state of permanent revolution, a series of commotions and permutations which have only the pathos of experience as cause and norm'.[39] A poetry given over entirely to an expression of the 'pathos of experience' is one which acquiesces completely in the 'conditions of its existence', committing the 'sin of materialism' with impunity. *Missouri Sequence* advocates, albeit obscurely, a very different dependence of poetry on experience from surrealism. In the concluding section of the sequence poetry is said to bear 'the truth of all', to live 'whenever everywhere', voicing a universal 'love' which, nevertheless, does not occlude the irreducible particularity of the text:

> Poetry becomes humankind. . . .
>
> Watch the slender swallow flash its wings,
> dive, sheer sky in two,
> never before, never again,
> and such is poetry.   (*PV*, p. 86)

These lines are usefully compared with Maritain's claim in 'The Frontiers of Poetry' that the *artifex* is answerable to – constrained by – 'humanity'. Art is in 'the service of our common culture'; rooted in 'twisted man' (*PV*, p. 86) poetry is thus *'for man'*. The poem's recourse to this over-arching 'truth of all' is, however, extremely problematic, and reveals an ethnocentrism (and unconscious sexism) equally present in Maritain's vague reference to *'our'* culture. *Missouri Sequence*'s concluding pronouncements resolve the debate conducted in the course of the poem only by shifting it onto a vatic plane. We need to turn to Coffey's later poetry to follow through this ethical dimension to his metapoetic concerns.

Advent and *Death of Hektor*

Advent (1975) is not as self-reflexive a poem as *Missouri Sequence*, nor are its themes as centred on the aesthetic. My discussion, therefore, will focus on merely a single aspect of this long and multi-faceted poem.

One approach to the poetic issues raised by *Advent* is Maritain's claim, in *Creative Intuition in Art and Poetry*, that modernist poetry possesses two spiritual 'countenances': the 'ardor of acceptance' and the 'ardor of refusal'. The latter prompts, according to Maritain, 'the search for transmuting reality through the power of words', a search related to that which Maritain, in another context, labels 'Angelism': the striving of human intelligence to attain the spiritual autonomy reserved, in Thomism, for creatures unbound by material individuation.[40] 'Angelism', Maritain believes, has its origins in Descartes, and, as Ellman Crasnow has demonstrated, provides a convenient trope for the ambitious idealism of writers like Wallace Stevens, Rainer Maria Rilke and Paul Valéry.[41] These are poets who, wishing to forget matter, commit what *Art and Scholasticism* terms the 'suicide of an angel'. Towards the close of *Advent* Coffey opines that such forgetfulness is a pernicious human failing:

> We are always in human circumstances
> no angels and prone to forget
> we can work only from point to point   (*PV*, p. 149)

The poem, as a whole, treats humanity's propensity for 'angelism' — its chronic suppression of its utter dependency upon the earth — through the social, political and, above all, environmental results of such collective amnesia: humankind 'soils the sea to calm the mighty wave/ravishes maternal earth to make deserts grow' (*PV*, p. 121).[42] Implicated in this process are those poets whose 'Dark mind[s]' project 'the pure image sought/on glass of bent desire' (*PV*, p. 119). Their 'arrogance of angelism', in Crasnow's words, springs from 'the temptation to see themselves as perfected intelligences with worlds at their disposal'.[43] Such idealism is viewed by Coffey as escapist, a 'false advent idol'; they are 'distracted while earth [goes] on yielding fruit' (*PV*, p. 119). Like *Missouri Sequence*, *Advent* binds the poet to the 'here and now', the 'earth', yet develops that theme (as does *Death of Hektor*) to embrace the complex relationship between poetry and history. *Advent* views the poet not as having worlds at his or her disposal, but as imbricated in the history of *this* world; and, further, as morally bound to imaginatively re-cognizing the historical forces of which he or she is a part. It is in this sense that the poem builds upon *Missouri Sequence*'s claim that poetry 'bears the truth of all': 'poetry is ontology' in *Advent* to the extent that it is granted an important ethical role in humankind's ongoing endeavour to achieve self-understanding.

In section 3 of the poem Coffey invokes the Muse of history, Klio, and proceeds to outline the fashion in which poetry works upon history:

> in poem quickening clear view of what we are
> allowing tale-teller chance of prudence after event
>
> (*PV*, p. 125)

In support of this the poem gives a synopsis of Aeschylus's bloody triology the *Oresteia* — 'incest rape murder obscenity' — and concludes:

> Poet then displayed to wakening eyes
> the drama   what now goes on
> and humbled men maybe began to be wise   (*PV*, p. 126)

Stan Smith says of this passage: 'Story here redeems history from that vast panorama of futility and anarchy that is a mere pointless unfolding of event on event. . . .'[44] Tales become 'exempla' from which, due to their imaginative shaping of historical material, we may perhaps learn 'to be wise'. The 'truth' of these tales lies not in their historical veracity, but in the response they elicit from their readers or auditors: 'history works still against the rounded tale' (*PV*, p. 126). Smith's astute commentary allows us to read the poetic of *Advent* as, in part, a reply to Mallarmé's *Un coup de dés*, which Coffey was translating at the same time as he was working on his own major poem.[45] In Mallarmé's poem 'angelism' implodes as the imposition of order reaches its negative apotheosis in the randomly thrown dice of the poetic act. As its full title suggests, *Un coup de dés jamais n'abolira le hasard* is concerned with chance and contingency. More precisely, 'Mallarmé's "hasard"', in the view of one critic, 'is the abidingly unstable medium of thought', an image for the actions of 'the vulnerable and inventive self' in the midst of 'a universally accidental world'.[46] The text's Byronic protagonist, the master-mariner, can be interpreted as a figure of the poet, confronting 'the tempest', within and without himself, with 'the unique Number', hoping 'to undo division and pass on proud'. But the mariner's shipwreck suggests that there is no uniquely revealing order; thinking can only be provisional, to an extent arbitrary: 'All Thought utters Dice Thrown'.[47]

The close of *Un coup de dés* contains modernist suppositions about language that, in various forms, reach down to the present day. The poem can be interpreted as debunking any claim that we can 'grasp' reality (history included) except as a creation of the conceptual schemes our linguistic structures impose upon us. More drastically, it is a short step from such an understanding of *Un coup de dés* to a textualist one, that is, to a reading that perceives in the poem the dizzying movement of *différance*. For Jacques Derrida the Mallarméan word, through its 'undecided allusion' or suggestiveness, severs the link with 'all meaning (signified theme) and . . . referents (the thing itself, and the conscious or unconscious intention of the author)'. Signs in a poem like *Un coup de dés* 'finally refer only to their own game, and never really move toward anything else'.[48] Or, in Mallarmé's enigmatic words: 'NOTHING/WILL HAVE TAKEN PLACE/BUT PLACE'.[49] Coffey's dedication to poetry's 'truth', that is, the poet's ability to give his or her reader a 'quickening clear view of what we are', and thus, by extension, to refer to history, is clearly at odds with this strand of modernism and postmodernism. Such 'truth', so conceived, is necessarily far from absolute: it consists, as Smith puts it, of our human need to turn history into story; the urge to make sense or find meaning in what *Advent* terms 'earth's unfinished business' (*PV*, p. 127) from the limited vantage-point of the present.

Coffey explores the interface between poetry and history at greater length in his treatment of Homer in the 1979 sequence *Death of Hektor*. In section 6 of this poem Coffey states that, though basic biographical facts about the author of the *Iliad* are unavailable ('where born where buried of whom the son/what journeys undertaken not know'), 'His work/abides witness to unfaltering sad gaze constrained':

> A harp he   uses background for verses sung
> He pared no fingernails not indifferent   not masked . . .
> His ears open to spoken word and words down time like
>   wind-blown sand
> words of triumph unsleeping enmities wound-up spells malice
> swirl of sound continual mixed in a perfect ear
> surfacing coherent truer than history all and everything
>
> (*PV*, p. 156)

The passage's allusion to Joyce's *Portrait* draws a distinction between the humanity encapsulated in Homer's text and the arrogant 'angelism' of the young Dedalus: 'The artist', says Stephen to his friend Lynch, 'like the God of creation, remains within or behind or beyond or above his handiwork, invisible, refined out of existence, indifferent, paring his fingernails'.[50] If Stephen's ideal artist has no 'existence' in the artifact he or she creates, Coffey's Homer is an *artifex* whose work is an abiding 'witness' to the historical conjuncture which 'constrained' him. This of course accords with Coffey's belief that, in reading a poem, one is in some sense 'meeting another person'. Yet *Death of Hektor* also reiterates the larger claim of *Missouri Sequence*: 'Poetry becomes humankind.' For despite the socio-political and literary historical 'constraints' upon Homer – the embeddedness of his poetic making – Homer's words are said to possess an importance which transcends their moment of production. In fact, their significance is that they comprise a narrative which is 'truer than history all and everything'. As with *Missouri Sequence* truth and poetry are conjoined, and again we are forced to consider what content this theory of 'truth' contains. It is not a correspondence theory of truth (namely, a judgement is true if and only if it corresponds to the facts) because Homer's account is said to be 'truer' than the raw events of history. Instead, truth we are told lies in the *coherence* of the poem; in the interanimation of beliefs, events, characters, etc. which comprise Homer's representation of the Trojan War. It is a 'world-version', in Nelson Goodman's terminology, the truth of which is metaphorical or allegorical rather than literal.[51] The metaphorical truth of the *Iliad*, its rounding of history into story or exemplar, is the inhumanity of war: 'Homer has shown us /. . ./ False picture false childhood standards war not human not good' (*PV*, p. 164). Coffey thus politicizes Maritain's woolly belief that the 'constraints' on the artist are in 'the service of our common culture'. Homer's 'world-version' is neither the seemingly self-contained 'world' imagined by modernist 'angelism', nor the textualist prison-house of language of a deconstructed Mallarmé. It is a version of the world 'common' to all; a world which, from Homeric tribes to the nuclear powers of this century, Coffey views as being at the mercy of humanity's destructive capacity: 'And/Doom now in the air like a cloudy mushroom swags above Troy' (*PV*, p. 160).

This aspect of the metapoetic reflections of *Death of Hektor* branches out to include the reader-reception of the *Iliad*, both in the past and present:

> Prudent Homer who survived to make his poems
> did he keep unsaid wordly in innermost anguished heart
> what would not have pleased his client banqueters
> not reached by resonance the hearts of self-approving lords
> yet at last might reach our raddled selves   (*PV*, p. 156)

Homer's contemporary audience, those 'self-approving lords', are partisan, their interests leaving them deaf to the 'resonance' or suggestive power of the poet's narrative. They are subject to the fault Coffey isolates in section 4 of *Missouri Sequence*: 'The habit of withholding love/unfits us for poetry' (*PV*, p. 86). But in what way are readers in the late twentieth century in a more privileged position to comprehend the implications or 'resonance' of the *Iliad*? Surely the significance which reverberates through the poem is constructed out of the beliefs of readers ('our raddled selves') as interested as, if in different ways from, Homer's original audience. The 'truth' of the epic can *only* be a contextually circumscribed interpretation. In section 14 Coffey is quite explicit that the *Iliad*'s truth content is not only related to what Homer actually says, but equally depends on how 'we' respond to the poem's gaps and blanks, which can only be made to speak through the interpretative activity of a reader:

> By what he has not said we judge ourselves
> He showed us hero bad compassion none hero good
> idolatry of spoil   fightmanship   glory   (*PV*, p. 164)

Death of Hektor shows that poetry 'lives whenever everywhere' because readers bring their own preconceptions and pre-understandings to a text, and read it according to their cultural, political and ideological lights. As Hans Robert Jauss argues, the historical 'horizon' in which a text is received is as co-productive of its 'meaning' as the 'horizon' in which it was written.[52] The poem, in other words, demonstrates that Homer's epic serves 'the common culture', possesses 'resonance' in the late 1970s, through functioning as a sounding board for Coffey's pacifist, anti-nuclear beliefs.

This powerful poetic, I have argued, has its roots in Coffey's resistance to certain currents within modernism, as viewed through the prism of Neo-Thomist aesthetics. Coffey is wary of, firstly, surrealism's desire to realize the 'pathos of experience' in poetic form; and, secondly, and more significantly, the implications of pure art's belief that, in the words of Mallarmé: 'The only Reality is Beauty and Its only perfect expression is Poetry.'[53] Coffey's disparaging view of both these strains of modernism reveals a larger dissatisfaction with aesthetic modernity. Coffey's rejection of art's autonomy, and his concomitant emphasis on the artwork's connections with its author's and readers' lifeworlds, constitute an implicit critique of the post-Kantian separation of science, morality and art. Modernism, stripped of a social dimension, its double-edged autonomy laid bare in its elevation of form over content, represents the culmination of art's disengagement from the political and ethical spheres of society. (Surrealism's 'revolutionary' aim of wresting the aesthetic realm from its bourgeois consumers simply renders that realm anarchic. It by no means reintegrates art with other areas of social life.)[54] In this light, Coffey's desire to relocate art within human experience as a whole can be seen to be inseparable from the conservative Catholicism he shares with, and partly derives from, Maritain. Maritain's rosy portrayal of a medieval society in which art and religion are fused, in which Baudelaire's 'modern' uncertainty over the origins of poetic beauty is inconceivable, is diametrically opposed to the fragmented technocratic world represented by the 'Bullfrogs' in *Advent*:

> 'No going back' they bay 'Prophets of doom to the wall' So
> Bullfrog say as Bullfrog is 'Expand Bigger Better Expand'
> 'Only' says Bullfrog so mincingly croaky 'Only
> growth counts' while grinding salt-mills grind on   (*PV*, p. 122)

In the lifeworld of *Advent* Baudelaire's question in 'Hymne à la beauté' is inescapable: 'And Beauty that other inferred so often desired in gift of none/is to be longed for but where may it be seen' (*PV*, p. 121). From a neo-Thomist perspective Mallarmé's answer to Baudelaire's question – his excessive, 'blasphemous' valorization of poetic 'Beauty' – is, in the last instance, underwritten by the increasingly secular nature of capitalist society, which Maritain, in 1924, saw as 'a crisis affecting our whole civilization'.[55] Indeed, Mallarmé's equation of 'Reality', 'Beauty' and 'Poetry' comes from a letter in which he recounts his struggle with, and defeat of, 'that creature of ancient and evil plumage – God'. In *Creative Intuition in Art and Poetry* Maritain quotes this passage as an illustration of pure art's 'experience of the void'.[56] Coffey's headnote to a selection of his poems included in a recent anthology of Irish poetry cites, and concurs with, Maritain's judgement. Poets, Coffey writes, may be valuably studied, as 'either hav[ing] faced the void or chosen otherwise'.[57] Coffey chooses otherwise; for the 'experience of the void' is, for the Neo-Thomist, a consequence of pure art's 'ardor of refusal', its 'angelism'. In the final section of *Advent* Coffey expresses Maritain's contrary spiritual 'countenance', 'the ardor of acceptance', which finally leads to an 'experience of the presence of God and the wounds of the redeemer':[58]

> Why is this hanging wreck forsaken the remedy for
>   world . . .
>
> Must it be this way
>
> How would one better have had it done   (*PV*, p. 148)

In conclusion, if the hiatus after *Third Person* arguably attests, to some degree, to the disjunction Coffey felt in the 1930s between the claims of aesthetic modernism and Catholicism, it is equally noteworthy that he resumed writing at the time of the New Critical canonization of modernism. *Missouri Sequence*, for all its formalist 'devices', repudiates New Criticism's belief in the self-referential character of modern poetry, that a text's significance is generated through the internal cross-references of 'spatial form'.[59] In contrast, the sequence, as we have seen, inaugurates Coffey's neo-Thomist inaugurates Coffey's neo-Thomist attempts to ground poetry in 'humankind', in non-aesthetic spheres of human activity: ethics, politics and history.

Notes

1 'The Notion of Order According to St Thomas Aquinas', *The Modern Schoolman*, 28, 1, 1949, pp. 1–18.

2 For an example of the reliance of Coffey's philosophical views on Maritain's in this period see Brian Coffey, 'The Philosophy of Science and the Scientific Attitude: I', *The Modern Schoolman*, 36, 1948, pp. 23–35. Coffey's argument in this essay follows, at times verbatim, Jacques Maritain, *Distinguish to Unite; Or, The Degrees of Knowledge*, fourth edition, trans. Gerald B. Phelan, Geoffrey Bles, London, 1959.

3 See Coffey's letter to MacGreevy, 30 March 1935, housed at Trinity College Dublin (TCD MS 8110/18).

4 See Jacques Maritain, *Art and Scholasticism with Other Essays*, trans. J.F. Scanlan, Sheed and Ward, London, 1930, p. 69.

5 Maritain, *Art*, pp. 90, 119.

6 Charles Baudelaire, *The Complete Verse*, ed. Francis Scarfe, Anvil, London, 1986, p. 81.

7 Jacques Maritain, *Creative Intuition in Art and Poetry: The A. W. Mellon Lectures in the Fine Arts*, Meridian, New York, 1955, p. 136.

8 'Brian Coffey, An Interview by Parkman Howe', *Éire/Ireland*, 13, 1, 1978, p. 119.

9 Percy Bysshe Shelley, *A Defence of Poetry or Remarks Suggested by an Essay Entitled 'The Four Ages of Poetry'*, *Shelley's Poetry and Prose*, eds. Donald H. Reiman and Sharon B. Powers, Norton, New York, 1977, p. 508.

10 Brian Coffey, 'Of Denis Devlin: Vestiges, Sentences, Presages', *University Review*, 2, 2, 1967, p. 12.

11 Maritain, *Art*, p. 7.

12 See Fredric Jameson, *Postmodernism; Or, The Cultural Logic of Late Capitalism*, Verso, London, 1991, p. 307; and Jerome McGann, *Black Riders: The Visible Language of Modernism,* Princeton University Press, Princeton, 1993, especially Ch. 1.

13 Coffey, 'Of Denis Devlin', p. 16; Brian Coffey, 'A Note on Rat Island', *University Review*, 3, 8, 1966, p. 26.

14 Brian Coffey, introduction, *Poems of Mallarmé*, trans. Brian Coffey, Menard/New Writers' Press, London/Dublin, 1990, p. 7.

15 Maritain, *Art*, pp. 91–2. The phrase 'poetry is ontology' is taken from Charles Maurras's *La Musique intérieure* (Maurras's words are an adaptation of Boccaccio's comment on the *Divina Commedia,* 'poetry is theology').

16 'Coffey, An Interview', p. 119.

17 Maritain, *Art*, pp. 93, 94.

18 Coffey, 'The Philosophy of Science and the Scientific Attitude: I', p. 24.

19 Coffey, 'The Philosophy of Science and the Scientific Attitude: I', p. 31.

20 In a response to Maximilian Beck, however, Coffey, citing Aquinas as his authority, does declare: ' "the beautiful" is transcendental'. ('Remarks on Maximilian Beck's "Existential Aesthetics", *The Modern Schoolman*, 25, 1948, p. 267.) Coffey's reflections in this article on artistic beauty as viewed from a Thomist perspective are, sadly, somewhat cursory.

21 See Coffey's letters to Thomas MacGreevy, 5 August 1952 and 19 December 1952 (TCD MSS 8110/36 and 8110/39), and the editors' introduction to this volume.

22 Coffey, introduction, *Poems of Mallarmé*, p. 7.

23 John Berryman, *Collected Poems 1937-1971*, ed. Charles Thornbury, Faber, London, 1990, p. 201.

24 See Victor Erlich, *Russian Formalism: History - Doctrine*, third edition, Yale University Press, New Haven, 1981, pp. 194-5. (I say the function of autobiography in the poem is 'akin' to the formalists' 'motivated device' in order to distance my use of the term from their term's purely synchronic dimension. The sequence, after all, is plainly concerned with the diachronic, the historicity of the literary object, as I argue below.)

25 Indeed, Coffey's ardent belief that a poem is produced by 'making' rather than through the vagaries of inspiration makes a formalist model a germane one for his work. As I noted above, Coffey's Thomism requires that, after Aristotle, making is the working of 'form' on matter. The similarity between Aristotle's *eidos* and the Russian formalists' 'form' is not lost on Erlich, who perceives in the latter 'a formative principle of dynamic integration and control' that is 'closely akin to Aristotle's *eidos*, which . . . connotes the "inward shaping power applied to raw matter" '. (Erlich, p. 189.)

26 'Coffey, An Interview', p. 114.

27 Stan Smith, 'On Other Grounds: The Poetry of Brian Coffey', *Two Decades of Irish Writing: A Critical Survey*, ed. Douglas Dunn, Carcanet, Manchester, 1975, p. 59.

28 James Joyce, *A Portrait of the Artist as a Young Man*, Grafton, London, 1977, p. 184.

29 See Terence Brown, *Ireland: A Social and Cultural History 1922-1985*, Fontana, London, 1985, pp. 168-9. Anthony Cronin reflects briefly on the 'external reasons' for MacGreevy's limited output in 'Thomas MacGreevy: Modernism not Triumphant', *Heritage Now: Irish Literature in the English Language*, Brandon, Dingle, 1982, pp. 155-60.

30 Quoted in Michael Smith, 'Irish Poetry Since Yeats: Notes Towards a Corrected History', *Denver Quarterly*, 5, 1971, p. 7.

31 TCD MS 8110/41. The passage is dated 11 January 1953.

32 W. B. Yeats, *The Poems*, ed. Daniel Albright, Dent, London, 1990, p. 375.

33 Coffey, 'A Note on Rat Island', p. 25.

34 Jack Morgan reports that, during his time at St Louis, Coffey's identity

as a poet was virtually unknown to his colleagues at the college. Only Leonard Eslick, a professor of philosophy at St Louis, and to whom the second section of *Missouri Sequence* is dedicated, knew about his work. See Morgan, '"Missouri Sequence": Brian Coffey's St Louis Years, 1947-1952', *Éire/Ireland*, 28, 4, 1993, pp. 100-13.

35 On the topic of female figures in Devlin, and their function in his modernist 'private language', see Alex Davis, '"Foreign and Credible": Denis Devlin's Modernism', forthcoming in *Éire/Ireland*, 30, 2, 1995; and Anne Fogarty's essay below.

36 Elsewhere Coffey has described 'the central element of Devlin's poetic activity' in words which bear fruitful comparison with this section of *Missouri Sequence*. Devlin's 'aim and search' is 'for what is most distant, most different and distinct from us humans.' His poetry 'attempt[s] to bring that most distant beyond all sensible or imagined horizons into human proximity' ('Denis Devlin: Poet of Distance', *Place, Personality and the Irish Writer*, ed. Andrew Carpenter, Colin Smythe, Gerrards Cross, 1977, p. 151).

37 Maritain, *Art*, p. 90; authors italics.

38 Renato Poggioli, *The Theory of the Avant-Garde*, trans. Gerald Fitzgerald, Harvard University Press, Cambridge, Mass., 1968, p. 204.

39 Poggioli, p. 204.

40 Maritain, *Creative Intuition*, pp. 137, 150.

41 See Ellman Crasnow, 'Poems and Fictions: Stevens, Rilke, Valéry', *Modernism 1890-1930*, eds. Malcolm Bradbury and James McFarlane, Penguin, Harmondsworth, 1976, p. 380. Maritain develops his notion of 'angelism' in *Three Reformers: Luther-Descartes-Rousseau*, Sheed and Ward, London, 1928, pp. 53-89.

42 See also *PV*, p. 135:
    Up some north face where cultures climbing rise only to fall
    not as skilled as flies on wall they come and they go
    never foresee the final fatal step of failed mastery
    blind to the speech of signs

43 Crasnow, p. 380.

44 Stan Smith, 'Against the Grain: Women and War in Brian Coffey's "Death of Hektor"', *Etudes Irlandaises*, 8, 1983, p. 171.

45 Coffey published his translation of *Un coup de dés* in 1965 (Dolmen Press, Dublin). As early as 1952 Coffey discusses *Advent* at some length in a letter to MacGreevy; see TCD MS 8110/38. For comments on the composition of *Advent* see 'Coffey, An Interview', pp. 113-4.

46 Malcolm Bowie, *Mallarmé and the Art of Being Difficult*, Cambridge University Press, Cambridge, 1978, p. 132.

47 Stéphane Mallarmé, *Dice Thrown Never Will Annul Chance*, trans. Brian Coffey, *Selected Poems and Prose*, ed. Mary Ann Caws, New Directions, New York, 1982, pp. 112-3, 127.

48 Jacques Derrida, 'Mallarmé', trans. Christopher Roulston, *Acts of Literature*, ed. Derek Attridge, Routledge, London, 1992, pp. 120-1. See also Derrida's

long essay on Mallarmé, 'The Double Session', in *Dissemination*, trans.
Barbara Johnson, Athlone, London, 1981, pp. 173-285. The connection
between modernist conceptions of language and more recent 'relativist'
or deconstructive theories is made in Gerald Graff, *Literature Against Itself*,
Chicago, Chicago University Press, 1979.

49 Mallarmé, *Dice Thrown*, pp. 124-5.
50 Joyce, pp. 194-5.
51 See Nelson Goodman, *Ways of Worldmaking*, Hackett, Indianapolis, 1978,
    p. 18: 'In a scientific treatise, literal truth counts most; but in a poem or
    novel, metaphorical or allegorical truth may matter more, for even a literally
    false statement may be metaphorically true and may make new associa-
    tions, change emphases, effect exclusions and additions'.
52 See Hans Robert Jauss, *Towards an Aesthetic of Reception*, trans. Timothy
    Bahti, University of Minnesota Press, Minneapolis, 1982.
53 Stéphane Mallarmé, 'To Henri Cazalis', 14 May 1967, trans. Bradford
    Cook, *Selected Poetry and Prose*, p. 88.
54 See Jürgen Habermas, 'Modernity versus Postmodernity', *New German
    Critique*, 22, 1981, pp. 3-14.
55 Maritain, *Art*, p. 142.
56 Maritain, *Creative Intuition*, p. 137.
57 Brian Coffey, 'About Poetry', *Dedalus Irish Poets: An Anthology*, Dedalus,
    Dublin, 1992, pp. 253-4. Of Mallarmé's *Un coup de dés* Coffey has said:
    'it's really the statement of somebody who sees the whole as a void bubble'.
    ('Coffey, An Interview' p. 118.)
58 Maritain, *Creative Intuition*, pp. 138-9. Maritain instances Paul Verlaine,
    T.S. Eliot and Charles Péguy as poets whose work voices 'the ardor of
    acceptance'.
59 See Joseph Frank's influential essay, 'Spatial Form in Modern Literature',
    Criticism: The Foundations of Modern Literary Judgement, eds. M. Scorer, J.
    Miles and G. McKenzie, California University Press, Berkeley, 1958.

'The Poetry is Another Pair of Sleeves':
Beckett, Ireland and Modernist Lyric Poetry[1]

Patricia Coughlan

'God love thee, Tom, and don't be minding me. I can't think of
Ireland the way you do. Ever, Sam'
(Letter from Samuel Beckett to Thomas MacGreevy,
31 January 1938).

Beckett's poetry and his relations with Ireland have both been rather
neglected subjects. This essay takes the occasion of the re-examination
of Irish modernist poetry in general to investigate the two by each
other's light, and to analyse Beckett's 1930s poetry in particular
within this context. The 'Irish Beckett' has fared less badly than the
poetry: after the invaluable pioneering work of J.C.C. Mays, and
John Harrington's book-length study, comes W.J. McCormack's
recent incisive probing of the problem of Beckett and Ireland, all
of which serve in a salutary way to complicate the narrative account
in Deirdre Bair.[2] But the sheer intensity and importance of
Beckett's reaction to Ireland can do with further exploration, especial-
ly as the too-often ignored or suppressed social and ideological
ground of his work. Against this background this essay addresses
the poetry Beckett wrote during the crucial decade from his early
twenties to his early thirties (i.e. 1929–1939), while his own
individual aesthetic project within European modernism was being
developed and tested in his work. A further task also needs to be
performed: to bring that body of writing into detailed relation with
the projects, gradually and variously diverging from his, of his fellow

Irish poets whose work is the subject of the rest of this volume, with whom he shared some common goals, and with whom he was in close contact at times during the period. Much thought and some research still remains to be done before we can achieve this second task; my aim is to move towards it by means of the discussion below.

I have said that the poetry remains neglected by criticism; it is worth reflecting on why this is so. There is a number of reasons, some good and others less acceptable. There is the general judgement that Beckett is a very much more distinguished writer of narrative and of drama than of poetry, and the view that the war marks a watershed in his development and his thirties' writings are more or less prentice-work. Both of these are, however, debatable points, as I shall go on to argue. More indisputable are the following factors: the uneven quality of the very early poetry, its relative inaccessibility, the uncertainty of the canon (some poems which appeared in the 1930s, later effectively suppressed by Beckett himself, others rumoured to be still awaiting publication in any form), the very long delay of the promised collected edition, and the poems' formidable intellectual difficulty, obscurity of allusion and quality of gnomic resistance to interpretation. There is, finally, the fact that the best work, from late in the decade, is in French: while it is probably not tactful to say so, this may have helped to deter many primarily Anglophone critics from venturing there.

Further, the existence of a long and very thoroughly researched book, by a scholar — Lawrence Harvey — who was privileged to have a wealth of information direct from Beckett, has unfortunately and paradoxically not stimulated a process of active ongoing interpretation of the poems.[3] The information in Harvey covers the whole range of facts which could conceivably be of relevance in a commentary, from the biographical background, intentions as to theme, and circumstances of composition of the work, on the one hand, to specifically literary considerations — such as allusions of all kinds and formal influences — on the other. A particular difficulty is that a close analysis of Harvey's text reveals both a large number of disambiguating decisions about semantic and syntactic matters, and a certain tendency to fall back upon biographical explanation (see my discussion below of the poem 'Arènes de Lutèce'). Beckett's poems are usually difficult texts, sometimes because of their obscure vocabulary both English and French, sometimes on account of a looseness in syntax which is a highly characteristic effect of this work, and sometimes from an equally Beckettian ellipsis both in syntax and in referential function. Is the reader to take it that Harvey's readings emerged during his conversations with Beckett, and how far should one, as a result, accept them and build one's own interpretation of the poems on them? Assuming that we do take these readings to be sanctioned by the author Beckett, then to adopt them to the exclusion of others which might be textually justifiable or possible would be to take a strongly intentionalist position and impoverish the texts. It is particularly ironic that this situation should arise in the interpretation of a writer so dedicated to opposing the whole institution of the unitary self and to its tyrannical continuities, and one who in his later narrative writings conducted a virtual test to destruction on the transcendental subject. Ann-Marie Lecercle has remarked on the centrifugal quality of Harvey's discussion of the collection *Echo's Bones*; he provides so much detail that it is hard for the reader to gain a sense of the poems (often fragile and volatile objects anyway) as general, properly aesthetic utterances, however unsatisfactory.[4]

Besides Harvey's nevertheless indispensable study, there is a surprisingly small body of criticism specifically on the poetry. This is of varying quality, and has tended to keep recommencing at the same point: it is still true – as John Pilling's searching and sensitive essay, the best single discussion, observed in 1976 – that we have little sense still of the 'shape' of the poetry as a whole.[5] A routine disclaimer, almost an apology, about the quality of the poetry in itself is almost universal at the outset of the discussion, as if by a self-denying ordinance we were obliged to pretend that the poems exist in some kind of generic vacuum and we could only judge them by pretending that Beckett had written nothing else.[6] In my view the result of this has been the loss of the opportunity offered by these texts, as a body of writing produced at the outset of his career, for a fuller understanding of his literary thought in general. Furthermore, the negative valuation of the poems which has prevailed is unwarranted in many cases, especially in the work of the later thirties. Certainly some of the poetry is not fully realized aesthetically, but that in itself, in the case of an author whose texts offer so much resistance to interpretation, affords a view of Beckett's distinctive vision and techniques in the making. Further, as I have said, there is room to develop our discussion of the Irish contexts of the early work, whether literary, cultural or to do with the formation of Beckett's aesthetic ideas in relation to and in contradistinction from his Irish background. W.J. Mc Cormack has remarked on the domination of Beckett criticism by what he calls 'rival campaigns' which link him to 'French existentialism, the British theatre, an Anglo-Irish tradition'; the institution of literary criticism is, unfortunately, at least as much governed by competing interest groups and unthought conventions as by disinterested intellectual attention to the disorganized, enigmatic, and half-apprehended processes of history and ideas in it.[7] My own attempt to gain a clearer view of the poetry, and the particular nature of its modernist aims, has been greatly helped by reflecting on Beckett's letters to MacGreevy during the decade insofar as they concern Beckett's own sense of the creative process, his discussion of painting and literature, his expressed responses to Ireland, social, topographical, and cultural-ideological, and his judgements at the time of the quality and direction of his own work.

It is, of course, part of the project of this whole volume to investigate what relations may be proposed between the master narratives of international modernism, with all their internal variations and contested issues, and the nature of Irishness and how it was framed in terms of institutions, on the one hand, and selfhoods, on the other. How may we locate Beckett in those relations? It was within the ideological macrocosm of newly assured Irish national legitimacy that he lived his formative years – he was fifteen in 1921 – and it was against this background that he had to embark upon his own early self-placing in terms of culture and ideology. As David Lloyd has persuasively argued, the narrative of Irish nationalism, which had been inaugurated as one of difference and otherness – a narrative perforce subordinate to that of hegemonic imperialism – from an early stage had itself begun to mirror the features of that dominant rhetoric which it sought to displace.[8] By their mirroring of the adversary's face, a perhaps unconscious and virtually unavoidable fate, Irish nationalists had after all been doing no more than seeking to assert the validity and viability of their own vision as a totalizing one which would be adequate and therefore genuinely alternative to that of their opponents. Post-colonialist theorists, Lloyd and others, argue that this replication or mirroring happened because both, albeit competing, visions and discourses were being produced within the framework of identity thinking, which held as self-evident the origin of meaning in a unitary self. From this point of departure, liberal ideology enjoined it upon individuals as an ethical imperative to seek unity between that self and a social world (even in Hegel, specifically a state) felt, however mutely or obscurely, to be ultimately benign.[9] Nationalism had to move towards, to promise the acquisition of, the institutions which defined legitimacy in late nineteenth-century terms. This process took place in spite of the other, revolutionary and creatively destabilizing moment within Irish nationalism (and also within specifically Literary Revivalism), whose disruptive energies are also apparent at this distance.

It is evident that this latter characteristic, of making or discerning a radical break in the given continuities, which allows us to perceive Irish nationalism between the 1840s and 1921 as the working out of a revolutionary process resembling those elsewhere in Europe and in the world, became less and less a prominent feature of the ideological and cultural life of Ireland from 1922, at the founding of the new state, onwards. Nationalism seemed, in terms of its own previous aims, to have succeeded: it had displaced and toppled the institutions of its oppressor, and could now become, like that quondam oppressor, itself a dominant ideology. The official over-printing at independence of British George VI postage stamps with 'Saorstát Éireann' is a piquant emblem of the situation; though we should perhaps acknowledge that our late twentieth-century awareness of the extent to which one form of hegemony may come to resemble, even mirror, another in all its repressive solidity is a form of hindsight.[10] Certainly, as Terence Brown again shows in his essay in this volume, by the 1930s the intense sense of newness and of more or less Utopian experimentation – which at least some Irish cultural revolutionaries had had in common with the prophets of the European avant-garde in the period of high modernism – no longer figured prominently in the public discourse of Irish letters and culture generally.

What of the other term in the nationalism-modernism relation? The danger of taking modernism as having a monolithic referent is rightly emphasized by other contributors here; but some tentative placing is necessary. Thus, attempting to classify and order the

various modernisms or modernist phases, Fredric Jameson considers
Charles Jencks's category of 'late modernism', in which one would
put the 'last survivals of a properly modernist view of art and the
world after the great political and economic break of the Depres-
sion', when various brands of social realism were gaining cultural
dominance. In this category Jameson finds

> names like Borges, Nabokov, Beckett, poets like Olson or
> Zukofsky, composers like Milton Babbitt, who had the misfortune
> to span two eras and the luck to find a time capsule of isolation
> or exile in which to spin out unseasonable forms.[11]

If we consider the 'engaged' poetry of the 1930s in England and
the still-urgent nationalist ideological imperatives enjoined on Irish
writers, especially, for example, the felt urgency to depict Irish local
realities — Corkery, O'Connor, the Abbey's testing for 'Peasant
Quality' — as variants of these social realisms, we can readily place
Beckett's implacable resistance to the Yeatsian influence in Irish
writing as a classic modernist refusal to allow what David Lloyd
calls 'ethical'[12] demands to deflect him from his commitment to
what were, after all, between 1930 and 1939 not yet evidently
'unseasonable forms'. The applicability of post-colonialist theory
to the Irish situation in general and in particular to Ireland's literature
in English is, of course, debatable. But the underpinnings of that
theory, in its more sophisticated forms, from the German
philosophical tradition and in particular from the Critical Theory
of the Frankfurt School provide, insofar as they deal with self-world
or subject-object mediation, very suggestive insights into the prob-
lems of disintegrating subjectivity in modernity. These problems
were recognized and faced, in different ways, by the Irish modern-
ists of the second generation in their poetic practice; Beckett himself
argued in 1934 that they were evaded by the neo-Revivalists. The
nature of subjectivity is necessarily a central preoccupation of lyric
poets, being the ground whereon lyric is built.

In that essay 'Recent Irish Poetry', considered in detail by other
contributors and now being understood as an Irish modernist
manifesto, Beckett is eloquent on the 'flight from self-awareness'
entailed by Revivalist thematics with their 'cut-and-dried sanctity
and loveliness': the nationalists' mission of constructing and express-
ing a national identity is the antithesis of Beckett's sense of the self

as process and of the gulf between the welter of consciousness and the equally disunited world.[13] He insists in the first paragraph (prefiguring Lyotard and his concept of the *événement* rather as Adam in the Bible is said to prefigure Christ) on a 'thing that has happened', namely the 'breakdown of the object'. He then, with rhetorical scorn, offers the reader the option of thinking of this as 'the breakdown of the subject' if that is easier. In other words, he insists on the processual qualities of *both* self *and* world. His account of Proust three years before was already emphasizing the constantly changing character of both subject and object, with its explanation of how the action of time on the subject results in 'an unceasing modification of his personality, whose permanent reality, if any, can only be apprehended by a retrospective hypothesis' and its definition of habit as 'the countless treaties concluded between the countless subjects that constitute the individual and their countless correlative objects'.[14] Reading Schopenhauer, who proposes to dissolve both the body-mind and self-world dichotomies, and whose language pervades his writings in this period, can only have worked to exacerbate his detachment.

Dougald MacMillan rather surprisingly defines Beckett's work in *Echo's Bones* (1935) as antithetical to the project of modernism in its various forms, marking in particular Beckett's distance from both Pound's and Eliot's strategies. He finds a restless, 'dynamic' quality in the work which he sees as an implicit rejection of imagism and of centripetal poetry whose centre is metaphor.[15] He rightly notices Beckett's insistence on the relation between terms and not the substance of the terms themselves, a point to which I shall return. But he is on shakier ground when implicitly defining modernism by its moment of *com*position, its claims to hegemony and self-constitution as a new master-narrative, rather than by what one might argue is its equally characteristic and constitutive moment of *decom*position and radical disjunction from a totalizing aesthetic. (Or, one might say, he is thinking of Eliot's modernism rather than Joyce's, and at that of Eliot's criticism rather than his earlier poetry.) In fact that aspect of modernism which is mythopoeic is deeply uncongenial to Beckett's mind. He is quite outside the kinship of Eliot and Yeats in shoring fragments against their ruins or seeking Unity of Being, just as he cannot share his Irish contemporaries' enthusiasm for the nation. In the letters we see him towards the end of the decade regretfully but gracefully distancing himself from MacGreevy's positing of, and willing identification with, forms of national aesthetic expression: in January 1938 he responds equivocally to MacGreevy's essay on Jack Yeats, apologizing for his own 'chronic inability to understand as member of any proposition a phrase like "the Irish people"'. It is characteristic, however, of the strong affection he shows towards MacGreevy that, in a turn of phrase perhaps humorously, though not sarcastically, Hiberno-English he adds, at the end of the letter: 'God love thee, Tom, and don't be minding me. I can't think of Ireland the way you do. Ever, Sam' (31 January 1938). As his eventual opting in to Ireland in 1941 shows, MacGreevy, born in Tarbert, County Kerry, son of a primary teacher and a policeman, shared even with the likes of Daniel Corkery a sense of belonging, an identification of things Irish, however dismaying, being his, 'ours'; Beckett, for a whole range of reasons, could not.

It is worth recalling his actual social position in Dublin, where on reaching adulthood he found himself on the margins in several senses: by background a Protestant in a state increasingly and aggressively Catholic in ideology, by conviction an atheist in a family devoutly low-church and Evangelical, member of the suburban middle class in a cultural milieu officially devoted to enthusiastic imaginative celebration of the rural peasantry, bohemian and cosmopolitan by taste and inclination, and, in a household governed by respectability and propriety, valuing the life of the intellect and the arts above bourgeois professional status or security. 'They want me to wear a bowler hat', he complained to MacGreevy upon one of his returns from Paris; and, more plaintively: 'I don't want to be a professor.' This marginality and the resultant self-alignment athwart Dublin social life in almost all of its available manifestations is quite clear in the Belacqua of both *More Pricks than Kicks* and *Dream of Fair to middling Women*, and no doubt it contributes to Beckett's negative aesthetic judgements in 'Recent Irish Poetry'; but his position is first of all a principled and intellectually coherent one, and of a piece with his radical and philosophically well-grounded scepticism. He scornfully convicts the antiquarians (followers of Yeats) of a belief that 'the first condition of any poem is an accredited theme, and that in self-perception there is no theme'. From this relegation to the 'circumference' only MacGreevy, Devlin and Coffey are given partial exemptions, in Devlin's and Coffey's case based on their potential rather than actual achievements. The terms in which he praises MacGreevy — whom with acute critical perception he places in a position intermediate between the 'antiquarians' and the 'others' — will serve as the best point of departure for our examination of Beckett's own poetic project in these years. MacGreevy, he says, 'neither excludes self-perception from his work nor postulates the object as inaccessible. But he knows how to wait for the thing to happen . . . And when it does . . . whatever happens to be dispensed, *gile na gile* or empty hearths, it is the act and not the object of perception that matters' (*Disjecta*, p. 74).

This privileging of the act rather than the object of perception is echoed in *Dream of Fair to middling Women* where a concern with the relations between terms rather than the terms themselves is celebrated in a virtuoso passage as the only *modus vivendi*:

> poised between God and the Devil, Justine and Juliette, at the dead point, in a tranquil living at the neutral point . . . For me the one real thing is to be found in the relation: the dumb-bell's bar, the silence between my eyes, between you and me . . . I can only know the real poise at the crest of the relation rooted in the unreal postulates, God-Devil, Masoch-Sade (he might have spared us that hoary old binary) . . . On the crown of the passional relation I live, dead to oneness, non-entity and unalone. . . . (*Dream*, pp. 27-8)[16]

This recalls the emptying out of the plenums of tradition performed by the modernist avant-gardes in general, and the surrealists and Dadaists in particular, down to the Sadeian references, which come from the period's vocabulary of resistance to normative bourgeois identity. This inventive refusal of the 'unreal postulates' finds its own flowering in those aporias, the staging of which is so intensely characteristic of Beckett's imagination and in which his skill was to grow in the various genres from decade to decade.

He insists upon the breakdown of a notionally pre-existing unity; this can be recognized as the founding bourgeois accommodation of self and world, achieved *par excellence* by classic-realist works of art, and which further is structurally parallel to Geulincx's preestablished harmonies, themselves to be the objects of Beckett's ironic protest in *Murphy*. He sees the Revivalists' recourse to myth ('Oisin, Cuchulain, Maeve, Tir na n-Óg . . . the Crone of Beare') as an unwarranted and inauthentic regression to enslaving forms. For him the need for radical breaks and fissures is not past: the imperative is to resist a unity he sees as like the waters closing over his head, the forming all over again of a seamless world of 'cut-and-dried sanctity and loveliness'. The very early text 'For Future Reference', said to be a dream-record, presents a narrative of the terror of drowning in or scarification by the rocks surrounding a deep pool, into which the narrator fears being thrown by one of a succession of jeering male authority figures, the first a chemist, the second a jeering, predatory anatomy professor, the third a mathematician (a figure identified as based either on Beckett's father or on his Portora swimming and mathematics teacher by Harvey and Bair respectively). Here, by extension, we can see an Oedipus in the making, rehearsing as yet only one phase of his destined plot, the fear of threatening, castrating fathers. The other phase, of fantasized symbolic parricide and union with a perhaps equally threatening feminine, is yet to follow, and does indeed manifest itself in the poems of the next four or five years; in 'Recent Irish Poetry' we see the break with the fathers of Irish Revivalism being staged with aggressive decisiveness.

In the long view, Mays's identification of Beckett's scepticism as especially Anglo-Irish, placing him in the tradition-rejecting lineage of Swift and Shaw, among others, is of course right.[17] There is a further specific content to his style and vision, however, which is the product of other influences. These are partly to do with the course of study he followed both officially at Trinity College, Dublin and later, concentrating on European rather than English literature, and with a strong philosophical emphasis. The letters of the mid-1930s show him only then, in his late twenties, reading English writers, especially novelists, of the eighteenth and nineteenth centuries (Richardson, Johnson, Fielding, Dickens); the texts which left the earlier and deeper impression on him were evidently those of Dante and Provençal poetry, of Racine and the German and French philosophers, and, however antithetically it is often invoked in his work, the Bible. His extensive reading during the thirties of the Austrian nominalist philosopher Fritz Mauthner — the '*Whoroscope* Notebook' has his many longhand transcriptions of lengthy passages — will have confirmed his existing position of scepticism.[18] The loss of positive content in language itself, matching the hollow claim of literary forms to ideological plenitude, was leading philosophers including Wittgenstein to Mauthner's signpost pointing towards 'laughter and silence'. Beckett's own steely rejection of false consolation led him both to extremes of disruption in his writing, and to amused acknowledgements of his own steadfast intellectual asceticism, such as the engaging remark to MacGreevy, while attacking 'Jesuitical' poems (referring to Mallarmé), that 'I suppose I'm a dirty low-church P.[rotestant; *sic*] even in poetry: concerned with integrity in a surplice' (18 October 1932). There is an irony in the atheist Beckett's lack of appreciation of Mallarmé, the atheist poet so admired by the Catholic writers MacGreevy, Coffey and Devlin. Further, the terms of the self-description are striking: while conducting a purely literary meditation he comically gives himself a label from the rhetoric of Irish sectarianism, which at the time could be virulent.[19] This derivation of an intellectual position from the givens of family religious background is mostly a joke, but not entirely so; the remark shows a very Irish and rueful sense of the ineradicability of confessional origins, at least in the eyes of the Irish majority.

Apart from his actual life in a literary Paris still devoted to creative *épatement* of the bourgeoisie, Beckett's versions of Crevel and Breton, made early in 1932, show his thorough exposure to the surrealists' radical eschewing of privileged topics, discourses or registers in poetry. In the short term this may perhaps only have increased the pressure on his own imagination, with its tendency both to seek and simultaneously to disparage forms of potential order; and the systematic and philosophical character of his mind must have limited the degree of his satisfaction with the playful automatist high jinks of surrealism and his sense of their adequacy.[20] Besides, his apprehension of the indivisibility of consciousness from material being and of the ferocious energies of the unconscious must have been all too vivid, tormented as he was by his own body's painful announcements of mental distress, translated into its own speech as fistulas, night terrors, and bouts of suicidal despair. For all his subscribing to the idea of 'Orphic creation' advanced by the 'Verticalist Manifesto' in Jolas's *transition* 1932, his own eventual direct recourse to psychoanalysis as a suffering analysand puts him in a rather different position from that of, say, André Breton, with his glad annexation of Freud's arguments to his own advocacy of the inner self, and at a distance from the willed experiments of the group in the simulation of states of mental disturbance.[21]

In this connection, Beckett's way of talking in the letters about his own poetry and about the creative process is revealing: it emphasizes the involuntary ('Orphic?') nature of the event of composition, and it simultaneously relates the process of composition metaphorically to the body, especially to sexual release, sometimes to disease. Thus: 'I'm enclosing the only bit of writing that has happened to me since Paris' (referring to a version of 'Serena I', letter of 8 October 1932) and one of the French poems 'dictated itself to me' (27 January 1938). In August 1932, discussing the merits of his own poems, he judges 'all the early ones − the Caravan ones' as 'talk' (except *Whoroscope*); later that year, making an exception also of 'Moly', alias 'Yoke of Liberty', from this negative judgement, he sets up an opposition between poems which seem merely willed (his word is *construits*) and those which do not, but 'represent a necessity'. He uses images of dirt and infection to characterize the successful poems 'the 3 or 4 [*sic*] I like and that seem to me to have been drawn down against the really dirty weather of one of these fine days into the gutter of the "private life", Alba and the long Enueg and Dortmunder, even Moly, do not and never have given me that impression of being *construits* . . . ' These, he says, have been written 'above an abscess and not out of a cavity' and are 'a statement not a description of heat in the spirit to compensate for pus in the spirit'. These disease metaphors ('abscess', 'pus') are an implicit rejection of conventional dualisms which would segregate an intellectual-aesthetic sphere from the physical, and strikingly replicate the exact form of his own acute physical illnesses in those years (literal abscesses and pus). Poetic creation is associated, then, with suffering, despair and deracination: in the same letter he quotes a couplet from Eluard:

> Quel est le rôle de la racine?
> Le désespoir a rompu tous ses liens.

The actual production of text, however, is also associated with ejaculation. He calls the production of two poems composed within a short space of time 'a double-yoked orgasm in months of aspermatic nights and days' (21 December 1931). The letters make little verbal doodles − in doggerel − about a sexualized creative process, with a comic-grotesque conceit of the brain as an erectile organ, even while 'my algos is puss in the corner', that is, emotional suffering is temporarily suspended.[22] He makes jokes about the Freudian, or mock-Freudian, symbolic equation of faeces and art object, each as something precious to its creator and something physically produced (or perhaps on other occasions blocked), for example the elaborately casual and self-deprecating remark in an early letter telling MacGreevy that four poems had been accepted for *European Caravan*: 'Bronowski [the co-editor, with Reavey and Putnam] says he is using three turds from my central laboratory [scored through, but so as to remain legible] lavatory' (7 July 1930). This body-talk with its studied crudity is one of the ways he marks his sense of difference not only from the life of Foxrock and its analogues, but also on occasion, as the letters show, from the contained polite dignity of his Irish contemporaries' poetic utterance. On 9 October 1933 he writes to MacGreevy about a meeting with Brian Coffey and Denis Devlin:

> I'm afraid I didn't get much kick out of Coffey and Devlin, their pockets full of calm precious poems . . . I gave them the Enueg [*Enueg I*] and we went to the Gallery (grosse erreur). . . . Coffey seemed to find the Enueg highly delightful amusing enlightening. Devlin didn't know what an algum tree was and I couldn't enlighten him . . .

In his continuing dialogue with MacGreevy he also makes a habit of commenting admiringly on the heroic representation of male figures in Renaissance religious painting; I would read this insistence on the sexualized body as a combination of the schoolboy's rebellious gesture, still being elicited by the various repressions of his Irish upbringing, and the impulses of the period towards systematic blasphemy and various forms of outrage against decency. Thus, on 22 December 1931:

> I've been three times to look at the new Perugino Pieta in the National Gallery here. . . . A dream-laden, potent Xist [*sic*] and a passion of tears for the waste. . . . But a lovely chee[r]y[23] Xist full of sperm, and the women touching his thighs . . .

It is difficult to imagine how such passages as this may have fallen on MacGreevy's ear, with his capacity for delicate reverential attention to art and his strong religious feeling. Six years later, writing from Germany at the beginning of 1937, Beckett regards with a similar attention the works he had just seen at Sanssouci: 'the Mabuses are sublime, there is one big bevelled penis, I forget whether Adam's or Neptune's'. In the same context of enthusiasm and even gaiety, he finds an insouciant group of female figures: 'And the Caryatids are all laughing, pretending to be bowed down' (18 January 1937). However facetious such passages may be, it is nevertheless clear that his figuration for art is a specifically male potency, a 'spermatic' production.[24] This is all aggressively masculinist, as are also the speaking selves of most of the poems up to 1936 and some later, and the Belacqua of the thirties' narratives; it is a quality which I shall argue is, however, considerably tempered in the 1937–39 poems. The laughing Caryatids, adjacent in his letter, imply his sense, here a charming and delighted one, of the coolness and envied paradoxical impenetrability of women. This is a theme evident elsewhere in the work of the period – clearly, for instance, in the poem 'à elle l'acte calme', and in the two pendents 'Dortmunder' and 'Alba'. It is one of the countercurrents running in the turbulent stream of mingled desire, disgust and anxiety about the feminine which sweeps along the masculine speakers of several of his works: yearning for and fear of erotic-infantile attachment to, and being overpowered by, a powerful feminine.[25] His analysis with Wilfrid Bion would cause him intense pain by dwelling on these themes, but it did begin to show him a route out of misery.[26]

    This analysis during 1934 and 1935 – pursued very intensively, sometimes at an astonishing six sessions a week – has been usefully discussed by Didier Anzieu.[27] Anzieu finds parallels between Beckett's working out of his creative philosophy in the thirties and forties and Bion's account of the 'vortex' of inward selfhood. Bion, who was not much older than Beckett at the time of their dealings with each other, had yet to develop his own, later important, theories, and was working within Kleinian perspectives. Melanie Klein's accounts of the self's defence against fundamental anxieties in what she calls 'the paranoid–schizoid position' by 'mechanisms of dissociation, denial, omnipotence, idealization and projective identification' seem (perhaps apart from the projective identification) a strikingly good description of the lyric personae, taken collectively, in Beckett's 1930s' poems.[28]

I turn to the nature of the material itself. The vast majority of the poems in English belong to the first half of the decade, and the period can be further divided into phases as far as Beckett's poetic production is concerned: there is a first phase, inaugurated in 1930 with *Whoroscope* and two other poems, then a group of four appeared together in the 1931 collection of experimental work, *The European Caravan*, and a further two appeared individually in magazines in that year. Then thirteen poems, the first nine of which had been completed before the end of 1934, were gathered and carefully juxtaposed in the 1935 collection *Echo's Bones*. This is the bulk of the poems in English: 1936 and 1938 produced only a further two, 'Cascando' and 'Ooftish' respectively. The most important works written from 1936 to 1939 are the group of twelve short lyrics in French, written between 1937 and 1939, which did not appear until after the war in 1946.

In the first phase, there are, then, nine very early pieces which did not find their way into *Echo's Bones*. These are: 'For Future Reference', 'From the Only Poet to a Shining Whore', 'Return to the Vestry', the four from the *European Caravan* – namely 'Hell Crane to Starling', 'Casket of Pralinen for the Daughter of a Dissipated Mandarin', 'Text', and 'Yoke of Liberty' – the sonnet Belacqua addresses to the Smeraldina in *Dream* (70–1), which is a rather special case, and another poem in *Dream*, 'Calvary by Night'. Few of these nine are successful in themselves; nevertheless a more determined and widespread analysis of them would pay dividends.[29] Beckett chose to exclude all eight from Calder's *Collected Poems 1930-1978*, which has made them difficult to find for readers who do not have easy access to the original. Harvey very helpfully provides texts of all the poetry, including these – in a category of 'Jettisoned Poems' – but they are dispersed throughout his discussion and consequently gaining an impression of them as a whole is difficult: this accidental constraint makes the permeability of the poem-commentary boundary in all criticism, *pace* formalism's well-wrought urns, even more apparent than usual.[30]

With the exception of the *Dream* sonnet, these earliest poems are clogged, obscure exercises in multiple allusiveness, often furiously choleric in tone and jagged with awkward movements which seem aimed at undermining the lyric speaker even at the very moment he is being constituted. They lurch uncertainly from irony to irony, constantly offering, and then ironically snatching away, instants of prospective beauty, order or fulfilment. This passage from 'Casket of Pralinen for the Daughter of a Dissipated Mandarin' (1931) will illustrate the less than effective handling of the procedure:

> . . . Now me boy
> take a hitch in your lyrical loinstring.
>
> What is this that is more
> than the anguish of Beauty,
> this gales of pain that was not prepared
> in the caves of her eyes? . . .
>
> Tonight her gaze would be less
> Than a lark's barred sunlight.

And more in a similar plangent lyric tone, ending:

> Fool! do you hope to untangle
> the knot of God's pain?

— which is immediately followed by:

> Melancholy Christ that was a soft one!
> Oh yes I think that was perhaps just a very little inclined to be
>   rather too self-conscious.
>
> Schluss!
> Now ladies and gents
> a chocolate-coated hiccough to our old friend.
> Put on your hats and sit easy.
>   ('Casket', 25-30, 32-3, 43-8; *schluss* means 'an end')[31]

The texture of these *Caravan* poems is a veritable montage, each passage violently at odds with its predecessor and successor. Montage is often described as the quintessential modernist technique, but even among modernist works Beckett's early texts are exceptionally close to Eisenstein's classic conception of sequence as a succession of disruptions, explained in his 1929 essays. As film historians point out, Eisenstein 'viewed montage as a kind of collision or conflict, particularly between each shot and its successor. He sees each shot as having a kind of potential energy . . . [which] becomes kinetic when the first shot collides with the succeeding one. . . . This conflict produced the tense, violent rhythms that became an Eisen-stein trademark.'[32] It is argued that this conflict 'was also important to Eisenstein because he took it to be an expression, in the realm of images, of the Marxist's dialectical principle'. While Beckett does not identify his own method as dialectical, its valuing of breaks and ruptures above continuity nevertheless keeps constantly before our consciousness the 'new thing that has happened' (*Disjecta*, p. 70) to lyric utterance. It is, however, unfortunately true that in many of the very early poems both the poetic method and the handling of theme emphasize disjunction in such a forced way as to wreck the whole enterprise of sequential or comprehensible utterance. This is the case in three of the four *European Caravan* poems, for example, all except 'Yoke of Liberty', which escapes it for reasons I suggest below. It is true to a somewhat lesser extent of *Whoroscope*, where the Descartes material acts as a unifying narrative, as Johannes Hedberg points out in his very useful discussion of the poem.[33]

The poems up to and including *Echo's Bones* are also full of often bewildering allusions: Dantean, biblical, Greek mythological, and orientalizing: in fact almost everything *but* Oisín, Maeve, and the Crone of Beare. Beckett's resort in this early phase of his work to such 'colours' recapitulates the earlier history of modernism; he pro-gresses towards finding these effects more or less dispensable by the late thirties. Many practitioners of the various arts in modernism's first generation sought, especially in their earlier work, to estrange the reader's, viewer's, or listener's response by exotic and deliberately esoteric references, and thus to decompose the oppressive unities of the bourgeois phenomenal world.[34] The strategy was already present in *fin de siècle* aesthetics and in French symbolist writings, especially in the work of Rimbaud, whom, as we have seen, Beckett admired much more than Mallarmé.[35] As the decade advances Beckett develops instead his more characteristic resources, of spare laconic syntax and verbal patterns involving repetition with ironic variation.

What all the poems have in common is the continual disperse-ment of the lyric subject of the *énoncé*, which is matched by the wilful scattering of the lineaments of the phenomenal world into disorder.[36] There have been some, I believe ill-judged, attempts to compose these shards into a coherent narrative. For example, Dougald McMillan (1976) reads the whole collection *Echo's Bones*, starting from a rather literal interpetation of the Ovidian story to which the title alludes, as devoted to the theme of lost love, an alleged episode of which in Beckett's life (evidently the relationship with Peggy Sinclair) McMillan treats as the *clef* to unlock the puzzles of the book — as if it were a *roman*. The psychological origins of the poems, so far as they are capable of being discussed, are in any case evidently much more complex and dialectical than McMillan allows. One might point out that the lyric speakers in the poems are anxious to an exactly equal extent about the failure of attachment — the loss of love — and the failure of *de*tachment: erotic desire and longing are matched by moments of recoil and fear of destructive immersion in the Other.[37] Besides the emphasis on the relations between terms (subject and object, body and mind, self and world, 'Shilly and Shally', son and mother) we should keep in mind Belacqua's hilarious attempts near the beginning of *Dream* to muster an adequate sense of loss at the departure of the Smeraldina on the Dun Laoghaire boat (*Dream*, pp. 3-6).[38]

All the poems of the period construct — with varying clarity of vision yet quite in accordance with his own 1934 requirement for 'self-awareness' — one isolated self, a frantic centrifuge, faced with many other, usually female, subjects or potential subjects, often defensively debased and crushed in the representation into mere objects, or more rarely, elevated in beauty, grace and composure above the narrators. The selves in these poems yaw between attempts at mastery and abject self-abasement, while simultaneously, as we have seen, oscillating between moments of lyrical poise and dishevelled interior antagonism and self-mockery. In theme, the texts perform an intense, even obsessive, rehearsal of male-female erotic confrontations, quite without arriving at any reconciling mediation. One might easily anatomize their misogyny, but to see Beckett's representation of sexual relations as offering him the paradigm case in which to interrogate and break apart the composed surfaces of the unitary, controlled self, is I believe, a more productive strategy.

It is worth remarking that these 1930s' poems attend more to sexual love and male-female relations than any other body of Beckett's work; this theme provides an especially clear lens through which to view the development of his competence in the genre. Partly this is because his preoccupation at this time with the obligation to arrive at adequate representations of interiority meets and clashes creatively with the central role played in Western culture by the sexual imperative to join together individual selves, those discrete particles, in pairs, with all the familiar and powerful resonances of cosmic complementarity (which, however, coexists with a familiar asymmetry in terms of power and status between women and men). The poems certainly exhibit signs of the mixture of fear, disgust and felt alienness of women all too familiar in masculine attitudes, adolescent and adult; we should also recall that modernism's great iconic works, in their different ways, are not themselves free from these disfigurements of misogyny. It is, however, striking that in *Dream* the anti-feminine invective is accompanied by an equally virulent self-denigration on the part of the protagonist Belacqua, an emotion not so prevalent in the poems, at least in those from *Whoroscope* on.

In many of the *Echo's Bones* poems Beckett systematically appropriates the whole system of Provençal poetry, itself largely or wholly predicated on the importance of a codified male-female encounter. As Lawrence Harvey shows in very helpful detail, this is done by a series of pastiches of individual forms: the *aubade*, the *serena* or evening-poem, the *enueg* or *planh* – the poet's complaint against the world about his desperate situation.[39] The Provençal influences play an important formally sustaining role in the collection, and offer, as Harvey well says, such resources as the constitutively discontinuous movement of the *Enueg* form, which answers so well to the pressing inherent demands of Beckett's own aesthetic. On the level of theme, by means of a courtly vocabulary and a set of conventional gestures which are heavily laced with scarcely adapted metaphors of religious adoration and desire for the divine, the originals compose an idealized vision of transfigured sexual desire. In these fictions the wished-for unity of self with self (subject and its other) makes up a powerful totality; it is highly characteristic of Beckett's imagination that he chooses such a set of conventions as his framework, and combines it with many allusions to Dante's version of idealized sexual love precisely in order to resist that world-formation *à deux* which is the central ethical and emotional presupposition of this tradition and of the subsequent centrality of the *topos* of romantic attachment in the European literatures.[40]

The very early writings repeatedly stage Stephen Dedalus-like encounters of a young male poet-protagonist with female figures characterized as Other, in classic and stereotypical struggles which rehearse the simultaneous need, and fear, on the man's part, of a kind of immersion in an overhwelming feminine which is matter (and mater) itself. The 1929 short story 'Assumption', Beckett's first work published in *transition*, deals with an initiation such as this, played out with a typical 'hesitation betwen fear and desire'.[41] More achieved works such as the poems 'Alba' and 'Dortmunder', significantly placed on facing pages in *Echo's Bones*, complicate such encounters: 'Alba' is the nearest Beckett comes to a capacity to represent the erotic as a route to, rather than away from, the ideal; but it is notable that in his hands what constitutes that ideal has become a blankness, a silence after the 'tempest of emblems' (*CPB*, p. 15). A certain dry apprehension of the emptiness of the mere structures persisting like the bones of Echo after the demise of values, especially of tenable collective or communal ones, becomes more and more evident throughout these poems, recalling the Saussurean axiom that 'in language there are only differences; there are no positive terms'. Thus, the many invocations of the aesthetically and metaphysically ordered and luminous (albeit morally flawed and corrupt) worlds of Dante only throw up in a clearer light Beckett's own present conviction of a complete absence of reliable system, whether metaphysical, moral, or aesthetic. It is this discovery which is rehearsed in 'Alba' (1931), early though it is. The ceremony of revelation, the Dantesque angelic vision, does not happen; instead what with hindsight we can see as a characteristic Beckettian aporia occurs: the desired woman's beauty produces a blank sheet and 'bulk dead', instead of the conventional 'sun' and 'unveiling'; the 'tempest of emblems' is quite obscured – like the whole inheritance of European poetic devices and the vision they were developed to express.

The pastiche sonnet Belacqua addresses to the Smeraldina in *Dream* deserves attention in this connection. In it, by contrast, the moment of ecstatic conjunction is duly envisaged in proper form (both thematically and prosodically). Belacqua, speaking in the parodic persona of the enamoured sonneteer, acknowledges his inadequacy as a single self, finding in his 'dark confused soul' the 'certitude that I cannot be whole' unless 'I be consumed and fused in the white heat / Of her sad finite essence' (*Dream*, pp. 70–1). Having undergone this process of erotic immolation, the couple will be granted, by virtue of their new wholeness – described by figures of assimilation into the sky and into elemental, cosmic fire – a stellar apotheosis: 'Like syzygetic stars, supernly bright,/Conjoined in the One and in the Infinite!' This very credible essay in the philosophical idealization of eros (a skilful pastiche recalling Sidney, Donne and Meredith, which is rather unjustly disparaged by Pilling) is, of course, surrounded in *Dream* by sardonic distancing, labelled in advance 'some of the finest Night of May hiccupsobs' and succeeded by a passage of equally perfectly phrased 'Nausicaa'-inspired prose.[42] Yet the effect of the sonnet is somehow not quite eradicated by these juxtapositions: it remains as evidence of Beckett's preoccupation with versions of philosophy's old problem of the One and the Many in terms of the self-world struggle in general and the problems of inter-subjectivity and sexuality in particular.

The figures of female power constructed in these poems are more often transcendent and enigmatic than merely dominant (versions of the terrible mother become more frequent in Beckett's work of the 1940s onwards).[43] The early 'Yoke of Liberty' (1931), the best of the Caravan poems, does, however, propose a predatory woman as sexual antagonist. Its alternative title is 'Moly', the herb Ulysses carried to protect him from the power of Circe: the poet imagines himself as armed with a power (the poetic faculty itself?) which prevents him from succumbing to the woman's attraction, but which is also a kind of burden (the paradoxical 'yoke of liberty' of the other title). Using atmospheric colour in a way similar to 'Dortmunder', the poem constructs the woman as a grey moon-goddess; it uses a chain of displaced metaphoric terms for the female genitals: 'lips', 'loop', 'wound', 'snare', 'crescent'. In a very brief compass of thirteen lines, it sets up, in subtly shifting perspectives, a gender confrontation in which the woman's power, while natural, animal-like, beautiful, 'will be broken' by the poet's capacity for detachment. He is one of the 'sensitive wild things' endangered by her 'grey, grave silk crouch' (a vocabulary recalling that used about the woman in 'Alba'). This poem addresses a theme similar to that in the later 'à elle l'acte calme', namely the problem presented for the self by its twin and antithetical impulses towards detachment and attachment. Here, as so often in earlier European love-poetry, but not in Beckett's poems from 1937 on, the fascinated description of the female Other serves to give boundaries to the speaking, masculine, self, who can define himself as that which eludes her threat of incorporation ('lips', 'loop', 'snare', even 'wound' – the last temptation, of compassion for the ultimately pitiable). The poem strikingly avoids the ranting, sneering tone and wild oscillation of others in the *Caravan* group, but is still dependent on an erotic thematics which Beckett will pass beyond.

'Serena II' (*CPB*, pp. 234) stands out amid the work of the decade in that it is concerned with a maternal figure, or more accurately splinters of one, consisting of a pet Kerry Blue bitch in pup, the earth as mother, and at the close a human mother, kneeling by whom the male protagonist says his night prayers. The resistance to linear sequence (the poem unreels backwards in time, ending in early childhood) and to unitary characterization in the poem, should be noted: too often interpreters, faced admittedly with texts of formidable difficulty, seek to recompose what Beckett has very carefully put asunder. This poem is also unusual in that it ranges over Irish landscapes, from those of the West (Clew Bay and Croagh Patrick) to 'Meath shining through a chink in the hills'. Among Beckett's works of the period it comes nearest to a symbolic deployment of the geography of Ireland which might be assimilated to the use of scenery and topography in Revivalist texts and the translations of early Irish material; it also shows interesting resemblances to MacGreevy's handling of landscape and place-names generally. Meath, besides 'shining' in an unreachable distance, is also described as a land of 'fairy tales'; half-suggesting its ancient role as the seat of Irish kingship; the language of the Mayo passage invokes equally blurred, distant images of numinousness, associated with the bitch's time of delivery (ll. 16 ff.) The bitch is simultaneously the narrator's pet (there shall be no loss of panic between a man and his dog') and an instance of femininity and the maternal (the 'she' who 'took me up on to a watershed' is not distinguishable from the 'she' who 'drops her young'); likewise the narrator himself shifts between adulthood – 'posses of larches there is no going back on' – and an infancy secured by rituals, luminously constructed in the closing passage:

> the fairy tales of Meath ended
> so say your prayers now and go to bed
> your prayers before the lamps start to sing behind the larches
> here at these knees of stone
> then to bye-bye on the bones.

Irony and disillusionment, however, are never far: the displacements between canine and human mothers are intentionally grotesque, the distant glory of 'Meath' shines only in the child's deluded vision, and the maternal knees in the poem are 'of stone': cold, hard, and associated with death.[44] Yet, in spite of Beckett's own verdict that it did not 'represent a necessity' (letter, 18 October 1932) the poem's sardonic harshness does not quite displace its poignancy – an effect present throughout his writings up to the last.

Matching 'Alba' – they are printed on facing pages in the original *Echo's Bones* (1935), though not in the Calder *Collected Poems* – is the undervalued 'Dortmunder', written in January 1932 in Kassel (*CPB*, p. 16). Set at dusk rather than dawn, it recounts the narrator's hurrying past a church towards a 'bawd' who is represented in orientalizing language with references to Chinese ('K'in') music and to 'jade'. Her strangeness is thus emphasized, and, as with the 'Alba' woman, a quality of repose which the protagonist himself lacks; her mystery, contrasting and matching that of the 'Alba', is associated with night and 'the eyes the eyes black'. A powerful associative context of exotic, almost narcotic sensuality and profane quasi-magical wisdom is skilfully established. Both poems invoke textuality and solemn scriptures, with the ambiguous twice-used 'sheet' and 'Logos' in 'Alba' and the 'scroll, folded' in 'Dortmunder'. Both use music and light in their symbolic texture, though differently. But unlike the way 'Alba' steers itself successfully towards white counter-revelatory emptiness, 'Dortmunder' ends with a kind of fall into a bitter moment in which the narrator finds himself the carrier, representer, of 'the glory' of the bawd's 'dissolution': a Habbakuk. Habbakuk names a short prophetic text in the Bible which is particularly choleric and notoriously obscure. He attacks the cruelty, excesses, and corruption of the Babylonians, and, like Job questioning God's providence, angrily interrogates God's having delivered the Jews into their hands. Beckett's narrator thus claims a prophetic role, while simultaneously abasing himself as 'mard [cf. *merde*] of all sinners'; and Schopenhauer, advocate of passing beyond desire to an unillusioned peace, 'is dead' and hence presumably defeated in the protagonist's inner self-debate. The exact nature of the encounter between poet and 'bawd' is obscure: he survives the occasion, but bitterly, in a stance of rage and disillusionment. The bawd, by contrast, remains a figure of enigmatic power, retaining an indeterminate mystery against which the self-arrogated and self-righteous prophetic anger batters in vain; at the end she 'puts her lute away'. In terms of technique in the representation of subjectivity, 'Dortmunder' and 'Alba' both represent a major advance not only on earlier work but also on most of the other *Echo's Bones* pieces; this may be because the theme of the erotic encounter provides for the poem a fixed position which can contain the decentring of the self he needs to stage. By contrast, in the journey-poems of the collection – conspicuously in 'Enueg II', 'Sanies I' and 'Serena I' – a disordered world, a veritable 'spray of phenomena', as Molloy calls it, forces an unwelcome wholeness of perspective on the self which observes it.

The twelve French poems represent a major advance on the previous two thirties' groups. There is a striking poise and spareness about the group as a whole: no more flagrant rafflesias or, for that matter, asses lepping with stout (as in 'Enueg I' and 'Hell Crane to Starling' respectively). The poems start to behave differently as to setting: the Dublin and occasionally London settings, topographically laden and often cumbersome, have also gone, and in the best of the French poems, with two exceptions, it is simply not appropriate to speak of setting at all. The exceptions are 'Ascension' and 'Arènes de Lutèce', which both emphasize urban actuality as a scene of alienation and self-fragmentation. In all these poems Beckett has solved the problem he wrestled with so strongly in his first poems, in which the speaking self is a frantic centrifuge. It is important to notice that the series is not uniform in method; he presents a range of means and tactics, all of them more assured and satisfying than those of the uneven earlier work. Sometimes it is done by diminution and sometimes by a kind of incremental repetition in reverse, paring away instead of adding material. In the most gnomic of the pieces – the second, sixth, seventh, and twelfth poems – he makes the skeletal structure of the syntax persist and complete itself in the mind, but with a degree of ambiguity or indeed polyvalence which mostly eluded his earlier, too fully furnished, efforts. What he wrote in 1937 (about Beethoven's Seventh Symphony) of how 'the sound surface is torn by enormous pauses . . . so that through whole pages we can perceive nothing but a path of sounds suspended in giddy heights, linking unfathomable abysses of silence' applies, on what is as yet a smaller scale, to the suite of French poems on which he was then beginning.

Turning to write in French is one of Beckett's few aesthetic decisions on whose motives we have very explicit comments of his own. These are in the 1937 letter to Axel Kaun from which I have just been quoting, itself, perhaps significantly, written in distancing German.[45] The key passages rehearse, with a pure intensity still recalling the sheer demolition drive of earlier modernism and in terms perhaps recalling Mauthner, the impulse against language itself:

> As we cannot eliminate language all at once, we should at least leave nothing undone that might contribute to its falling into disrepute. To bore one hole after another in it, until what lurks behind it — be it something or nothing — begins to seep through. (*Disjecta*, p. 172)

Noting that literature has lagged 'in the old lazy ways, so long abandoned by music and painting', he asks more or less rhetorically: 'Is there any reason why that terrible materiality of the word surface should not be capable of being dissolved . . .?' and with a highly characteristic witty sarcasm bemoans the 'lack of silence': 'For in the forest of symbols, which aren't any, the little birds of interpretation, which isn't any, are never silent.' At the end of the letter he remarks that he has, against a current incapacity to produce writings, 'the consolation, as now, of sinning willy-nilly against a foreign language, as I should love to do, with full knowledge and intent against my own . . .' (*Disjecta*, pp. 172-3). In this same year his silence was followed by a set of consistently effective gestures in the poetic genre towards 'the literature of the unword': the twelve French poems, only two of which he provided with English versions. There is a striking biographical event in the background of these poems. On 7 January 1938 Beckett was stabbed by a pimp in Montparnasse, late at night, as he walked home from the cinema with his friends Alan and Belinda Duncan. In his letters of 27 and 31 January to MacGreevy, he enclosed copies of 'Ascension', 'La Mouche', and the poem 'musique de l'indifférence', which he then called 'Prière' (which come fourth, fifth, and sixth in the series); he also describes how another poem 'dictated itself to me the night before last', and further mentions the first poem, 'elles viennent', by its English title 'they come'. 'Son sang gicla avec abondance', as the dying woman's does in 'Ascension': was this gush of inspiration a kind of 'dictation' produced by the trauma of the stabbing, a serious wound delivered by a stranger in the street (who when asked in court why he had done it, replied 'Qui sait?'); or was it that the stabbing allowed him to release the poems to MacGreevy?[46] On the other hand, real life is a complex and continuous collusion between event and insight, the adventures of the body and those of the imagination: a letter written two days before the stabbing tells MacGreevy that 'the entire works of Kant arrived from Munich' (5 January 1938); see poem 8, 'ainsi a-t-on beau', 1.8: 'sur Lisbonne fumante Kant froidement penché' (*CPB*, p. 48).

The first three of the series are misogynistic to varying degrees; these are the best-known piece — the relatively limpid 'elles viennent' — and the third ('être là sans mâchoires sans dents') a poem about sexual disgust and panic at the loss of positive affect which presents a lyric persona with a furiously choleric tone, and which, set as it is in an alienated urban milieu, is rather reminiscent of the Roman elegists. The second poem, 'à elle l'acte calme' (*CPB*, p. 42) is an example of elliptical ambiguity where, if one accepts Harvey's reading, the poem's liquid grace is disfigured by what seems scorn of the feminine, whereas another interpretation is possible which leads away from misogyny to suggest a common fate of sad detachment. Prefacing his interpretation with some rather jejune generalizations proposing to fit the poet into a stereotype of masculine psychological development — 'Beyond thirty a man's fancy turns, less than lightly, to more serious affairs. Not without a backward glance, however, for Eros still has its uses' — Harvey discerns in the poem a male subject who is expressing his state of world-weariness and his lack of erotic affect in comparison to his female partner. To my mind, this is a good example of a reading which diminishes the poem by disambiguating its poised indeterminacy: here, as elsewhere, Harvey offers us an emotional biography into which we can fit the poem and so disarm it of its disturbing *textual* qualities, such as the question of who owns the 'pores savants' and the 'sexe bon enfant' which are ambiguously allocated 'à elle': is this *to* her as in 'they belong to her, are her attributes', or is it *to* her as in 'this is what I have to bring to her'? Is it he or she who is capable of the 'calm act'? The text of the *poem* seems to me not to decide this question, and to be all the more effective an aesthetic object for not doing so. Finally, we might read the speaker's attitude here as an attempt at the detached stance of the Schopenhauerian artist-saint: the rain which stops at the end of the day is the moisture of the body and specifically of sexual arousal, while the blue sky which briefly supplants it offers cool elevation and the promise of transcendence; I would argue, however, that the point is precisely the failure, a *necessary* failure, of the attempt.[47]

The fourth poem, 'Ascension', is less elliptical and presents, at first sight, as narrative: it represents a coherent scene with an observing, listening speaker, already like Molloy and M[alone] a solitary man in a room. Through a thin partition he hears a radio football commentator and through the open window the crowd's passionate howls at the sporting spectacle; meanwhile a woman dies, her blood spurting out over the bedsheets and the sweet peas. Her eyes are closed by 'son mec' (equivocally a lowlife boyfriend, pimp, pal) during the noise.[48] A moving profane ascension concludes the poem, very sparely imagined in a mere seven words:

> elle rode légère
> sur ma tombe d'air   (*CPB*, p. 44)

The girl rises and floats lightly above the young man's tomb of air: *her* spirit is freed to rise, albeit at the cost of her death, as his is not; he is confined in quotidian life, his very breathing entombs him, set between the intolerable antinomies of the crowd's brutish enthusiasm for spectacle and his solitude in the room. As elsewhere in this series, and especially in the trilogy, the geography of the text suggests an allegorical gesture towards the psychophysical being of humanity: the 'mince cloison' (thin partition) suggests the skull, which would mean that what he overhears is other parts of himself, and in the 'next room' of his being the 'doigts dégoûtants' of the 'mec' are closing the large green eyes of the girl. She transcends his being, but again at the cost of her death. We may discern a reprise of the erotic-mystical encounter already rehearsed in earlier work, most notably in the sonnet to the Smeraldina (also green-eyed) and in 'Alba' and 'Dortmunder'. Like a Jungian *anima*, the female figure here is spiritually enabled as the poet is not; but he cannot as yet incorporate her being within his: she floats away above him angel-like in a moment of great aesthetic grace.

The lovely 'Arènes de Lutèce', penultimate of the series, shows a thematic development over 'Ascension': while initially allotting the woman the characteristically feminine role of an irresolute wandering about, it shows her as meeting the protagonist's gaze at the end in a kind of mutual clarity which passes beyond the prescriptions of neoplatonist eroticism and stages a recognition scene in which she can be taken as a splinter of himself rather than an Other:

> . . . Elle hésite,
> fait un pas vers la sortie de la Rue Monge, puis me suit.
> J'ai un frisson, c'est moi qui me rejoins . . .
>
> (*CPB*, p. 52)

The protagonist reacts here a little as one who has seen a ghost, an Other returning as himself. Following the poem's opening self-fragmentation: 'de là où nous sommes assis . . . / je nous vois entrer . . .' — 'from where *we* are sitting *I see us* coming in' — this transforms his vision, so that he now looks with 'd'autres yeux'. Like the earlier 'Ascension', but more insistently, this surely asks to be read as an *anima* encounter in which the male poet discovers how to accommodate the woman, with her not-him-ness, into his own state of being, and her strangeness and wandering away from him is overcome by self-recognition in mutuality. From that position he can recognize the world afresh, especially the poignant detail of the little girl dragging after her her toy hoop (a circle, a frame like the Paris square, near the Museum of Natural History, in which the poem is set, an 'arène' for experience and understanding). Transcendence is, once again, specifically ruled out of this enlightenment: the sky 'nous claire' only 'trop tard'. This recalls, though more drily, the poignant sentence which describes Murphy, excluded, circling round and round Pentonville prison: 'Even so, at evening, he had walked round and round cathedrals it was too late to enter'.[49] In each case a literal detail of the anecdote becomes vehicle and mask of the symbolic meaning: literally, the cathedrals are closed because it is after six o'clock and the sky brightens on the lovers too late not to have spoiled their walk; but symbolically it is too late to enter cathedrals because faith has been definitively lost, and the tardy hint of divine illumination postdates the understanding they have themselves secularly arrived at. The irony of this recalls the celebrated letter to Lord Chesterfield by Johnson (whose work preoccupied Beckett in this period).[50] The presence of the statue[51] of 'le savant Gabriel de Mortillet' — famous natural historian — and the name of the square — that of the Roman city which preceded Paris — places the poem's events in a long perspective which is reminiscent of the poem 'ainsi a-t-on beau' earlier in the sequence; there is an immemorial quality to all the items of the represented scene.[52] The content of the understanding reached, however, is still sombre: the woman he finds beside him still has a 'triste visage'.

Beckett's mature handling of the genre of poetry does not consist, however, simply of a linearly increasing minimalism. As I have said, the series shows a range of poetic means and techniques; the seventh poem, 'bois seul' (*CPB*, p. 47), is a paradigm example of his elliptical method and of the resultant resistance to interpretation. The poem is a first-person utterance, but even the 'je' required by normal speech is lopped off (an early example of, 'not I'), which trips up unsuspecting readers by leaving them undecided as to the grammatical category of 'bois': is it the verb '[I] drink' or the noun 'wood'? Line 2 clears this up, but not without leaving one radically unsettled and concentrating very closely on the meagre clues offered by syntax in the remaining six lines. The poem might be described as a philosophical meditation, as also are 'La Mouche' and 'ainsi a-t-on beau', which succeeds it in the series. It describes a series of activities of the body, all performed alone: drinking, scoffing food, burning (presumably with sexual desire in the manner of St Paul's account, since it is followed by fornication); then dying ('crève', an example of 'low' vocabulary, as also are 'bouffe' ([I] 'scoff' or 'stuff myself') and 'puent' ('they stink')). The poem represents existence as exclusively to do with what is actually there at a given moment: 'les absents sont morts' ('the absent are dead') an ironic revision of the more usual sententious complaints that the dead are absent. Faced with this account of the nature of life, the reader is familiarly and brusquely told to look aside from all this, towards the reeds: natural objects which nevertheless have some kind of intersubjective life, 'teasing' and therefore real and immediate relations with one another, as, by implication, people do not (we should note that sex, despite the fact that the sense of 'fornique' would seem to indicate a partner, is included in the list of acts one performs in an essential solitude):

> sors tes yeux détourne-les sur les roseaux
> se taquinent-ils ou les aïs

This passage is difficult because of the shortage of syntactic signals and also for a semantic reason. Are we to read 'détourne-les sur les roseaux . . . ou les aïs' or, on the other hand, 'se taquinent-ils ou [taquinent-ils] les aïs'? If the latter, then which of the two likely meanings of 'aïs', a plural noun, is the appropriate one?[53] Both Harvey and the 1959 German translator Elmar Tophoven interpret 'aïs' as referring to the three-toed sloth, a sense which puts some strain on our interpretative ingenuity, not least because it is a plural form, where mentioning one sloth would have been enough to make the point; surely another sense – a turbulence, a disturbance caused in running water by an obstruction – is at least equally, if not more appropriate? The intentionalist problem reasserts itself here (did Beckett tell Harvey he was thinking of the sloth? Should we take this as authoritative and obediently abandon the much more metaphorically appealing brief scene of reeds in a river disturbed by the wind?) The biblical injunction to consider the lilies of the field may lurk more or less ironically in the background, but in any case the advice is immediately cancelled: 'pas la peine . . .' ('not worth it'). The haunting ending, 'il y a le vent/et l'état de veille' ('there is the wind and the state of waiting') withholds all interpretatively comforting detail and thus produces a powerfully disturbing indeterminacy: one might read it either as a description of nature's indifference to human feelings, its anti-Romantic blankness – there is *only* or *nothing but* the wind and the state of waiting – or as a consolatory moment: there is *at least* the wind and the 'état de veille', which are an opening, other and better than the closed space between 'bois' and 'crève', drinking and dying. The semantic field of 'veille' is not readily conveyed in English, covering the ideas of vigil, of watching, perhaps anticipation, and of the eve of a religious feast. Here again, then, an instance of possible transcendence is held suspended, perhaps promised, perhaps not. These successive glimpses of escape, each time withheld from a subject more and more economical of utterance, and more and more cogently suffering and grieved, anticipate the protean guises of hope and disappointment endured together by the reader-narrator couple in the trilogy.

The final, haunting, poem, 'jusque dans la caverne ciel et sol' (*CPB*, p. 53) is based on a mythological, perhaps via a Miltonic, reference to the rape of Proserpina, but in spite of this recognizable cultural reference-point it resists facile decoding. The quintessential female victim-figure, Proserpina, is stolen away underground, but along with her go Atropos, the scissors-wielding Fate who cuts off life, and everything from the ancient world and the modern one following it: all the old voices, hair-raising wrongs ('qui . . . macérait naguère les capillaires') the old laws, the light itself: all disappear into 'la bouche d'ombre', the mouth of darkness. There is no possibility here of instants of transcendence and recognition, however fragile, such as irradiate 'Ascension' and 'Arènes de Lutèce'. (Indeed we might take it as a negative pendent to 'Ascension' in that it deals with an anti-moment of death as disappearance into extinction, rather than as a preface to any kind of ascension whatsoever.) The poem is especially striking because, rather like the zero-focalized 'Time Passes' section of Virginia Woolf's *To the Lighthouse*, it appears to manage without a narratorial or personal lyric speaker: here Beckett has solved the problem of arriving at a habitable and speakable subjectivity which bedevilled his first poetry and produced its incessant and awkward perspectival shifts and its gross ironies. This consciousness just barely voiced has been freed from that busy, intrusive, selfhood, but without falling back on any of the kinds of centred, assertive lyric mastery such as dominated the whole inherited tradition of previous lyric, even up to and including the late work of Yeats. The governing image presents this whole earth as a cavern's mouth ready to engulf not just a Proserpina but the myths themselves that generated her, and in its turn all human consciousness which generated them, in an indeterminate void:

> Proserpine et Atropos
> adorable de vide douteux
> encore la bouche d'ombre[54]

The implicit ideological position, of extreme, systematic and principled scepticism, is a recognizable and coherent development of that voiced in the furious snatches of the first poems; but the poetic means have changed almost out of recognition, and the tone and emotional colouring are irradiated by a sombre compassion and an incomparable sense of lyric repose. Beckett has not eliminated language but has 'bore[d] one hole after another in it, until what lurks behind it – be it something or nothing – [has begun] to seep through . . .' (*Disjecta*, p. 172).

Notes

1 From Beckett's letter to MacGreevy, 9 January 1935, relating a visit to Paris by Brian Coffey: 'I found him very *fort* on his subject but the poetry is another pair of sleeves.'

2 See especially J.C.C. Mays, 'Les racines irlandaises du jeune Beckett', Jean-Michel Rabaté, ed. *Beckett avant Beckett*, Presses de l'Ecole Normale Superieure 1984, Paris, pp.11-27, and 'Mythologized Presences: *Murphy* in its Time', Joseph Ronsley ed., *Myth and Reality in Irish Literature*, Wilfrid Laurier University Press, Waterloo, Ontario, 1977, pp. 197-218. John P. Harrington, *The Irish Beckett*, Syracuse University Press, Syracuse, 1991; Deirdre Bair *Samuel Beckett: A Biography*, Vintage Press, London, 1978.

3 Lawrence Harvey, *Samuel Beckett: Poet and Critic*, Princeton University Press, Princeton, 1970.

4 Anne Marie Lecercle, 'La formidable symètrie de l'oeuf pourri or ou Une poétique de la suture', in Rabate, pp. 47-78.

5 John Pilling, 'Beckett's Poetry', in *Samuel Beckett*, Routledge, London, 1976, pp. 159-83. Roger Little's briefer recent essay illuminates the neglected territory of the poems' formal strategies and usefully yokes together the work in English and French: 'Beckett's poems and verse translations or: Beckett and the limits of poetry', in *The Cambridge Companion to Beckett*, Cambridge University Press, Cambridge, 1994, pp. 184-95. See also my '*Entre le galet et la mer*: A Beckett Poem between Two Languages', in *Cross-Currents in European Literature*, ed. Catherine O'Brien, Dublin Italian Institute, Dublin, forthcoming 1995. Marjorie Perloff's two essays 'Between Verse and Prose: Beckett and the New Poetry', *Critical Inquiry*, 9, 1982, pp. 415-33; and 'The Space of a Door: Beckett and the Poetry of Absence,' *The Poetics of Indeterminacy: Rimbaud to Cage*, Princeton University Press, Princeton, 1981, pp. 200-47, though neither discusses the earlier poetry, do important and highly relevant work towards perceiving the nature and influence of Beckett's general aesthetic project in the context of possible literary practice after modernism.

6 A point noted by Melvin Friedman, 'Introductory Notes on Beckett's Poetry', Edouard Morot-Sir et al. eds., *Samuel Beckett: The Art of Rhetoric*, University of North Carolina Press, Chapel Hill, 1976, pp. 144-9.

7 W. J. McCormack, *From Burke to Beckett: Ascendancy, Tradition and Betrayal in Literary History*, Cork University Press, Cork, 1994, pp. 385-6.

8 David Lloyd, *Anomalous States: Irish Writing and the Post-Colonial Moment*, Lilliput Press, Dublin, 1993.

9 See the excellent discussion by Stanley Aronowitz, *Dead Artists Live Theories and Other Cultural Problems*, Routledge, London, 1994, ch. 8, 'Reflections on Identity', pp. 191-209, which addresses itself to the establishment of the category of the individual as 'the outcome of a long dialectical process in which the state is the material embodiment of the unity of humankind' and notes how 'for Hegel, individuality is *produced*, but neither by God nor the law but by social interaction with significant others' (p. 194).

10 I thank Piaras Mac Éinrí for bringing to my attention the overprinting of the stamps, which continued in the case of high-value denominations until well into the 1930s.

11 Fredric Jameson, *Postmodernism; Or, The Cultural Logic of Late Capitalism*, Verso, London, 1991, p. 305.

12 See Lloyd, especially pp. 41-7.

13 Reprinted in *The Lace Curtain*, 4, Summer 1971, pp. 58-63, and now available in, *Disjecta*, pp. 70-6.

14 Samuel Beckett, *Proust* (1931), Calder and Boyars, London, 1965, p. 15.

15 Douglas MacMillan, '*Echo's Bones*: Starting Points for Beckett', in Morot-Sir, pp. 165-6. J.C.C. Mays remarks elsewhere in this volume on MacGreevy's hostility to imagism, and casts doubt on his alleged enthusiasm for Pound (see Mays, p. 125 n.13 and n.33).

16 The passage anticipates the knife-rest in the trilogy which consists of two 'x'es joined by a line.

17 Mays, 'Les racines irlandaises', pp. 23-4.

18 See Linda Ben-Zvi, 'Samuel Beckett, Fritz Mauthner, and the Limits of Language', Harold Bloom ed., *Samuel Beckett: Modern Critical Views*, Chelsea House, New York, 1985, pp. 193-218: 'the highest forms of critique are laughter and silence'. The '*Whoroscope* Notebook' is in Reading University Library, MS 3000, and contains very long transcriptions from vols. II and III of Mauthner's *Betrage Zu einen Kritik der Sprache*, Leipzig, 1923. Richard Ellmann notes Beckett's reading aloud of Mauthner in the period 1932-35 to an interested Joyce (*James Joyce*, Oxford University Press, Oxford, 1983, pp. 648-9).

19 See J.J. Lee, *Ireland 1912-1985: Politics and Society*, Cambridge University Press, Cambridge, 1989, p. 77, on the existence of militant anti-Protestantism in the Irish Free State in the 1920s and on the claim to control of Protestant consciences by the Catholic bishops; see also the account by Beckett's contemporary, Mervyn Wall, both of the bigotry and philistinism of Irish public opinion and discourse, and of the ferocity of social regulation in the era of the Censorship of Publications Act 1929. Wall vividly describes the impression left on his generation of the hypocrisy and hollow patriotic triumphalism of certain public figures. See 'Michael Smith Asks Mervyn Wall Some Questions About the Thirties', *Lace Curtain*, 4, Summer 1971, pp. 77-86.

20 See Anna Balakian, *Surrealism: the Road to the Absolute*, revised edition, Allen and Unwin, London, 1972, and Whitney Chadwick, *Women Artists and the Surrealist Movement*, Thames and Hudson, London, 1991 for lively accounts of the communal dream-sessions, avant-garde costume parties, and other characteristic forms of aesthetic play and protest.

21 See Balakian, pp. 125 ff., on Breton and Freud; for Verticalism, see McMillan (1975), pp. 62-75.

22 Prefiguring 'love love love thud of the old plunger/pestling the unalterable/whey of words' in the 1936 poem 'Cascando'.

23 I have not been able to decipher the word, which may be either 'cheesy' or 'cheery'.

24 A sharp contrast with Coffey's 'maker'-poet: see Alex Davis's essay above.

25 The 'Becky' with whom the speaker pleads to be spared in 'Sanies II' is a rawer version impoverished, for once, by explicitness. 'Becky' alludes to Becky Cooper, madam of a Dublin brothel, where a picture of Lugarno depicting Dante and Beatrice hung: an ironic contradiction not lost on the author of Belacqua, for whom during a fevered meditation – owing a lot to the Stephen of Joyce's *Portrait* – on the Smeraldina and the whores, the one and the many, he thinks: 'a Beatrice lurked in every brothel' (*Dream* p. 40). See also the letter of 9 October 1931 which refers to consuming an overpriced bottle of stout at 1/- at Becky Cooper's.

26 The letters make clear the extreme difficulty and dismay he experienced during the analysis; and see Bair.

27 'Beckett et la Psychanalyse', *Revue Francaise de Psychanalyse*, fasc. 5, 1989, pp. 1405-14. Anzieu's monograph *Beckett et Bion* is, I think, less helpful, at least to those primarily interested in Beckett; I found its procedure of constructing a series of imaginary conversations between the two a good deal less illuminating than the more conventional discussion in Anzieu's article.

28 See Leon Grinberg et al, *Introduction to the Work of Bion*, Jason Aronson, New York, 1980, pp. 53-60.

29 J.C.C. Mays's interesting comment in this volume that they engage in a complicated dialogue with MacGreevy's work should be pursued further.

30 Texts of all the sanctioned poems and of some of his translations from French – Rimbaud and Eluard, but not Crevel or Breton – appear in *CPB*; a new, fuller collection of the poems has been for some time awaited from Calder.

31 *The European Caravan*, eds. Samuel Putnam et al., Part I, Brewer, Warren and Putnam, New York, 1931, pp. 476-8.

32 Gerald Mast and Marshall Cohen, eds. *Film Theory and Criticism*, Oxford University Press, New York, 1979. Eisenstein's 1929 essays, reprinted in Mast and Cohen, are 'The Cinematic Approach and the Ideogram' and 'A Dialectic Approach to Film Form'. Beckett considered film as a possible avocation during this period, and in 1936 actually wrote to Eisenstein, about whom he was enthusiastic, on the subject (Bair pp. 215-6).

33 Johannes Hedberg, *Samuel Beckett's* 'Whoroscope': *A Linguistic-Literary Interpretation*, Moderna Sprak, Stockholm, 1972. I have not discussed *Whoroscope* because of the magnitude of the task and the existence not only of Harvey's vast commentary, but also of Hedberg's eminently sensible essay.

34 Debussy's use of Javanese music in the 1890s is one among many examples. Beckett's deployment of such estranging effects should be carefully distinguished, however, from primitivism, to which he was strongly antipathetic.

35 Letter, 18 October 1932: 'I was trying to like Mallarmé again the other day, and couldn't'.

36 Compare Beckett's review of Rilke, *Criterion*, 13, July 1934, pp. 705-7: 'There is no position here, no possibility of a position, no faculty for one. He changes his ground without ceasing . . .'.

37 A structure similar to that outlined by Walter Benjamin (discussing the possible modes of approach to the aesthetic, rather than the erotic object) in his idea of the 'aura' as 'a phenomenon of distance, however close it may be'. See 'The Work of Art in the Age of Mechanical Reproduction' (1936), reprinted in *Illuminations*, trans. Harry Zohn, Fontana, London, 1970, pp. 219-53 (especially p. 224).

38 '. . . the hyphen of passion between Shilly and Shally, the old bridge over the river', *Dream*, p. 27.

39 See Harvey, pp. 67-169 for the fullest discussion of Beckett's use of Provençal poetry and of Dante.

40 In the case of 'Da Tagte Es' [Then came the dawn], whose title is from the medieval German poet Walter von der Vogelweide, Harvey shows helpfully how Beckett alters the optimistic view of dawn and of the glories of love in the original to a death-figure by replacing the lovers' temporary parting with death's definitive departure which will supplant 'surrogate goodbyes' with the real thing (pp. 84-5).

41 *transition* 16-17 June 1929, pp. 268-71.

42 Pilling: '. . . there is a fatigue in rhymes and scansion that suggests no formal mode would ever have suited Beckett' (p. 163).

43 See the excellent discussion by Angela Moorjani, *Abysmal Games in the Novels of Samuel Beckett*, University of North Carolina Press, Chapel Hill, 1982.

44 Besides recalling the bones of Echo, which in Ovid are turned to stone but still sing. Pursuing that allusion gives us a poet-child figure who only sleeps lying upon the 'bones' and is not even the echo-author of culture's texts.

45 Given in both the original form and in English translation in *Disjecta*, pp. 51-4 and 170-3.

46 Letters of 27 and 31 January 1938; Bair, pp. 294 ff.

47 And hence Harvey's presentation of a rather smug dispassionate thirty-year-old man is misconceived. On the weather of the poem, he somewhat puzzlingly comments: 'For Beckett a day of light rain with skies that clear just before dusk is a typically Irish phenomenon. From this climactic starting-point he develops the theme of "too late" . . .' (p. 187).

48 I find the scene equivocal: does the 'mec' murder the girl? Or is she dying, as Harvey reads it, presumably with authorial sanction, of phthisis like Peggy Sinclair, also green-eyed? This is a classic case of disambiguation by revealed authorial intention. The perhaps phantom murder a reader tends to discern has an imaginative truth: the poet is alive, the woman dead; his fingers are not felt to be clean, whether or not she has been murdered by his splinter-figure the 'mec' (Harvey pp. 190 ff.). Pilling, on the other hand, to me inexplicably, has the man penetrating the 'thin

partition' in a sexual act, whereupon 'an unequivocally human, sexual ascension takes place' (pp. 173 f.).

49   Beckett, *Murphy* (1938), Calder, London, 1977, p. 46. The idea of divine belatedness is a recurrence: see also 'Enueg II': 11.6, 28, 'too late to darken the sky' and 'too late to brighten the sky'. The 'Arènes de Lutèce' line was originally 'qui *vous* éclaire trop tard' (my italics); see *CPB*, p. 175.

50   The letter, a masterpiece of icy wit, points out the utter uselessness and hypocrisy of the powerful patron's belated offers of assistance. There are three notebooks full of Johnson material, meant for a play about his life, of which Beckett wrote in 1937 the fragment called 'Human Wishes'; see *Disjecta*, pp. 155-166.

51   Or perhaps merely of its plinth. The poem refers only to 'le socle' of the statue, and in March 1995 when I visited the Arènes de Lutèce, only the plinth remained. I have not to date succeeded in ascertaining whether the plinth was already vacant during the 1930s.

52   We should compare this long view, which shrinks human life to a fly-sized miniature, to the fine 'ainsi a-t-on beau', eighth in the suite, with its sardonic assumption of a transcendental philosophical viewpoint from which the ice ages and the Lisbon earthquake are viewed with equal detachment, and Kant leans coldly over the ruined city. The two similar meditations on the fly from this period (see 'La Mouche', poem five, and the conclusion of 'Serena I') are also part of a developing strain of more poised theological satire, which will culminate in the indifferent God-figures of *Watt* and the trilogy.

53   There are actually four dictionary senses: the others are a Champagne wine and an inflammation of the tendons, intriguing but not really assimilable even in Beckett's writerly poetic practice. I thank Paddy O'Donovan for finding out and discussing with me these various senses of 'aï'. See Harvey, pp. 202-3 and Elmar Tophoven and Eva Hesse, trans. *Beckett: Gedichte*, Limes Verlag, Wiesbaden, 1959.

54   Pilling reads this poem as a kind of allegory of subjectivity which concerns the persistence of the old dichotomies in the cavernous depths of the self: 'the same tension of sky and earth, the same light that consumes the darkness, and the same laws of attraction and repulsion' (pp. 177-8). But one could equally well interpret the plot of the poem as the loss of habitable structure or recourse ideologically, theologically, politically. Adorno's defence of Beckett thirty-seven years ago against Lukacs's charge of escapist bourgeois formalism comes to mind: see Adorno's 1962 essay 'Commitment', reprinted in Ernst Bloch et al., *Aesthetics and Politics*, Verso, London, 1965, pp. 177-95, especially pp. 190-1, where he insists that Beckett's works 'deal with a highly concrete historical reality: the abdication of the subject.' He contemptuously contrasts the effect of Kafka's and Beckett's art with 'officially committed works': 'Kafka and Beckett arouse the fear which existentialism merely talks about'. This curiously echoes Beckett's own early words about Joyce's *Work in Progress*: 'His writing is not *about* something. *It is that something itself*' (author's italics, *Disjecta*, p. 27).

8

Gender, Irish Modernism and the Poetry of Denis Devlin

Anne Fogarty

What should we be without the sexual myth,
The human reverie or poem of death?

Castratos of moon-mash – Life consists
Of propositions about life.

'Men Made out of Words', Wallace Stevens

In *A Room of One's Own*, Virginia Woolf notes that women appear to be more pointedly discouraged from the writing of poetry than of fiction.[1] She finds that whereas the notion of a woman novelist enjoys some currency, that of the woman poet is still viewed with suspicion. The purpose of this essay is to consider why Irish modernist poetry appears to be such an inveterately masculine and consequently patriarchal domain. Undeniably, several women produced poetry of merit during the earlier half of this century. Yet, even a cursory glance at the work of Rhoda Coghill, Mary Devenport O'Neill, and Blanaid Salkeld, to list but a few almost forgotten names, indicates that Irish female modernism belongs to a literary past which is even more irrecuperable than that of the supposed lost generation of male poets of the period.[2] To triumphantly reinstate their work by seeing it as part of a diffuse but coherent literary context which embraces male and female writing alike, would involve a self-blinkering and premature denial of the unremittingly androcentric and fragmented nature of the Irish modernist literary scene.

209

As a consequence, it would be facile to claim that the poetry produced by men and women in Ireland of the thirties should be seen as torn halves of the same whole. The lost work of Irish women poets cannot simply be salvaged and added victoriously to the imaginary, capacious, and all-embracing museum of national literary tradition. Nor, to invoke an alternative image, can we comfort ourselves by seeing the work of these women poets as nestling safely like a hitherto buried shell inside the Russian doll or *matrioska* of a male literary tradition which many have pronounced to be itself lost and blighted. Inequality of opportunity and sexual difference leave indelible marks upon the work of these early twentieth-century writers and may also be found to be at the root of the disparate and incommensurate achievements of male and female poets in the early years of the newly independent Irish state.

Thus, although my examination of these authors does not lead me to the conclusion that literary endeavour bears the hallmarks of essentialist and hence ineradicable biological differences, I hold that an appreciation of the varying achievements of men and women in this period calls for a separate examination of their work. For numerous reasons which this essay proposes to explore, sexual difference is inscribed as textual difference in the creative output of Irish writers of the thirties. A critical assessment of the 'sexual myths' which form the political unconscious of male modernist aesthetics will unearth many of the conflicts between notions of a creative and transcendent subjectivity and of an organic and impersonal tradition at the heart of this movement. It will also indicate the way in which Irish modernists contradictorily insist both upon the masculine energy and the feminine otherness of the national literary tradition which they are helping to found. Thereafter, I shall examine the way in which the poetry of Denis Devlin both contests and reinstates the sexual myths which Wallace Stevens views as an indivisible aspect of modern poetry. Although Devlin tries to resist the reification of the feminine in his work, he nonetheless, it will be seen, constructs a negative theology which still depends upon stereotypical images of women and of gender identity.

The Gender of Modernism

In his prescient and mischievous essay which inveighs against the poets who dominated the Irish Literary Revival, Samuel Beckett constructs a rival and in part impromptu tradition of his own (*Disjecta*, pp. 70-3). In effect, his description of a plurality of poetic practices in modern Ireland demonstrates what more recent criticism has proven in greater detail still, namely that there were many different kinds of modernism and that therefore to use this term as if it referred to a single monolithic literary movement is in fact to falsify and abnegate the variety and complexities of artistic endeavour in the early twentieth century. Furthermore, Beckett also has the foresight to predict how myths about supposed schools of poetry foreground certain authors to such an extent that they become calcified in a seemingly immutable canon of great writers and eclipse many others who are of equal if not greater interest. Nevertheless, even his revised taxonomy listing poets of merit and interest allows little room for female voices. In fact, he refers to only three women writers in the course of his review of the Irish poetic scene; two, Dorothy Large and Irene Haugh, are mentioned *en passant*, while the third, Blanaid Salkeld, is scrutinized in some detail and given the author's seal of approval.[3]

Thus, Beckett's broadside is an early contribution to a debate which is still in progress about what Raymond Williams terms 'the discrimination of modernisms'.[4] His ironic assessment of contemporary Irish poetry raises the spectres of tradition and authority and also puts forward the view that there are in effect two warring factions within modernism: the first, which is that of the so-called Irish antiquarians such as Yeats and James Stephens, is, for all its innovations, conservative and backward-looking, while the second, which Beckett links with the work of Thomas MacGreevy, Denis Devlin, and Brian Coffey, is marked by its radicalism, experimentalism, and rejection of insularity. This battle over poetic value is one, however, which appears to be fought almost entirely within the confines of a putative canon of male writers. Although Beckett's essay is uncannily prophetic of the way in which an unabashedly nationalist literary politics would lead to the neglect of writers whose work did not immediately conform to the methods and themes of the Celtic Twilight poets, it is also symptomatic of the manner in which even radical revisions of modernism still exclude and bypass the achievements of women. Indeed, Beckett's very division of poets into two camps is itself a gesture which is characteristic of modernist polemic. As Michael Levenson points out, the urge of modernist writers to use dualist oppositions in order to set themselves apart from Romanticism, classicism or, in the present case, the Irish Literary Revival has the effect not only of severing all links with tradition but also of abolishing any possibility of a *tertium quid*.[5]

Hence, the Beckettian genealogy of modern Irish poetry must itself be viewed with some suspicion. As recent literary criticism has shown, almost any attempt to designate a canon of literature is necessarily predicated on exclusions and omissions. Thus, although the poetry of Devlin, MacGreevy, Niall Sheridan, and Brian Coffey still fails to be given proper weight and continues to be overlooked in histories of modern Irish literature, the poetry of Blanaid Salkeld and of Mary Devenport O'Neill has fallen still further from the horizon of critical attention. It may be fruitless to try to rank what Tillie Olsen calls the 'unnatural silences' which have marked the careers of all of the unorthodox and unacknowledged Irish writers of the thirties.[6] Yet, it still seems undeniable that the silences which affected the women writers were at once more hidden and more per-nicious than those which also blighted the careers of the male poets.

A review of the terms used by modernist criticism to describe the nature of poetic creation provides some insight into the masculinist bias which underwrites notions of literary production in the first three decades of this century. In analysing the ways in which cre-ativity was conceptualized in early twentieth-century essays and manifestoes, my objectives are both to probe the nature of this philosophical debate and to establish links between it and the declara-tions made in a similar vein by Irish writers during the same period. The largest question looming over such an exploration is whether the various forms of modernism in Ireland may be said to have much in common with literary movements elsewhere. Indeed, several critics have suggested that Irish modernism has a peculiar local cast because of the political problems which beset the country. As J.C.C. Mays argues, the wish to found a fresh culture and tradition and, in Ezra Pound's phrase, 'to make it new', took on a particular urgency in Ireland because of the simultaneous desire to achieve independence from English rule in every sphere including the literary.[7] To some extent, too, this meant that Irish modernism does not coincide chronologically with the modern movement in England and America; as it enacted itself in the Irish Literary Revival, it is in ef-fect a modernism *avant la lettre*.[8]

Similarly, the pitched battle between a new, defiant mode of alienated, cosmopolitan consciousness and an older, more parochial, national tradition which Raymond Williams sees as one of the key aspects of modernism takes on a peculiar dimension in the Irish context.[9] Here, the determination to celebrate the local and the national is initially at least as revolutionary as the aim to explore an anti-bourgeois and decidedly urban world marked by its transience, restlessness, and lack of fixity. Indeed, Joyce may be said to have exploited the tension between these two countervailing moments in *Ulysses.* During the course of this novel, Dublin with its paralysing confines is transformed because it is viewed through a modernist lens and shown to be endowed with the ambiguous and potentially liberating flux of the metropolitan centre.[10] However, equally, it must be recognized that the battle between traditionalists and a literary avant-garde in Ireland is particularly virulent because of the way in which it is interwoven with the struggle to achieve a separate national identity. Most of the adversarial energies of the modernist impetus seem either to have been hijacked by the nationalist cause or else ostracized as marginal or deviant.

Moroeover, if as Raymond Williams claims, the radical estrangement of modernist texts quickly becomes a spent force or readily aligns itself with ideologies such as fascism or nationalism, then it may be claimed that the problem faced by the generation of Irish poets under consideration in this essay was that they were attempting to create a modernism *a posteriori* in a cultural climate now inimical to any other form of literary revolution.[11] Terence Brown has convincingly demonstrated that literary activity in the Irish Free State and later in the Republic of Ireland, which was established in 1949, was increasingly stifled by the narrowly defined nationalism, social conservatism, and blinkered Catholicism that formed its ideological bedrock. Indeed, provincialism and censorship, those very forces which were anathema to the modernist spirit, became the hallmarks of the Irish cultural scene for many decades.[12] The ominous apocalypticism that inspired Antonin Artaud's visit to Inis Mór in August 1937 in a fruitless search for the saving wellsprings of Irish primitivism may be seen symbolically to mark an ebbtide in the fortunes of the Irish modernist movement.[13]

A cross-comparison of two Irish literary journals published during this period, *The Dublin Magazine* and *The Bell*, provides a telling map of the increasing constriction and oppressiveness of the Irish cultural scene.[14] Both magazines display an eclectic and far-ranging set of cultural interests. In *The Dublin Magazine*, essays on Shakespeare, Joyce, and Synge find a place alongside discussions of Dadaist art and the work of Goethe, Marguerite Yourcenar, Nietzsche, and Villiers de L'Isle-Adam. Similarly, *The Bell* publishes critical accounts of both the contemporary Irish and European literary scenes. However, a comparison of the issues of *The Dublin Magazine* published throughout the 1930s and those of *The Bell* published a decade later in the 1940s indicates a considerable darkening of the general cultural climate and consequent narrowing of the range of representative voices finding an outlet in print. *The Dublin Magazine* seems far less compromised by external pressures than *The Bell* in its endeavour to publish a broad spectrum of literature and critical opinion. Moreover, although they never predominate, there is a significantly higher proportion of female contributors, as creative writers, critics, and reviewers, to *The Dublin Magazine* than to *The Bell*. The former magazine publishes the plays of Teresa Deevy and of Mary Devenport O'Neill, the short stories of Mary Lavin, Patricia Lynch and Mona Godden, and the poetry of Lorna Reynolds, Temple Lane, Blanaid Salkeld, and Sheila Wingfield. *The Bell*, by contrast, which was founded in 1940, contains far fewer original literary texts and reviews. Instead, its attentions, due of course to the political courage of its editor, Seán O'Faoláin, are centred primarily on the overwhelming problems caused by state censorship. The egalitarian albeit genteel atmosphere of *The Dublin Magazine* seems to have dissipated, although this publication continues throughout the forties and fifties to give space to burgeoning literary talents, both male and female.[15] In comparison, *The Bell*, for all its liberalism and outspokenness, appears no longer capable of providing that broad-minded and non-discriminatory forum which existed in *The Dublin Magazine* during the 1930s. The Victorian gentility of *The Dublin Magazine* seems ironically to have provided a more encouraging environment for women writers than the ideological stridency of *The Bell*.

T.S. Eliot's essay 'Tradition and the Individual Talent' has been seen, some would say unaccountably, as a key attempt to constitute a form of modernist aesthetics. Eliot's vision in this essay of a necessary physical labour by the poet masculinizes and heroicizes this figure. In effect, Eliot rehearses problems which he has inherited from the Romantic period, including the nature of poetic genius and the difficulty of mediating between self and world and between knowledge and experience.[16] The declarative insistency of Eliot's statements acts an an inadequate screen for the all-too apparent inconsistencies which riddle his arguments. Thus, the trait of impersonality which he purportedly supports is confusingly grounded in an equally heartfelt belief in the individualism of the writer. Similarly, his insistence on the longevity of tradition and the magnetic pull of preceding voices and texts appears at odds with his simultaneous emphasis on the innovatory powers of the poet with his pioneering ability to open new horizons and displace everything that went before him. Yet, despite his claims to the contrary, Eliot's essay, in fact, evinces anxieties both about the nature of tradition and the prowess of the sovereign, creative genius. He tells us that 'hard labour' is necessary in order to ensure that the wisdom enshrined in previous works of art is passed on. Thus, tradition is not guaranteed; it has to be painfully reconstructed and, it is also suggested, remade. A dedicated scholastic austerity becomes the hallmark of this new type of writer who sees Homer as his ultimate progenitor. In this manner, the poet's subservience to tradition safeguards the transmission of his birthright.

Eliot's use of kinship metaphors and of biological images gives added dimensions to his account of the imperishable legacy of male genius. Through his strenuous endeavours and self-sacrifice, the writer finds that he is genetically imprinted with the literary accomplishments of past ages. Eliot declares that 'the historical sense compels a man to write not merely with his own generation in his bones, but with a feeling that the whole of the literature of Europe from Homer and within it the whole of the literature of his own country has a simultaneous existence and composes a simultaneous order'. Clearly, there is a sense in which the feminine is written out of this account of the triumphant self-generation of the male artist. His powers of autogenesis ensure his accession to the visionary company of great writers.

Accordingly, Eliot insists that 'no poet, no artist of any art, has his complete meaning alone. His significance, his appreciation is the appreciation of his relation to the dead poets and artists'. However, even when Eliot takes refuge in such gnomic pronouncements, tensions can be discerned. Indeed, his most sententious statements about the nature of poetry are the aspects of his arguments which beg the largest questions. Thus, the claim that the development of a writer depends on 'a continual self-sacrifice, a continual extinction of personality' and the related contention that 'the more perfect the artist, the more completely separate in him will be the man who suffers and the mind which creates'[17] lead one inevitably to interpret such renunciations and divisions as repressions and to ask what freedoms are rejected in favour of these vocational sublimations.[18]

Eliot's concept of art as mastery and his views that aesthetics are necessarily severed from the experiential and that the poet transcends history by incorporating within himself the best of literary tradition are echoed and reshaped in many different ways during the varying phases of Irish modernism. W.B. Yeats, for example, repeats the Eliotic paradox of the commingling of the personal and the impersonal in the figure of the poet. Thus, in his essay 'Poetry and Tradition', he sees the 'ancestral memory' which is a necessary component of the pursuit of a literary vocation as leading both to 'the perfection of personality' and to 'the perfection of its surrender'.[19] In his preface to *The Oxford Book of Modern Verse*, he tellingly conceptualizes poetic endeavour in masculine terms despite his inclusion of a number of women poets whom he held in high regard in the collection.[20] Hence, he praises Synge for restoring 'masculinity' to Irish verse and lauds the other writers of the Literary Revival for 'creating masterful personality'. However, in a radio-broadcast on modern poetry, he is careful to draw distinctions between Irish modernism and the Anglo-American tradition which Eliot describes.[21] He insists that Irish poetry in contradistinction to the reigning cult of impersonality in England is experiential and local because of its roots in a native folk tradition. Accordingly, Yeats deems Irish modernism, which of course is confined in his analysis to a selective group of authors that co-ordinate with his view of things, as inflected by difference. The distinctiveness of modern Irish poetry derives thus in Yeats's eyes from a marriage of masculine craftsmanship to a feminine otherness.

Critics and writers who come after Yeats are, however, far less sanguine about the positive difference of Irish poetry. Rather, they see themselves as epigones in a tradition that has run aground on its own ambiguities or which has uselessly expended itself in petty rivalries and squabbles. Thus, Louis MacNeice's essay 'Poetry To-Day', published in September 1935, ventures the view that discussions of aesthetics by practicing writers are by definition hypothetical, tentative, and often contradictory[22]. Like Yeats, he distinguishes modern Irish from English poetry. But, while Yeats locates the alterity of Irish modernism in its ethnic otherness, MacNeice says that it is its political content that is the mark of its difference. In addition, he deploys Eliot's notions of individualism and tradition with a decided scepticism. He puts increased emphasis on the conflicts between the single writer and his literary heritage and claims 'that we want to have the discoveries of other poets in our blood but not necessarily in our minds'. However, even this critical contestation of some of the central terms of modernist critical discussion does not in the final reckoning lead to a refutation of the key tenets of Eliot's aesthetics. MacNeice ends his exposition by reinforcing, however reluctantly, the view that poetry is the result of 'the paradox of the individual and the impersonal'.[23]

A brief essay on contemporary Irish poetry by Austin Clarke, published over a decade later in 1946, provides evidence of an even more embattled and oppressed literary scene. Clarke opens his discussion by rebutting the claim that Irish poetry is in a state of decline.[24] He contends rather that the fickleness of literary taste has led to the ostracism of Irish writing which was once held in high regard in England during the 1890s. The otherness of Irish poetry is no longer a guarantee of its popularity. In his view, the setting up of the Free State has necessitated a philosophy of literary Home Rule not so much because of any new-born nationalist fervour in the Irish cultural establishment but ironically because of what he terms the 'Sinn Féin policy' of the English literary scene. In his eyes, it is English nationalism which is responsible for the fact that Irish poets are currently neglected, misunderstood, and, more importantly, unpublished.

While Clarke's essay is of value for the insight which it gives into the material effects of changes in the mechanisms of literary production on the later generations of Irish poets who followed on from the Revivalists, it is of even more moment for the contradictory picture which it paints of the belated modernism of the poets of the thirties and after. Clarke insists on a literary separatism and claims that 'Irish poetry has its own problems, and they are not those of contemporary England'.[25] Yet, at the same time, in a contradictory gesture which may be seen as typical of a post-colonial worldview, he holds the lack of publishing opportunities for contemporary Irish poets to be the fault of the English literary establishment. Thus, Clarke acclaims the separate and unique nature of modern Irish poetry, whilst simultaneously lamenting the disarray of the Irish literary scene. The transition to a genuinely independent literary tradition created a void, he suggests, and as a result collected editions of most of the poets whom he mentions, such as John Lyle Donaghy, are unavailable. Tellingly, he concludes by contrasting the timidity of the critics with the vigour of the creative writers. His comments indicate a stagnation and lassitude in Irish publishing and a concomitant crisis of confidence about the value of the poetry being written. Thus, Clarke indicates, despite his vaunting of contemporary talent, that the absence of England as a literary other rather than providing an impetus for creative activity led to a breakdown in the Irish literary scene. The modernism which he describes is now aware of its difference not in the positive, though potentially restrictive, Yeatsian terms of its ethnic rootedness, but in the negative sense of its disconnectedness and lack.

Writers such as Denis Devlin, Brian Coffey, Rhoda Coghill, and Blanaid Salkeld seem to make good this feeling of lack and of conflict mentioned by MacNeice and Clarke, not by reaching for a further compensatory notion of a national organic tradition but by utilizing multifarious cultural contexts to motivate their writing. In their greater sense of an affiliation with a wide span of European literature, they provide evidence of a more expansive view of cultural heritage. Devlin translates, amongst others, St-John Perse, René Char, and Paul Eluard, and Coffey writes 'versions' of Pablo Neruda, while Coghill produces translations of Rainer Maria Rilke and Salkeld of Alexander Blok and Anna Akhmatova.[26] However, simply to state matters thus is to accept without further question Beckett's notion of two opposing camps within the history of Irish modernism: the nationalist antiquarians, on the one hand, and the followers of a pluralist avant-garde unaffected by nationalist loyalties on the other. Such a stark opposition of poetic practices and of political beliefs does not accord with the given situation. While none of these writers may have perceived Ireland as enabling their work, none explicitly rejects or denounces the country either.

What draws this group together, if one brackets the figure of Beckett, is a sense of tentativeness and impediment about the pursuit of a literary career. Yet, even here, further qualifications need to be made because it is evident that poets such as Coffey and Devlin still devote themselves to a literary *métier* with a sense of purpose and direction which does not obtain to the same degree in the case of O'Neill, Salkeld, and Coghill. Even in sharing the female fate of marginalization, the male poets of the thirties' generation still continue to subscribe to modernist myths of universal transcendence and impersonality, or to romantic notions of the *poète maudit*. Thus, Devlin in an article on St-John Perse indicates his admiration for the universality and impersonality of the French poet, while Thomas MacGreevy as signatory of a revolutionary manifesto published in Paris in 1932 gives his assent to a poetry which although abolishing the transcendent 'I' aims at 'the illumination of a collective reality and a totalistic universe'.[27] Thus, although they attempt to cut through the cultural prejudices of the Literary Revival, many of the male poets in this forgotten backwater in the history of Irish modernisms still overtly replicate much of the sexual bias of modernist aesthetics. The mystifying universalisms which they invoke are ultimately exclusionary even though they may serve a purpose in indemnifying the diversity of the poetry they themselves were writing. The creative talent either at the centre or in the margins of Irish modernism is conceived of in terms which do not take what Mary Loefllelholz calls 'the experimental lives' of modern women into account and which fail to acknowledge the significance and otherness of their writing.[28]

'The Absolute Woman of a Moment': Self as Other in the Poetry of Denis Devlin

> You shall make of the non-existent soul a man better than her.
> Denis Devlin, 'To The Health of the Serpent'
>
> (*CPD*, pp. 312-16)

In his introduction to his collected edition of Devlin's work, Brian Coffey claims that this writer achieves mastery rather than singularity in his poetry. In thus assessing his literary achievement, Coffey invokes some of the key tenets of modernist writing and intimates that Devlin sacrifices his individual talent to the impersonality of literary tradition (*Devlin*, p. xiv). He further suggests that in fulfilment of his hieratic calling he surrenders himself to language and eschews the use of poetry as a vehicle for self-expression. In the discussion that follows, I wish to examine the way in which subjectivity is both constructed and deconstructed in Devlin's first two collections which were published in 1937 and 1946 respectively, namely *Intercessions* and *Lough Derg and Other Poems*. In particular, I shall focus on the centrality of the encounter between self and other in Devlin's love poetry both secular and religious. I shall make the claim that his work is involved in a constant struggle to free the subject which is helplessly confined within the circle of its own immanence or transfixed by the illusion of its transcendence by positing an other which does not simply turn out to be its own reflection or its negative opposite. However, this attempt to break the spell of selfhood is constantly foiled by the reabsorption of alterity into identity. As a consequence, to borrow a phrase from Adorno's *Negative Dialectics*, the 'individual survives himself' in Devlin's poetry and remains trapped in his sense of alienated isolation.[29] By the same token, the feminine figures of alterity which serve the function of initiating a negative dialectics which will both break down absolute oppositions of subject and object and obviate the necessity falsely to unify them also become realigned with various hypostatizing abstractions which reproduce rather than contest stereotypical views of gendered identity.

Marshall Berman in his study of modernism notes the dual propensities of the literature of this period in which a sense of doom and constant disintegration is often pitted against a belief in the possibility of renewal.[30] He cites the following passage from Karl Marx's 'Manifesto of the Communist Party' which he sees as epitomizing this battle between becoming and dissolution and between a utopian view of modernity and a vision of modernism as heralding apocalyptic destruction which marks twentieth-century literature:

> Constant revolutionising of production, uninterrupted disturbance
> of all social conditions, everlasting uncertainty and agitation
> distinguish the bourgeois epoch from all earlier ones. All fixed,
> fast-frozen relations, with their train of ancient and venerable pre-
> judices and opinions, are swept away, all new-formed ones become
> antiquated before they can ossify. All that is solid melts into air,
> all that is holy is profaned, and man is at last compelled to face
> with sober senses, his real conditions of life, and his relations with
> his kind.[31]

It is just such a sense of instability and of uninterrupted disturbance
that one encounters in the poetry of Devlin. Yet this very realiza-
tion that 'all that is solid melts into air' which underpins his work
is simultaneously used as a basis for the construction of a negative
theology capable at least of describing if not circumscribing the
meaning of the 'real conditions of life'.

Two poems included in the volume, *Intercessions*, may be used to
pick out this twofold movement. Both 'Death And Her Beasts,
Ignoble Beasts' (*CPD*, pp. 49–50) and 'Victory of Samothrace' (*CPD*,
pp. 51–3) involve a supplication to, and an exorcism of, a death-
dealing goddess figure. The former poem opens with a description
of the feelings of revulsion inspired by the physical decay induced
by death. The speaker who represents himself as a hapless victim
of this marauding mother who 'smoothes me like cambric on an
infant's flesh' probes his ambivalent desire simultaneously to embrace
and to recoil from this figure. His divided state of mind leads to
a self-cancelling declaration of love: 'There is none so much as you,
none you, I think of.' Thereafter, however, childlike submission
becomes transformed into defiant rebellion against the treachery of
this false mother and lover:

> Attack me in the dark, I'll extreme fear
> With the first of all landscapes given its eyes
> In the frantic group of naked man and horse;
> With the cheering of shredded men in lost forts
> And to go on with, the length of to-day and to-morrow,
> The evidence that lifting needles make the cloth.

The enticing 'numbness that looks like peace' and dangerous passivity
offered by death are countered by the images of social and cultural
activity in the final stanza. The frantic heroism of the 'naked man

and horse' and of the 'shredded men' derives further strength from the feminine images of the watchful landscape and of the silent industry of the cloth-making needles. The merging of feminine powers of creativity with masculine bravado permits a momentary laying of the feelings of terror which haunted the poem. The ghastly spectre and unremitting otherness of death have been transformed into the more amenable figure of Cybele, invoked in the third stanza, who is both a goddess of fertility and of war. The 'frightened antimonies' of the poem are brought ultimately into a precarious balance.[32]

'Victory at Samothrace', by contrast, allows no such sense of equilibrium to emerge. The goddess conjured up in the initial stanza is 'A sweet lady! not alas! the invented lady of stasis'. Like death in the previous poem, she is seen as a figure of discord and chaos who is capable of 'disturbing the exact harmony of the stars'. The speaker once again represents himself as a supplicant caught between desire and dread, being and nothingness:

> A man is swung between two lilies tall as pines. Terror!
> Increasing loudness of a thousand feet of men tramping
>   down wooden stairs. Throbbing wooden stairs
> I will make another prayer
> Give me an object of art, a statuette of Diana: I will caress
>   her limbs closely with my fingers
>
> For these graces, spirit of movement, I will build you an
>   altar, to be destroyed immediately,
> And make offering of promise
> Of heroes once again
> Of women's eyes before love has drowned their sweetness.
> The moment is poised in fear
>
> Our Lady of Victory!

The devotion inspired by this goddess proves the grounds of its own undoing. Yet it also seems the occasion for the poet's art as it is his caress that produces these self-consuming altars with their tantalizing but evanescent promises. The poem ends, however, with the extinction of the self and the victory of this ambiguous goddess who holds sway over the forces of creativity and destruction alike:

And your voice, which has the opulent contentment of a
    June stream, babbles
And I feel with relief;
Better in danger with a goddess than float safe like a barge
    on the sea:
Fingers again at my throat

Baptism by immersion in the numerous sea

As the water closes over me, I look up while life keeps
    interest
To see the impersonal gleam in your eyes
And the soft ebb and flow of your breasts.

The 'baptism by immersion' is of course also a death by drowning. The languid but needy gaze of the 'I' is foiled by the impersonal life-force of the goddess.[33] The tidal imagery in the final line, while it suggests the fusion of the heroic, creative artist with the natural rhythms of the world around him, also indicates that such balance and unity are impossible. The goddess remains other; her aloofness and distance highlight and give dimension to the male subject's needs and desires. The opposition between self and world is reinforced rather than cancelled in this final moment of imaginary fusion. The oceanic desire for the danger and energy of this female deity brings about the destruction of the poet. Self and other represent an ultimate duality rather than an ultimate unity.

Problematically, however, for a feminist reading, Devlin's discovery of the non–identity at the core of identity does not alter the fixed repertoire of tropes which he utilizes in order to depict either femininity or the female beloved and muse. Like Sartre, he portrays consciousness as pure negativity and as capable of knowing the world only as that which it is not.[34] Similarly, too, his poetry shows the nihilating activity of consciousness on the one hand and the failure of being on the other to be paradoxically the very preconditions of existence. In a manner akin to that of the Sartrean subject, the self in Devlin's work is engaged in an impossible quest to overcome its facticity by cancelling both its lack of being and its fear of mortality and thus achieving transcendence. This struggle to act upon the world and to reconcile being-in-itself, or mere existence, with being-for-itself, or consciousness, is mediated by images of a reified feminine other who alternately mirrors or opposes the male subject.

Simone de Beauvoir in her feminist rereading of the principles of existentialism points out that women like men are split and threatened by the fall into immanence. However, they find that their situation is more conflicted and ambiguous than that of men because the latter consistently cast them as other, that is as objects to their subjects:

> Now, what specifically defines the situation of woman is that she – a free and autonomous being like all human creatures – nevertheless discovers and chooses herself in a world where men compel her to assume the status of the Other. They propose to turn her into an object and to doom her to immanence since her transcendence is for ever to be transcended by another consciousness which is essential and sovereign. The drama of woman lies in this conflict between the fundamental aspirations of every subject -which always posits itself as essential- and the demands of a situation which constitutes her as inessential.[35]

Thus, in 'Victory at Samothrace', despite the poet's insistence on the fragmentation of the lyric persona and of his object of veneration and his refusal to integrate the two, it remains nonetheless the case that the figure of the woman plays a predictable role in this drama of alienated consciousness. She may be viewed as an allegory of repressed desire and of plenitude on the one hand and of lack and destitution on the other. It is her function to act as an insentient canvas for his projected meanings and to become the impossible referent for his poem as a whole. She is the vehicle for a truth that remains always out of reach. The fetishized images of this elusive female body captured in the parting description of the 'soft ebb and flow of your breasts' operate as an objective correlative of the poet's divided consciousness and not of that of the feminine other. Even though the goddess remains a symbol of the ineluctable nature of human desire, she herself is trapped in the essentializing optics of the poem. The dissolution of the male subject depends upon the retention of the objectified image of the female other with all of its attendant contradictions.

The image of woman as an absence that constitutes and frames the alienated presence of the male speaker constantly recurs in the love poems contained in *Lough Derg and Other Poems*. In 'West Pier' (*CPD*, pp. 148-9) the poet tells us that 'I love and lose her with an ever love', thus indicating that the renewed experience of loss merely confirms the strength of his love. The incessant invocation of the absent other becomes the instigation for this intercessionary mode of writing. In 'Argument with Justice' (*CPD*, pp. 170-1), the poet rails against the remote figure of allegorized justice:

> Virtue all men stand under, what wonder, blinded on thy
>   column transcendental, thou art
> Sterile, since not bedded with man thy secular wooer who
>   could waken thy
> Dreams to bloom; and why blinded?
> Darest not take, not take to thy sight these anarchic, thy
> Realms of thy reign abandoned?

Here, he seeks to break down the opposition between the impassive female object and the active male subject. In doing so, however, he invokes another set of oppositions which ensure that the divisions against which he battles will stay in place. The virginal sterility of justice is opposed to the saving virility and mortality of the speaker. In deconstructing the idealist myth of the female body as a vehicle for high-minded, transcendent truths, he invokes the alternative myth of the fallen female body as an epitome of contingency, sinfulness, and sexuality:

> Virtue of all men, fear not that we thy temple crumble, flesh
>   crumbles, but
> Not till the mind's raped out. Fear rather thy name be
>   forgotten from father to
> Son, or by thy saints. Come down, let there be
> Justice though the heavens fall, be virtue of our
> Temporary measure.

The allegory of justice is rejected in favour of an impossible androgynous union of flesh and spirit and of ideal and counter-ideal. The commutation of the feminine is depicted as the means by which this unreachable aim may be achieved.

In 'Eve In My Legend' (*CPD*, pp. 206-7) and 'A Dream of Orpheus' (*CPD*, pp. 217-220), the process of what Alice Jardine terms 'gynesis', or the putting into discourse of woman, becomes emblematic of the operations of the imagination as a whole and of its attempt to compensate for the rifts in being.[36] Both poems end with a formulation of love that rescues the self from its solipsism by representing it as an object of knowledge produced by the

consciousness of the other. Thus, 'Eve In My Legend' concludes
as follows:

> As she from my drugged side took life.
> I feel like Adam who in sleep
> Gave birth to Eve, daughter and wife
> Whence his far brood would sow and reap,
> Half monster, half philosopher,
> Movement by mood conceiving her.
>
> And now stop for a mental spell
> The forest-eyed, obsidian After!
> Yet let that hundred-headed tell
> My arms full of her blond laughter
> Nothing to know that is not she
> Nor she know anything but me.

The clotted and abstruse language of these lines captures the effort
involved in trying to describe this love which depends upon a
metaphysics of absence rather than of presence. The riddling declara-
tion that closes the poem indicates that the woman who can only
be depicted metonymically as 'blond laughter' is a shifting horizon
of meaning rather than someone tangible and concrete. The pro-
cess of knowing devolves into an endless series of displacements.
Moreover, the attempt to imagine the perspective of the other, what
the woman might know, founders. In the end, it is the self's failure
to grapple with anything outside itself that becomes the only thing
that can be imagined by this self-defeating ontology. All we are left
with is a mirage of truth and a recognition not of the presence of
the other but of the endless spirals of otherness that constitute the self.

Similarly, 'A Dream of Orpheus' ends with a wistful attempt to
project the consciousness of the other and to see it as separate from
that of the orphic poet:

> But Orpheus
> Grieves for her still; in the shell and web of her body,
>   beauty
> Dreamt the forms his love made substance of and that she
>   dreams in him.

The tragic separation of Orpheus and Eurydice in the classical legend mirrors the divisions within human experience. The substantiality of the self depends here upon an eternal opposition between dream and reality, being and nothingness, and truth and illusion. Yet, ultimately, the self is not so much constituted as undone by the existence of these dualisms. His internalized sense of division underlines his inability to project the other as anything other than an illusion or a figment of the imagination. Orpheus absorbs Eurydice back into himself and views her as an image of the unknowable nature and nonentity of his own being. The loss of the beloved becomes transposed into an allegory of the voided subject-ivity which is the central theme and instigating moment of all of Devlin's poetry.

A comparison of Devlin's aesthetics of loss with a poem by Rhoda Coghill entitled 'To His Ghost, Seen After Delirium' may provide a final measure of the differences between Irish male and female modernism and of the role played by seemingly ineradicable sexual myths in this androcentric literary movement. In Coghill's poem, Eurydice addresses Orpheus and asks for some sign of recognition of her identity:

> Since I have fought the pigmy host
> that has besieged me so, those wanton thoughts
> and not-thoughts, which would steal from me
> all memory of being, and at last
> steal me from life: − since I have found
> again my mind's dear garden, will you not praise me?
> will you not give me, victor now,
> a crown of olives? − will you not come
> bearing a flower from fields of asphodel?
>
> I never see you in that sunlit place.
> Yours is a footstep heard on the threshold;
> yours is a presence made known only to the blind.
> Your gifts are new-born sensation, new-born suffering. −
> Tantalus, Eurydice, Echo, −
> I am all these at once and individually,
> waiting your daffodil
> waiting your tribute,
> your olive-crown.[37]

The divisions between self and other still obtain in this version of the myth. Here, however, the other speaks and protests at being turned into a figure of absence. Eurydice, despite her exile from the world, rediscovers herself as presence in Coghill's revisioning of things and demands some tangible sign that confirms her consolidation of herself. But the daffodils and olives, or signs of achievement, which she craves remain ultimately beyond her reach.

In the traditions of Irish modernism, Orpheus remains forever separated from his Eurydicean other because he banishes her to the realms of myth and allegory and is capable of seeing her only as a projection of facets of his own psyche. The poetry of Denis Devlin registers the contradictions and conflicts involved in this co-optation of the feminine and tries desperately to imagine the place of the other as something more than a void within the self. This attempt fails, however, because the subjectivity which he explores still depends upon sexual myths which oppose masculine and feminine identities. His work suggests that it is the fate of the poet to discover that the legendary Eves of his creation are simply aspects of a monstrous and tormenting philosophy of being which endlessly perpetuates its own illusory truths. Like the druid elms in the closing stanza of 'Royal Canal' (*CPD*, p. 142), however, his poetry can do no more than depict with harrowing precision the existential 'panic' and sense of despair induced by this discovery. In a poem published towards the end of his literary career, Devlin's Turcoman diplomat wryly announces to the wraiths of his past: 'Ladies, I call you women now' (*CPD*, pp. 95-301). Yet, his vision of these ghostly women permits of no ultimate readjustment. They remain ciphers of loss and unshifting allegories of his own emotional and spiritual impasse.

Notes

I am grateful to my colleagues, James McCabe, Gerard Quinn, and Susan Schreibman for their advice on aspects of this essay.

  1 Woolf contends that women have been able to mould the novel to suit their own purposes and hence to make a mark in the sphere of fiction but 'it is the poetry that is still denied outlet'. See Virginia Woolf, *A Room of One's Own/Three Guineas*, ed. Morag Shiach, Oxford University Press, Oxford, 1992, p. 101.
  2 Rhoda Coghill, *The Bright Hillside*, Hodges Figgis, Dublin, 1948 and *Time is a Squirrel*, Dolmen Press, Dublin, 1956; Mary Devenport O'Neill,

Prometheus and Other Poems, Jonathan Cape, London, 1929; Blanaid Salkeld, *Hello, Eternity*, Elkin, Mathews and Marrot, London, 1933, *The Fox's Covert*, Dent, London, 1935, *A Dubliner*, Gayfield Press, Dublin, 1942, and *Experiment in Error*, Hand and Flower Press, Aldinton, Kent, 1955.

3   Dorothy M. Large wrote many novels for children and popular poetry; the latter work concentrates on rural and religious themes. Her best-known collection of verse is *Songs of Slieve Bloom*, Talbot Press, Dublin, 1926. Irene Haugh published only one work, *The Valley of the Bells and Other Poems*, Basil Blackwell, Oxford, 1933. This collection includes several pieces inspired by the music of modern composers, including Debussy, Ravel and César Franck, and poems which explore various aspects of religious belief. A despairing meditation on the problems of being a woman called 'A Song of Defeat' which closes this single volume may explain why she did not pursue her writing career.

4   This phrase which is attributed to Raymond Williams is cited in 'Editor's Introduction: Modernism and Cultural Theory', *The Politics of Modernism: Against the New Conformists,* ed. Tony Pinkney, Verso, London, 1989, p. 1.

5   Michael H. Levenson, *A Genealogy of Modernism: A Study of English Literary Doctrine 1908-1922*, Cambridge University Press, Cambridge, 1984, pp. vii–xi.

6   Tillie Olsen, *Silences*, Virago, London, 1980.

7   See James Joyce, *Poems and Exiles*, ed. J.C.C. Mays, Penguin, London, 1992, pp. xl–xlii.

8   J.C.C. Mays uses this notion of a proleptic modernism to analyse the poetry of Joyce; see *Poems and Exiles*, pp. xvii–xlvii.

9   Raymond Williams, 'When Was Modernism?', *The Politics of Modernism*, pp. 31-5.

10 For a suggestive discussion of the way in which Joyce and Beckett harnessed that instability and lack of identity which were aspects of Ireland's colonial condition, see Terry Eagleton, *The Ideology of the Aesthetic,* Basil Blackwell, Oxford, 1990, pp. 317-23.

11 Williams, 'What Was Modernism?', p. 35. For a cognate but far more pessimistic reading of the conservative ideological underpinnings of modernism, see Georg Lukács, 'The Ideology of Modernism', *The Meaning of Contemporary Realism*, trans. John and Necke Mander, Merlin Press, London, 1963, pp. 17–46.

12 See Terence Brown, 'The Counter-Revival: Provincialism and Censorship 1930-65', *The Field Day Anthology of Irish Writing*, gen. ed. Seamus Deane, Field Day, Derry, 1991, vol. 3, pp. 89-93.

13 For a discussion of the way in which the Aran islands were seen in a type of *fin-de-siècle* fervour as a final refuge of primitive energies by Synge and Yeats amongst others, and for an account of Artaud's visit, see Patrick Sheeran, 'Aran, Paris and the *Fin-de-Siècle*', *The Book of Aran*, Tír Eolas, Galway, 1994, pp. 299-305.

14 *The Dublin Magazine* was founded by Seamus O'Sullivan (James Sullivan

Starkey) in 1923 and continued to be published until 1958. *The Bell*, under the editorship of Seán O'Faoláin, was launched in October 1940 and ceased publication in December 1954.

15 W.J. Mc Cormack's assessment of *The Dublin Magazine* is more negative than mine. He condemns it on the grounds of its 'genteel provincialism'. See *The Battle of the Books*, Lilliput Press, Dublin, 1986, p. 9. Terence Brown similarly dismisses the magazine because of its lack of literary energy and its dependence on the interests of an 'insecure self-regarding coterie remembering past glories'. See *Ireland: A Social and Cultural History 1922-79*, Fontana, London, 1981, p. 167.

16 T.S. Eliot, 'Tradition and the Individual Talent,' *Selected Prose of T.S. Eliot*, ed. Frank Kermode, Faber, London, 1975, pp. 37-44. For a perceptive account of the interconnections between Romanticism and modernism, see Edward Larrissy, *Reading Twentieth-Century Poetry: The Language of Gender and Objects*, Basil Blackwell, Oxford, 1990, pp. 1-50.

17 Eliot, pp. 38-41.

18 For further accounts of the contradictions embedded in the modernist philosophy of the disengaged and transcendent writer, see Maud Ellmann, *The Poetics of Impersonality: T.S. Eliot and Ezra Pound*, Harvester Press, Brighton, 1987, and Thomas E. Yingling, *Hart Crane and the Homosexual Text*, University of Chicago Press, Chicago, 1990, pp. 1-23.

19 W.B. Yeats, 'Poetry and Tradition', *Essays and Introductions*, Macmillan, London, 1961, pp. 255.

20 See W.B. Yeats, 'Introduction to *The Oxford Book of Modern Verse*', *Selected Criticism*, ed. A. Norman Jeffares, Macmillan, London, 1964, pp. 217-37.

21 'Modern Poetry: A Broadcast', *Essays and Introductions*, pp. 491-508.

22 Louis MacNeice, 'Poetry To-Day', *Selected Literary Criticism of Louis MacNeice*, ed. Alan Heuser, Clarendon Press, Oxford, 1987, pp. 10-44.

23 MacNeice, p. 43.

24 Austin Clarke, 'Poetry In Ireland To-Day', *The Bell*, 13, 1946, pp. 155-61. For a discussion of the constant spectre of decline that haunts accounts of modernism and the resultant fear that this movement is not only on the wane but may lead to the end of all art, see Peter Bürger, *The Decline of Modernism*, trans. Nicholas Walker, Polity Press, Oxford, 1992, pp. 32-47.

25 Clarke, p. 158.

26 See Denis Devlin, *Translations Into English*, ed. Roger Little, Dedalus, Dublin, 1992, Brian Coffey, *CPV*, pp. 223-43, Rhoda Coghill, *Rilke: Angel Songs*, Dolmen, Dublin, 1958, and Blanaid Salkeld, 'Anna Akhmatova', *The Dublin Magazine*, 8, 1933, pp. 50-5, 'Dialogue About Love, Poetry and Government Service by Alexander Blok', *The Dublin Magazine*, 22, 1947, pp. 18-47.

27 Denis Devlin, 'St-John Perse À Washington', *Cahiers de la Pléiade*, 10, 1960, pp. 86-9, and 'Poetry Is Vertical', *transition*, 21, 1932, pp. 148-9. The latter manifesto is signed by Hans Arp, Beckett, and MacGreevy *inter alia*.

28 Mary Loeffelholz, *Experimental Lives: Women and Literature, 1900-1945*, Twayne, New York.

29 Theodor W. Adorno, *Negative Dialectics*, trans. E.B. Ashton, Routledge, London, 1966, p. 343.

30 Marshall Berman, *All That Is Solid Melts Into Air: The Experience of Modernity*, Verso, London, 1983.

31 Karl Marx, 'Manifesto of the Communist Party', *The Marx-Engels Reader*, ed. Robet C. Tucker, Norton, New York, 1972, pp. 473-500 (p.476).

32 For a discussion of Devlin's use of paradox and antinomy, see Stan Smith, 'Frightened Antinomies: Love and Death in the Poetry of Denis Devlin', *Advent VI*, Denis Devlin special issue, 1976, 24-31.

33 In the revised version of this poem included in *Lough Derg and Other Poems* the gaze of the 'I' is given far less force. Also, the ebb and flow of the goddess's breasts are described as 'lax' rather than soft thus rendering this half-suggested apotheosis even more uncertain. See *CPD*. pp. 196-8.

34 For a persuasive interpretation of Devlin's work in the light of Sartre's theory of the imagination, see Alex Davis, '"Foreign and Credible": Denis Devlin's Modernism', forthcoming, *Éire/Ireland*, 30, 2, 1995. For an analysis of Sartre's philosophy of being, see *The Cambridge Companion to Sartre*, ed. Christina Howells, Cambridge University Press, Cambridge, 1992.

35 Simone de Beauvoir, *The Second Sex*, trans. and ed. H.M. Parshley, Penguin, London, 1972, p. 29. See also Toril Moi, *Simone de Beauvoir: The Making of an Intellectual Woman*, Basil Blackwell, Oxford, 1994.

36 Alice Jardine, *Gynesis: Configurations of Women and Modernity*, Cornell University Press, Ithaca, 1985.

37 Rhoda Coghill, *The Bright Hillside*, p. 20.

9

'Precarious Guest':
The Poetry of Denis Devlin

Stan Smith

Denis Devlin spent little more than a third of his life in continuous
residence in Ireland. Born of *émigré* Irish parents in Greenock on
the Clyde, in 1908, he did not return to Dublin until he was twelve.
In the thirties, after three years of study in Paris and Munich, and
two as a lecturer at University College Dublin, he joined the Irish
Department of External Affairs. From 1938 he held a succession of
diplomatic posts in Italy, the USA, England and Turkey. He died
in 1959, a year after his appointment as Irish Ambassador to Italy.
Sign ificantly he returned in his last weeks to die on 'home' ground
in Dublin.

The choice of diplomatic career seems in retrospect a key to the
enigmatic identity of the poet. Like that other poet-diplomat whose
work he successfully translated, St-John Perse,[1] Devlin saw himself
as essentially the 'precarious guest of the moment, man without proof
or witness', regretting that 'On too many frequented shores have
my footsteps been washed away before the day'.

Impelled to find in the impalpable community of language a home
he could not locate in any specific time or place, he glimpsed there
too the emptiness and evanescence of the forms on which the
soul relies:

> Those who, each day, pitch camp farther from their birthplace,
> those who, each day, haul in their boat on other banks, know bet-
> ter, day by day, the course of illegible things; and tracing the rivers
> towards their source, through the green world of appearances, they

are caught up suddenly in that harsh glare where all language loses
its power.

This indeed is the central paradox for Devlin: if language is the
tract on which the soul constructs itself from moment to moment,
it is also an impermanent and treacherous ground. The temporiz-
ing self, like its words, is easily erased. All utterance is pitched in
the tension between allegiance and silence, where the restless spirit
seeks a provisional coherence:

> And it is no error, O Peregrine,
>> To desire the barest place for assembling on the wastes of exile
> a great poem born of nothing, a great poem made from nothing. . . .
>> I have built upon the abyss and the spindrift and the sand-smoke.
> I shall lie down in cistern and hollow vessel,
>> In all stale and empty places where lies the taste of greatness.

St-John Perse's link between spiritual evacuation (as the precondition
of poetry) and the weary personal renunciation of place must have
seemed an inevitable one for Devlin:

> You shall not cease, O clamour, until, upon the sands, I shall
> have sloughed off every human allegiance. (Who knows his birth-
> place still?)

Absence is at the heart of Devlin's absolutes: an unaccommodating
emptiness pursued by the stringently self-denying conscience, a
greatness 'made for nothing'. Devlin's perpetual question is that set
out in The *Heavenly Foreigner*[2]: 'How I might make my soul/In a
freedom that might destroy it?' But there is, too, a complementary
quietism. The 'protesting' self, striving to forge its own salvation,
acknowledges a possible recusancy, in a gesture towards that mode
of Christian resignation which equates activity with sin, ambition
with insurrection:

> Like those who will not surrender a small liberty
> Which they cannot cultivate in any case.
> Rebellion is imperfection like all matter
> Mirror without reflection, I am helpless. . . .

His editor, Brian Coffey, has commented of Devlin: 'I, for one, always associated with the seminary that mass of reserve of his, which struck so many people as noteworthy' (*Devlin*, p. xi). Educated at Belvedere College, Dublin, the Jesuit institution which left such a mark on James Joyce's intellect, and at Clonliffe, Dublin, Devlin for a time intended to enter the priesthood. The ascetic hauteur of Loyola's spiritual *corps diplomatique* probably appealed to Devlin for complex biographical reasons.

In an illuminating article, W.M. Walker has discussed the state of mind of the Irish immigrant community in Scotland at the turn of the century.[3] Walker attributes to the Catholic ghetto the 'siege' mentality of 'a community which . . . feared for its reputation and for the preservation of its historically nurtured uniqueness'. Such a community sought refuge in a willed abstentionism, in the world yet not of it, which combined a canny, guarded superiority with defensive defence: 'Catholic social organization was inimical to free expression and suspicious of spontaneity. The training in self-effacement began in the home.'

In 'Celibate Recusant', the double withdrawal implied in the title – from the flesh and from subscription to the civil power – uses the analogy with Catholic dissent to present Devlin's attitude as one of abstemious and even squeamish disengagement from an abandoned world – a stance summed up in the final terse exchange of the poem: ' "Touch me not!" . . . "It's as you wish." ' The mere fact of physical existence, of having a body, is enough to soil one with complicity. In *The Heavenly Foreigner*, he speaks of 'My busy, alien lip and eye' as if the business of the world were something which estranged body from spirit, soul from itself. Devlin is preoccupied with this tension between hypostatized self and other, in a way which leads him into innumerable paradoxes. For one's own body can become part of the other ('the fiery circle cataracting outer-world'). Yet the Other is also the 'heavenly foreigner', one's own elusive soul which is also Christ and (in an extension which draws on Sufi mysticism and its troubadour variants) the Beloved who is *anima* and completion of one's own true being. The numinous is only revealed subversively, through the dangerous phenomenal forms of this material world, the 'divine/Dissidence in river and wheat':

Something there was other
Always at my elbow. . . .
When the foreign power intervened and made all the difference
Between the bog and the road,
Making the present, making life. . . .
The world glows with mortal divinity . . .
O heavenly foreigner! Your price is high.

Characteristically, Devlin thinks of this negotiation between self and other in diplomatic terms, as if only protocol preserved that necessary composure without which self might be overwhelmed and its hard-won autonomy abolished. Devlin's position is, in fact, self-confessedly Jansenist, despite his early Jesuit training. In 'Jansenist Journey' the transition from guilt to innocence is associated with indifference and renunciation and, symptomatically, with distrust ('But I put no trust in him, no trust'); the goal is merely a continuation of the present in which pilgrimage is, punningly, a 'retreat':

> We entered cloisters with a priest,
> Sat on the stone wall, listening
> To his plans for our retreat,
>   . . . . No rapture;
> The plain virtue of the chosen few.
>
> (*Devlin*, p. 44; *CPD*, p. 146)

Jansenism has been classically defined by Lucien Goldmann as the reaction of the seventeenth-century French 'legal nobility' to the decline of its social power. Potential leaders of the central bureaucracy, members of this class found themselves, instead, in the role of depressed administrative élite,

> economically dependent, as officers, upon a monarchical state whose growth they opposed from an ideological and political point of view. This put them in an eminently paradoxical situation . . . where they were strongly opposed to a form of government which they could not destroy or even alter in any radical manner.[4]

Enough similarities exist between this experience and Devlin's own social dilemma to make Jansenism a fruitful source of analogies for him. The paradoxes are revealed in his 'The Investiture of D'Artagnan' through a harshly convoluted language which in its unnatural inversions reproduces the spiritual tergiversations of which it speaks. D'Artagnan, reluctant servant and even embodiment of the state, preserves his self-respect through an aristocratic disdain for the mediocrity his squandered merit serves:

> With you is my last dignity in retreat from these the precise great.
> By Clio squandered. I have pacted with the time unworthy of my
>   chance,
> Embroidered, twisting a feckless baton, first marshal of France
> Who should have ridden the times in spasm, have been I the State.
>
> (*CPD*, p. 107)

Principled withdrawal within an active life ('the saviour lighthouse solitude') is sustained by the conviction that service of Caesar is a chastisement which only enhances worth:

> Foreclosed. Not to be captain conqueror of kneaded minds is my gift
> To resignation, smile to the King, Sire I cannot leave
> These lawns the hereditary breezes bevel, this soft life a reprieve
> From my intended life. . . .   (*CPD*, p. 108)

It is the dilemma of the poet-diplomat whose 'intended' vocation, as spiritual viceroy, has been twisted into this 'bitter' (l. 9) secular parody. The resolution of these tragic paradoxes, within Jansenism, lay in a theology of grace as the interruption of the worthless material world by intimations of a nobler, juster dispensation ('the foreign power'), modest faith in a collective election substituting for loss of secular autonomy.

Such a theology is explored in that strangely anachronistic poem, 'The Passion of Christ', which sketches, in a series of vignettes , the whole of divine history from Fall to Transfiguration. Significantly, Devlin cannot avoid a surreptitious admiration for the figure of Pilate, whose silent diplomatic gesture preserves a self-absolving composure in an impossible colonial cul-de-sac:

> The scene's complete! the filthy, wine-lit bands
> Forgive Barabbas who shed blood,
> Pilate, the surgeon, cleans his distant hands,
> In sage disgust, praises the Good.
>
> (*Devlin*, p. 12; *CPD*, p. 290)

But Devlin overtly shows this to be bad faith, and sets against it the acknowledgement of Christ by the Good Thief. The latter's rueful self-criticism reverses Pilate's posture, by remorsefully accepting complicity; ironically, however, he sees himself in terms which mimic Pilate's consular authority:

> It is not right for me to talk to You,
> To wait on You with ministerial bow. . . .
>
> The huge and foreign universes round me,
> The small dishonours in me coat my heart. . . .
>
>   . . . my understanding less imperious . . .
> Loses whole continents where in my childhood
> I was Your Viceroy, and approved the Just
> And condemned my natural evil thoughts. . . .
>
>   *(Devlin, p. 13; CPD, p. 292)*

Devlin's recurrent antinomy of justice and nature is focused here in the orthodox belief that original sin is a fall from the state of grace to the state of nature. The poet's skill lies in playing up the statist metaphor to the point at which he can speak of the 'majesty of Christ' as that of 'God's Son foreign to our moor'. But Christ is also the supersession of the state, and the Last Supper man's initiation into this negativity, taking the self beyond the compromising loyalties and betrayals of a fallen political world:

> Outside the window, the world was still,
> Absence of principalities and powers:
>   The world His will,
> He broke bread and said He would be ours.
>
>   *(Devlin, p. 10; CPD, p. 289)*

The characteristic supplication of the poem's last line ('Oh, come, Unworldly, from the World within!') leaves the reader with an absence that can be filled only by faith, by the conviction of the Good Thief 'That You are there and are not there'.

God is simultaneously absent from and immanent in creation, and this negative mode of divine presence is specifically that of the Jansenist Pascal's 'hidden God', a tragic theology salvaged from defeat and disillusion. Pascal's influence pervades Devlin's work. In

'Meditation at Avila' it is there in the idea of the 'saving presence' of a grace that is not habitual but momentary, which 'Is never a promise, comes without warning/Or, being most wanted, fails', yet is nevertheless sustained by a faith founded in the unanswering void that validates each 'doomed and sunny moment'.

Christ's emissary, the soul which is precarious guest of an alien empire, is constructed by the mundane self out of a dialogue in which one side is always silent. And yet the self, like those 'Fountain waters' which 'Bloom on invisible stems', rides this apparent absence, which is 'the seed, the sap and the fruit':

> Magnificence, this terse-lit, star-quartz universe,
> Woe, waste and magniflcence, my soul! . . .
> Welcome as always;
> Fibrous listener in the darks of mind
> Till my confession
> Articulate your silence. . . .
>
> You shall see blue arches of emptiness marching into the horizon
> Over the yellow and black, the intolerant
> Excellency of the Castilian highlands. . . .
>
> If I could not talk to you
> Fear would oppress me.   (*Devlin*, p. 53; *CPD*, p. 162)

Devlin seeks to intercede between the two orders, between the intransigence of a material, political world (picked out by the enjambment which allows 'Excellency' a double meaning) and the 'impalpable' fluidity of grace. In sifting out the 'magnificence' from the 'waste', he rejects St Teresa's brutal dichotomy of spirit and flesh, which inverts his own terms:

> God being star-froze heaven
> And Devil, fluent earth.
> O Santa, Santa Teresa,
> Covetous, burning virgin!
> Scorning to nourish body's
> Farmlands with soul's
> Modulating rains,
> You lost your eyes' rich holdings
> To rubble, snakes and swine
> And like the skeptical miser

> You lost the usufruct
> Of heaven, this floral life.
>
> *(Devlin,* p. 54; *CPD,* pp. 163-4)

For Devlin, soul transfigures this alien world with 'comfort'. The concept of 'usufruct' to redefine the parable of the good steward is apposite and precise. But such comfort is rare and not to be presumed upon: the world easily falls apart into discrepant antitheses. When self 'call[s] in alien silence' out of the grief of a collective mortality, towards an infinite which looks mutely back, it confronts that eternal silence of space in which Pascal felt the terror of the divine. At the same time (as in 'The Colours of Love') the world remains a 'fluent fantasy' that 'makes a mock' of the self, tempting it to 'throw off [its] absolutist devices/And dissemble in the loose resplendent sea'. Resolution lies in the Pascalian act of faith:

> Yet think on how, San Juan, bitter and bare,
> Wrapt in his drama, sent his cry above,
> And though, through layer on suffocating layer
> Nothing came back, he loved; and so I love.
>
> *(Devlin,* p. 20; *CPD,* p. 279)

As 'Obstacle Basilisk' indicates, one must always be on guard against a world where the 'treacherous years' and 'each bandit land-mark' of time and place threaten the careful distinction of the soul. The only proper stance is a 'scrupulous alarm' that keeps the 'mean groom' of the flesh at bay. The 'justified' self in this poem (in its theological sense, having been reconstructed in grace) fears that it may be assimilated into the alien, degrading universe around it. The anxiety is that of the recusant minority in a squalidly hostile environment, careful of a spiritual election which is also its guarantee of class superiority:

> I have lived with nobility of emotion
> Thought out my honour, justified my rise:
> Is this mean groom my measure? he, my harm?
> Shall thus his fear degrade me, slow my arm?
>
> *(Devlin,* p. 69; *CPD,* p. 188)

Dissolution, subversion, assimilation: it is this which appals the poet in 'Est Prodest', where 'Tablelands of ice', image of that 'identity' which is 'Other' ('He is me otherwise'), can easily thaw into the 'eternal horror' of the middle section:

> Murmur of cities . . .
> Its voices, panic,
> Cataracting, bestial . . .
> The loosened universe flowing
> Loathsome, limpid. . .   (*Devlin,* p. 48; *CPD,* p. 152)

It becomes clear, at this point, why Devlin's work is so dominated by the tone of the diplomat. In language alone can the anxious self be guaranteed a breathing space, a *cordon sanitaire* within which to conduct its negotiations with an alien and always potentially destructive world. This accounts for the peculiarly aureate, mannered quality of Devlin's language, its almost hieratic distance. Language is a specious resolution of antinomies for Devlin, the reduction of objective conflict to verbal paradox. The respectful rhetoric of the *amour courtois* tradition, which abounds in his love poetry, is finally admitted, in 'Edinburgh Tale', to be a device for keeping down 'the ungovernable, scared birds of the heart and the blood risen' (*Devlin,* p. 79; *CPD,* p. 204). The vocative mode of much of his poetry is an attempt to mediate between two worlds without being compromised by either (his second volume was called *Intercessions*),[5] like those birds in 'Memoirs of a Turcoman Diplomat', characteristically seen as 'Imperial emblems', who 'in their thin, abstract singing,/Announce some lofty Majesty whose embassies are not understood' (*Devlin,* p. 3; *CPD,* p. 295).

Islam, in this remarkable poem, seems almost a mirror image of Devlin's Catholicism, reconciling ascetic rigour with a worldly hedonism, in the same way that the persona of the Turcoman diplomat expresses, with wry, resigned maturity, an abiding preoccupation. The retired diplomat may reflect, nostalgically, that the 'puritanic temperament's outgrown', but the casual rumination is qualified, given savour, by the inkling that this is not an absolute fact, but the reflection on a particular life, as the evening's lapsing ('Evenings ever more willing lapse into my world's evening') is seen to be simply the reflex of a personal acquiescence.

The impermanency of residence in such a world is indicated by the title of the first memoir, 'Oteli Asia Palas, Inc.', admitting good-humouredly that one is a precarious guest in the hotel of the world,

as the evening itself is only one of many rooms in the father's house.
The old man casts himself as the emissary of a superseded past:

> . . . the yellow and blue skies changing place,
> I hold my stick, old-world, the waiters know me,
> And sip at my European drink, while sunlight falls,
> Like thick Italian silks over the square houses into the Bosphorus.
> Ladies, I call you women now, from out my emptied tenderness,
> All dead in the wars, before and after war,
> I toast you my adventures with your beauty!

Time and place continually change, the only 'absolute kingdom' is
'far in the sky'; one is always left with the passing and accidental
present, and such a realization brings its own compensations. The
slow assimilation of the volatile spirit of youth – that empty freedom
which is all potential – into a shabby and specific actuality, a career
and a past, may be a lapse from distinction to mediocrity, but it also
brings the maturity, and the self-awareness, to see this and not be
overwhelmed by it, an 'emptied tenderness' that does not equate
transitoriness with vanity:

> You are not what you thought, you are someone like all these,
> The most ardent young man turn, at the drop of a black hat,
> Into some rabbity sort of clerk, some heart-affairs diplomat,
> A John of the Cross into a Curia priest.
> It was years ago. It is not now like when the century began –
> Though apple and peach lie brilliant on the dark,
> And mineral worlds on the dark sky shine,
> And the red mouth breathes in; thine is mine,
> And the careless Atlantic inhales the Thames, the Tagus and the
> 　　Seine.

The syntax, hingeing on that qualifying 'Though', suggests the
discrepancy is a subjective one, depending on point of view: there
is no absolute change, for the same awakening, the same fruitions
and disappointments, go on for other lives, here and in other places.
It is a salutary recognition.

Self is a construct, not easily tampered with ('My father thought
my feeling could take fire by the vibrant Seine/And a tough intellect
be constructed in Göttingen'), but the ceremonious distance of
protocol may be a necessary way of endowing the transient with
a more absolute dignity:

In the Foreign Office, they humorously ask my advice,
My father had money, I was posted from place to place:
What can I tell them? even if I got it right?
There would be protocol about the right time and the right place.

But, of course, there is no such thing as the right time and the right place: both alike in this poem are adjectival, fortuitous concurrences that speak always of elsewhere, attributes of the subject or its objects: 'my European drink,' 'Italian silks', 'our salaried Levantine admirals', 'some international Secretary General', 'our Westernising dictator', 'the up-country captains', 'my Frankish Friend's one wife,/In a far Latin Villa'. The absurdity of the attempt to endow place with absolute value is disclosed by the nomadic ancestry of the Turks themselves, late inheritors of the residue of several empires – an experience crystallized in the title of the shortest piece in the sequence: 'The Turkish for Greek is Roman'.[6]

The resolution of the poem is unusual in Devlin for its earthy colloquiality. The old man moves from nostalgia to opportunism, grasping at the compensations of a post-war world short of men and looking for paternal reassurance:

Tuck in your trews, Johannes, my boy, be led by me,
These girls are kind. And we're all the rage now, whiskey-flushed men
of our age,
The callow and the sallow and the fallow wiped off the page!

Asia seems to offer Devlin a territory, beyond Christendom, in which he can relax his prickly defences. In 'Ank'hor Vat', as if protected by his role as envoy-discreet, tactfully reserving his own opinions in the presence of an alien authority – he can face the flux of things with an unruffled equanimity where 'the dung-filled jungle pauses' and 'Buddha has covered the walls of the great temple/With the vegetative speed of his imagery' (*Devlin*, p. 51; *CPD*, p. 159). An ambassadorial *sang-froid* enables him to patronize this colonial deity with an easy deference, while taking notes on comparative anthropology, making a scholarly pun ('vegetative speed') and remaining quietly unperturbed by his ignorance of the local flora. A world of overflowing motions, of fecund disturbing energies, is thus contained by a cool 'mental distance from passion' which allows him to stand impassive and attendant. Such a stance can translate even 'the lissome fury of this god' into the composure of script ('quiet lettering on vellum'), holding the world 'at my mental distance from passion'.

Yet the consolation offered by this flexible quietism can turn to ashes in the mouth, for there is an immediate, urgent world, where nature and justice are inextricably intertwined, that will not easily be denied, that demands voice and commitment. At times Devlin, who shared the political enthusiasms of the thirties' generation, seems to regard that very diplomatic discretion as his own particular version of the Sartrean *huis clos*. This at least seems to be the point of 'Tantalus', in which the charge laid against Pilate comes home to roost, as the diplomat now finds himself dumb, his hands tied, for 'Shame like an Alderman in Hell/Has broke me down till I have cried' (*Devlin,* p. 66; *CPD,* p. 182).

One of those laments is 'The Tomb of Michael Collins' (*Devlin,* p. 15-16; *CPD,* pp. 283-5). The assassination of the Free State leader by that section of the republican army which refused to endorse the Treaty with the British occurred in 1922, shortly after Devlin's family returned to Ireland.[7] This intersection of the personal and the public is crucial to the poem, which links the birthpangs of the new state with the trauma of adolescence, the initiation into mortality and fallenness. There is an incipient Oedipal dimension to the poem, which equates the Jesuit teachers of Devlin's youth with the 'voracious fathers' who 'bore him [Collins] down', as if the suppression of the hero-figure were also, for the boy who identifies with him, a personal death ('O Lord! how right that them you love die young!/ He's what I was when by the chiming river/Two loyal children long ago embraced').

The nexus in which the persecutors meet is, significantly, literature: the news of Collins's death coincides with a classroom reading of Whitman's poem on the assassination of Lincoln, and beyond this lies a whole tradition of pastoral elegy which reaches back through 'Lycidas' to Theocritus. What the poem records is the deepening conviction on the young Devlin's part that we, the children, are accomplices of the 'voracious fathers':

> Then, Oh, our shame so massive
> Only a God embraced it and the angel
> Whose hurt and misty rifle shot him down.

That transferred epithet ('hurt and misty rifle') suggests the general complicity: the death testifies to a universal fallenness, to some original sin that makes a sacrificial martyr of its liberators (the analogy with Christ is implicit throughout):

> And sad, Oh sad, that glen with one thin stream
> He met his death in; and a farmer told me
> There was but one small bird to shoot: it sang
> 'Better Beast and know your end, and die
> Than Man with murderous angels in his head.'

Devlin is haunted by these equivocal angels, who lurk in the stony places of the soul. He is insistent that this is an Irish guilt ('No one betrayed him to the foreigner'), one more instance of that Irish tradition of keeping murder within the family. 'It is inside our life the angel happens', announcing that foreign power which is our own mortality and otherness. The ending is richly ambivalent, framing the death with the poet's reception of it, in his own separate life, distinguishing the rawness of the immediate, unformed and inchoate response from its placing now, in an explicit act of retrospect which locates it as just one more betrayal in a whole history of defections and dereliction:

> Walking to Vespers in my Jesuit school,
> The sky has come and gone: 'O Captain, my Captain!'
> Walt Whitman was the lesson that afternoon –
> How sometimes death magnifies him who dies,
> And some, though mortal, have achieved their race.

That final, outrageous 'Metaphysical' pun, recalling Dryden's elegy on Oldham but also Stephen Dedalus's ambition to 'forge the un-created conscience of [his] race' suggests the homiletic purpose of this poem. Like Pascal, Devlin was preoccupied with the imposs-ibility of justice in a world divided by custom and state, convinced that of all possible evils, civil war was the worst. The 'frightened antinomies' of his poetry transpose into a spiritual and personal dimension the whole condition of Ireland in this this century. The dissension is reproduced in Devlin's poetry as an internal schism in human nature, embodied in the oxymoronic construction which history unfolds as a paradox and truth: 'murderous angels'. 'Old Jacobin' (*Devlin*, pp. 56-7; *CPD*, pp. 167-8) is a fine poem which combines the fervent political commitment of 'Michael Collins' with the poised and worldly relaxation of 'Turcoman Diplomat'. Like many of Devlin's poems, it specifies the civil war within the self in terms of a clash between past and present, fanaticism and scepticism, this-worldly and other-worldly values. Yet neither invalidates the other. Selfhood is the equilibrium that can admit 'the tragic teaching of Jansenism [which] insisted upon the essential vanity of the world and upon the fact that salvation could be found only in solitude and withdrawal', and yet seek that 'solitude and withdrawal' within the hectic arena of history. As Goldmann puts it:

> Prevented by the presence of God from ever accepting the world, but prevented at the same time by His absence from abandoning it altogether, he is constantly dominated by a permanent and fully justified awareness of the radical incongruity between himself and everything around him, of the unbridgeable gulf which separates him both from any real values and from any possible acceptance of the immediate reality of the ordinary external world. The situation of tragic man is paradoxical and can be explained only by paradoxes: for he is in the world and conscious of it from within, but refuses the world because of its inadequate and fragmentary nature.[8]

The poem is another retrospect, in which the Old Jacobin makes his reckoning with God and history:

> In the light of innocence
> The slag is washed away
> I make my soul, am peaceful
> As though I had never sinned. . . .

But those same sins are acknowledged, as the necessary evils a man takes upon himself in trying to reform an unregenerate world. The discrimination is Jesuitical in its separation of intention and consequence.

> Never lied to the people
> Lying to themselves
> As I flagged them on with promises
> Like the lover loving less than the beloved
> Looking in her gentle face
> Comforting her with lies.

That acknowledgement is crucial: the revolutionary cares *less* (i.e., is more *disinterested*) than those he leads on, and in that fine carelessness lies the secret of his gift. For him, history is a drama (as for St John in 'The Colours of Love'), an unreal scenario to which the intending communicant must commit himself until his faith is vindicated, made real, as the soul is constructed from the self's dialogue with silence:

> The sun was gone from my father's garden
> The white bodies vanished from the stream
> And gunmetal twilight steeled my madness;
> And I wore the pandemonium of the heroes.
> But the antique stuffs I wrapt my virtue in:
> Porous they proved to the maleficent winds
> When prison walls
> Roared in my ears high and black like thunder
> The time I signed away the men I loved.
> Where were the hero-selves that my imperium
> Summoned from the *Odes*, the Roman *Lives*
> To walk with me on the lawns in my green time?

What calls him to this sacrifice, of himself and those he loves, is a more pressing reality, the grief of others which is always real and absolute in a way that one's own never is, the ghosts of starving children and their weeping fathers:

> I shouted in the Assembly; the deputies
>
> Blushed in the drama. They knew and I
> The Goddess Reason's treasonable trance. . . .
>
> Still to quiet the children's crying, how I would give
> My one blood and heart! But that was done, Christ!
> Nor did that Tree bear like a round apple
> The all good here; nevertheless
> As the water bears the light equably
> As I will have no shame before my father
> I bear my life
> Without regret or praise.

The 'garden' cannot be restored in this world; the children still cry. But it was enough to try, to throw oneself unequivocally into the theatrical embarrassments of history. The repeated 'bear' gathers to it innumerable resonances: life is a cross to bear, a bringing to birth, and an enduring which in the end is beyond 'regret or praise', a bearing of the self well; for 'we must endure/Our going hence even as our coming hither'. Precarious guest in the green world of appearances, the self must trace the rivers to their source, to 'that harsh glare where all language loses its power', where all allegiances are sloughed. But that glare can turn to grace, for it is precisely in these 'stale and empty places', amidst the 'bitter watercress' of disillusion, disappointment and defeat, that the self whose only pursuit was justice can find its absolution. The fine balance of lyric plangency and ascetic rigour with which the poem ends catches the equipoise of chastity and charity which is Devlin's own particular gift − the precarious resolution of antinomies[9] in the unique tones of an individual voice:

> Bitter watercress
> Long water widening to where
> There is but water and light and air.

Notes

1 St-John Perse, *Exile and Other Poems*, bilingual edition with translation by Denis Devlin, Pantheon Books, New York, Bollingen Series, 15, 1953. The poem cited is 'Snows'. The text of subsequent quotations from Devlin with the exception of *The Heavenly Foreigner,* follows that of Coffey's 1964 edition (*Devlin*); page-references to *CPD* are also given.

2 Denis Devlin, *The Heavenly Foreigner*, variorum edition, edited with introduction and notes by Brian Coffey, Dolmen Press, Dublin, 1967. Text also available in *Devlin* (in an earlier form) and *CPD*.

3 W. M. Walker, 'Irish Immigrants in Scotland: Their Priests, Politics and Parochial Life', *The Historical Journal*, 15, 1972, pp. 649-67.

4 Lucien Goldmann, *The Hidden God*, trans. Philip Thody, Routledge and Kegan Paul, London, 1964, pp. 103-41.

5 Denis Devlin, *Intercessions*, Europa Press, Paris, 1937.

6 The Turkish word for Greece is 'Yunanistan'. 'Yunani' is a corruption of 'Romani', as applied to the inhabitants of the Eastern Roman Empire in Constantinople.

7 Edward Norman, *A History of Modern Ireland*, Penguin Books, London, 1971, pp. 296-7.

8 Goldmann, pp. 55-6.

9 I have discussed this aspect of Devlin's work at greater length in 'Frightened Antinomies: Love and Death in the Poetry of Denis Devlin', edited by Brian Coffey, *Advent VI,* Denis Devlin special issue, Advent Books, Southampton, 1976, pp. 24–30.

10

'Unificator':
George Reavey and the Europa Poets of the 1930s[1]

Thomas Dillon Redshaw

Four months before Prime Minister Chamberlain flew back from Berchtesgaden, on May Day in 1938, four British surrealists – Roland Penrose, Julian Trevelyan, James Cant, and T. Graham – acted out their left sympathies by organizing a procession in London's Hyde Park to indict the advance of fascism in Spain. Perhaps just newsreel stills, numerous monochrome photographs document this cortège.[2] Broadcasting Spanish republican ballads from a van that housed a skeleton hung in a cage, the protesters also rigged up an ice-cream tricycle with a wire horse's head filled with balloons. Following that in pantomime came four Chamberlains complete with wing collars, tailcoats, top hats, and umbrellas, and each wore a caricature mask fabricated by the Belfast sculptor F.E. McWilliam.[3] Around the neck of each Chamberlain impostor hung a placard reading 'Chamberlain Must Go'.[4] Curiously, the photographs of this political moment retain more *élan* than do either the several group portraits of the London surrealists – stills from Gaumont footage – or such intentional compositions as that of Sheila Legge posed as a rose-headed 'Surrealist Phantom' among the pigeons of Trafalgar Square.[5] That photograph ornaments the fourth *International Surrealist Bulletin* (1936) which Zwemmer issued to celebrate the arrival of Continental surrealism in London. Welcomed by Herbert Read, Roland Penrose, and David Gascoyne, surrealism documented well its own migration from Paris's cafés, studios, and galleries. Likewise, the British artist Julian Trevelyan (1910–1988) had come to London in 1934, after he had worked witn S.W. Hayter for three years at Atelier 17. In the same year, Trevelyan's *confrère* the poet, translator, and publisher George Reavey also left Paris to settle in London.

A decade earlier, and before the devaluation of sterling, both Trevelyan and Reavey sought in Paris what others of their generation sought — romance, literary apprenticeship, artistic induction into an avant-garde. And, by the early 1930s, the Anglophone milieu of the Rive Gauche had its 'diary' in Wambly Bald's 'La Vie de Bohème' column of the American *Paris Tribune*. In this column Bald noted the doings of socialites and Bohemians, famous and infamous, and several columns featured anecdotes about George Reavey (1907–1976).[6] Reavey's presence at the Dôme, or in Sylvia Beach's Shakespeare and Company shop, or in Samuel Putnam's *New Review* offices, or further south in Cagnes-sur-Mer, precisely coincided with an efflorescence in Paris of expatriate avant-garde publishing in English between 1926 and 1934, the year of the Stavisky riots and the rise of the *Front Populaire*. The American dollar financed many of these avant-garde presses — the Crosbys' Black Sun (1922–31), or Titus's Black Manikin (1926–32) — and most of them strove to bring into print the work of an earlier generation — of Lawrence, Pound, and Joyce, whose *Work in Progress* regularly appeared in Eugene Jolas's *transition* (1927–38). Chief among competitors with Jolas were, first, Walsh's and then Titus's *This Quarter* (1925–32) and *The New Review* (1930–32), edited by the American translator Samuel Putnam (1892–1950).[7]

Putnam saw the last of the *New Review* books into print in 1932, including the poems of Reavey's *Faust's Metamorphoses*. Since Thomas MacGreevy (1893–1967) had introduced Reavey to Samuel Beckett, to the Joyce circle, and to *transition* writers in 1928,[8] Reavey might well have come directly under Eugene Jolas's wing, but Reavey spent his first months in France, before he moved to Villa Brune in Paris with Julian Trevelyan in 1930, as a private English-language tutor in Fontainebleau.[9] Owing to Gurdjieff's presence there, Reavey had contact with *emigré* Russians, as well as with Ilya Ehrenburg in Paris, and so he continued to translate *fin-de-siècle* Russian and early Soviet writing, some of which later appeared in his *Soviet Literature* (1933) after Putnam failed to bring out the second volume of *The European Caravan*. After moving to the Villa Brune — where the sculptor Alexander Calder and the jazz guitarist Django Reinhardt, for instance, had studios – Reavey frequented such cafés as the Dôme and the Flore, and he came to meet such literary figures as Walter Lowenfels and André Breton, as well as such painters as R.O. Dunlop, the van Velde brothers, Model, and those artists like Trevelyan who worked at Hayter's Atelier 17. In 1933, just before the death of his mistress Andrée Conte, whom he called 'Karma', Reavey set up the Bureau Littéraire Européen with the translator Marc Slonim. Despite his disappointment over *The European Caravan*, Reavey had hopes of imitating Putnam's example as a literary agent, as a translator, and as an editor and publisher.

Reavey had moved to Paris from London in the autumn of 1929 under the pretext of polishing his French for the Indian civil service examinations. His parents – Daniel Reavey (1876–1938), a Belfast flax engineer, and Sophia Turchenko Reavey (1883–1957) – had managed to send him up to Gonville and Caius College, Cambridge University, as an exhibitioner in history and literature. Reavey's fluency in Russian came from his mother, from his birth and infancy in Vitebsk, and from his early schooling in Nizhninovgorod, where the Reavey family lived from 1909 to 1919. After his father's arrest during the Russian civil war, Reavey went with his mother to live at Stramore, in Chichester Park, Belfast. Reavey continued his schooling at the Royal Belfast Academical Institution (1919–21) and then at the Sloane School (1921–26) in London, after the family had settled in Fulham. During the summers, Reavey was often sent back to Belfast, and his school notebooks record ballads and Gaelic verses learned from Joseph Reavey, his County Down uncle, as well as transcriptions from the Russian.[10] Armed with Russian as his mother tongue, at Cambridge Reavey gravitated towards the *Experiment* circle dominated by William Empson and Jacob Bronowski, but including the American Richard Eberhart, as well as Charles Madge, Kathleen Raine, and Julian Trevelyan. To the pages of *Experiment* (1928–31) Reavey contributed prose experiments, verse, and translations – chiefly of Pasternak. From *Experiment*'s pages Eugene Jolas later selected some thirty pages for his 'Revolution of the Word' issue of *transition* (1930).[11] Despite this entrée, and despite Reavey's affiliation with MacGreevy and Beckett, it was Samuel Putnam, rather than Jolas, who first helped Reavey into print.

Reavey's Cambridge translations from Pasternak[12] and his contributions to *Experiment* fitted him for a part in the grand project of Putnam's two-volume *Anthology of the New Spirit in European Literature*, or more briefly *The European Caravan* (June 1931), whose first and only published volume included work by Beckett, Mac-Greevy, John Lyle Donaghy, and Geoffrey Taylor – all introduced by Bronowski.[13] Reavey researched, introduced, and translated many of the Russian pages of *The European Caravan*'s proposed but unpublished second volume. His *New Review* (December 1932) article on Andrei Biely, for instance, had probably been intended for the *Caravan*'s second volume.

Though immersed in Russian writing, Reavey was also recomposing *Faust's Metamorphoses* from his collegiate drafts. Announced for publication in April 1932, *Faust's Metamorphoses* bore Putnam's 'Foreword to a Sunken Continent' which claimed Reavey as one of the 'after-Joyce Irishmen' who had been able 'to take Surrealism with no bad after-effect.'[14] By identifying Reavey with the Joyce 'circle' by way of his acquaintance with MacGreevy and Beckett, Putnam suggests that Reavey's Marlovian Romanticism has postmodern predilections in two senses: first, that Reavey's surrealism derives from a sensibility prone to premonitory bricolage, and second, but more importantly, that Reavey's sensibility derives not from cosmopolitanism but from a displacedness that expresses itself in masks, personae, and the ventriloquism of translation. In *Faust's Metamorphoses* Reavey's tonalities prove largely Eliotic, but the linguistic method is 'after' Joyce, as in 'Post-Mortem of Faust: An Evening Elegy':

> After the wars and Vasco de Gama
> florid false-gothic
> Browning puffed
> in slowpuffs syllabic factorial.
> Trains mechanically brought
> Les Fleurs du Mal[15]

Reavey's twenty *vers libre* monologues, or 'metamorphoses', employ the mask of Marlowe's Faust in an effort to shape a personal and romantic aestheticism: '. . . I am in revolt against the brute fact – the realism – the naturalism – the insignificant saturation.'[16] Reavey had rather heretical hopes for these poems, hopes appropriate to the transcendentalism of the 'Montparnasse Meditation Company', but his colophon to the collection betrays the weaker aspirations of an undergraduate aestheticism. Because S.W. Hayter illustrated

Faust's Metamorphoses with six engravings pulled at Atelier 17, both his signature and Reavey's appear under the colophon.[17]

Published from the Bureau Littéraire Européen, Reavey's three Paris printings — *Nostradam, Signes d'Adieu*, and Beckett's *Echo's Bones* — constitute the 'Europa Poets', numbers I through III. In these first Europa Press examples Reavey has clearly followed the basic design of *Faust's Metamorphoses* as issued by Putnam. Likewise, as the colophons and illustrations, by Hayter and Roger Vieillard, of the first two titles suggest, Reavey intended these titles for collectors and his own Paris circle. But Reavey had begun to find in London a consistent market for his prose translations of Nicolaevsky and Berdyaev. In 1934, a year after Wishart issued his *Soviet Literature*,[18] Reavey moved the European Literary Bureau and Europa Press to London. Thus, *Echo's Bones and Other Precipitates* (November 1935), though it was Reavey's last Paris printing, addressed chiefly avant-garde Anglophone readers, for whom Reavey had also planned to publish poems by Denis Devlin in 1935.[19] Compared with Reavey's monologues, the clarity of tone and focus in Beckett's lines gives a sharp sense of place and voice, as in the echoed memories of 'Enueg II':

> doch I assure thee
> lying on O'Connell Bridge
> goggling at the tulips of the evening
> the green tulips
> shining round the corner like an anthrax
> shining in Guinness's barges[20]

Owing to Beckett's eventual 'after-Joyce' mastery of the existential monologue in fiction and then drama, the thirteen titles in *Echo's Bones*, such as 'Dortmunder' or 'Malacoda', have come to figure rather more pertinently in literary history than the sixteen poems of Reavey's *Nostradam* (May 1935) or the thirteen brevities of his *Signes d'Adieu* (May 1935). These Pierre Charnay had selected to translate into French from the 'Frailties of Love' which Reavey composed from December 1933, through January 1934, for Andrée Conte, who died later in 1934.[21] Charnay's introductory note asserts that Reavey sought 'à découvrir un point d'appui dans le remous du monde moderne et parmi son effroyable vide', but these lyric *pensées* seem now to pose a conventional erotic melancholia. In contrast, the rhymed lines of *Nostradam* seek to 'build' a theme connecting Reavey's 'emotive life and the world of historical experience', and Reavey attempts this through masking and ventriloquism, again, in a period that he sees as an historical reiteration because 'Faust's twelfth hour is so poignantly like our own.'[22] The poems of *Nostradam* fall into two 'cycles' or sequences: 'A Word for Nostradamus', ten titles dedicated to Hayter, Pasternak, Essenin, among others; and the six titles of 'À La Belle Dame Sans Merci'. Dated from 1930 through 1932, these poems indulge in hyperbole both romantic and prophetic, as in 'Bombs for All', dedicated to Mayakosky:

> O Dynamite! The soul's explosion wrought
> Will start the dead with crash of buildings tall;
> Look where flames' thongs shall lash the sky's face torn![23]

The inversions suggest syncopation, the lines suggest the declamatory habits of Russian public verse, and the apocalyptic imagery suggests, if not futurism, then a future shortly to be foretold in Abyssinia and Spain. While Hayter's white decoration for the black wrap of *Nostradam* suggests amorphous and pent-up energies, Reavey's poems exercise those energies through the personae and poses of the Occidental past.

Reavey's return to London was part of a larger migration.[24] From 1934 through 1936, David Gascoyne, Herbert Read, E.L.T. Mesens, and Roland Penrose transplanted surrealism in prose and paint from Paris into London's galleries and salons chiefly through highly publicized exhibitions at, for example, the Mayor and New Burlington galleries. Zwemmer issued the 1936 *International Surrealist Bulletin*, while Mesens edited and published the *London Bulletin* through the 1940s. Gascoyne's *Short Survey of Surrealism* (1935), followed by Herbert Read's essays in *Surrealism* (1936), marked the movement's critical arrival in the milieu of London letters.[25] More importantly, the occasional presence in London of Max Ernst and René Magritte, or of Paul Eluard and André Breton, helped to graft Continental sensibilities onto British painting, graphics, assemblage, 'performance art' — like the 1938 May Day procession mocking Chamberlain — and writing, as in Hugh Sykes-Davies's *Petron* (1935), Gascoyne's *Man's Life This Meat* (1936), or in the pages of Roger Roughton's *Contemporary Poets and Prose* (1936–37). Both Roughton's 'little' magazine and *Man's Life This Meat* were published from David

Archer's Parton Street bookshop just around the corner from the offices of Reavey's European Literary Bureau in Red Lion Square.

With the opening of the International Surrealist Exhibition in June, 1936, at the New Burlington galleries came Reavey's Europa Press edition of Paul Eluard's poetry entitled *Thorns of Thunder*. Perhaps more important to literary history than Putnam's *European Caravan*, Reavey's edition of Eluard's selected poems contains translations chiefly by Beckett, Devlin, Gascoyne, and himself, with a few by Eugene Jolas, Man Ray, and Ruthven Todd – all identified in print by their initials.[26] Quoting Eluard's claim that '. . . everything has its echo, its reason, its resemblance, its opposition, and its becoming everywhere . . .', Reavey's foreword also claims that 'The systematic application of Eluard's concept to art is one of the main features of the surrealist movement to-day . . .'. While Herbert Read's short preface stresses 'imaginative faculty', Reavey's introduction prefers Romanticism by identifying Eluard as 'one of the few genuine love poets writing in an out-of-love world'.[27] Of the forty-four titles in *Thorns of Thunder*, Beckett rendered seven into English and Devlin five, and their choices interestingly forecast themes yet to come in their own writing. Beckett's version of 'Second Nature', for instance, anticipates the entropy of *Endgame*:

> In honour of the dumb the blind the deaf
> Shouldering the great black stone
> The things of time passing simply . . .[28]

Likewise, Denis Devlin's version of 'Girls in Love' foretells the fideism of *The Heavenly Foreigner*: 'They must be believed on a kiss/On a word and a look/Only their kisses are to be kissed.'[29] Reavey translated seventeen of the poems in *Thorns of Thunder*, many appropriately titled after such artists as Ernst, Klee, Miró, and Picasso, for Ernst designed the book's lilac wrapper and Picasso provided the frontispiece portrait of Eluard. The latter of Reavey's translations in *Thorns of Thunder* express his aestheticism a bit more programmatically, for Reavey chose three fragments entitled 'Poetic Objectivity', which 'only exists in the succession, the linking together of all the subjective elements of which the poet, until the beginning of the new order is not the master but the slave.'[30] Although Reavey made sure of closing *Thorns of Thunder* with an insistent notice of future 'Europa

Publications' by Devlin, Apollinaire, Pasternak, Mayakovsky, and Dylan Thomas, the practical matters of printing, binding, and distributing *Thorns of Thunder* were all overseen by Stanley Nott.

From 1936 through 1939 Reavey tenaciously continued to publish poetry and critical prose in publications of a surrealist inclination – contributing, for example, to Mesens's *London Bulletin* and to Read's *Surrealism* (1936) – while he was also translating much of Nicolai Berdyaev, even through the 1940s, for the Centenary Press.[31] Marc Slonim having kept an office in Paris, Reavey reconstituted the European Literary Bureau as a literary agency devoted to the translation or 'transmission', really, of Continental and expatriate writing. Although Reavey did help secure the London publication of *Murphy* (1937) for Samuel Beckett,[32] his offices in Red Lion Square served mainly as a haven for Europa Press, which issued four titles in 1939. Of these, *Intercessions* (1937) by Denis Devlin and, to a lesser degree, *Third Person* (1938) by Brian Coffey have won a place in Irish literary history owing to their aboriginal context in the translated and transplanted milieu of British surrealist publishings.

Reavey issued Devlin's *Intercessions* and Coffey's *Third Person* in limited editions of three hundred. Just as Beckett's *Echo's Bones* gives a plain example of French book-making, so *Intercessions* offers an example of chaste British printing. That restraint distinguishes *Intercessions* from *Thorns of Thunder* and, later, from both *Third Person* and Reavey's own *Quixotic Perquisitions* (1939), for those titles evidence Reavey's inclination towards the connoisseur's taste. While both were students at University College, Dublin, Coffey and Devlin had published *Poems* (September 1930) together, and Coffey had his *Three Poems* (February 1933) printed in Paris, where both learned of Reavey and the Europa Press, and from Beckett rather than from MacGreevy.[33] Devlin's letters to MacGreevy suggest not only that Devlin argued Reavey out of producing a 'precious' private edition of *Intercessions* in favour of a more proletarian one, but that Devlin also subsidized its printing, just as Beckett had backed *Echo's Bones*.[34] Despite Reavey's usual financial and managerial distractions, *Intercessions* proved to be the most substantial of the Europa books after *Thorns of Thunder*. Technically and thematically, *Intercessions* contributes more decisively and rewardingly to Devlin's canon than does *Echo's Bones* to Beckett's canon, composed, as it is, of fiction and drama. Five poems from *Intercessions* reappear in Devlin's *Lough Derg and Other Poems* (1946): 'Victory of Samothrace', 'Daphne Stillorgan', 'Bacchanal', 'Est Prodest', and 'The Lancet'.[35] While 'Est Prodest' anticipates Devlin's Catholic and transcendental preoccupations to come – as implied, as well, by the title *Intercessions* – poems like 'Communication from the Eiffel Tower' and 'Bacchanal' establish in their respectively futurist and surrealist manners the ground for those preoccupations:

> Those with hands like shrinking linen that
>   deprecate the state of affairs,
> Parsing their attitudes, fleas in intricate corri-
>   dors of interlocking hairs,
> Those that are Not so sure that the poor in
>   pogrom will not be rather a Bore,
> Lips bitter-sweet, they know by Culture they
>   know Human Nature can grow no more; . . . (*I*, p. 29)

Often overlooked as a period piece, 'Bacchanal' retains the rich tonalities created by the dreadful energies of the 1930s. Devlin took care to revise 'Bacchanal' over a span of some six years. In response to MacGreevy's comments on the typescript of *Intercessions*, Devlin defended the long loaded lines of 'Bacchanal': 'I want to avoid telescoping and thus gnomic poems'.[36] 'Bacchanal' has its original text in 'News of Revolution', composed between 1931 and 1933. Consequently, not only does the poem have its origin in Devlin's early contact with, say, Eluard's poetry in Paris, it also spans the time of Devlin's entry into the Irish diplomatic corps, including his service with de Valera at the League of Nations in Geneva.[37] Those same years saw the rise of Nazism, the bombing of Guernica during the Spanish civil war, the appearance of Haile Selassie before the League of Nations, and the Berlin Olympiad of 1936.[38] In consequence, 'Bacchanal' lets athleticism melt into militarism in a scope more epic than that provided by, say, William Carlos Williams in 'The Yachts'. Sometimes using urban speech in Louis MacNeice's syncopated way, the poem also loads repeated journalese with a sense of fatal totalitarianism, as in Dylan Thomas's 'The Hand that Signed the Paper'. Given its mythologizing sweep of scene and tone, resembling that of a St-John Perse poem, 'Bacchanal' also resembles a very large canvas by Max Ernst.

> Forerunners run naked as sharks through water,
>   nose to their prey, have message by heart
> Their thighs will be tackled, Look Out They're
>   Away clipping the wind, they've gained on
>   their start
> The wind thrusts knives in their teeth, harrows
>   the stubble of parched throats
> The front line licks its fire, leaderless, can they
>   cut their way to the boats?
> They have never eaten nor drunk nor slept
>   their fill, and have no quick-wit means,
> Only envy learnt in feeding the shutfist pistoned
>   right machines.
> Canaille, canaille, what red horizons of anger
>   for humbled lives lie
> Tumbled up in the old times, the long-ferment-
>   ing now, canaille!   (*I*, pp. 26-7)

Devlin's reworking of 'News of Revolution' into 'Bacchanal' partly answered MacGreevy's comments and partly responded to the darkening vistas of the 1930s. By juxtaposing human exploits with human victimization, the poem leaves the reader with a tingling sense of fatality, of the impossibility of individual heroism, of the inevitable advent of the mass-man.

Like Devlin, Brian Coffey sent a typescript of eighteen poems, entitled 'Image at the Cinema', to MacGreevy as well as to Reavey, who announced it for publication in 1935 as 'Europa Poets II'.[39] This typescript did not become the Europa Press book that was published in 1938. *Third Person* shares with the earlier typescript 'Image at the Cinema' only one title: 'A Drop of Fire'.

> If memory which does not err
> holds a garden farthest back
> where the flowers cast no shadow
> what is that to you or to me
> The way up is the way down
> when blood has soured in the breast.   (*TP*, p. 19)

Coffey's withdrawn or abstract, gnostic and gnomic lines received no plain printing in *Third Person*. S.W. Hayter supplied for those fourteen poems an engraved frontispiece in the collector's binding — copies I through XXV — and Reavey chose deckle edge paper for the text of all copies. Not only does *Third Person* embody Reavey's aesthetic aspirations, its interior and wrapper advertisements also list seven titles for the 'Europa Poets' — all 'limited editions in collaboration with modern artists and engravers' — and announce Reavey's *Quixotic Perquisitions* and *The Burning Baby*, short stories by Dylan Thomas (see *TP*, p. 30).

Another Parisian expatriate, the American Charles Henri Ford, provided Reavey with the sixth Europa Poets book: *The Garden of Disorder*. Ford and Parker Tyler had published a notorious novel *The Young and the Evil* (1933) with Obelisk Press in Paris. Ford's connection with Reavey came not just through Bald's gossip page in the *Paris Tribune*, which reported on both, but also through Putnam's *New Review*. Ford appealed to Reavey's Slavophilia by introducing him to the artistry of Pavel Tchelitchew, who drew the frontispiece for *The Garden of Disorder*. Ford's lines also brought to the Europa Poets list an American dialect flavoured with novel rhythms and tones more syncopated than plangent, bluesy rather than mauve:

> When I was a candy kid down in Dixie
> an all-day sucker went all too quickly;
> and now that I'm a grown-up man,
> sweet things melt as fast as they can.[40]

Ford's jazzy diction, his 'dicty-glide', juxtaposed with his affection for sonnet rhymes and Marlowe, helps *The Garden of Disorder* fit into the setting of migrant surrealism and of, in Reavey's words, the Europa Poets 'Dante-Marlowe-Rimbaud perspective'.[41] In his collection Ford gathered forty-four poems into four groups: 'The Garden of Disorder, to Pavel Tchelitchew', 'A Pamphlet of Sonnet', four dedicated to Djuna Barnes and five to Tchelitchew; 'Early Lyrics'; and 'Later Lyrics', including 'Plaint': 'I, Rainey Betha, 22,/from the top-branch of race-hatred look at you'.[42]

Owing to Ford's publications in *Pagany* in the United States, William Carlos Williams supplied the introduction to *The Garden of Disorder*. In 'The Tortuous Straightness of Charles Henri Ford' (June 1937), Williams's view of the poems proves both critical and clever: the poems 'form an accompaniment to the radio jazz and other various, half preaching, half sacrilegious sounds of a Saturday night in June with the windows open and the mind stretched out attempting to regain some sort of quiet and be cool . . .'[43] Because

New Directions Press had become the champion of Williams's writing, James Laughlin acquired from Reavey bound copies of *The Garden of Disorder*, with tipped-in title page, for publication in North America (October 1938). Laughlin also contracted to purchase from Reavey's European Literary Bureau the printed sheet of Dylan Thomas's 'The Burning Baby'.

Not only did Reavey acquire 'The Burning Baby' stories in December, 1937, he also obtained rights to reissue Thomas's famous *18 Poems* (1934) early in 1938. Reavey hoped to decorate his Europa edition of Thomas's stories with a frontispiece portrait of Thomas by Augustus John, but John proved recalcitrant. Then, having scented in Thomas's prose the offending odour of lewd *double-entendre*, Reavey's English typesetters balked, which encouraged Reavey to shift the printing to Paris and produce a 'fine' collector's edition. That prospect, in turn, offended Thomas. Finally, James Laughlin bought the American rights for New Directions printings of both the poems and the stories, which Dent issued as *The Map of Love* (1939) in London.[44] Reavey's fruitless efforts to publish Thomas underscore the tenuity of his financing and the limits of his diplomacy. Though very much a 'small' publisher, Reavey was not alone in his troubles, for British publishing as a whole was undergoing a troubled period. Even large and well-financed publishers, unless they had private supplies of printing stock stored up, had to circumscribe their efforts after the Munich crisis and during the 'Bore War' of 1939–40. Moreover, during the opening months of World War II, London's literary life metamorphosed in ways even the London surrealists might not have dreamed of: Bloomsbury became the Ministry of Information; Eliot's *Criterion* closed down and in its place appeared *Lilliput*; and the pub-talk of Fitzrovia carried on the discourse of the arts.[45]

Similar problems thwarted Reavey's other plans for the Europa Poets. In 1936 Reavey had hoped to print David Gascoyne's poems as well as translations of Apollinaire, Mayakovsky, and Pasternak. Only the latter came into print, but more than two decades later in 1959. Likewise, in 1935 Reavey had announced Brian Coffey's 'Image at the Cinema' as 'Europa Poets II', as well as collections from his own hand: the English poems of 'Frailty of Love', 'The Damnation of Faust', to be decorated by Hayter; and a selection of manifestos and essays to be entitled 'At the Crossroads of Time'. These projects, however, hung fire through 1939, and even then Reavey announced new collections by Frederick Brockway and by Henry Treece, a founder of the 'New Apocalypse' movement. Ever hopeful, late in 1938 Reavey prepared a mock-book typescript of 'The Endless Chain', his 'Selected Poems, 1930–38'.[46] The contraction of literary publishing after the Munich crisis, however, prompted Reavey to get just his *Quixotic Perquisitions* into print.

Published in the spring of 1939, *Quixotic Perquisitions* proved to be the eighth and last of the Europa Poets books, although the wrapper and verso of the half-title page announced five more titles 'In Preparation', including, Reavey's second series of 'Quixotic Perquisitions', the book of essays retitled as 'The Rape of Europe', and the selected poems of 'The Endless Chain'. By writing extensive notes and a 'Postscriptum' for *Quixotic Perquisitions* in October, 1938, weeks after the Munich crisis, Reavey not only offered a thematic frame for the poems, he also provided a foretaste of the interrogations that motivated his unpublished essays. Some of these, of course, were pioneering composition in Soviet literary history while other essays were to extend such philosophical queries as this, which closes the 1938 'Postscriptum':

> . . . Hence the paradox of socially applied solar mechanics, that of the human psyche trapped on an escalator paradise. But accident must speak for itself. May not 'l'homme machine' be washed another man in the waters of reflection and viscissitude?[47]

The external dialectic of accident and 'solar mechanics' remained Reavey's chief concern even after World War II, for by then it had acquired experiential immediacy for him, not just aesthetic or philosophical perquistiveness. Reavey reprinted 'De Revolutionibus: A Copernican Poem' several times in the 1970s, for instance, long after it had appeared in *Quixotic Perquisitions*:

> . . . earth's, stars' revolution,
> – man's is a different dream, –
> signing hymns in your honour, O Sancho Proles!
> Where's your place, destiny's wheel?[48]

In contrast, Reavey never republished his 'Christmas and New Year Greetings' of 1938 in which, in the very mixed mood of that season, he invokes the past 'Builders of Europe' in order to contradict

> The travail of our gnawing doubt
> The Commerce of false reasoning,
> The endless chain of circumstance. . . .[49]

Reavey prepared the poems in *Quixotic Perquisitions* from a body of work dating from 1932 and collected since 1935 for 'The Endless Chain', as the typescript dates of July – October, 1938, suggest. Both that typescript and the finely printed pages of *Quixotic Perquisitions* allude, moreover, to the Belgian surrealist painter René Magritte (1898-1967).

During the 1930s Reavey collected paintings by Magritte and by Paul Delvaux, as well as collages by Max Ernst and E.L.T. Mesens,[50] and Magritte's tropes and *trompe l'oeil* effects clearly figure in Reavey's poetry. Expecting to use it as a frontispiece, Reavey titled his selected poems after Magritte's painting *La chaîne sans fin* (1938). For *Quixotic Perquisitions*, however, Reavey used an engraving of Cervantes' hero by John Buckland-Wright, a student of S.W. Hayter. For 'The Endless Chain' Reavey selected thirty-three poems, including a prose-and-verse sequence based on the imagery of Magritte's painting. *La chaîne sans fin* clearly and colourfully presents a horse being ridden off to the viewer's left by three men: the first in boots and bowler, behind him a second and a twin in Italian or English Renaissance hose and doublet, and behind him a Roman or Greek triplet in white toga or chiton – all depicted 'superrealistically', to use Herbert Read's term. As set and printed by René Hague and Eric Gill, *Quixotic Perquisitions* alludes to Magritte's *Le pont d'Héraclite* (1935) twice, once in the 1938 'Postscriptum':

> The gulf between illusion and reality is no less: the halfway house of realization – *The Bridge of Heraclitus* – is more than ever our destiny, for time has forged a new and more efficient machinery against us (*QP*, p. 32).

The fifteen poems of the collection also borrow motifs from Cervantes in Reavey's ventriloquizing manner, and nowhere more clearly than in the poem 'The Bridge of Heraclitus'. In the mere nine lines of that terse parable Reavey proposes himself as the idealist Quixote stopped on a bridge spanning 'limpid water' that conceals where

> Real eddies surged, decades', days' increasing now;
> And Don Quixote urging Rozinante to excel,
> Was in the waters' mirror washed another man,
> His goal half-won, but Dulcinea still his talisman.   (*QP*, p. 4)

In Magritte's painting there is no Quixote or Rozinante, but there is a concrete bridge that reaches the left bank only in its watery reflection. The 'real' bridge, however, dissolves into a bank of impossibly low clouds. In Reavey's poem, Quixote's horse, an emblem of animal and perhaps Marxist materialism, refuses to budge. Yet, Quixote strains forward toward the connected ideal he can imagine, while the flowing waters reflect him baptized, accepting a 'goal half-won'.

In the typescript of 'The Endless Chain', however, the bleaker personae of Faust and Nostradamus dominate the Cervantesque masks of *Quixotic Perquisitions*, in accord with the implications of Reavey's draft of the preface: '. . . our world is that of Marlowe or Faust in the twelfth hour . . . [not] that *the* world is coming to an end, but that *a* world is approaching its tragic dénouement.'[51] So, almost inevitably in 1938–39, the poses of Reavey's customary *personae* became only the symptoms of a two-fold problem that had motivated Reavey's poetic speculations since his Cambridge years. First, given the distresses of World War I and its totalitarian aftermaths, how might human individuality plausibly be asserted in an inhospitable mass culture? Or, second, given the increasing internal antipathies of that culture, how might its positive qualities be asserted by the discrete human subject? Futurists, Dadaists, and finally the surrealists cultivated both aphasia and intuition so as to salvage from the wreck and from the mass a place for personal idealism. However limited by a certain collegiate aestheticism, that salvaging had become Reavey's ambition as well, and he was fitted by his educations and his literary career to hope that even traditions created by the High Culture had survived in the delusory 'escalator paradise' of mass culture. Consequently, in the early months of the 1930s Reavey was sometimes emboldened to entitle himself 'unificator', but in the latter months of the 1930s he had arrived at an increased sense of his own circumscription:

> I am endeavoring to suggest a whole experience, . . . an experience
> of contradictions. . . . The real protagonist is Western Man − a

very definite and limited psychological type . . . one divided against
himself when seen from within. . . .[52]

Reavey's decade-long interest in the subjective, in philosophical
contradiction, in types of cultural divisions bounded by the individual
all secured for him a sense of the precarious rarity of idealism —
his 'Dulcinea' — and that sense founded, in turn, a deeper dismay,
as expressed in the essays and the poem entitled 'The Rape of Europe':

> . . . Expectant Europe armed, air-raided,
> Perplexed in this uncertain weather;
> Involved, inconstant but determined,
> In sawing winds', sharp whirlwind's swirl,
> She dares her destiny, stars' whirl.   (*QP*, p. 31)

Though published by Mesens in the surrealist *London Bulletin*, 'The
Rape of Europe' is one of Reavey's most conventional compositions.
Orthodox in poetic language, its four-stress lines allude canonical-
ly to Milton, to Blake, and especially to Pope — to the vision of
entropy that closes *The Dunciad*. As in a canvas by Max Ernst, the
poem offers imagery on a large scale, but its vision of kinetic disorder
itself proves to be static — as still as a Magritte canvas. The suspended
syntax of Reavey's lines picks up Beckett's bleaker tones, and some
of Devlin's early scorn, and so the MacNeice-like jauntiness of the
opening lines winds up registering little but desperation:

> Ptolemy fades among the stars:
> Goodbye the static world's seclusion,
> Gunpowder rent the seamless robe
> Of one-way-world-safe-from-delusion; . . .   (*QP*, p. 30)

After the dismemberment of Poland, Reavey made his way to the
Soviet-occupied zone of eastern Poland in November, 1939, to rescue
his mother and bring her back to London. Reavey then suspended
the Europa Press and the European Literary Bureau, joined the British
Foreign Office in Madrid, and afterwards was sent to the Soviet
Union via Murmansk. From 1942 through 1945, first in Kiubyshev
in the Urals and then in Moscow, Reavey served as a press attaché
and as an editor of *Britanski Soyuznik* ('British Ally'). On his return
to London in 1945, Reavey quickly composed *Soviet Literature*

To-Day (1946). That book enabled him to emigrate to New York, where he taught Russian literature and published translations of, for example, Pasternak (1959), Yevtushenko (1967), and Biely (1974). Reavey's remarriages – first to Irene Rice Pereira (1901–1971) in 1950 and then to Jean Bullowa (1917–1987) in 1960 – drew him into the New York milieu of postwar painting at the Whitney and theatre in Greenwich Village. Nevertheless, Reavey never revived either his literary agency or his publishing enterprise. While Grove Press issued his *Colours of Memory* (1955), which contains poems from 'The Endless Chain' typescript supplemented by others based on his ill-fated voyage to Murmansk, Reavey's poetry appeared after that only in such private editions – *Seven Seas* (1971), for example – as published by Brian Coffey's Advent Books in England. In the early 1970s Michael Smith included seven poems by Reavey in *The Lace Curtain* (Dublin, 1971), and John Montague two in his *Faber Book of Irish Verse* (1974), just before Reavey's death in 1976. One of Montague's choices was 'The Bridge of Heraclitus'; the other was 'Never', which begins with an ending:

> When the bones walk out of me
> Down the hill and the flesh falls limp
> And lies all still as the wind blows back
> And ever until . . .[53]

Despite excursions back to Paris and London, to Dublin and even Belfast, in the 1950s and 1960s Reavey all but disappeared from English, and thus Irish, literary history – his own poetry thwarted by his war-time experience.[54] In effect, mass event and public history had swept over Reavey's life, as over the lives of so many others, and had submerged his chances for some second poetic parturity. Unwillingly, Reavey found himself 'situated' in Jean-Paul Sartre's sense:

> And our life as an individual . . . seemed governed down to its minutest details by obscure and collective forces, and its most private circumstances seemed to reflect the state of the whole world. All at once we felt ourselves abruptly situated. History flowed in upon us. . . .[55]

While, in consequence, his own poetry may now seem an idiosyncracy redolent of the period, Reavey's ambitions as a publisher did create more than fine editions for the collector and connoisseur. As his advertisements from 1935 through 1939 show, Reavey brought together under the Europa imprint the translations and poems of three Irish writers of Continental character and resources: Brian Coffey, Denis Devlin, and Samuel Beckett. Certainly neither Beckett nor, to a lesser degree, Devlin now lack either academic commentators or international critics.[56] Even so, while the late *Crane Bag* or the Field Day pamphlets have claimed revisionist understandings of Irish writing after Joyce, the accomplishments of the Europa poets have yet to find their place in contemporary Irish criticism, a discourse often bedevilled by Gog-Magog dualisms.[57] Reavey's example as both a publisher and a poet displays, at least, an interplay of influences and resources not usually accounted for as pertinent to Irish literary history, a history itself thwarted in some degree by the 'Great Emergency'. To view the small Europa Press canon in the context of British surrealism, and especially in the situation of the late 1930s, is to view differently from another periphery a period of Irish writing once overruled by Yeats and Joyce and now overshadowed by Kavanagh and MacNeice.

Notes

1 I thank the editors of *The Linen Review* (Belfast) in which a different version of this article appeared (Spring, 1988) for their kind permission to reprint much of it, and I thank Professor R.H. Buchanan and the fellows of the Institute of Irish Studies, The Queen's University of Belfast, for supporting much of my research concerning Reavey during 1986-87.

2 *British Surrealism – Fifty Years On*, The Mayor Gallery Ltd., London, 1986, p. 11. Two other anniversary catalogues provide much documentation: *Surrealism in Britain in the Thirties*, Leeds City Art Galleries, Leeds, 1986 and *Surrealism in England, 1936 and After*, Herbert Read Gallery, Canterbury College of Art, Canterbury, 1986.

3 Mel Gooding, *F.E. McWilliam: Sculpture, 1932-1989* The Tate Gallery, London, 1989, p. 18.

4 Julian Trevelyan, *Indigo Days*, MacGibbon and Kee, London, 1957, pp. 78-80; photograph facing page 112.

5 *International Surrealist Bulletin*, 4 September, 1936, 1; Eileen Agar, *A Look at My Life* Methuen, London, 1988, photograph 8a, facing p. 53.

6 Wambly Bald, *On the Left Bank, 1929-1933*, ed. Benjamin Franklin V, Ohio University Press, Athens, 1987, pp. 57-8, 103, 107-9, 127-8.

7 Hugh Ford, *Published in Paris: American and British Writers, Printers, and Publishers in Paris, 1920-1939*, Macmillan, New York, 1975, pp. 318-22.

8 See the introduction, *CPM* as well as Deirdre Bair, *Samuel Beckett*, Harcourt Brace Jovanovich, New York, 1978, pp. 98-9.

9 Some details in this paragraph and others derive from my transcriptions of George Reavey's letters to Julian Trevelyan, dated 5 April 1929, through 20 May 1935. Other details are informed by letters from Reavey to Prof. Emile Delavenay as well as an informal memoir concerning Reavey by Prof. Delavenay, 18 April 1986. Delavenay knew Reavey at Cambridge and, moreover, had both MacGreevy and Beckett as English tutors at the École Normale Supérieure.

10 Most of Reavey's extant papers are housed in the Harry Ransom Humanities Research Center, University of Texas, Austin. I thank Reavey's third wife and widow, the late Jean Bullowa Reavey (1917-1987) for permission to quote from those papers. The Delavenay memoir, 18 April 1986, notes that Daniel Reavey was arrested twice in Russia – once during the 1905 revolution for siding with his workers and again after 1917 as an 'imperialist agent'.

11 *transition*, 19-20, June 1930, pp. 105-38. The standard history is Dougald McMillan, *transition: The History of a Literary Era, 1927-1938*, George Braziller, New York, 1976. Irish contributors to *transition* included: Joyce, MacGreevy, Beckett, Reavey, Geoffrey Taylor, John Lyle Donaghy, and Niall Montgomery.

12 Reavey collected many of these translations in *The Poetry of Boris Pasternak, 1917-1959*, G.P. Putnam's Sons, New York, 1959, prefaced by an extensive introductory essay probably first composed in the 1930s and including a memoir of Reavey's own literary life in the 1920s and 1930s.

13 *The European Caravan: An Anthology of the New Spirit in European Literature*, ed. Samuel Putnam, Maida Castelhun Darnton, George Reavey, J. Bronowski, Part I, Brewer, Warren and Putnam, New York, 1931. Contributions from Beckett, MacGreevy, and Donaghy appear on pp. 475-80, 493-7, and 439-41 respectively.

14 *Faust's Metamorphoses*, pp. 7-9.

15 *Faust's Metamorphoses*, pp. 53-4.

16 George Reavey to Julian Trevelyan, 30 November 1929. See also George Reavey to Julian Trevelyan, 17 November 1930: 'Faust for the last months has been abominally [*sic*] tortured by Mephistopheles, has wept many bitter and metaphorical tears . . .,' and: '. . . I cannot admit imitation of Eliot, as I want to find something positive & dynamic. . . .'

17 Trevelyan, *Indigo Days*, pp. 25-6.

18 *Soviet Literature: An Anthology*, ed. and trans. George Reavey and Marc Slonim, Wishart and Company, London, 1933, 430 pp. The new publishers Covic and Friede issued an American printing of *Soviet Literature* in 1934.

19 *Echo's Bones*, [p. 38]. The same advertisement lists a selection of poems by Paul Eluard 'by various hands'.

20 *Echo's Bones*, [p. 15]. Since Beckett had subsidized the printing of *Echo's Bones*, he was displeased with Reavey for not distributing the book properly. See Bair, *Beckett*, pp. 185-8, 216-17.

21 In Julian Trevelyan's file of letters from Reavey there is a photograph of a painting by Ronald Ossary Dunlop (1894-1973) of Andrée Conte. The photograph was enclosed in a letter dated 28 November 1930. Conte apparently died of tuberculosis in 1934. Reavey collected twelve of the twenty poems entitled 'Frailties of Love' in a mock-book typescript dated 1934. The poems, which were to have decorations by Hilda Ainscough, were never published in English, but Reavey persistently listed that title as 'in preparation'. Later, when stationed in Kiubyshev and Moscow during World War II, Reavey repeatedly retyped from memory many of these poems in the backs of cyclostyled communiqués and press releases.

22 *Nostradam*, p. 7.

23 *Nostradam*, p. 19. Like Sergei Essenin (1895-1925), Vladimir Mayakovsky (1894-1930) committed suicide.

24 Reavey moved to London with Gwenedd Vernon (b. 1900), whom he married on 18 July 1937, in a ceremony witnessed by Thomas MacGreevy. From a family with South African connections, Vernon exhibited as an 'independent' painter, along with Julian Trevelyan, at the London Gallery early in 1939. See *The London Bulletin*, 8-9, January-February, 1939.

25 Brian Coffey reviewed Gascoyne's *Short Survey of Surrealism* in *The Criterion*, 15, 60, April, 1936, pp. 506-11. The essential literary studies of the period are: Valentine Cunningham, *British Writers of the Thirties*, Oxford University Press, Oxford, 1988; Samuel Hynes, *The Auden Generation: Literature and Politics in England in the 1930s*, Princeton University Press, Princeton, 1972; Paul C. Ray, *The Surrealist Movement in England*, Cornell University Press, Ithaca, 1971, and A.T. Tolley, *The Poetry of the Thirties*, St Martin's Press, New York, 1976.

26 Reavey had conceived of the project of translating Eluard earlier in 1935. Denis Devlin noted that the translations were originally to have come from himself, Beckett, and Brian Coffey. Denis Devlin to Thomas MacGreevy, 15 March, 1936, Trinity College, Dublin (TCD), MacGreevy Papers: 8112/9.

27 *Thorns of Thunder*, Europa Press, Paris, 1936, pp. vii-viii.

28 *Thorns*, p. 23. Reavey had Beckett's translations on file, but he asked Beckett to supply improved versions, which Beckett could not do. When *Thorns of Thunder* appeared containing the unimproved translations, Beckett condemned both the book and Reavey in a letter to MacGreevy. See Bair, *Beckett*, p. 218. Clearly, Bair overly dramatizes this episode, for Beckett's displeasure did not prevent him from entrusting to Reavey negotiations for the publication of *Murphy*.

29 *Thorns* p. 39. Aside from translating Breton and Eluard, and later René Char and St-John Perse at some length, Devlin also put poems by Apollinaire, Baudelaire, Mallarmé, Nerval, and Rimbaud into Irish. See *CPD*, pp. 123-9.

30 *Thorns,* p. 51.

31 Reavey's translations of Berdyaev for the Centenary Press are: *The Meaning of History* (1936), *Spirit and Reality* (1939), *Leontiev* (1940), and *Solitude and Society* (1947). Also, in the early 1940s Reavey provided the British Broadcasting Corporation with translations from the Russian.

32 Bair, *Beckett,* pp. 241-4, 247-8, 269-70.

33 Brian Coffey to Thomas MacGreevy, 30 March, 1935, TCD, MacGreevy Papers: 8110/18; also, 6 December, 1935, 8110/20.

34 Denis Devlin to Thomas MacGreevy, 15 March, 1935, TCD, MacGreevy Papers: 8112/9; also 28 November, 1936, 8112/10.

35 *I,* pp. 10-12, 22-25, 26-31, 51-57, 61-63; Denis Devlin, *Lough Derg and Other Poems,* Reynal and Hitchcock, New York, 1946, pp. 59-60, 52-3, 39-42, 18-22, 61-2, respectively. Robert Penn Warren provided the jacket note for *Lough Derg,* whose title suggests Devlin's religious concerns and whose text places 'Est Prodest' much before 'Bacchanal', not following it as in *Intercessions.*

36 Denis Devlin to Thomas MacGreevy, 15 February, 1937, TCD, MacGreevy Papers: 8112/2; also, 22 January, 1937, 8112/11.

37 Brian Coffey, 'For the Record', *Advent,* 6, 1976, p. 21. This note introduces the text of 'News of Revolution', *Advent,* 6, 1976, p. 22-4.

38 While Beckett, writing in the *Bookman* (August 1934), asserted the importance of Devlin and Coffey as Irish writers in a Continental context, J.C.C. Mays argues against seeing Devlin as 'a member of the avant-garde, whose starting point is polemic and whose career is defined in terms of opposition to the established canon' (*CPM,* p. 9). Such a caveat prefers, in effect, the late Devlin of *The Heavenly Foreigner* (1950), as forecast by 'Est Prodest', to the early Devlin of 'Bacchanal' and 'Communication from the Eiffel Tower'. Nevertheless, by offering his translations to Reavey for publication in *Thorns of Thunder* and by, a little later, helping Reavey issue *Intercessions* as a Europa Press book, Devlin proved willing to let his poetry be received in an obviously polemic and 'oppositional', because avant-garde, context.

39 Brian Coffey to Thomas MacGreevy, 6 December, 1935, TCD, MacGreevy Papers: 8110/20; see also the typescript of 'Image at the Cinema' (1935), 8110/17.

40 *The Garden of Disorder,* Europa Press, Paris, 1938. For a sample of the range of Ford's poetry, see *Flag of Ecstasy: Selected Poems,* ed. Edward B. Germain, Black Sparrow Press, Los Angeles, 1972.

41 *Nostradam,* p. 7.

42 Ford, *Garden,* p. 60.

43 Ford, *Garden,* p. 9.

44 Dylan Thomas, *The Collected Letters,* ed. Paul Ferris, Macmillan, New York, 1985, pp. 267, 303-4, 314, 339, 412.

45 See Andrew Sinclair, *War Like a Wasp: The Lost Decade of the Forties,* Hamish Hamilton, London, 1989, pp. 14-42; Robert Hewison, *Under Siege: Literary Life in London, 1939-1945,* Weidenfeld and Nicolson, London, 1977, pp. 5-26.

46 The typescript mock-book of 'The Endless Chain' (WB1/F3/F), as well
    as the typescripts of *Quixotic Perquisitions* (WB2/F9/B and WB2/F9/G), are
    housed in the Reavey Papers, Harry Ransom Humanities Research Center,
    The University of Texas, Austin. To the staff of the Harry Ransom
    Humanities Research Center, and particularly to Cathy Henderson, I owe
    many thanks for their help.
47 Reavey's prefaces and introductions in *Soviet Literature: An Anthology* (1933)
    became the foundations of Reavey's *Soviet Literature To-Day*, Lindsay
    Drummond, London, 1946, which Yale University Press reissued in 1947,
    thus helping Reavey earn a Rockefeller Foundation fellowship for 1948-49.
48 *QP*, p. 22. The poem was reprinted in *The Lace Curtain*, 4 (1971) and in
    1973 as a broadside by the Mirage Press, Boston, in an edition of two
    hundred copies, twenty-six lettered and signed by the author.
49 Reavey did not collect this broadside poem, but its theme, imagery, and
    rhymed lines link it strongly to 'The Rape of Europe', *QP*, pp. 30-1. It
    is printed on deckle edge, Homeric Antiquarian laid paper, folded, but
    carries no colophon. Reavey did collect 'The Rape of Europe' in *The Colours
    of Memory* Grove Press, New York, 1955, pp. 36-7.
50 Reavey's letters suggest that he sold much of this collection before 1942
    in order to equip himself for service in the Soviet Union. Reavey lost much
    of this 'kit', including literary papers, when his transport the *S. S. Jutland*
    was torpedoed on its way to Murmansk.
51 'The Endless Chain', Reavey Papers WB1/F3/F, Harry Ransom Humanities
    Research Center.
52 'The Endless Chain', Reavey Papers, WB1/F3/F, HRHRC.
53 *The Colours of Memory*, p. 56. *The Faber Book of Irish Verse*, ed. John
    Montague, Faber and Faber, London, 1974, p. 299.
54 To date, the only comprehensive record of Reavey's career has been pub-
    lished in *The Journal of Beckett Studies*, 2, Summer 1977.
55 Jean-Paul Sartre, 'The Situation of the Writer in 1947', in *What is Literature?*
    trans. Bernard Frechtman, Methuen, London, 1950, p. 157.
56 For example, see Stan Smith on Coffey, *The Lace Curtain*, 5, Spring 1974,
    pp. 16-32; and on Devlin, *Advent VI*, 1976, pp. 24-31, and the *Irish Univer-
    sity Review*, 8, 1, Spring 1978, 51-67. See J.C.C. Mays on Devlin, *Advent
    VI*, 1976, pp. 9-14; and on Coffey, *Irish University Review*, 13, 1, Spring
    1983, 65-82. Academic and critical studies of Beckett are so numerous
    as to require no citation.
57 While the historian Roy Foster claimed in 1986 that 'We Are All
    Revisionists Now', in respect to literary history, revisionism does not yet
    account well for Irish writing of the 1930s. The chief Irish critics – Terence
    Brown, Seamus Deane, Edna Longley, for example – have so far but
    blinked at Reavey's share of Irish poetry in the 1930s. More *outré* critics,
    such as David Lloyd or Norman Vance, have hardly done better recently.
    Two exceptions to this state of affairs need noting. First, in 1985, Dillon
    Johnston's *Irish Poetry After Joyce* proposed a connection between Irish

writing of the 1930s and contemporary Irish poetry, especially in his chapter 'Devlin & Montague'. Second, quite recently, W.J. Mc Cormack examined Beckett's contributions to Nancy Cunard's *Negro Anthology* (1935), in *Hermathena* (1992), pp. 73-92, in a manner that takes the literary and political preoccupations of the 1930s seriously, and as pertinent to present-day Irish writing.

The Europa Press: Descriptive Checklist

1

FAUST'S METAMORPHOSES   1932

George Reavey / Faust's Metamorphoses / poems / illustrated / by / Stanley William Hayter / The New Review Editions / 42bis rue du Plessis, Fontenay-aux Roses, Seine, France.

End leaf verso: colophon.

Colophon: There have been printed on this book 1 copy on Japanese paper with the original drawings and an autographed manuscript; a 106 copies on Holland Van Gelder Zonen paper of which a 100 are numbered 1 to 100, and 6 hors commerce marked A, B, C, D, E, I; and 30 press copies on Edita Prioux.

Pp. 63. Vanilla wrap with black lettering over stiff card. 26 x 20 cm.

2

NOSTRADAM   1935

George Reavey / Nostradam / A Sequence of Poems / Europa Press / 13, Rue Bonaparte, Paris VIe / 1935.

Verso: *Europa Poets No. I. / colophon / Copyright by author.*

Colophon: There have been printed of this book 250 copies on Alpha of which the first 200 are numbered and the first 50 signed; 25 copies on Japon impérial paper and two copies on Japon nacré paper of which the first twenty and the first respectively are numbered and signed. The copies on Japanese paper are illustrated with an engraving by *Stanley William Hayter* who has also done the cover engraving. Only the numbered copies are for sale.

End leaf verso: *Achevé d'imprimer / le premier mai 1935 / sur les presses de Charles Bernard / maitre imprimeur / a Paris.*

Pp. 34. Black wraps with white lettering and decoration by Hayter. 24 x 16 cm.

3

SIGNES D'ADIEU 1935

George Reavey / Signes d'Adieu / (Frailty of Love) / poèmes mis en français / par Pierre Charnay / Éditions Europa / 13, Rue Bonapate, Paris VIe / 1935.

Verso: *Europa Poets No II / colophon / Copyright by Author.*

Colophon: Il a été tiré de cet ouvrage 150 exemplaires sur bouffant, dont vingt-cinq numérotés de 1 á 25 et signes par l'auteur et le traducteur, et soixante-quinze numérotés de 26 à 100; vingt exemplaires sur japon impérial avec une gravure de *Roger Vieillard*, dont les quinze premiers numérotés de I à XV et les autres H. de C.

End leaf verso: *Achevé d'imprimer / le premier Mai 1935 / sur les presses de Charles Bernard / maitre imprimeur / a Paris.*

Pp. 24. Cream wrap with black lettering over stiff card. 18 x 12 cm.

4

ECHO'S BONES 1935

Echo's Bones / And Other Precipitates / by Samuel Beckett / Europa Press / 1935 / 13, Rue Bonaparte / Paris.

End leaf verso: colophon.

Colophon: This edition is limited to 327 copies of which 25 on Normandy vellum signed by the author are numbered I to XXV; 250 on Alfa paper numbered 1 to 250; and 50 copies marked hors commerce. 2 copies on Normandy vellum marked A and B are reserved for the author and publisher respectively. Printed by the G.L.M. Press. Paris. November 1935.

Pp. 40, unnumbered. Cream wrap with black lettering over stiff card. 2.5 x 16.7 cm.

5

THORNS OF THUNDER 1936

Paul Eluard / Thorns / of Thunder / Selected Poems / with a Drawing by Pablo Picasso / star / Edited by George Reavey / star / Translated from French by / Samuel Beckett, Denis Devlin, David / Gascoyne, Eugene Jolas, Man Ray, / George Reavey and Ruthven Todd / star / London / Europa Press & Stanley Nott.

Verso: Colophon / *Printed in England by Henderson and Spalding Ltd. / at The Sylvan Press, Sylvan Grove, S.E. 15, for / Stanley Nott Ltd., 69 Grafton Street, Fitzroy Square, W. 1 / All rights reserved.*

Colophon: This, the first edition of THORNS OF THUNDER, is limited to 600 copies, of which No. 1, printed on hand-made paper, contains an original drawing by Pablo Picasso and an original MS. by Paul Eluard, and is signed by the Author, Artist, and the translators; Nos. 2 to 51 are signed by the Author; Nos. 52 to 575 constitute the ordinary edition; and 25 copies have been reserved for the use of the Author and Publishers.

Pp. 70. Blue cloth lettered white on spine. Lilac wrap with red lettering and illustration by Max Ernst. 22.5 x 14.5 cm.

6

INTERCESSIONS   1937

Intercessions / Poems / by / Denis Devlin / London / Europa Press / 30 Red Lion Square, W.C. 1.

Verso: *Europa Poets V* / colophon / *Printed by the Temple Press, Letchworth, Herts / for the Europa Press / All Rights Reserved. 1937.*

Colophon: This, the first edition of 'Intercessions', is limited to 300 copies, of which the first 25 are signed by the author.

Pp. 66. Blue cloth lettered white on spine. White paper wrap lettered black. 22.5 x 14.5 cm.

7

THE GARDEN OF DISORDER   1938

The / Garden of Disorder / and Other Poems / by / Charles Henri Ford with an Introduction by / William Carlos Williams / and a Frontispiece by / Pavel Tchelitchew / London / Europa Press / 7 Great Ormond Street, W.C. 1.

Verso: *Europa Poets VI* / colophon / *Printed by the Temple Press, Letchworth, Herts / for the Europa Press / All Rights Reserved 1938.*

Colophon: This, the first edition of *The Garden of Disorder*, is limited to 500 numbered copies, of which those numbered I to XXX are signed by the Author. Copies A to K are not for sale, and are reserved for the Author and Publisher. Copies 41 to 500 constitute the ordinary edition.

Pp. 82. Green cloth lettered yellow on spine. White paper wrap with black lettering and illustration by Tchelitchew. 22.5 x 14.5 cm.

8

THIRD PERSON 1938

Third Person / by / Brian Coffey / London / George Reavey The Europa Press / 7 Great Ormond Street, W.C. 1.

Verso: *Europa Poets VII* / colophon / *All Rights Reserved 1938 / Printed in Guernsey, C.I., British Isles, by the Star and Gazette Ltd. for / The Europa Press.*

Colophon: This, the first edition of *Third Person* printed on toned hand made rag antique wove deckle edge paper, is limited to 300 numbered copies. Copies numbered I to XXV are illustrated with an original engraving by S.W. Hayter and are signed by Author and Artist. Copies A and B are not for sale and are reserved for Author and Publisher. Copies 28 to 300 constitute the ordinary edition.

Pp. 30. Red cloth with black lettering on spine. Blue wraps with red lettering. 22.5 x 14.5 cm.

9

QUIXOTIC PERQUISITIONS 1939

Quixotic / Perquisitions / First Series by / George Reavey / London / The Europa Press / 7 Great Ormond Street, W.C. 1.

Verso: *Europa Poets VIII* / colophon / *All Rights Reserved 1939 / Printed & Made in Great Britain for the Europa Press.*

Colophon: This, the first edition of *Quixotic Perquisitions*, is limited to 340 numbered copies printed by Hague & Gill Ltd., High Wycombe, on Arnold & Foster's mould-made paper. The 40 special copies, illustrated with an original engraving on copper by John Buckland-Wright and signed by author and artist, are numbered as follows: 10 copies not for sale, A to J; and 30 copies I to XXX. Copies 1 to 300 constitute the ordinary edition.

Pp. 38. Yellow cloth boards and white cloth spine lettered in red. Red wrap with yellow lettering. 22.5 x 15 cm.

11

New Writers' Press:
The History of a Project

Trevor Joyce

New Writers' Press was formed and published its first volumes in the summer of 1967. It came about as the result of eighteen months or so of discussion between Michael and Irene Smith and myself about the stagnancy of the Irish poetry scene relative to what had happened in the U.S. and Europe. We felt that the mainstream of contemporary poetry was passing us by. Only the Dolmen Press, under Liam Miller, was publishing substantial collections in Ireland at that time, but the Dolmen was reliant on the small stable of writers it had helped establish, it still leaned heavily on the legacy of Yeats, and it favoured the book as art–object rather than as a cheap, fast, and effective means of getting new poetry before its prospective public. We aimed to change that.

Both Mike and I were in the process of assembling our first collections, and neither of us anticipated a favourable response from the Dolmen, still less from those few English publishers who extended themselves to consider Irish work: their expectations were of a provincial literature, unambitious in its concerns, formally conservative, and rural in its outlook. We failed on all counts. In addition to our own work, Mike was interested in promoting the interests of a number of poets whose work, which we found sympathetic, had appeared in John Jordan's *Poetry Ireland*, and in the journal *Arena*, edited originally by James Liddy and Liam O'Connor.

What small expertise we had in the technicalities of printing and publishing had been gathered by Mike during a brief stint working for a Dublin newspaper. Being more interested in the effect than in the niceties of its delivery, we searched out the cheapest printer who could handle the job, and set to work. The first two volumes, first collections both for myself and for Paul Durcan and Brian Lynch, took advantage of new photo-offset print technology. Although the books were relatively cheap to produce, my own volume could be retrieved only in lots of fifty or a hundred copies at a time from the printer, as we did not have the money to pay off the whole bill at once. It took several years to get our hands on the whole edition. Mike's own first collection came out in the early summer of 1968.

For their money, readers of NWP's first volume also got a statement of editorial policy by Michael Smith. It was prefaced, in characteristically combative style, by the ironic injunction from Pound to 'give up verse, my boy, there's nothing in it.' It then outlined the publisher's intent as being:

> . . . to bring out a series of small books each of which will give a young poet the chance of finding the audience so necessary to him. The nature of such an audience – of any artist's audience – precludes any question of coercive advertising and this is not a commercial venture for the publisher's part. Poetry is one of the few disinterested offerings made by the individual to society and the publisher's role in this venture is a participation in such an offering.
>
> Most of the poets whose work will be included in this series are Irish and under thirty. Believing poets should be beyond the herd-instinct, they belong to no school, movement, club or clique. They are all serious poets that is, human beings for whom writing poetry is, morally, a profoundly central activity, not a mere hobby or ornamental grace.[1]

Publicity and distribution were both handled, then as later, by Mike's brother Peadar, who got us noticed in all the principal Dublin papers, and the response was generally favourable, both to the body of work we had brought out, and to the overall project of the press.

The next stage for NWP was to get our own printing capability. After several false starts we at last laid hands on an Adana handpress, whose salesman warned us that it could be used to print dance tickets and raffle tickets but definitely not books. The funds were raised by converting all expected gifts from my twenty-first birthday into ready cash.

We used the new flexibility given us by having our own press to pursue our interests in two new directions: experimental poetry in English from outside Ireland, and little-known foreign-language poetry in translation. These were represented initially by Spicer's *Billy the Kid*, then tied up by litigation in the US, and Borges's *Selected Poems*, translated by Anthony Kerrigan, Borges's finest translator, into English. The Borges volume was, to the best of my knowledge, the first collection anywhere, in English, completely given over to his poetry.

We also started out on yet another track at this time by publishing issue 1 of *The Lace Curtain, A Magazine of Poetry and Criticism*, whose concise editorial made clear our intent:

> Poetry magazines, anywhere, have, like butterflies, an all too short life; and in our mean Irish climate this brief span is even more cur-tailed. Maybe it's as well: maybe a poetry magazine shouldn't stay about too long and become institutionalized and editorially retrogressive.
>
>   But *The Lace Curtain* is here now, and for however long or short a time it lives, it will do its best, first of all, to provide poets with a more immediate contact with an audience than, for the lucky few, a book every two or three years can; and, after that, to supply criticism that, whether expository or directive, will always be rele-vant, lively and, we hope, honest.[2]

Once we were in a position to print our own books, and so to ignore the economics of viable print runs, the pace of our publishing picked up considerably. In 1969, apart from *The Lace Curtain*, we managed to bring out six additional books. We were, however, still severely constrained by lack of money to replace damaged type, for example, and this sometimes resulted in somewhat Procrustean editing (see the remarks on items 8 and 9 in the Checklist below). To raise cash we had recourse at times to eccentric methods: I believe it was over the Christmas of 1969 that we sat around the table in Mike's unheated kitchen, dressed in scarves, hats, and overcoats, set-ting monotype with numb fingers for the union rulebook for a Dublin hotel. Everything was undertaken communally: editing, set-ting, printing, making tea and sandwiches. Discussions of editorial policy were carried on in a context of baby-minding, shopping, and drink. Text written by one hand was more than once appended to an article signed by another, wild moneymaking schemes were thought up, and unlikely aspirations concocted to satisfy the compilers of reference books.

With some achievements behind us we grew more ambitious. In a letter to *The Irish Times*, Mike asked for one hundred Irish poetry-lovers to contribute each £1 towards the purchase of an electric-powered press for NWP. The appeal raised £110, and one of the first contributions received was £10 from Douglas Gageby, editor of *The Irish Times*. We brought out Michael Hartnett's *Selected Poems* as the first in a new, high-quality series, named Zozimus Books, after the nineteenth-century balladeer of Dublin's Coombe. This title was chosen since the address of NWP had changed from Lawrence's Mansions, Sherriff Street, the innner-city working-class area from where the first books had issued, to Blackpitts, near the Coombe, where Mike had set up home. We also negotiated with Hartnett for permission to bring out his version of the *Tao*, first published in *Arena*. He eventually acceded in exchange for the promise of a pint of stout for each of its seventy-odd sections. Hartnett's later attack on some of NWP's work is the more unfortunate and inexplicable given this dedicated early championship of his poetry. A few months later, we brought out the first in an extensive planned series of *Versheets*, folded broadsheets intended as a cheap and effective way of bringing out new poetry and prose. Sadly, the promised texts and translations were too frequently not forthcoming, and the series ceased after just four issues.

At this point, a good-humoured disagreement, which had been running between Mike and myself for some years, came to a head. We both complained of the rarity of good new writing, and both felt the urge to do something about it. Our disagreement concerned the means: Mike felt that relevant and acute criticism could do the job, while I despaired of such oblique approaches and decided that the only way to get poetry written of the sort I would be interested in reading was to write it myself, and if this helped anyone else do likewise, then, good. As a result, I withdrew increasingly over the course of *Lace Curtains* 3 and 4, from active involvement in the running of the press, and left it to Mike to achieve one of NWP's major successes.

Mike had seen work by Brian Coffey in the pages of the *Irish University Review*, edited by Lorna Reynolds, and knew him as the editor of the edition of Denis Devlin's *Collected Poems* which had appeared first as a special edition of that journal, before its later manifestation as a Dolmen book: same inside, different cover and title-page. He began a lengthy correspondence with Brian in early 1970, and with Brian's support and expert direction, uncovered a number of Irish poets of the 1930s whose overall, if only implicit, project seemed in significant ways continuous with ours. One of Brian's own lasting concerns was 'the elimination of the term irishness [*sic*] from the critical vocabulary'[3] and he constantly encouraged Mike to use the press towards that end; given its original aims, NWP needed little encouragement. Brian, however, could both suggest the names and texts to support such a policy, and focus it through expressing his own pithy arguments:

> The phrase: *recognizably Irish quality* is a bad one for either it refers to the purely physical effects of biological kind and as such says nothing of interest about the poetry, or it sets up a very dubious criterion of a limiting kind almost certainly bound to bias the critical judgement which accepts it . . . Poets work in words and how they work in words is the first object of a critic, not whether they are actually, nearly or remotely Irish . . .[4]

One of the contacts made possible through Brian was Niall Montgomery. Niall designed the cover of *Lace Curtain* 3 for us, and carried on a protracted defence against our attempts to get from him for publication a collection of his own poetry. We eventually prevailed against his lack of literary ambition, and he gave us the text of *Terminal*, with permission to bring it out when we were ready. Unfortunately, that text is among those yet to be published by NWP, and Niall, always a good friend to the press, is not alive to see it. Niall's generous support extended so far beyond the merely literary as to get jobs for both Gerry Smyth, an NWP poet, and myself, during the seventies.

Another name turned up in the course of Mike's researches on the thirties was that of Charlie Donnelly, an active Marxist, who joined the International Brigade and was killed in the Spanish civil war. His poetry was virtually unknown in the early seventies. In fact, when a friend and comrade of Charlie's, from the Brigade, approached us after hearing a paper Mike read on him for, I think, a fiftieth anniversary commemoration of the war, it emerged that even he had been entirely unaware that Charlie wrote poetry, and knew him only for his courage under fire and his humanity. Mike's article on Donnelly in *Lace Curtain* 4 made his name known, and some of his texts available for the first time.[5]

Due to the stigma involved in acknowledging a practicing Marxist in an Irish Catholic family, however, we could not gain permission to publish a collection of his work, and it was only through the mysterious intervention of the Irish College in Salamanca that a *Collected Poems* at last appeared in 1978. I know of no other volumes published under this imprint. The collection was available through some Dublin bookshops, as well as free in several pubs, but it was notable that the Irish Communist Party bookshop concurred with Irish Catholic sentiment in that they stocked the book under the counter, rather than having it on open display. Perhaps they considered it subversive.

This interest in the thirties reached its highest achievement in the publication of Thomas MacGreevy's *Collected Poems*, and Brian Coffey's *Selected Poems*, and in the assembling, in *Lace Curtain* 4, of a fine anthology of the poetry of this period, together with relevant criticism. This anthology included some criticism by Samuel Beckett, previously published anonymously during the thirties, along with some of his later poetry. This contact with Beckett was another product of Brian Coffey's tireless enthusiasm in support of the press. Some unsold copies of each of these publications were distributed by Raven Arts Press, with new wrappers to hide the NWP covers, during NWP's dark ages.

After this flurry of activity, the pace slowed down again. Mike, assisted by his critical workshop, twice elaborated his critical introduction to *Lace Curtain* 3,[6] a rebarbative attack on Brendan Kennelly's *Penguin Book of Irish Verse*, into extended considerations of the canon of recent Irish poetry written in English.[7] These pieces made explicit, in retrospect, what had emerged as NWP's editorial policy in relation to the tradition of Irish poetry. Publication of poetry in translation, and of work by non-Irish poets, continued, but finally, however, the scarcity of good contemporary Irish work took its toll on NWP, and its publications became less frequent. Arts Council funding had at last become available to us, on a book by book basis, but there was not enough good work around to publish, and neither Mike, Irene, nor myself felt inclined to switch to promoting second-rate writing. NWP in its heyday published some work that on second thoughts might have been better left alone, and with hindsight we did not wish to do so again.

Between 1979 and 1993 NWP was in a period of quiescence, with less than a dozen books over fourteen years. Mike and I turned our attention to other things: he to translation from the Spanish, in addition to his original work, and I to reading and learning from Chinese and Japanese poetry. It seemed as if we had done our job, and we assumed that now we had established that Irish poetry did not have to be rural, provincial, and technically and intellectually naive, other writers and publishing houses would take up the fight. We were disappointed: few heeded Beckett's observation that 'the issue between the conventional and the actual never lapses' (*Disjecta,* p. 70-1).

When I moved to Cork in 1984 I tried, briefly, to continue with the NWP programme, publishing volumes by Mike and by Brian Coffey under the imprint of the Melmoth Press.[8] It did not work; I had not the necessary time to give to the project, and it was too difficult to work remotely with printers in Dublin. Somnolence resumed.

NWP's resurrection eventually started in late 1992. Recent developments in desktop publishing, together with a mounting frustration with the current situation in Irish poetry, prompted us to try again. With two books behind us now, and another one due out in spring of 1995, NWP is back on the scene, as the only policy-driven poetry press in Ireland. The aim now, as always, is to print work that we believe is worth printing, to encourage good writing through good editing and criticism, and to make available to our readers the best work from other languages, in the best translations. The sixth issue of *The Lace Curtain* came out in 1978. We always described it as an occasional journal. Maybe the time is right for number 7.

Notes

1   Michael Smith, 'Introduction to New Irish Poets', Trevor Joyce, *Sole Glum Trek*, New Writers Press, Dublin, 1967.
2   Michael Smith and Trevor Joyce, 'Editorial', *The Lace Curtain,* 1.
3   Brian Coffey to Michael Smith, personal correspondence, 20 November 1986.

4   Brian Coffey to Michael Smith, personal correspondence, 8 September 1970.
5   Michael Smith, 'Charles Donnelly: 1914-1937', *The Lace Curtain*, 4, 1971, pp. 64-9.
6   Michael Smith, 'Irish Poetry and Penguin Verse', *The Lace Curtain*, 3, 1970, pp. 3-10.
7   Michael Smith, 'Irish Poetry Since Yeats: Notes Towards a Corrected History', *The Denver Quarterly*, 5, 4, Winter 1971, pp. 1-26, and 'The Contemporary Situation in Irish Poetry', *Two Decades of Irish Writing*, ed. Douglas Dunn, Carcanet Press, Manchester, 1975, pp. 154-65.
8   Michael Smith, *Selected Poems*, Melmoth Press, Cork, 1985. Brian Coffey, *Chanterelles, Short Poem, 1971-1983,* Melmoth Press, Cork, 1985.

New Writers' Press: A Checklist of Publications

Information enclosed in brackets is supplied either from memory or from the NWP Descriptive Catalogue, printed in the summer of 1971. All dimensions are approximate, as NWP books tended to vary in size from copy to copy.

1

Title:	*Sole Glum Trek*	Date:	(June) 1967
Author:	Trevor Joyce	Size:	21x14.5 cm.
Editor	Michael Smith	Pages:	30
Series:	New Irish Poets	Price:	3/6
Edition:	(500pb)		
Cover	(Trevor Joyce)		
Printer:	Museum Bookshop		

Remarks: Author's first collection. Contains 'Introduction to New Irish Poets' by Michael Smith. Front cover featured the 'man in the moon' design which later became NWP logo. Back cover lists 'Forthcoming Volumes by Paul Durcan, Brian Lynch, Michael Smith, Leland Bardwell'.

2

Title:	*Endsville*	Date:	(August) 1967
Authors:	Brian Lynch, Paul Durcan	Size:	21x14.5 cm.
Editor:	Michael Smith	Pages:	59
Series:	New Irish Poets	Price:	5/-
Edition:	(500pb)		
Cover	John Behan		
Printer	Museum Bookshop		

Remarks: First collection for both authors. Authors acknowledge financial assistance from Anthony and Elaine Kerrigan. Division of pages: pp. 5-32, Durcan, pp. 33-59, Lynch.

3

Title:	*With the Woodnymphs*	Date:	(May) 1968
Author:	Michael Smith	Size:	20.5x14 cm.
Editor	Michael Smith	Pages:	32
Series:	New Irish Poets	Price:	5/-
Edition:	300pb		
Cover	Donal Byrne, wraparound		
Printer	Pronto Print		

Remarks: Author's first collection. Inside of back cover lists 'To be published shortly Leland Bardwell: I'll Do the Messages'.

#3a

Title:	*With the Woodnymphs*	Date:	1968
Author:	Michael Smith	Size:	20.5x14 cm.
Editor:	Michael Smith	Pages:	32
Series:	New Irish Poets	Price:	7/6
Edition:	(20 approx.)		
Cover	(Michael Smith), wraparound		
Printer:	Pronto Print		

Remarks: This edition consisted of a small number of #3, with the original grey wraparound replaced by a deep blue, and with a new price. As the new wraparound was printed on the NWP handpress, the publication date is certainly later than October 1968, and probably later than that indicated in the volume.

#4

Title:	*Dedications*	Date:	(November) 1968
Author:	Michael Smith	Size:	21x15.5 cm.
Edition:	200pb	Pages:	18, unnumbered
Cover:	(Michael Smith), wraparound	Price:	5/-
Printer	NWP		

Remarks: This was the first volume produced on NWP's Adana handpress. It appeared in at least two different colour covers, green and blue, and with several variants on the cover design.

#5

Title:	*Billy the Kid*	Date:	1969
Author	Jack Spicer	Size:	21x16.5 cm.
Edition:	150pb	Pages:	14, unnumbered
Cover	(Michael Smith), wraparound	Price:	none given
Printer	NWP		

Remarks: End-note states that 'some copies are not for public sale'. These were probably given to James Liddy, who suggested the edition. The 1971 Descriptive Catalogue gives publication date as November 1968.

#6

Title:	*Poems*	Date:	(August) 1969
Author:	Jorge Luis Borges	Size:	26x16.5 cm.
Trans:	Anthony Kerrigan	Pages:	23

Edition: 300pb, numbered   Price: none given
Cover   Trevor Joyce, wraparound
Printer   NWP

Remarks: Contains 'A Tangential Comment on a Borgesian Theme: or Translator's Bio-Bibliographical Note' by Kerrigan. Dedication reads:

>   TO JORGE LUIS BORGES LAPRIDA LAFINUR
>   SUAREZ ACEVEDO LYNCH
>   and his idea of Ireland
>   as   a   vast   theatre
>   where a ritual drama
>   is ceaselessly enacted
>   under the direction
>   of a Great Director & Dreamer
>
>   AND TO THE RE-CREATED
>   AND RE-ENACTED
>   SINN FEIN AND I.R.A.
>   OF THE FUTURE

Permission to publish this edition came by way of a letter from Borges to Kerrigan, dating from the period before his fame in the Anglophone world, granting Kerrigan English rights to all his works.

#7

Title: *The Lace Curtain No. 1*   Date: (Autumn) 1969
          A Magazine of Poetry and Criticism Size: 21x13.5 cm.
Editors: Michael Smith, Trevor Joyce   Pages: 73
Edition: 1000pb   Price: 5/-
Printer: Dorset Press Ltd.
Contents:

Editorial	
Poetry	
Brian Lynch	'To The Unloving'
	'LLano'
Kay Boyle	'The Lost Dogs of Phnom Penh'
	'Thunder Storm in South Dakota'
James Hogan	'The One Bright Spot'
	'For Dolly Wyse'
	'Image'
	'Amhaireadh'
Pearse Hutchinson	'Brave Galinsoga strode up the aisle'
Michael Smith	'Quietly the Memory'
	'Particulars'

Criticism

James Hogan	'Death and Contacts'
Michael Smith	'Pablo Neruda: The Passionate Sage'
Trevor Joyce	'Ideologist of Love (The Poetry of James Liddy)'
David Polk	'A Short Introduction to Jack Spicer's Poetry'
Jim Chapson	'Letter from San Francisco'
James Liddy	'Open Letter to the Young about Patrick Kavanagh'
Leon Trotsky	'Lesson of the Dublin Events'
D.R. O'Connor Lysaght	'Conor Cruise O'Brien'

#8

Title:	*No Die Cast*	Date:	(June) 1969
Author:	Brian Lynch	Size:	20.5x12.5cm.
Edition:	75pb, numbered	Pages:	11, unnumbered
Cover	Wraparound	Price:	private circula-
Printer	NWP		tion only

Remarks: We chose the title as the longest meaningful phrase we could extract from the few letters of display-sized type we had available – those used for the cover of Michael Smith's *Dedications*.

#9

Title:	*Watches*	Date:	(September) 1969
Author:	Trevor Joyce	Size:	21x14 cm.
Edition:	150pb, numbered, 71 signed	Pages:	16, unnumbered
Cover	(Trevor Joyce), wraparound	Price:	7/6
Printer	NWP		

Remarks: The text of some poems had to be modified due to a shortage of certain letters in our few cases of type.

#10

Title:	*Homage to James Thomson (B.V.) at Portobello*	Date:	(November) 1969
Author:	Michael Smith	Size:	26x16.5 cm.
Edition:	50pb	Pages:	9, unnumbered
Cover	(Trevor Joyce), wraparound	Price:	private circula-
Printer:	NWP		tion only

Remarks: The cover design was arrived at by modifying the cover linocut for *Watches*, and using different colours. The text occupied only two pages.

#11

Title:	*The Hag of Beare*	Date:	(November) 1969
	A Rendition of the Old Irish		
Author:	Michael Hartnett	Size:	26x17cm.
Edition:	100pb, numbered	Pages:	10, unnumbered
Cover	Wraparound	Price:	5/-
Printer	NWP		

#12

Title:	*The Flags are Quiet*	Date:	(November) 1969
Author:	Gerard Smyth	Size:	26x19.5cm.
Edition:	90pb	Pages:	12
Cover	(Michael Srnith), wraparound	Price:	7/6
Printer	NWP		

Remarks: Author's first collection.

#13

Title:	*Survival*	Date:	(November) 1969
Author:	Augustus Young	Size:	25x18 cm.
Edition:	(250pb)	Pages:	11
Cover	(Front: Michael Smith, back:		
	John Maher), wraparound	Price:	(50p)
Printer	NWP		

Remarks: Author's first collection.

#14

Title:	*Friend Songs*	Date:	(January) 1970
	Mediaeval Galaicoportuguese		
	Love Poems		
Trans:	Pearse Hutchinson	Size:	25x17 cm.
Edition:	130pb, numbered	Pages:	19
	only 100 for sale	Price:	none given
Cover	John Maher, wraparound		
Printer.	NWP		

Remarks: Endnote acknowledges material assistance from Liam Miller.

#15

Title:	*The Lace Curtain No. 2*	Date:	Spring 1970
	A Magazine of Poetry and Criticism	Size:	21x13.5 cm.
Editors:	Michael Smith, Trevor Joyce	Pages:	44

Edition: 1000pb   Price: 5/- (75c.)
Cover   John Maher
Printer   Dorset Press Ltd.
Contents:

      Editorial

      Poetry

Pearse Hutchinson	'Ringing Changes on the Mistral'
	'It Still Happens'
	'Quinze Juillet, Early Morning'
	'Birdsong'
Jorge E. Eielson	'Mystery'
Augustus Young	'Hero'
Gerard Smyth	'Ghosts'
	'It's a Sad Walk After'
	'I Have Decided to Divide Myself . . .'
	'Enormous Crimes Have Kept us Close Together'
Geoffrey Hazard	'A Sequence of Four Poems'
James Tate	'The Artificial Forest'
John Montague	'Summer Storm'
Javier Heraud	'The River'
	'I Don't Laugh at Death'
Georg Trakl	'The Autumn of the Lonely One'
	'Rest and Silence'
	'Birth'
	'To the Dumbfounded'
	'Decline'
Trevor Joyce	'I Know These Streets'
Michael Kane	'A Poem for Frank'
	'Good Taste'
Anthony Kerrigan	'Silhouette of Joseph Casey (et al)'
Antonio Machado	'On the Burial of a Friend'
	'Childhood Memory'
P.M. O'Brien Burkley	'After Insult'
	'Dirges'
Knute Skinner	'The Customs of Queens'
Michael Smith	'Dedication XXXI'
Niall Montgomery	'It's Warmer Down Below'
	'Now I Lay Me'
	'Pious Ejaculation'
Lorna Reynolds	'A Dream'
Peter Prachar	'Morrow'

Paul Durcan	'Atonement'
	'from Letter to Sailorson'
Michael Hartnett	'Enamoured of the Miniscule'
	'How Goes the Night, Boy'
	'Birds Cross'
Pamela Good	'High Dive'
Macdara Woods	'Decimal's Liberal Schooling – and After'

Criticism

| D.R. O'Connor Lysaght | 'Memorandum for a Socialist Programme for the Irish Labour Party' |
| Michael Kane | 'A Letter from Zurich' |

Remarks: The inside covers list Notes on Contributors. Publication assisted by Paul O'Dwyer and the New York Irish Institute.

#16

Title:	*The Mad Cyclist*	Date:	(June) 1970
Author:	Leland Bardwell	Size:	25x15cm.
Edition:	300pb	Pages:	20
Cover	Michael Smith, wraparound	Price:	10/6 ($1.50)
Printer	Dorset Press Ltd.		

Remarks: Acknowledges assistance from the Arts Council. Probably the first NWP publication to receive such assistance.

#17

Title:	*Decimal D. Sec Drinks in a Bar in Marrakesch*	Date:	(June) 1970
Author:	Macdara Woods	Size:	25x14.5
Edition:	200pb	Pages:	8
Cover	Michael Smith, wraparound	Price:	7/6 ($1.50)
Printer	Dorset Press Ltd.		

#18

Title:	*Twenty Poems*	Date:	(June) 1971
Author:	Gerard Smyth	Size:	22x14.5cm.
Edition:	80 boards, signed and numbered	Pages:	28
Cover	(Michael Smith)	Price:	£2.00
Printer:	NWP		

Remarks: Note inside cover states that 'This book was printed by hand in the summer of 1970. Through an error of its amateur printers 80 copies and not 100, as stated, in the book, were finally printed. Of these, 50 copies only are for sale.' The 1971 catalogue gives the publication year as 1971.

#19

Title:	*The Lace Curtain No. 3*	Date:	Summer 1970
	A Magazine of Poetry and Criticism	Size:	24.5x15 cm.
Editor	Michael Smith	Pages:	56
Assoc. Ed:	Trevor Joyce	Price:	6/- ($1)
Edition:	700pb		
Cover:	Niall Montgomery		
Printer	Dorset Press Ltd.		
Contents:			

Editorial	
Michael Smith	'Irish Poetry and Penguin Verse'
Poetry	
Gerard Smyth	'My Poor Lazarus'
	'I Woke Up'
Mathieu Bénézet	'The landscape is a madwoman. . . .'
Desmond O'Grady	'Limerick: Ireland'
Leland Bardwell	'Reward to Finder'
Brian Coffey	'Eleison I'
	'Eleison II'
	'24 from Daybreak'
Geoffrey Hazard	'After Charles Baudelaire'
	'Image'
Augustus Young	'A Party for a Stillbirth'
Michael Hartnett	'Fairview Park: 6 a.m.'
	'Woman at Sad Canal'
Denis Devlin	'Adventure'
	'Donna Mia'
Michael Smith	'Dedication XXXIV'
John Jordan	'The Feast of St Justin'
Trevor Joyce	'Elegy of the Shut Mirror'
	'Surd Blab'
Paul Murray	'A Kind of Palmistry'
	'Poem'
Brian Lynch	'Historical Poem'
Gottfried Benn	'Alaska'
	'Hebbel'

	'Warning'
	'Mother'
	'Songs'
	'Icarus'
Howard McCord	'For Chris'
Eiléan Ní Chuilleanáin	'Two Poems on a Change'
Georg Trakl	'Summer'
	'Evening Song'

Criticism

Samuel Beckett	'Denis Devlin'
Michael Smith	'Considering a Poetic'
Niall Montgomery	'Le Déjeuner sur Malherbe –
	Homage to Charles Baudelaire'

Notes on Contibutors

Remarks: Publication assisted by Paul O'Dwyer and the New York Irish
Institute, and by the Arts Council of Ireland. This was, to the best of my
knowledge, the first time Beckett granted permission for his piece on Devlin
to come out under his own name. It had originally appeared anonymous-
ly in the *Bookman* in the 1930s. Michael Smith's editorial article in this edi-
tion later took on more weight to form his 'Irish Poetry Since Yeats: Notes
Towards a Corrected History', published in *The Denver Quarterly*, 5, 4, winter
1971. A different version appeared as 'The Contemporary Situation in
Irish Poetry', in Douglas Dunn's *Two Decades of Irish Writing,* Carcanet,
Manchester, 1975.

#20

Title:	*Selected Poems*	Date:	(November) 1970
Author:	Michael Hartnett	Size:	19x11.5 cm.
Series:	Zozimus Books	Pages:	61
Edition:	1000pb	Price:	75p
Printer:	Dorset Press Ltd.		

Remarks: Publication assisted by the Arts Council.

#21

Title:	*How We Died*	Date:	(December) 1970
Author:	Thomas Tessier	Size:	23.5x15cm.
Edition:	200pb	Pages:	14
Printer:	NWP	Price:	none given

#22

Title:	*Un Hombre Pasa*	Date:	(December) 1970
Author:	César Vallejo	Size:	n/a
Trans:	Michael Smith	Pages:	n/a
Edition:	40pb	Price:	n/a
Cover:	n/a		
Printer:	NWP		

Remarks: I have been unable to locate a copy of this volume.

#23

Title:	*Versheet 1*	Date:	(March) 1971
Author:	Brian Coffey	Size:	23.5x13.5 cm.
Editor:	Trevor Joyce		44.5x25.5 cm.
			opened
Edition:	500pb, broadsheet	Pages:	6
Printer:	Dorset Press Ltd.	Price:	(20p)

Remarks: First publication in the *Versheet* series, intended to get new work, verse and prose, into circulation cheaply, and with minimum delay. Projected issues included essays by Adorno.

#24

Title:	*Versheet 2*	Date:	(March) 1970
Author:	Robert Pawlowski	Size:	23.5x13.5 cm.
Editor:	Trevor Joyce		44.5x25.5 cm.
			opened
Edition:	500pb, broadsheet	Pages:	6
Printer:	Dorset Press Ltd.	Price:	(20p)

#25

Title:	*Hellas*	Date:	(April) 1971
Author:	Desmond O'Grady	Size:	26x17 cm.
Edition:	500pb	Pages:	16, unnumbered
Cover:	Dmitri Hadzi, wraparound	Price:	50p ($1.50)
Printer:	Dorset Press Ltd.		

Remarks: Publication assisted by the Arts Council.

#26

Title:	*Patrician Stations*	Date:	(May) 1971
Author:	John Jordan	Size:	19.5x14.5 cm.
Edition:	500pb	Pages:	26
Cover:	(Michael Smith), wraparound	Price:	50p ($1.50)

Printer: Dorset Press Ltd.

Remarks: Publication assisted by the Arts Council.

#27

Title:	*Ritual Poems*	Date:	(July) 1971
Author:	Paul Murray	Size:	22x14.5 cm.
Edition:	500pb, of which 100 signed	Pages:	26
Cover:	(Michael Smith)	Price:	50p ($2.00)
Printer:	Dorset Press Ltd.		

Remarks: 1971 catalogue gives edition as 400 copies.

#28

Title:	*The Lace Curtain No. 4*	Date:	Summer 1971
	A Magazine of Poetry and Criticism	Size:	24.5x15 cm.
Editor:	Michael Smith	Pages:	95
Asst. Ed.:	Brian Coffey	Price:	40p ($1.25)
Edition:	2000pb		
Cover:	John Maher		
Printer:	Dorset Press Ltd.		

Contents:

Editorial

Michael Smith

Poetry

Samuel Beckett	'Alba'
	'Serena 1'
	'Da Tagte Es'
	'Malacoda'
	'Gnome'
Brian Coffey	Three Poems from 'Daybreak' (Numbers 28, 33, 43)
	'Dead Season'
Denis Devlin	'Mr Allen'
	'The Statue and the Perturbed Burghers'
	'To Me: A Greek Country School-teacher'
	'Commercial Attaché'
	'Wickey'
	'Animals'
Lyle Donaghy	'The Hermit'
	'The Grave'

Michael Smith	'Charles Donnelly: 1914-1937'
Samuel Beckett	'Humanistic Quietism'
Niall Montgomery	'Farewells Hardly Count'
	'An Aristophanic Sorcerer'
Michael Smith	'Interview with Mervyn Wall about the Thirties'
Austin Clarke	'The Thirties'
Notes on Contributors	
T.D. Redshaw	

Remarks: This issue was dedicated to the memory of Charles Donnelly. Publication assisted by Paul O'Dwyer and the New York Irish Institute, and by the Arts Council. A number of the Devlin poems were previously unpublished. Unsold copies of this issue were later re-covered and sold under the imprint of the Raven Arts Press.

#29

Title:	*Tao*	Date:	1971
	A Version of the Chinese Classic of the Sixth Century B.C.		
Author:	Michael Hartnett	Size:	24.5x15 cm.
Edition:	500 boards	Pages:	20
Cover:	Trevor Joyce	Price:	£1.50 ($5.00)
Printer:	Dorset Press Ltd.		

Remarks: This text had been first published in *Arena* in 1964.

#30

Title:	*Versheet 3*	Date:	1971
	Homage to Patrick Kavanagh	Size:	23.5x13.5 cm.
Author:	James Liddy		44.5x25.5 cm.
Editor:	Trevor Joyce		opened
Edition:	500pb, broadsheet	Pages:	6
Printer:	Dorset Press Ltd.	Price:	25p ($.75)

#31

Title:	*Versheet 4*	Date:	1971
	Such a Heart Dances Out		
Author:	Thomas Dillon Redshaw	Size:	23.5x 13.5 cm.
Editor:	Trevor Joyce		44.5x25.5 cm.
			opened
Edition:	500pb, broadsheet	Pages:	6
Printer:	Dorset Press Ltd.	Price:	20p

#32

Title:	*Collected Poems*	Date:	1971
Author:	Thomas MacGreevy	Size:	23.5x16 cm.
Series:	Zozimus Books	Pages:	77
Edition:	1000pb, 250 boards	Price:	£3.00 boards
			£1.05 paper
Cover:	(Michael Smith), incorporating drawing by Jack B. Yeats		
Printer:	Dorset Press Ltd.		

Remarks: Publication assisted by the Arts Council. The Foreword by Samuel Beckett was a reprint of his piece 'Humanistic Quietism'. The volume also included the text of the manifesto 'Poetry is Vertical', signed originally by Hans Arp, Samuel Beckett, Carl Einstein, Eugene Jolas, Thomas MacGreevy, Georges Pelorson, Theo Rutra, James J. Sweeny, and Ronald Symond. There was an Afterword by Thomas Dillon Redshaw.

#33

Title:	*Selected Poems*	Date:	1971
Author:	Brian Coffey	Size:	23.5x16 cm.
Series:	Zozimus Books	Pages:	68
Edition:	1000pb, 250 boards	Price:	£2.00 boards
Printer:	Dorset Press Ltd.		£1.05 paper

Remarks: Publication assisted by the Arts Council.

#34

Title:	*On Loaning Hill*	Date:	1971
Author:	Augustus Young	Size:	23.5x16 cm.
Series:	Zozimus Books	Pages:	80
Edition:	1000pb, 250 boards	Price:	£1.50 boards
Printer:	Dorset Press Ltd.		75p paper

Remarks: Publication assisted by the Arts Council.

#35

Title:	*Pentahedron*	Date:	1972
Author:	Trevor Joyce	Size:	23.5x16 cm.
Series:	Zozimus Books	Pages:	53
Edition:	1000pb, 250 boards	Price:	£1.50 boards
Cover.	(Trevor Joyce)		75p paper
Printer:	Dorset Press Ltd.		

Remarks: Publication assisted by the Arts Council. Distinct cover designs were used for the paperback and hardback editions, the former featuring The Morgue, an etching by Charles Meryon, the latter a Chinese glyph.

#36

Title:	*Ceremonies for Today*	Date:	1972
Author:	Robert Pawlowski	Size:	24x15.5cm.
Edition:	(500 pb. 200 boards)	Pages:	40
Cover:	(John Maher), wraparound	Price:	none given
Printer:	Dorset Press Ltd.		

#37

Title:	*Blood Relations*	Date:	1972
Author:	Tom MacIntyre	Size:	23.5x16 cm.
Series:	Zozimus Books	Pages:	35
Edition:	500 boards	Price:	£1.50
Cover:	(John Maher)		
Printer:	Dorset Press Ltd.		

#38

Title:	*The Wood-Burners*	Date:	1972
Author:	Patrick Galvin	Size:	Unknown
Series:	Zozimus Books	Pages:	Unknown
Edition:	500 boards	Price:	£1.50 boards
Cover:	(Michael Smith)		45p paper
Printer:	Dorset Press Ltd.		

#39

Title:	*Collected Poems 1950–1973*	Date:	1973
Author:	Anthony Cronin	Size:	20.5x12cm.
Edition:		Pages:	109
Cover:	(Michael Kane)	Price:	£3.00 boards
Printer:	Dorset Press Ltd.		75p paper

Remarks: Publication assisted by the Arts Council.

#40

Title:	*The Lace Curtain No. 5*	Date:	Spring 1974
	A Magazine of Poetry and Criticism	Size:	24.5x15 cm.
Editor:	Michael Smith	Pages:	101
Edition:	(1000)	Price:	£1.00 ($4)
Cover:	Michael Smith		

Printer: Dorset Press Ltd.

Contents:

Tom Phillips	'If I Were to Tell You'
Gerard Smyth	'Suicide Notes'
Sean Connolly	'Agony Column'
Neil Belton	'Blacklist'
	'Obverse'
	'Poem'
	'Prelude'
	'Poem'
Paul Murray	'Tenebrae'
Jorge Carrera Andrade	'The Stroke of One'
	'Klare von Reuter'
	'The Guest'
A.C. Dawe	'Lantern'
	'Operation'
Thomas Kinsella	'A Hand of Solo'
	'Sacrifice'
	'At the Crossroads'
Derek Mahon	'Fire-King'
Asa Benveniste	'Change'
	'Arousing'
	'Blue'
Máire Mhac an tSaoi	'Ceangal Do Cheol "Pop"'
	'Muiris ag Caoineadh Phádraig'
Mairtń O Direáin	'Teangmháil'
	'Dorchú'
	'Gníomh Dóchais'
Micheál Ó hUanacháin	'Leannáin'
Michael Davitt	'dathanna' . . .
Gabriel Rosenstock	'. . . Go mbeidh an Seó Déanach Thart'
Tomás MacSíomóin	'1847'
	'Liodán le hAghaidh Liadain'
Seán O Leocháin	'An Carbadóir'
Pablo Neruda	'Twenty Love Poems & One Poem of Despair'

Remarks: The back cover featured Notes on Some Contributors. Publication assisted by the Arts Council. The long sequence by Neruda, in this translation by Michael Smith, later appeared as a separate NWP volume.

#41

Title:	*Drowned Stones*	Date:	1975
Author:	Geoffrey Squires	Size:	21.5 x 14.5 cm.
Series:	Zozimus Books	Pages:	76

Edition:	(500 pb.)	Price:	£1.00
Cover:	(Patrick Dunne)		
Printer:	Elo Press Ltd.		

#42

Title:	*The Poems of Sweeny Peregrine* *A Working of the Corrupt Irish Text*	Date:	(June) 1976
Author:	Trevor Joyce	Size:	24.5x15.5 cm.
Editor:	Michael Smith	Pages:	50, unnumbered
Edition:	(500 pb.)	Price:	£1.00
Cover:	Trevor Joyce		
Printer:	Elo Press Ltd.		

#43

Title:	*Early Poems*	Date:	1976
Author:	Antonio Machado	Size:	24x15.5 cm.
Trans:	Michael Smith	Pages:	57
Edition:	500	Price:	£1.00
Cover:	Natalie d'Arbeloff		
Printer:	Elo Press Ltd.		

Remarks: A version of the poems from Machado's volumes *Soledades* and *Del Camino. The versions from Del Camino were revised and corrected from a 1974 Gallery Books edition.*

#44

Title:	*World Without End*	Date:	1977
Author:	Gerard Smyth	Size:	24.5x15.5 cm.
Edition:	(500 pb.)	Pages:	46
Cover:	Michael Smith	Price:	£1.00
Printer:	Elo Press Ltd.		

Remarks: Publication assisted by the Arts Council

#45

Title:	*The Lace Curtain* No. 6	Date:	Autumn 1978
	A Magazine of Poetry and Criticism	Size:	25x15 cm.
Editor:	Michael Smith	Pages:	59
Edition:	(800)	Price:	75p
Cover:	(Michael Smith)		
Printer:	Elo Press Ltd.		

Contents:

Anthony Cronin   'Thomas MacGreevy: The First of
the Few'

Notes on Contributors

Remarks: The cover features a drawing of Thomas MacGreevy by Seán O'Sullivan.

#46

Title:	*Stopping to Take Notes*	Date:	1979
Author:	Michael Smith	Size:	24.5x15.5 cm.
Edition:	(500 pb.)	Pages:	46
Cover:	(Michael Smith)	Price:	£1.50
Printer :	Elo Press Ltd.		

Remarks: The cover featured La Rue des Mauvais Garçons, an etching by Charles Meryon.

#47

Title:	*Six Poems*	Date:	1984
Author:	Michael Smith	Size:	23x16 cm.
Edition:	100 pb, signed	Pages:	10
Printer:	NWP	Price:	private circula-tion only

#48

Title:	*Eight Love Poems*	Date:	1986
Author:	Francisco de Quevedo	Size:	21x15 cm.
Trans.:	Michael Smith	Pages:	18
Edition:	20, numbered and signed	Price:	private circula-tion only
Printer:	NWP		

#49

Title:	*Flower of Nido*	Date:	1987
Author:	Garcilaso de la Vega	Size:	21x15 cm.
Trans.:	Michael Smith	Pages:	18
Edition:	50, numbered and signed	Price:	private circula-tion only
Printer:	NWP		

#50

Title:	*Irish Love Poems*	Date:	1987
	Dánta Gradha	Size:	21x15 cm.
Trans.:	Michael Smith	Pages:	18

Edition: 20   Price: private circula-
Printer: NWP   tion only

#51

Title:	*Dark Night*	Date:	1987
Author:	San Juan de la Cruz	Size:	21x15 cm.
Trans.:	Michael Smith	Pages:	15
Edition:	20	Price:	private circula-
Printer:	NWP		tion only

#52

Title:	*10 Poems*	Date:	1988
Author:	Michael Smith	Size:	21.5x 15.5 cm.
Trans.:	Luis Huerga	Pages:	16
Edition:	(200 pb)	Price:	
Cover:	Wraparound		
Printer:	Elo Press Ltd.		

#53

Title:	*Poems of Mallarmé*	Date:	1990
Trans.:	Brian Coffey	Size:	21x29.5 cm.
Edition:	(500 pb)	Pages:	34
Printer:	Icon Impressions Ltd.	Price:	£5.00

Remarks: This volume was co-published with The Menard Press, London. Publication was assisted by the Arts Council.

#54

Title:	*Twenty Love Poems*	Date:	1991
	from the Greek Anthology	Size:	21x15 cm.
Trans.:	Michael Smith	Pages:	25
Edition:	20 pb, numbered and signed	Price:	private circula-
Printer:	NWP		tion only

#55

Title:	*Lost Genealogies and Other Poems*	Date:	1993
Author:	Michael Smith	Size:	23x15 cm.
Edition:	400 pb	Pages:	84
Cover:	(Patrick Dunne)	Price:	£4.95
Printer:	ColourBooks Ltd.		

Remarks: First publication of the resurrected NWP.

#56

Title:	*stone floods*	Date:	(January) 1995
Author:	Trevor Joyce	Size:	23x15 cm.
Edition:	400 pb.	Pages:	52
Cover:	(Trevor Joyce)	Price:	£5.99
Printer	ColourBooks Ltd		

#57

Title:	*Landscapes and Silences*	Date:	1995, forth-
Author:	Geoffrey Squires		coming
Remarks:	Assisted by the Arts Council.		

Index